God is a Capitalist: Markets from Moses to Marx

Roger D. McKinney

God is a Capitalist: Markets from Moses to Marx published by the Christian Capitalist, 25898 Lariat Circle, Broken Arrow, OK, 74014

www.rdmckinney.blogspot.com

ISBN-13: 978-1-9735-1712-2

Table of Contents

Preface

In his book, *Jesus in Beijing*, author David Aikman describes a lecture that he attended in Beijing in 2002. The speaker, a scholar from one of China's premier academic research institutes the Chinese Academy of Social Sciences, said the following:

> One of the things we were asked to look into was what accounted for the success, in fact, the pre-eminence of the West all over the world . . . We studied everything we could from the historical, political, economic, and cultural perspective. At first, we thought it was because you had more powerful guns than we had. Then we thought it was because you had the best political system. Next we focused on your economic system. But in the past twenty years, we have realized that the heart of your culture is your religion: Christianity. That is why the West has been so powerful. The Christian moral foundation of social and cultural life was what made possible the emergence of capitalism and then the successful transition to democratic politics. We don't have any doubt about this.

While college professors in communist and atheist China embrace the paternal role of Christianity in forming the culture that has made the West wealthy and powerful, few in the West itself hold even a suspicion of that truth. In fact, academia had taught a different history for the past three centuries in which Christianity bludgeoned progress after the fall of Rome and plunged Europe into the Dark Ages. Then the Renaissance and Enlightenment broke the chains of "monkish ignorance and superstition," as Thomas Jefferson wrote, and allowed reason and science to burst forth. Scholars reached back to the wisdom of ancient Greece and Rome to issue on stage freedom, human rights and democracy.

Fortunately, academia began killing off the old history with its myths of the Dark Ages, Renaissance and Enlightenment beginning in the 1960's as that history began to be viewed as less a history of progress and more of an apologetic for the white race oppressing the darker races. The old Western Civilization classes that introduced students to the classics were thrown out. Students have been left without a history of their culture and encouraged to be ashamed of it. The result has been, as Rodney Stark wrote in his introduction to *How the West Won*,

> They are in danger of being badly misled by a flood of absurd, politically correct fabrications, all of them popular on college campuses: That the Greeks copied their whole culture from black Egyptians. That European science originated in Islam. That Western affluence was stolen from non-Western societies. That Western modernity was really produced in China, and not so very long ago.

Also, the lack of history of the West has led to dozens of theories from top economists that explain the massive increase in wealth in the West as the result a purely random accident. However, at the beginning of this new millennium a few Western scholars have exposed the charades. The Dark Ages were a myth. The fall of the Roman Empire launched Europe into a period of greater progress and prosperity. Church monasteries then universities preserved and advanced scholarship. The Renaissance and Enlightenment did not break with history but bore the fruit of centuries of progress.

Ironically, academics in the West began to abandon traditional Christianity on the eve of its greatest economic success, the Industrial Revolution. Even with the enormous reductions in poverty evident everywhere around them, atheists and deists invented socialism in the early nineteenth century. Socialism replaced Christianity as the religion of intellectuals as well as much of the rest of the population and today is the dominant paradigm for structuring the social sciences and humanities. Socialism gave us Nazi Germany where the state murdered over twelve million of its own citizens, and the U.S.S.R where Stalin murdered over thirty million. Then there were fascist Italy, communism in Eastern Europe, communist China, North Korea and Cuba.

While residual Christianity thwarted the full instantiation of socialism in the United States and much of Western Europe, nothing barred China from getting drunk on the old wine. China fully implemented the most extreme versions of socialism under Chairman Mao Zedong. His desperate attempt to purify socialism in China of the 1960's in what became known as the "Cultural Revolution" nearly destroyed the nation and caused death by starvation of more than thirty million people. The disaster of the Cultural Revolution cured many Chinese of their zeal for socialism and opened their minds and hearts to foreign ideas.

A few Chinese scholars have become Christians as a result of their studies of Western history. Most Christian converts in China followed a different path to belief, as do most believers in the world, but the paths of those academics to faith in Christ differs little from those taken by C. S. Lewis and T. S. Eliot for whom the intellectual evidence pushed them toward reluctant belief. They demonstrate that an accurate history of how the West became great can be a powerful apologetic for Christianity.

Christians in the West need to understand their history as the Chinese intellectuals do in order to bequeath that Christian culture to their children in the hope of restoring it to the nations of its birth because our children will create their own culture with their values and institutions. But they will not create it in a vacuum as so many humanists assume. They will borrow from competing ideas today, such as democratic socialism, Chinese communism or radical Islam. They will assert that their ideas are new, revolutionary, and scientific, but since they know little about the past they will have no clue that they are merely resurrecting philosophies that have failed miserably the many times they were tried throughout history. Only one culture has succeeded in rescuing humans from endless cycles of famine and starvation and it arrived just three centuries ago and only in the West, but our young people know nothing about it.

This book is the outcome of about two decades of research. I did not start out trying to defend Christianity using the West's history. The impetus came from years of reading articles in a prominent evangelical magazine in the 1990s that openly promoted Marxism as Christian economics. I had recently earned an MA in economics, but had taken no history classes. I discovered later that all history of economics classes had been removed from the economics curriculum of most schools a generation ago. Experts had decided that the best of the past had been incorporated into modern mainstream economics so there was nothing students could learn from the past. They were wrong.

I began reading books on economic history and the history of economic thought in order to determine if the magazine was correct that capitalism was a gross distortion of God's plan for humanity and that Marxism would restore humanity to the "Garden of Eden" as Marx asserted it would. The stakes were high. Europeans had speculated for centuries that mankind had lived in a state of innocence, peace and prosperity before the enforcement of private property. Marx, and the many socialists before and after him, promised that if we followed his system we would create a world without poverty or crime. Socialists assume that humans are born innocent and resort to evil only because something oppresses them. Private property is the worst oppressor of all so eliminating property would allow human nature to return to its natural state of innocence and evil would evaporate like shallow water on a hot summer day. At the same time, poverty existed only because some people hoarded more than their share of wealth. Spreading wealth more evenly, eliminating inequality, would make everyone rich. What is there not to like about socialism?

The evangelical magazine seemed to think that Marxism was a shortcut to the Kingdom of God on earth. Evangelism was unnecessary. By the advent of the new millennium the magazine had changed editors and jettisoned its strident Marxism without embracing capitalism. The new editors followed the uncontroversial path blazed by most evangelical pastors and abandoned the field of economics completely except to complain once a year about the commercialism of Christmas. Few Christian leaders seemed satisfied with the reigning system, which everyone called capitalism. If the U.S. represented the pinnacle of capitalism, as the Western media proclaimed, then life could not get any better than it is in the U.S. and many people found that depressing.

A few Christian economists have written to defend capitalism, but I know of no prominent evangelical theologians who have done so. Most have declared that God is above concerns about economic issues and is neither capitalist nor socialist, implying that God's way must be somewhere between the two extremes. Without knowing it or having given it much thought, and certainly without having put any study into the subject, they have endorsed the democratic socialism popular in the West since World War II.

I thought that Adam Smith would provide quick answers to my questions about the origins of capitalism because he is considered its father. So I read his book, *The Wealth of Nations*. I had not read it in school, which is a sad admission for someone with a postgraduate degree in economics. But Smith only deepened the mystery. He does not say where he got his ideas. He assumes they are just sound reasoning based on solid observation. One thing stood out, though. Several times Smith referred to the Dutch Republic as the best example of his system of natural liberty.

So I plunged into the history of the Dutch Republic. It became clear that the Dutch had invented capitalism. They had achieved the highest degree of protection for private property;

their workers were the first in European history to enjoy rapidly rising standards of living; they had very limited government, honest courts and respect for business. Dutch individualism, freedom and love of business scandalized the rest of Europe even as their wealth inflamed envy in England and France. They quickly became the wealthiest and most powerful nation in Europe and that defied the reigning wisdom about how nations grow rich and powerful. The Dutch had won their independence through eighty years of war against the West's superpower – Spain. The wisest people at court had assumed that Spain would only grow more powerful as it stole shiploads of gold and silver from the New World. Yet Spain grew poorer in spite of its plunder.

The contrasts between the Dutch and the rest of Europe were striking and other Europeans wrote about it frequently. Unfortunately, the Dutch wrote very little economic theory and did not seem as surprised by their success as were other Europeans. Why were they so different? The great sociologist Max Weber speculated a century ago that the Reformation gave birth to capitalism, so I investigated the economics of the major reformers, especially Luther and Calvin, only to learn that they had opposed the free market principles of the Dutch. Calvinists in the Dutch Republic wanted the church to control prices, labor standards, quality, interest rates and most other aspects of the market. Puritans absorbed Calvinist economics and made their colonies in the New World as constrained as any in Europe in economic terms.

Before long, I discovered the writings of the theologians at the University of Salamanca, Spain, from the sixteenth and seventeenth centuries. In some ways they continued to cling to the principle of state and church controlled markets of the past, especially regarding charging interest on loans which they called usury. But in most ways they championed the freest markets in the history of writing about business and wealth. After more than a decade of searching, I finally discovered what the Chinese intellectuals had learned three decades before: God is a capitalist!

If any scholars read this book they will find plenty to pick apart because I did not write it for scholars. To write for a scholarly journal one has to pick a very narrow topic, say, how many angels can dance on the head of a pin, then survey the history of it, provide the arguments on both sides and make a small, innovative contribution. Such articles are tedious to read and that's why no one reads them. If I treated all of the controversial topics as required by an academic journal, this would not be a book but a set of encyclopedia volumes. I wrote for the average reader who wants to get to the heart of a matter quickly. I have tried to become as well informed on each issue as possible and present to the reader what the truth is. On theological issues I take the conservative evangelical side and on economics that of the Austrian school, not because I am unaware of opposing views but because I am convinced they are closest to the truth. For those who want a more scholarly debate, I have provided my sources and most of them offer both sides of the controversy.

Introduction

The physicist who is only a physicist can still be a first-class physicist and a most valuable member of society. But nobody can be a great economist who is only an economist - and I am even tempted to add that the economist who is only an economist is likely to become a nuisance if not a positive danger." Friedrich Hayek, "The Dilemma of Specialization."

Economists who aspire to be good economists must learn something about history, culture, religion, anthropology, technology and other subjects because good economics is about the totality of humanity, not just their money. The great Austrian economist Ludwig von Mises emphasized that point by naming his most important book *Human Action*.

One example of the danger of specialization shows up in attempts to explain the polarization of voters on the left and right. Commentators respond to this development like a calf looking at a new gate, as if it magically appeared out of nowhere. But the origins of the left/right divide are ancient, more ancient than people think. Most pin it on the Enlightenment in France. For example, Hayek tracked it to the father of modern socialism, Saint-Simon in France in the early nineteenth century. Some, like Murray Rothbard trace the origins of the right to Daoism in medieval China. Others recognize the leftist policies in Plato's *Republic* and the right in Aristotle's opposition to his mentor's philosophy.

This book pushes the birth of the debate to the earliest date of any proposed, back to 1500 B.C. when Moses led the Israelis out of slavery in Egypt and into their own land on the eastern shore of the Mediterranean Sea. Moses was one of the world's most vigorous proponents of free markets while pharaoh was an early Marxist.

Economics alone offers an emaciated, one-dimensional picture of capitalism. Weaving the complete history of capitalism from Moses to Marx required pulling threads from other disciplines, including history, philosophy, anthropology, theology, sociology and more as well as economics. The rest of this introduction summarizes the process by chapter.

Chapter 1 – What is capitalism?

Before we can journey to the origins of the debate, we must know what we are looking for by defining our terms. Chapter 1 looks for a definition of capitalism. Adam Smith, one of the earliest English economists and author of the classic *The Wealth of Nations*, called his system one of "natural liberty." The term "capitalism" came from followers of Marx and opponents of private property and free enterprise. If readers search for definitions of capitalism on the internet they will be overwhelmed with their number, variety and sheer ridiculousness.

One of the most common misconceptions conflates capitalism with commerce. Anywhere commerce for profit has taken place scholars have seen proto-capitalism. But if we accept that definition, then we have no explanation for the explosive growth in wealth and standards of living that took place in the seventeenth century in the Dutch Republic first, then England, because commerce has always existed. Something unusual must have happened in the seventeenth century to cause the unique event in world history that some economic historians have characterized as a hockey stick effect. In other words, if we graphed standards of living across time, the line would be flat like the shaft of a hockey stick from the beginning of history until the seventeenth century. Then suddenly the graph shoots upward like the blade of the hockey stick. Many economic historians do not seem to grasp that a unique event requires a unique explanation. Most explanations for that event were common through time and across geography, which begs the question: why did not the hockey stick inflection point in per capita G.D.P. happen before the seventeenth century or in other cultures?

Even under communism in the Soviet Union commerce existed in the form of the "black" or free market. So in addition to commerce being a non-unique cause, the co-existence of communism and capitalism in the same society at the same time is confusing. Capitalism must be more than just commerce for profit. Essentially, it is a set of institutions, formal and informal. The formal institutions are private property and the rule of law, but rule of law means more than just some parliament passing legislation. It means that people recognize a law existing above the mere legislation that parliaments and congresses may pass and that law binds governments as well as citizens. The essentials of that law can be summarized by the rights of individuals to life, liberty and property. And it means that the state enforces those laws for all citizens regardless of status.

Informal institutions are the values of the citizens that are instantiated by the culture. Citizens must hold to certain values in order for capitalism to work. Economic historian Deirdre McCloskey calls them the "bourgeois virtues." Until the advent of capitalism, the public, intellectuals and religion held commerce in low esteem. McCloskey points out that even if the formal institutions existed, capitalism would not have happened without the informal ones.

Finally, capitalism is mass production for the masses. All production before capitalism was craft production, small lots of hand crafted goods intended for the wealthy elite because only they could afford them. Common people and peasants got by with homemade goods. Capitalism standardized products and made them cheaper through mass production so that the masses of poor people could afford them. The history of capitalism has been the record of making luxury products cheaper for the masses. Marshmallows offer a trivial example. When first invented only the nobility could afford them, but mass production put them within grasp of even the poorest families today.

Chapter 2 – How individualism broke the envy barrier

The values needed for the appearance of capitalism took thousands of years to reappear after they were lost and chapter 2 explains why – envy. This chapter is a review of the great book by Helmut Schoeck, *Envy: A Theory of Social Behavior*. Schoeck explained that envy is part of human nature and is so powerful that it determines how people organize societies. For most of human history, envy kept economic development and capitalism in irons as traditional cultures labored to achieve equality of wealth among the common people while avoiding wealth accumulation out of fear of the envy of others. Envy aborted the bourgeois virtues necessary for capitalism and stifled innovation by crushing individualism. The history of the world is little more than the history of how societies have dealt with envy.

Schoeck argued that Christianity catalyzed economic development and capitalism by finding a way to suppress envy without eliminating it. Christianity accomplished that through the invention of individualism, according to Larry Siedentop in his book *Inventing the Individual: The Origins of Western Liberalism*. The West has a unique sense of the individual that took close to fifteen hundred years to birth, but when it finally appeared, it transformed the world.

Chapters 1 and 2 lay down a foundation for the search for the origins of capitalism, knowing that history is so vast and contradictory that we will find in it what we are looking for. Those chapters ensure that we are looking for the right things.

Chapter 3 - The Torah economy: the first capitalist nation

Solomon, known by Christians and Jews as the wisest man who ever lived, said there is nothing new under the sun, and that is true of much of economics and politics because human nature has not changed. The search for the birth of capitalism goes all the way back to Moses. The ancient Egyptian society out of which Moses led the Hebrews was essentially a socialist command economy. Pharaoh and the state were the same institution and controlled all of the land and the people. Some historians have been confused by the existence of markets in ancient Egypt, but markets existed for the common people to trade among themselves the small amount of goods that the state had left them, such as crumbs of food and rags for clothing. Common Egyptians could trade in land among themselves and the law prohibited theft, so some property rights existed, but they applied only to the dealings of the common people with each other. Pharaoh, owned the land and could confiscate it at will and give it to whomever he pleased.

The Egyptian model has proven to be the most robust form of government in the history of mankind as Douglass North and the New Institutional School of economics have discovered. In that model, a pharaoh, king, Caesar, dictator, general, etc., assumes absolute power. But he needs help maintaining control, so he bribes a small group of people, usually known as the nobility, to help him. Pharaoh gives them a monopoly on police power and the authority to pillage the common folk with impunity in exchange for their support.

The common people put up with the abuse from the nobility because of their envy of each other. As Schoeck pointed out, human nature causes common people to envy those closest to them in status. They do not envy the nobility and pharaoh because they are so distant from the commoner in every way that 1) the commoner entertains no hope of ever achieving noble status; 2) their religion tells them that the gods have ordained the structure of society, and 3) the extreme wealth of the nobility is justified by their status and role in society. In turn, the commoner relies on the power of the elite to maintain the status quo, keep everyone equal in poverty and punish upstart peasants who think they are better than the rest.

Then along came Moses. Reasonable people can be forgiven for thinking that Moses might have modeled his new nation on the very successful state created by Egypt. After all Moses had grown up in the school that groomed future pharaohs as well as the children of the nobility and foreign diplomats. He had mastered the Egyptian system of organization and statecraft. It was one of the most successful in terms of endurance and power in all of history and admired across the known world. But Moses did not create Israel in Egypt's image.

Chapter 3 explains the differences between the Egyptian and Israeli governments. Moses established a nation with a minimalist state that would be a modern libertarian's dream. The structure of the new nation could not have been more different from that of Egypt. The government of Israel had no state, no president or executive branch, no legislative branch, no standing army or police. It had only judges to settle disputes while citizens enforced judicial decisions. Individual leaders were similar to Supreme Court justices in the U.S., except they were the top generals during war.

Most law in Israel was common law. God had given Moses a mere 613 pieces of legislation according to some counts and most of those referred to the practice of religion or moral laws. Some scholars believe that the courts, or the government, did not enforce the religious and moral laws, such as giving to the poor, because they understood that coerced morality is not morality and forced religion has no value to God. The government, that is, the courts, enforced only the civil law which dealt with the protection of life, liberty and property issues such as theft, murder and slavery.

This "libertarian" society lasted by some estimates more than four hundred years before collapsing. During that time neighboring states occasionally conquered Israel and forced their tyranny on the people for a generation, but God always called a judge to lead the people to throw off the oppressors and re-establish freedom and prosperity. For impatient readers who demand an immediate response to the Apostle Paul's insistence on obeying the established authorities in Romans 13 of the Bible, the examples of the judges overthrowing such authorities in the book of Judges in the Old Testament offers a challenge to an absolutist interpretation of Paul. God clearly approved of some rebellions against the state.

A foreign power did not invade and end prosperity and freedom in ancient Israel. The people grew tired of freedom and voluntarily gave it up in one of the saddest incidents in the Bible. The people told God they wanted a king, a tyrant, like the nations around them. So God honored their wish, but with a warning of how terrible the tyranny would become. That is how the true dark ages began.

Chapter 4 – The dark ages

Most historians refer to Europe after the fall of Rome as the dark ages, but as historian Rodney Stark demonstrates that is due to their anti-Christian bias. Chapter 4 describes the dark age with respect to freedom and prosperity that began with the end of Israel's libertarian government and the establishment of the monarchy. Tyranny did not immediately arise because the first three kings, Saul, David and Solomon, were relatively godly men. But under Saul and David the nation continually marched to war. Solomon introduced peace, but taxed the nation so heavily that when his son succeeded him and refused to lighten the burden he ignited a civil war from which the nation never recovered. After Solomon, most kings practiced pagan idolatry, which often included human sacrifice. Tyranny, immorality and poverty increased under the kings to the point that God allowed the Babylonians to conquer the nation and relocate most of the population to Babylon. Eventually, Nebuchadnezzar destroyed the city of Jerusalem and the temple.

Chapter 4 covers a lot of real estate, from the end of the libertarian society in Israel to the beginning of the Dutch Republic in the sixteenth century. That may seem rash and unreasonable to most historians, but in terms of economics and government not much of any significance happened in between. Per capita income remained flat the entire period. Wealth did not increase; it merely sloshed from one conquering nation to another. Technology changed little. Hollywood tries to depict a gradual evolution from the oldest societies to the later ones, but economic historians disfigure that portrait. This long dark age made up the shaft part of the hockey stick graph in which standards of living remained almost flat. A peasant or nobleman living in sixteenth century Spain would have noticed little change from the days of ancient Egypt. This period can take up volumes in conventional history, but it is a record of little more than war, murder, tyranny, brutality and theft with brief interludes of sanity.

The darkness did not begin to recede until church scholars gained the confidence to criticize Aristotle and to reason for themselves. Then modern science began to take form, but for freedom and prosperity the change happened with the abandonment of Aristotle's economics. Then Church scholars began to examine the real world of commerce and reject Aristotle's prejudices. Scholastic thought on commerce reached its highest level in the sixteenth and seventeenth centuries at the school of Salamanca, Spain, where the scholars codified the essentials of capitalism – the rule of law, respect for private property, free markets as the instantiation of private property, honest courts and limited government. They established the role of government as that of protecting the life, liberty and property of the citizens and nothing more.

Chapter 5 – The Dutch Republic

The scholastics laid the philosophical foundation necessary for commerce to morph into capitalism, but the philosophy needed someone willing to practice it. Chapter 5 tells the story of how capitalism finally found a home in the Dutch Republic. Protestantism had invaded the low lands and captured the hearts of the bourgeois. The King of Spain claimed the authority to rule the territory and he was a Catholic. Alarmed by the growth of Protestantism, he first decided to persecute, and then annihilate all Protestants in the Netherlands. The princes of the region tried to persuade the king to relent, but he grew more obstinate. Eventually, the princes saw no alternative to rebellion and, led by Prince William of Orange, raised an army to defend their countrymen.

After dethroning the Spanish king, the princes, in agreement with the people, searched desperately for a monarch to replace him. They appealed to princes in France and to Queen Elizabeth to rule over them, but all refused out of fear of Spain's military power. So at first the Dutch settled for a republican form of government without a monarch. In the process of creating the institutions of the new nation they relied on the guidance of the Dutch scholar and student of the School of Salamanca, Spain, Leonardo Lessius. As a result, the Dutch created a nation with the capitalist institutions of free markets, respect for property and the rule of law. Two centuries later Adam Smith would recognize the Dutch as the first and most complete implementation of his system of natural liberty, or capitalism.

Chapter 6 – Fading empires

Chapter 6 considers the fates of the nations that opposed the Dutch system, France and Spain, and the superpower of the sixteenth century, the Ottoman Empire. France tried state directed commerce under the plan of the Great Colbert, with disastrous results. Spain limped along trying to survive on the gold and silver it could steal from its American colonies and eventually faded from the scene as a world power.

Like Spain and France, the Ottoman Empire never embraced the changes in attitude toward commerce, freedom and markets that swept parts of Western Europe. The Sultans retained the old traditional command and control economies that had existed since ancient Egypt. In the sixteenth century, the Empire had larger cities than Europe and a trading network that reached from Morocco to China, yet these advantages that so many economists trumpet as the cause of Europe's development mysteriously did not help the Empire. It never declined in absolute terms; each new century found it slightly richer than the previous one. But its wealth never increased at anywhere near the rapid pace of Western Europe, and that relative decline caused it to fall behind in military technology. The Empire achieved its deepest penetration into Europe with the failed siege of Vienna in 1688. From then on it continually lost real estate until its defeat in World War I. The Ottoman Empire created the institutions for most of the Middle East and that is the reason the region today is so far behind Europe, North America, and much of Asia in terms of economic development and freedom.

The Dutch enjoyed over 200 years of freedom and prosperity, becoming the world's wealthiest nation with one of its most powerful militaries and navies. Because of the close relationship between the Dutch and English, the Dutch system spread across the channel quickly, then to the English colonies in North America and parts of Western Europe.

Chapter 7 – The envy barrier resurrected

Chapter 7 explains the decline of capitalism in Europe and the U.S. No one took freedom and prosperity from them. As in ancient Israel, they gave it away and this chapter tells the sad story. In the eighteenth century, atheism and deism became fashionable in much of Western Europe. Atheists and deists offered no proof against God or for atheism. Many people hated the Catholic Church in France because of its wealth, corruption and political power. Its opponents lacked the intellect to challenge it either theologically or philosophically, so they resorted to ridicule. For most French, their hatred was so great that ridicule was enough.

French intellectuals decided they did not need the Church. They could create from scratch their own moral codes and theology using reason. Of course, envy began to reassert itself without the restraining power of Christianity, as Schoeck explained. The first of the Church's moral codes to be jettisoned were those relating to sex and property. Sex outside of marriage became a new moral act while property became the greatest of all evils. Henri de Saint-Simon led the assault against property and free markets and gave birth to socialism. Today, Karl Marx is the image of socialism and communism, but Marx contributed very little to Saint-Simon's system.

Saint-Simon's economics spread rapidly through France and Germany where people were the first to abandon traditional Christianity. After flirting with classical liberalism and free markets in the middle of the nineteenth century, most of Germany embraced Saint-Simon's socialism. It became so popular in Germany that the Chancellor, Bismarck, found no way to preserve the monarchy but to co-opt socialism's principles. Bismarck created the first welfare state by implementing most of the socialist agenda while retaining power in the monarchy. The socialist parliament had no real power.

In addition to the welfare state, German academics who had abandoned traditional Christianity invented a new form of Christianity without the Christian God. They denied the deity of Christ, his virgin birth and resurrection. They relegated all miracles in the Bible to mythical status. The sole message of Christ was to love your neighbor. Retaining the terminology of traditional Christianity, they emptied the words of their historical meaning and filled them with their own. This new version of Christianity without a Christ and worshipping an impotent god perfectly suited the growing ranks of deists. It spread to the U.K. and the U.S. As traditional Christianity receded, envy advanced and with it socialism. By the election of Roosevelt as President of the U.S., most of the West had embraced some form of socialism. The U.S. adopted Mussolini's brand of fascism under F.D.R., but continued to call it capitalism.

In fact, most people considered Nazism and fascism to be forms of capitalism. When Hayek grasped that, he wrote his most popular book, *Road to Serfdom*, to explain to the British the socialist origins of fascism and Nazism. Both ideologies fooled people because they left owners with the paper titles to their property while the state took all control. But common people failed to see that property without control is not property. Most people in the West are still fooled by this fascist sleight of hand.

Chapter 8 – Christian capitalism

Chapter 8 looks at what a real Christian capitalism based on Biblical principles would look like. It starts with the different views of human nature that socialists and Christians have. Christian economics must begin with a Biblical view of human nature. Socialism is a counter-gospel to that of the Bible. It teaches that humans are born innocent and turn to evil only because of oppression. The greatest oppression is private property. If socialists could eliminate property, human nature would return to its natural state of innocence and end all crime and violence. Of course, socialists in the U.S.S.R. and China discovered that human nature is not as elastic as they thought and some force might be required. As a result, the socialist states murdered over sixty millions of their own citizens. That figure does not include the tens of millions of citizens murdered in other nations that embraced socialism.

Mainstream economics assumes a human nature more like a robot that responds to stimuli and has predictable ranges of preferences. Entrepreneurs do not exist and everyone involved in markets knows everything a Ph.D. economist knows as well as the plans of everyone else. At least, those are the assumptions necessary for the equilibrium theory on which mainstream economics has been built.

A Biblical view of human nature says that humans are born with a tendency toward evil that only God can change. Parenting, religion and education can bend the will, but people choose whether to be moral or not. The state does not have the power to change people even if it used all at its disposal. Economically, humans make choices that are revealed in the markets as prices based on supply and demand. They are ignorant, but not irrational, and cannot predict the future. The school of economics that has been built on assumptions about human nature closest to those of Christianity is the Austrian school. Chapter 8 applies Biblical and Austrian economics to the issues of poverty, inequality, government, money, taxation, conservatism, and libertarianism.

Chapter 9 – Romans 13

Finally, chapter 9 briefly looks at the issue of how Christians should relate to government in light of the passage in Romans 13 in which Paul exhorts Christians to submit to governmental authorities. It concludes that Christians have a right, and sometimes an obligation to rebel.

Chapter 1 – What is capitalism?

Until recently few trees succumbed to the demand for books on the origins of capitalism. The consensus simply explained the system as the outcome of a Darwinian process involving innumerable mutations over centuries; as mankind crowns biological progress, so capitalism formed the apex of mankind's economic evolution.

"It is as if capitalism has always been the destination of historical movement and, more than that, the movement of history itself has from the beginning been driven by capitalist 'laws of motion,'" wrote Ellen Wood, a neo-Marxist professor at the University of Toronto. Wood wrote *The Origin of Capitalism* out of frustration with the circular reasoning of both capitalist and neo-Marxist historians who assumed the conclusion they tried to explain. In other words, the ember of capitalism has glowed in the hearts of men since prehistoric times, patiently awaiting the peeling away of the smothering layers that prevented it from bursting into flame:

> Even those who most emphatically insist on the system's roots in human nature and its natural continuity with age-old human practices would not claim that it really existed before the early modern period, and then only in Western Europe. They may see bits of it in earlier periods, or detect its beginnings in the Middle Ages as a looming threat to a declining feudalism but still constrained by feudal restrictions, or they may say that it began with the expansion of trade or with voyages of discovery—with, say, Columbus's explorations at the end of the fifteenth century. Some might call these early forms 'proto-capitalism,' but few would say that the capitalist system existed in earnest before the sixteenth century, and some would place it as late as the eighteenth, or perhaps even the nineteenth, when it matured into its industrial form. Yet, paradoxically, historical accounts of how this system came into being have typically treated it as the natural realization of ever-present tendencies.

Wood follows Marx by locating the birth of capitalism in seventeenth century England when the structure of land ownership changed from common to private as part of the enclosure system. Many farmers had to rent land to farm while peasants worked for wages. Renting forced farmers to invent new ways to improve the land, Woods wrote, and squeeze more profit from it in order to pay the rent. One of the problems with Marx's theory, and there are many, is that most farmers had paid rent for centuries before enclosure began in England. By the fifteenth century, feudalism in England had changed to the point that peasants paid a portion of their produce in rent instead of working in the fields of their lords, yet capitalism did not sprout in that ground.

The critical element in the expedition for the headwaters of capitalism is the definition, because historians tend to find what they are looking for. One of the greatest evils of any time, and undiminished in ours, is the dishonest method of attempting to win a debate by redefining terms in such a way that the side who defines the terms automatically wins. As a result, words often have many definitions. Capitalism has suffered more than most terms with the number of definitions it has to bear, so any discussion of the origins of capitalism has to begin with some sort of corralling of the roaming herds of definitions.

For most historians, a capitalist is nothing more than someone who accumulates wealth through business activity, so it is understandable that they find capitalists existing throughout history. In their eyes, ancient Phoenicians, the merchants of Rome and Venice, monks at monasteries that brewed beer and the wealthy Fuggers of Germany were pioneer capitalists. The transition to a capitalist system came about gradually through the growth of cities and expansion of international trade along with the consolidation of markets through the rise of nation states.

Until Marx, the system of private enterprise did not have a name. Smith had called it the natural system of liberty and contrasted it with the mercantilism of his day in which the state tried to control commercial activity for its own benefit. Socialists resurrected mercantilism and renamed it socialism. Late in the nineteenth century, followers of Marx invented the term "capitalism" as an insult to the free enterprise system. Capitalists were the owners of capital, which meant money, equipment, land, buildings, etc. - the things used to produce goods. Capitalists opposed labor, who Marx thought he championed. Capitalism to Marxists meant the control of the means of production by private individuals, or private property enterprise. But the concept of private property predates the advent of capitalism by millennia as does profit derived from commerce.

Lately, socialists have redefined capitalism again to mean a system in which large corporations control economic policy for their own benefit. The irony of this definition seems to have eluded socialists. First, Smith warned readers that businessmen were no friends of freedom. They often conspired to take advantage of consumers and used the power of the state to do it. Smith warned against the system that socialists mistakenly call capitalism.

Second, corporate control of policy was the definition of the systems of the national socialists in Germany and the fascists in Italy in the decades before WWII. The fascists and NAZIs considered themselves socialists who fought communism for political power while agreeing with them in principle. The differences between the two were small. Communists were more honest. They wanted the state to have legal and actual ownership of property. Fascists and Nazis wanted to maintain the illusion that private individuals retained ownership by letting them keep the paper title to property while the state controlled all aspects of the property. Of course, ownership without control is an oxymoron, but it fooled the people and that is all the fascists wanted. The deception worked so well that when Hayek realized his fellow Brits had fallen for it and considered the German system to be capitalist, he wrote his bestselling book, *Road to Serfdom*, to rescue his countrymen from the delusion.

Capitalism involves commerce and revolves around private property, but it is so much more. To begin, a definition of capitalism has to take into account the "hockey stick" shape of the explosion in per capita income around the beginning of the seventeenth century in Western Europe.

The hockey stick

Adam Smith titled his book *An Inquiry into the Nature and Causes of the Wealth of Nations* (1776) because he and many other people had noticed that some nations grew wealthier while others became poorer. In the two centuries preceding Smith, the Dutch Republic had risen from being a minor territory of Spain to one of the wealthiest and most powerful nations on earth, while its former master had deteriorated from being the super power of its day to an insignificant, poor has been. Proto-economists found the switching of roles remarkable for the fact that in the sixteenth and seventeenth centuries Spain has stolen hundreds of ship loads of gold and silver from its American colonies. By the economic reasoning of those centuries, the Dutch should have grown poorer while the Spanish waxed wealthier and more powerful because wealth came from the accumulation of greater amounts of gold and silver.

University of Chicago economist Deirdre McCloskey refers in her book *The Bourgeois Dignity: Why Economics Can't Explain the Modern World* to the event that Smith noticed, the rapid rise of wealth in the Dutch Republic and England, as the "hockey stick" effect for the shape that a graph of world per capita G.D.P. takes when plotted against millennia. If the graph begins with, say 5,000 years BC, and runs to 2000 AD, the line is almost perfectly flat from the beginning until about 1800 AD, at which point it launches upward at about a forty-five degree angle, giving it the shape of a hockey stick. In other words, most people in the world in 1800 AD were just as poor as their ancestors living ten thousand years earlier.

Illustrations of the hockey stick graph printed below come from Google pictures. The first starts with the year 1500, but readers can imagine that the previous ten thousand years were flat.

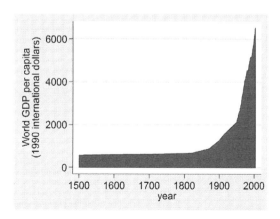

The graph below shows the divergence of the West from China and India after 1700:

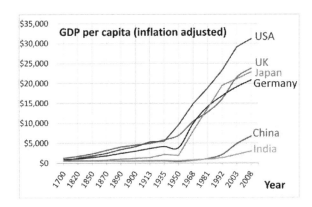

McCloskey has written that this hockey stick effect is the most important event in economic history and the main event that economists need to explain although their models and theories of growth cannot explain the explosion in wealth that occurred.

> The heart of the matter is sixteen. Real income per head nowadays exceeds that around 1700 or 1800 in, say, Britain and in other countries that have experienced modern economic growth by such a large factor as sixteen, at least. You, oh average participant in the British economy, go through at least sixteen times more food and clothing and housing and education in a day than an ancestor of yours did two or three centuries ago. Not 16 percent more, but sixteen multiplied by the old standard of living. You in the American or the South Korean economy, compared to the wretchedness of former Smiths in 1653 or Kims in 1953 have done even better.

> In 1800 the average human consumed and expected her children and grandchildren and great grandchildren to go on consuming a mere $3 a day, give or take a dollar or two. The figure is expressed in modern-day, American prices, corrected for the cost of living. It is appalling.

And that increase in standards of living happened in spite of the fact that the world's population has grown by a factor of almost seven since 1900. Writing before McCloskey, the economist William J. Baumol would have agreed. He wrote in *The Free Market Innovation Machine* the following:

> The virtual absence of any explicit attempt to explain the fabulous growth record of the free-enterprise economies in general, with their transformation of living standards and creation of technological innovations undreamed of in any previous era, is perhaps the most glaring omission of recent economic growth theory, despite all of its substantial contributions. I have been unable to find any systematic theoretical work seeking to account for this incredible record, or any investigation of why this economic system

is so different in its productivity accomplishments from all other economic systems that have ever been tried.

Baumol argued that the chief cause of this spectacular growth was the capitalist economic system that demands innovation of its participants. Without it, "the story appears as one great set of coincidences with little internal coherence, one that could just as easily have happened elsewhere, in radically different circumstances, and that could end as abruptly as it may appear to have begun."

Innovation for Baumol is not the same as invention, for many items have been heralded as great inventions for which no one could discover a use. Innovation means "the recognition of an economically promising opportunity for change and the carrying out of whatever steps are necessary to implement that change." Of course, the launching of per capita G.D.P., the most commonly used measure of standards of living, happened only in Western Europe and the U.S. for the first century. But if you break Western Europe down into its respective nations, the inflexion point moves backwards to around 1600 where it happened first in the Dutch Republic, quickly spread to England then the rest of Western Europe over the next two centuries.

A preliminary definition of capitalism might be the system that caused the hockey stick effect in per capita incomes. Even Marxists could agree on that definition because Karl himself endorsed it. In his theory of historical determinism, he believed the world had to go through the capitalist stage in order for productivity to raise enough to create the wealth that would be needed for an equal distribution of it to enrich everyone. Marx got everything wrong about history and economics except his admiration for the massive increase in productivity caused by capitalism. He was certain that under developed countries like China and Russia could not succeed with socialism without having gone through the wealth creating phase of capitalism.

The role of institutions

To complete the picture of real capitalism, we need to add to the definition the concept of institutions. The relatively new field in economics known as New Institutionalism has increased our appreciation of the role of institutions in the history of economic development and the definition of capitalism. "Economic institutions determine the incentives of and the constraints on economic actors, and shape economic outcomes," according to economists Daron Acemoglu and Simon Johnson in "Institutions as a Fundamental Cause of Long-Run Growth" published in *Handbook of Economic Growth*. Acemoglu and Johnson use North and South Korea as examples of a natural experiment in institutional change.

> North and South Korea shared the same history and cultural roots. In fact, Korea exhibited an unparalleled degree of ethnic, linguistic, cultural, geographic and economic homogeneity...In terms of natural resources North Korea is better endowed with significant reserves of coal, lead, tungsten, zinc, graphite, magnetite, iron ore, copper, gold, pyrites, salt,

fluorspar, hydropower. South Korea's natural resources are coal, tungsten, graphite, molybdenum, lead, hydropower potential. Both countries share the same geographic possibilities in terms of access to markets and the cost of transportation. The North enjoyed a significant advantage over the South in the advance of industrialization, but per capita incomes were identical.

By the late 1960's South Korea was transformed into one of the Asian "miracle" economies, experiencing one of the most rapid surges of economic prosperity in history while North Korea stagnated. By 2000 the level of income in South Korea was $16,100 while in North Korea it was only $1,000. By 2000 the South had become a member of the Organization of Economic Cooperation and Development, the rich nations club, while the North had a level of per-capita income about the same as a typical sub-Saharan African country. There is only one plausible explanation for the radically different economic experiences on the two Koreas after 1950: their very different institutions led to divergent economic outcomes. In this context, it is noteworthy that the two Koreas not only shared the same geography, but also the same culture.

Institutions create wealth and improve standards of living by protecting private property. Investment in new businesses that create jobs and raise standards of living is risky enough in societies that protect private property. Without that protection, people will hoard their wealth by investing in land or gold, or they will send it out of country for safe keeping, as many people from Africa do who export their wealth to Europe and the U.S.

Historians, socialists, and journalists tend to confuse capitalism with business for profit. As a result they see capitalism existing everywhere and at all times in history. If that were true then capitalism would not have contributed to the hockey stick effect of world development because it would have always been with us. Capitalism as defined by Adam Smith and others requires specific institutions. Those include the rule of law, limited government, respect for private property, equality under the law and relatively honest police and judges.

What distinguishes the economy of one country from that of another? Each has access to the same technologies. All countries, even communist ones, have people who understand double-entry accounting. Every nation has large cities with banks and access to the world's capital markets. They can train their people in the knowledge and skills necessary for any task. They have internal and external trade. In theory, every country could improve its productivity growth by adopting the appropriate technologies and management models, but most haven't. Why? The answer resides in their institutions.

Dr. Alexander Kondonassis of the University of Oklahoma wrote in "Economic Development: Issues and Problems" that, "The institutional framework, i.e., system of values, economic, social and political institutions, exercises a critical influence on the productivity of the production input." Institutions pose a serious problem for modern economics: they're messy. Institutions make difficult variables to wedge into the mathematical models that dominate the discipline. Yet, Kondonassis contended that "a main reason for our deficient knowledge on economic development is that no adequate attention has been given to the non-economic aspects of development."

Changes in technology and institutions are the deep wellsprings of development. The economic historian Cameron wrote in *A Concise Economic History of the World* the following:

> The interrelationship of population, resources, and technology in the economy is conditioned by social institutions, including values and attitudes… A complete list of all the social institutions of relevance to the economy would cover many pages, and the analysis of their interactions with other relevant variables is the most frustrating aspect of the study of economic history. But any attempt to comprehend the nature and modalities of economic development without reference to them is foredoomed to failure.

Rigid institutions, characterized by the resistance of interest groups, create "obstacles to productivity growth because every economic improvement requires additional efforts to break down the barriers to change, which increases the costs of (or lowers the returns to) innovation," according to Maarten Prak in *Early Modern Capitalism*. Examples of rigid institutions that have blocked, and continue to block technological innovation include guilds, unions, and common field farming. These institutions provided stability in highly volatile situations. But as the history of the Ottoman Empire in chapter 6 illustrates, inflexible institutions impede change and innovation.

One way that institutions affect productivity is through their impact on the supply of entrepreneurs and the freedom they have to act. Prak wrote, "The limits of entrepreneurial decision-making are dictated by the institutional framework of economic activity. In early modern Europe these limits were exceedingly narrow due to a high level of risk, the inadequate protection of property rights, and the rigidity of economic institutions." But the most important way that institutions control productivity is in their protection of private property, or the lack of, according to Prak.

> The creation of new technologies and ideas depends to a large extent on the protection of property rights. A dependable system of property rights guarantees investors a rate of return that reflects the social rate of return and thus encourages further innovation. Without sufficient protection private rates of return will fall short, creating a disincentive to investors.

> North considers the inadequate protection of property rights the main reason for the slow rate of technological change in the pre-industrial era. The rate of progress accelerated from the late eighteenth century on, when substantial legal improvements raised private returns, and became sustained when market forces began to dominate the process of invention.

Private property rights require laws that define and protect property, enforce contracts, and prohibit theft and fraud. Other laws must restrict governments from taking property without compensation, appropriating surpluses through overbearing taxation, and taking control of property away from the owner through regulations and price controls. In addition, property rights demand courts and a police force that will enforce the laws untainted by corruption or favoritism as well as politicians with enough humility to accept limited government.

Institutions determine the rules of the game that in turn create the demand for particular types of knowledge and sets of skills. For example, using a sports analogy, the rules of soccer encourage the development of footwork and teamwork; golf emphasizes individualism; poker reinforces secrecy. The institutions that have existed throughout most of the history of mankind and still dominate the Third World, "overwhelmingly favor activities that promote redistributive rather than productive activity, that create monopolies rather than competitive conditions, and that restrict opportunities rather than expand them. They seldom induce investment in education that increases productivity," wrote Douglass North in *Institutions, Institutional Change and Economic Performance*.

Nobel prize-winning economist Gunnar Myrdal, quoted in Michael Todaro's *Economic Development in the Third World*, wrote, "Included among social institutions needing change are outmoded land tenure systems, social and economic monopolies, educational and religious structures, and systems of administration and planning. In the area of attitudes, the concept of 'modern man' embodies such ideals as efficiency, diligence, orderliness, punctuality, frugality, honesty, rationality, change-orientation, integrity and self-reliance, cooperation and willingness to take the long view."

The military and political establishments that dominated the Ottoman Empire illustrate Myrdal's point. Ottoman educational institutions trained students in skills necessary to succeed in the military and government bureaucracy. Meanwhile, those people involved in productive activities, such as farming and manufacturing lacked security for their property and had no incentive to invest or attempt innovations. In Russia, efforts to create a free market economy without the supporting institutions, especially protection for private property, allowed criminals to steal the most valuable resources of the nation. A more developed definition of capitalism should include the institutions that made the hockey stick effect in per capita income possible.

Bourgeois values

Many definitions of institutions include the values of the majority of people, but some see those values as so important as to need a separate category. McCloskey has pointed out the institutions of private property and the rule of law are necessary, but not sufficient to launch economic growth of the magnitude enjoyed by the West since 1800. The institutions so valuable to development existed in England centuries before the industrial revolution as well as elsewhere:

Legal developments in England that happened many centuries or many decades after (not to speak of their prevalence in China and Japan) cannot explain the exceptional applied innovations of northwestern Europe beginning in the late eighteenth century. Security of property was a very old story in the England of 1689, as it was in the Chinese or Ottoman empires at the same time. The depredations by the Stuarts were minor, if infuriating to the wealthier Londoners of a non-Conformist disposition. The merely prudential incentives to innovate were just as great in the thirteenth century as in the eighteenth. Property rights, that is, were pretty full at both dates. Money was to be made. As Alan Macfarlane declared in 1978, "England was as 'capitalist' in 1250 as it was in 1550 or 1750."

So institutions such as property are necessary for development, but are impotent unless the majority of people adopt the bourgeois values. McCloskey demonstrates that routine economics cannot explain the striking growth in northwestern Europe. Only rapid innovation can, but for a culture of innovation to surface along the North Atlantic coast, popular attitudes toward business had to change. "I claim here that the modern world was made by a new, faithful dignity accorded to the bourgeois – in assuming his proper place – and by a new, hopeful liberty – in venturing forth. To assume one's place and to venture, the dignity and the liberty, were new in their rhetorics." To help readers appreciate McCloskey's thesis, he captures for the reader in *The Bourgeois Dignity* the extent of the debasement of commerce from ancient times.

> People of business (declared aristocratic Plato and aristocratic-admiring Aristotle) are motivated by apeiros (unlimited) greed. Thus Aristotle in the Politics. The "no limit" in Aristotle is about buying low and selling high, which is supposed not to exhibit the diminishing returns that, say, agriculture does. In the thirteenth century St. Thomas Aquinas, referring to Aristotle with a little less than his customary enthusiasm for the Philosopher, retails the usual complaint against retailing, which depends on "the greed for gain, which knows no limit and tends to infinity."

> In the middle of the thirteenth century Thomas Aquinas had written in the style of his ancient and antibourgeois authorities, especially of Origen and St. Augustine and the desert fathers, and of Aristotle the teacher of aristocrats, that "trading, considered in itself, has a certain debasement attaching thereto, in so far as, by its very nature, it does not imply a virtuous or necessary end."

> Merchants in Japan and China ranked for three millennia close to night-soil men. In Christian Europe they were considered for two millennia the enemies of God. Innovations were long viewed as threats to employment. And so the best minds went into war or politics or religion or bureaucracy

or poetry. Some still do, often on antibourgeois grounds taught to them by the clerisy after 1848.

In 44 BCE Cicero declared that "commerce, if on a small scale, is to be regarded as vulgar; but if large and rich...it is not so very discreditable...if the merchant...contented with his profits...betakes himself from the port itself to an estate in the country." A merchant, said Cicero, lived by making the worse product seem the better, which was shameful (though an orator like himself, who earned the price of his tenement houses in central Rome and his country estate by making the worse legal case seem the better, was of course one of nature's noblemen). In 1516 the blast by Thomas More – or, rather, by his character Raphael Hythloday ("peddler of nonsense"...) – can stand for the abuse directed for millennia at the vulgar traders and innovators of the towns: "They think up...all ways and means...of keeping what they have heaped up through underhanded deals, and then of taking advantage of the poor by buying their labor and toil as cheaply as possible...These depraved creatures, in their insatiable greed,...are still very far from the happiness of the Utopian commonwealth. [Where] once the use of money was abolished, and together with it all greed for it, what a mass of troubles was cut away!" The Earl of Leicester, sent by Elizabeth in the 1580's to meddle in the politics of the already bourgeois Dutch, did not trouble to conceal his contempt for the "Sovereign Lords Miller and Cheeseman" with whom he had to deal. And even the commercial Dutch had a proverb, *Een laugen is Koopmans welvaart*, "A lie is a merchant's prosperity."

Imagine the anti-business assault from the left and popular culture, especially motion pictures such as *Wall Street* and the *Wolf of Wall Street*, multiplied by a factor of ten. That gives a taste of how much most people through all of history have hated businessmen. They held prostitutes in higher esteem. They blocked the despised Jews from participation in the "noble" pursuits of the military, government and the Church and forced them to earn a living in the most reviled ghetto – business. Then change happened, according to McCloskey in *The Bourgeois Dignity*.

An old class of town dwellers, formerly despised by the clergy and the aristocracy and the peasantry, began to acquire a more dignified standing, in the way people thought and talked about it, in European rhetoric about the middle-class activities. And along with a new dignity the bourgeoisie began to acquire a new liberty. Both were rhetorical events.

As the economist Deepak Lal put it recently, "Capitalism as an economic system [I would call it 'innovation'] came about when the merchant and the entrepreneur finally were given social acceptance ['dignity'] and protection from the predation of the state ['liberty'].

If bourgeois dignity and liberty are not on the whole embraced by public opinion, in the face of the sneers by the clerisy and the machinations of special interests, the enrichment of the poor doesn't happen, because innovation doesn't. You achieve merely through a doctrine of compelled charity in taxation and redistribution the "sanctification of envy," as the Christian economist the late Paul Heyne put it. The older suppliers win. Everyone else loses. You ask God to take out two of your neighbor's eyes, or to kill you neighbor's goat. You work at your grandfather's job in the field or factory instead of going to university. You stick with the old ideas, and the old ferry company. You remain contentedly, or not so contentedly, at $3 a day, using the old design of sickle. You continue having to buy food for your kids at the liquor store at the corner of Cottage Grove and 79th Street. And most of us remain unspeakably poor and ignorant.

The shift in values to those of the bourgeois came together for the first time in European history in the Dutch Republic of the sixteenth century after it rebelled against Spain. Of course, the conception was not a miracle. Chapter 4 on "The Dark Ages" explains the historical development.

Zombie theories

The progress made in economic history and development economics over the past century has failed to slay many bad theories that attempt to explain the unique development of the West. Like zombies, the bad theories come back from the dead and have to be slain again and again. McCloskey takes on the zombie theories in his second book, *The Bourgeois Dignity*. For the most part McCloskey finds that the conventional wisdom on development fails to put forth a unique cause for the development of the West. Almost all of the features used to explain development in the West were present, often in greater abundance in the Ottoman Empire or China, elsewhere in the West or in the West at an earlier date, but did not spur development in those places or at those times. Development in the West was a unique event which requires a unique explanation, not an explanation shared with areas that did not develop.

Also, many theories of development in the West rely on a faulty view of human nature. They claim prudence as the sole motivation when in fact we know that humans are much more complex than that and let their religion guide them more than prudence. Or they treat people as animals who cannot plan, anticipate the future, or overcome obstacles but merely react to random events like beasts. McCloskey's trophies of slain zombie theories include thrift, capital accumulation, greed, the Protestant ethic, colonialism, education, transportation, geography, energy, trade, slavery, exploitation, commercialization, genetics, institutions, and science. Here are brief summaries of some of his trophies:

Colonialism

Marx attributed the industrial revolution to "primitive accumulation," by which he meant theft. In his theory, the revolution required massive amounts of capital to invest in the new factories and saintly savings could not provide it. He gave credit to the enclosure movement and the slave trade. Later writers look to colonialism, especially the theft of gold and silver from the Americas by Spain. But those cannot explain the West's rapid growth:

> After all, conquest, enslavement, robbery, murder – briefly, force – has characterized the sad annals of humankind since Cain and Abel. Why did not earlier and even more thorough expropriations cause an industrial revolution and a factor of sixteen or twenty or one hundred in a widened scope for the average European, or non-European?

Babylon, Greece, Rome, the Ottoman Empire and Spain all practiced "primitive accumulation." Their capitals became the wealthiest in their day and the envy of the world by conquering others and stealing their wealth. But none sparked an industrial revolution because capital decays. Capital cannot be accumulated and held on to for centuries. The owners spend it on consumption so they must continually replenish it either through conquest or through the market. Entropy destroys capital in the form of buildings and equipment. All of the ancient empires succumbed to decay when they had extended their borders to the limit and could no longer conquer and steal the wealth to replenish what they had consumed. Besides, McCloskey shows that the cotton weavers who launched the industrial revolution in England had modest capital needs that were easily met through meager savings of family and friends supplemented with short term bank loans.

Some argue that colonization actually benefited the colonized. India endured centuries of colonization under the British, but Vishal Mangalwadi, an Indian intellectual, maintains that India would never have been able to develop institutions and a self-understanding capable of sustaining independence without the social, political, educational, and judicial reforms forced upon the subcontinent by the British in his book, *India: The Grand Experiment*. One could mention the thousands of miles of railroads, train stations, government buildings, dams, roads, schools and utilities built by the British, also.

Education

Americans are possessed by the spirit of education. If only we could force enough people to go to school long enough we can educate away all of our problems. Yet economic historians and modern development experts have shown that education is a result, not a cause of economic development: as people grow richer they enhance their quality of life through education.

> Yet education without the new bourgeois rhetoric is merely a desirable human ornament, not the way to human riches. It makes for a clerisy that

may in fact be hostile to bourgeois values, and very willing to be of professional service to the antieconomic projects of the emperor or the lord bishop...Education proved to be of little use without the liberal political rhetoric, as in Holland and then in England and Scotland, that made economic and intellectual innovation dignified and free.

Again, other places (Ancient Greece, Rome, China and Japan) were well-educated and did not enjoy an industrial revolution.

Commercialization

Some historians and economists attribute the increase in trade and the money supply in Europe, partly as a result of the Spanish looting of the Americas and partly as a result of the common practice by kings of debasing their coinage. However, China used paper money long before the West and expanded the supply to a far greater degree than any nation in the West. England had used money extensively millennia before the Industrial Revolution.

> Contrary to what most educated people believe, Europe and certainly England was from the earliest times thoroughly "monetized" and was nothing like a "subsistence" or "barter" economy. It would be difficult otherwise to explain, to take an early sort of evidence, the English *danegelt* beginning in 991, assessed in silver and paid to the Vikings, or the hoards of precious metals found in England at every chronological level from the pre-Roman era on, or the ubiquity of money measures in the earliest records, such as the Domesday Book of 1086.

If increasing trade caused Europe to develop in the seventeenth century, then why did not the vast trade in the Roman Empire bend the per capita G.D.P. graph into a hockey stick? Why did China, India and the Ottoman Empire not grow rich as well? After all, the trade between the three empires extended from Morocco to Shanghai and dwarfed European commerce before the West was launched. Muslim Ottomans desired as little contact with Christian Europe as possible because they viewed Europeans as dirty savages with nothing to offer in trade but slaves, while Muslim nations, China and India offered everything the Ottoman's wanted to purchase. As for cities, the Ottoman Empire could boast of thirteen cities with populations greater than 50,000 as early as 800 AD, while Europe could point only to Rome.

Genetics

This argument simply asserts that the richest families out bred the poor and spread bourgeois values by procreation. One author claims that the wealthy of China and Japan did not have as many children and that explains why the East did not develop as did the West. Marxist materialism buttresses the argument and admits no place for ideas to launch change.

Of course, socialists could have it no other way. Their ideology requires an irrational faith in the natural goodness of mankind. Material circumstances must cause bad behavior, otherwise socialism could not save mankind from private property and restore humanity to its princely natural state.

As McCloskey points out, the genetics argument does not explain how the bourgeois out bred the rest of society when the towns they lived in were so unhealthy that until the late nineteenth century more people died than lived in them. Also, it does not explain why the nobility when they were the richest people (through most of humanity's existence) failed to out breed the bourgeois and pass on their anti-bourgeois values.

Institutions

While the institutions of the rule of law and protection for private property are necessary for development, and do not exist in most of the poorest nations, they are not enough to launch explosive growth:

> I gradually realized that the timing of institutional change in England fits poorly with its economic change. The curves moved out violently, by a factor of two and then sixteen and more, far too much to be explained by routine changes in institutions, even educational institutions, which after all had come and gone many times before in human history. There was by contrast, I realized decades later, an obvious and historically unique improvement in the dignity and liberty of the bourgeoisie, apparent for example in the invention of the science of political economy itself. The surrounding institutions of the economy were old.

Science

Modern science is another popular stud nominated for the fatherhood of Western economic growth. But Baumol points out that while medieval China, ancient Rome, and other civilizations produced an "astonishing profusion of inventions, virtually none of them possessed a mechanism that induced, let alone rendered mandatory, the cascade of innovation that has characterized free enterprise."

The ancient Romans built roads, aqueducts, baths, dams, and coliseums admired today, and in some cases, still used. They constructed sophisticated water wheels and a working steam engine. Medieval Chinese invented paper, movable type, water wheels, clocks, gunpowder, spinning wheels, cotton gins, hydraulic trip hammers, porcelain, umbrellas, matches, toothbrushes and many more clever items. They built ships that were larger and more seaworthy than those of Europeans and with much better maneuverability due to superior sail design.

Arabs remind the West that they introduced us to science, medicine, mathematics, astronomy and navigation. For centuries, Arabs, Persians and Turks dominated the world in the sciences. But science sat on the bench throughout most of the Industrial Revolution, Cameron informs us.

> In the eighteenth century dawn of modern industry the body of scientific knowledge was too slender and weak to be applied directly to industrial processes, whatever the intentions of its advocates. In fact, it was not until the second half of the nineteenth century, with the flowering of chemical and electrical sciences, that scientific theories provided the foundations for new processes and new industries… Indeed, one of the most remarkable features of technical advance in the eighteenth and early nineteenth centuries was the large proportion of major innovations made by ingenious tinkers, self-taught mechanics and engineers.…

McCloskey emphasizes the point that modern science was a product of economic development, not the cause, especially in the earliest years:

> But of course one problem that has to be faced by advocates of science as a cause, and to some degree even by the advocates of the Enlightenment as a cause, is that Chinese, and at one point Islamic, science and technology, separately and together, and their humanistic scholarship, were until very lately superior to Western science and enlightenment in most ways, and yet resulted in no industrial revolution…The historian of technology Nathan Rosenberg noted that "before the twentieth century there was no very close correspondence between scientific leadership and industrial leadership," instancing the United States, which had negligible scientific achievement by 1890 and yet industrial might, and Japan, ditto, by 1970.

> Like imperialism and trade, science was more a result of economic growth than a cause.

The former Soviet Union stands out as the most fascinating example in modern times of the impotence of pure science to generate wealth. The Soviets put the first man in space and matched the scientific advances of the free world until the atomization of the USSR. At the same time, the Asian Tiger nations impressed no one with a reputation for world leadership in scientific research, but they have surpassed Russia many times over in per capita income. In the twentieth century, the defunct USSR had among the best scientists in the world, but disintegrated because the state could not feed its people without massive loans from the West guaranteed by the U.S.

Any effort to expose the roots of capitalism must account for the differences between the ways in which people gained wealth in traditional societies and the methods used in capitalist societies. In medieval and early modern Europe, favoritism by the king provided the key to wealth accumulation. For example, the Spanish king provided armies to conquer the natives of the Americas and steal their gold. A king could grant a merchant a monopoly on the importation of goods in high demand. But the easiest way to wealth was simply to do a favor for the king and get appointed to a government office where holders could earn a high salary, take bribes, bribe judges, extort money from merchants, and siphon off funds from the public treasury. However, the wealthy never achieved respectability until they owned land; so many people who achieved wealth through these means invested it in land and bought titles of nobility. This pattern of wealth accumulation persisted in much of Europe and most of the world until the end of the nineteenth century.

Capitalist societies, on the other hand, outlawed these traditional methods of wealth accumulation. The only acceptable methods became trade, rent (either from land or interest on loans) and innovation. Those methods achieved respectability only under capitalism.

A definition of capitalism

Yes, capitalism requires institutions, investment, capital accumulation and all of the other variables of routine economics, but none of them will engender the explosive growth of the past 300 years without a change in attitude toward business. Therefore, any honest definition of capitalism must include the institutions and bourgeois values that account for the hockey stick effect in per capita G.D.P. growth. But I must add one more element – mass production.

Many scholars date the rise of capitalism with the city-states of northern Italy, such as Venice. While those states embraced commerce, manufacturing followed the ancient model of small scale craft production for the wealthy. Capitalist production is different. The great Austrian economist Ludwig von Mises wrote in *Human Action*, "Modern capitalism is essentially mass production for the needs of the masses."

In the Italian states, the masses made their own goods at home for the most part. Capitalism was born when the Dutch began using mass production methods to lower the costs of the goods that only the wealthy could afford under the old system of craft production. Not only did large scale mass production increase wages for laborers, it reduced the prices of goods so that the same laborers could afford to buy them. Mass production requires investment of money capital in capital equipment, which demonstrates the appropriateness of the name, "capitalism." Capitalist modes of production are distinct from traditional craftsmanship. In addition, capital intensive production requires larger firms and greater amounts of investment, which forced many investors to pool their resources. That inspired new ways of financing larger firms that spreads the risks over more investors.

Finally, capitalism requires individualism. That topic is too vast to deal with in this chapter so I have reserved the next one for it. But without the rise of Western individualism, none of the other aspects of capitalism could have developed or produced economic growth.

So here is my attempt at an honest definition of capitalism: capitalism is that set of values and institutions, including individualism, that encourage innovation and private investment in capital intensive modes of production, that is, mass production for the masses, and explains the rapid increase in per capita G.D.P. in Western Europe beginning in the seventeenth century.

Chapter 2 – How individualism broke the envy barrier

Economists and historians have fabricated as many theories to explain the economic divergence of the West from the rest of the world as there are economists and historians. There seems to be little consensus on what happened. The previous chapter summarized Deirdre McCloskey's dismissal of most of them in his books *The Bourgeois Virtues* (2006) and *Bourgeois Dignity* (2010). McCloskey teaches that the bending of the hockey stick of per capita G.D.P. could never have happened without a change in values. Pre-capitalist Europe held nothing but contempt for commerce, even manufacturing, and instead admired war, plunder, bribing government officials and accepting bribes as officials as the "honorable" means of acquiring wealth. Around 1600, the Dutch and then the British began to change toward what he calls the "bourgeois virtues," which include hard work, thrift, commerce, trade, etc. What caused such revolutionary change in the thinking of so many people?

Many streams had to converge to generate the powerful river of economic growth that lifted Europe out of regular assaults of famine and starvation, but chief among them was the tributary that overflowed the envy barrier and allowed differences in wealth among social equals. The medieval world saw little problem with extremes of wealth as long as the disparity existed between the nobility and peasants. Theologians justified the extreme inequality on grounds that the different roles assigned by God required different levels of wealth. But within the nobility or between peasants envy reigned and inequality was anathema.

Helmut Schoeck introduced the envy barrier back in the 1960's with his book *Envy: A Theory of Social Behavior*. Schoeck's masterpiece impressed many economists in the Austrian school, but because he did not include a single equation, the rest of the economics world dismissed it. The rebirth of institutional economics1 offers the opportunity to resurrect Schoeck's work. For while the revolution in values was necessary for the launch of capitalism and the growth of per capita incomes, the unmovable object against which all efforts at development had broken was human nature, especially the natural inclination to envy others. When institutions had reduced the envy barrier to scalable proportions then society liberated the bourgeois virtues to perform their miracles. Envy derails economic development by destroying three essentials to growth – coordination of plans, incentives to innovate, and capital accumulation.

While mainstream economists fixate on equilibrium analysis, Hayek insisted that any state of affairs resembling equilibrium can exist only if producers and consumers can coordinate their plans, which refer to the future. Hayek won the Nobel Prize in economics partly for his work on the "knowledge" problem that makes coordination possible or hinders it. Producers must coordinate with suppliers and buyers of their goods while the producers of final goods

---

[1] Pieter De la Court may have been the first institutional economist with his book *The True Interest and Political Maxims of the Republic of Holland* published in 1662. A century later, Adam Smith introduced institutional economics to England with his *Wealth of Nations*.

must coordinate with the desires of consumers. Business failure is nothing but the collapse of coordination. Coordination requires knowledge about the plans of others upon whom producers and consumers depend Hayek wrote in "Economics and Knowledge."

> In the first instance, in order that all these plans can be carried out, it is necessary for them to be based on the expectation of the same set of external events, since, if different people were to base their plans on conflicting expectations, no set of external events could make the execution of all these plans possible. And, second, in a society based on exchange their plans will to a considerable extent provide for actions which require corresponding actions on the part of other individuals. This means that the plans of different individuals must in a special sense be compatible if it is to be even conceivable that they should be able to carry all of them out. Or, to put the same thing in different words, since some of the data on which any one person will base his plans will be the expectation that other people will act in a particular way, it is essential for the compatibility of the different plans that the plans of the one contain exactly those actions which form the data for the plans of the other.

A short video on the internet with the title "I, Smartphone" makes the point well. The phone talks to two beautiful little girls and explains how it came into existence. The raw materials were mined in many different countries. Workers in still other nations fabricated the parts from the raw materials, and employees who assembled the parts lived in different countries from most of the people who bought the phones. Yet no government agency coordinated the whole process. Coordination happened as a result of entrepreneurs creating and observing prices.

A failure of coordination results in waste, which is the destruction of wealth. Often, producers make too much of some goods because other producers they depended on created too few complementary goods. The modern structure of production is vast and complex, requiring the knowledge of the plans for the future of others. Schoeck demonstrated that envy silences knowledge and poisons any attempts at coordination:

> The future, the only field where the fruits of any development are to be reaped, lends itself to a co-operative approach, to exploitation by men able to exchange and co-ordinate their ideas, knowledge and desires. But this is conceivable only when fear of the other's envy, of his possible sabotage or malicious sorcery, has to some extent been overcome. No one can even begin to have rational aspirations for the future unless he has a realistic view of what that future may be; but no such prognosis can be made as long as each member of the group carefully keeps hidden *his* view of the future. Nor can a view that is conducive to social and economic development be formed within a group until its individual members are able, in frank discussion, to compare, weigh and synchronize all their different pictures of

the future. It is precisely this, however, which more than anything else is impeded by the ever-present fear that basically everyone, more especially our near neighbor, is potentially envious and that the best defense against him is to pretend complete indifference about the future.

In our distant past, envy ranked as one of the seven deadly sins and inspired volumes of poetry. Today, the social sciences and humanities have neglected it to the point that it has become a joke. People have no shame in claiming to envy someone, meaning nothing more than a complement to the other's accomplishments, good luck or advantages. Schoeck scoured major academic journals of sociology and anthropology covering three decades and found "not a single instance of 'envy,' 'jealousy' or 'resentment' in the subject indexes..." Americans have defined envy into oblivion.

> The emphasis in the definitions of "envy" and "envying" in Webster's third edition is laid on the desire to possess what belongs to the other, not to see it destroyed. Indeed, this shift in emphasis corresponds almost exactly to the present American view of envy. Thus an American advertisement is able to declare that one should buy this or that in order to be envied – that is to say, so that the other man should at once do his utmost to get the same thing, not, as in earlier cultures, that he should try to damage it out of spite.

Envy has not ceased to exist because human nature has not changed in the last two generations; we have only ignored it. Since WWII we have absorbed envy into the definition of social justice. Social justice requires equality of outcomes, especially wealth, not just equal treatment under the law. Schoeck demonstrates that the insistence on equality of outcomes is the leading symptom of the disease of envy. By defining envy as justice we have expunged it from the deadly sins and elevated it to a virtue, Schoeck wrote.

> In socialist economists such as Abba P. Lerner, we find the envy-motive used indirectly, appearing now as a social virtue. Thus, a progressively rising income tax is proposed on the grounds that, for the psychological good of the collective, the appeasement of envy in the normal wage-earner – on witnessing the penalties of the highly paid – was quantitatively more important and beneficial than the discomfiture of the few, despoiled by the state for the benefit of the envious. This thesis overlooks the fact that there are countless, and often far more painful, occasions for envy than those few really large incomes or inheritances which can be mulcted; it also overlooks the fact that by raising envy to the status of virtue in the interest of the state one only intensifies the suffering of those with a truly envious disposition because politicians feel compelled continually to reveal new "inequalities" in the society.

The French economist Thomas Piketty has tossed fuel on the fire of envy in the West with the release of his book *Capital in the Twenty-First Century* in 2013. Piketty has built his career around the subject of inequality and the book became a bestseller in the U.S. He warns that unless governments punish high earners, inequality will spiral out of control and lead to revolutions. He wrote, "A rate of 80 percent applied to incomes above $500,000 or $1 million a year would not bring the government much in the way of revenue, because it would quickly fulfill its objective: to drastically reduce remuneration at this level…" And later he said, "The primary purpose of the capital tax is not to finance the social state but to regulate capitalism." The tax will not lift the poor because it will not bring in enough revenue; it will only punish high income earners. That is a confession of envy.

We need to rediscover the old vice in order to understand its ubiquitous nature and iniquitous consequences. Envy is a close relative of covetousness and jealousy, but covetousness has the positive goal to obtain something that another possesses while jealously seeks to protect what one has from loss. Currently, American English has no word for the deadly evil so feared throughout history and literature. Schoeck had to fall back on a definition of envy from the 1912 edition of the *Encyclopedia of Religion and Ethics*:

> Envy is an emotion that is essentially both selfish and malevolent. It is aimed at persons, and implies dislike of one who possesses what the envious man himself covets or desires, and a wish to harm him. Grasping-ness for self and ill-will lie at the basis of it. There is in it also a consciousness of inferiority to the person envied, and a chafing under this consciousness. He who has got what I envy is felt by me to have the advantage of me, and I resent it. Consequently, I rejoice if he finds that his envied possession does not give him entire satisfaction – much more, if it actually entails on him dissatisfaction and pain; that simply reduces his superiority in my eyes, and ministers to my feelings of self-importance. As signifying in the envious man a want that is ungratified, and as pointing to a sense of impotence inasmuch as he lacks the sense of power which possession of the desired object would give him, envy is in itself a painful emotion, although it is associated with pleasure when misfortune is seen to befall the object of it.

And Schoeck found a definition from a German dictionary that includes the essential elements of envy:

> Today, as in earlier language, envy [*Neid*] expresses that vindictive and inwardly tormenting frame of mind, the displeasure with which one perceives the prosperity and the advantages of others, begrudges them these things and in addition wishes one were able to destroy or to possess them oneself: synonymous with malevolence, ill-will, the evil eye.

The nature of envy becomes clearer through illustrations from travels through ancient literature psychology and anthropology. For example, Schoeck noted that Genesis 26:14, 15 in the Bible records, "For he had possession of flocks, and possession of herds...and the Philistines envied him. For all the wells which his father's servants had digged...the Philistines had stopped them, and filled them with earth." Schoeck pointed out that "In this respect, human nature has changed little since Old Testament times. Envy of a neighbour's herd of cattle and an assault on his water supply are the order of the day in many a village community in present-day South America, for example."

Classical Greek used the word *phthoneo* to "express the envy which makes one grudge another something which he himself desires...," according to *The New International Dictionary of New Testament Theology*. Aristotle defined jealousy as the desire to have what another has without harboring any ill feeling against the other, while envy seeks to deprive the other man of the thing rather than possess it. Xenophon wrote, "The envious are those who are annoyed only at their friends' successes." The Apostles Mark and Matthew attribute to envy the motive for the Jewish leadership handing over Christ to Pilate for execution (Mark 15:10). In the Epistles, envy is portrayed as a typical feature of the lives of non-Christians and something over which believers should gain victory through the power of the Holy Spirit.

But the most powerful passage on envy in the New Testament does not use the word for envy. In the Sermon on the Mount Jesus taught about the proper relationship to wealth of those who claim to follow him. Matthew 6:19-21 instructs believers to focus less on amassing wealth in this life and more on investing in heaven. Verse twenty-four is the famous passage on the impossibility of serving two masters, God and mammon, or material wealth. He did not mean that material wealth is evil; only that we cannot allow the desire for it master us.

In verse twenty-three, sandwiched between the two passages on material wealth, Jesus said, "The eye is the lamp of the body. So if your eye is sound, your whole body will be full of light; but if your eye is not sound, your whole body will be full of darkness. If then the light in you is darkness, how great is that darkness." One would think that the context would suggest to interpreters that the passage has something to do with the attitude of the believer to wealth, but all of the commentators I read missed the point. Most make the verses mean something about spiritual sight. It is more likely that Jesus is playing on the idiom of the "evil eye." Readers outside of the West will recognize the true meaning instantly because fear of the evil eye is ancient and permeates most non-Western cultures. Jesus is warning believers of the deadly sin of envy.

Schoeck wrote that poets throughout history have stressed aspects of envy: envy requires social proximity; few peasants envy the prince; the envious person afflicts all places and times; his imagination nourishes envy and makes it live long. Chaucer mentioned envy more than eighty times. "The Parson's Tale" in the *Canterbury Tales* concerns the seven deadly sins.

> But Chaucer sees envy as the worst of sins because nearly all the rest oppose only one virtue, whereas envy turns against all the virtues and against everything that is good. It denies, as we would now say, every value

in the scale or table of values. Because the envious man takes exception to his neighbour's every virtue and advantage, the sin of envy is distinct from all others. Every other kind of sin is in itself pleasurable, to some degree productive of satisfaction, but envy produces only anguish and sorrow. Chaucer holds envy to be a sin against nature because it consists in the first place of distress over other people's goodness and prosperity, and prosperity is naturally a matter of joy. In the second place envy consists of joy in the ills and suffering that befall others. This envy is like the devil, who always rejoices in human suffering.

Milton shows the function of envy in the story of the creation of mankind in his *Paradise Lost*:

> Who first seduced them to that foul revolt?
> Th 'infernal serpent! He it was whose guile,
> Stirred up with envy and revenge, deceived
> The mother of mankind...
> Satan – so call him now; his former name
> Is heard no more in heav'n – he of the first
> If not the first Archangel, great in power,
> In favour and pre-eminence, yet fraught
> With envy against the Son of God, that day
> Honoured by his great Father, and proclaimed
> Messiah King anointed, could not bear.
> Thro' pride that sight, and thought himself impaired.

The myth of primitive innocence

Schoeck explored the great literature of ancient Greece, Rome and Europe to demonstrate the sensitivity of pre-modern intellectuals to the problem of envy and their deep understanding of its destructive consequences. Then he turned to anthropology to discover if envy exists in primitive cultures. He paid particular attention to primitive tribes because of the long standing myth in the West that such cultures were the remnants of an ancient Golden Age free from envy. According to historian Richard Pipes, the myth of a Golden Age for mankind deep in the pre-historic past has roots in the opposition to inequality:

> The outstanding quality of this mythical past is the absence of private ownership: in the Golden Age everything is said to have been held in common and the words "mine" and "thine" were unknown. Since...no society has ever existed without some kind of property, the vision of an ideal propertyless world must be grounded not in collective memory but in collective longing. It is inspired by the belief that inequalities of status and

wealth are 'unnatural.' They have to be man-made, not God-made: for are not all beings born equal and, upon death, do they not turn alike to dust?

Europeans in the middle ages believed that on the edges of civilization primitive people still lived out the Golden Age without private property and therefore without the crimes that afflicted their own societies. When Columbus discovered the tribes of the Americas, Europeans assumed he had stumbled upon one of those Golden Age tribes and that mistake birthed the idea of the "noble savage." Schoeck devoted large sections of his book to examining the anthropology of primitive tribes in an attempt to dispel that myth. The following offers a small sampling of his discoveries.

Among the Navajo, the largest tribe in the U.S., there was no concept of personal success or achievement, good or bad luck. Any kind of success came only at the expense of others. Tribal members responded to their own success with lavish hospitality and gifts in order to prevent other members from becoming envious and using magic against them. The Navajo believed that those who attained old age had done so at the expense of younger people through magic and were suspicious of the rich and the poor as well as talented singers. They assumed the rich and talented had used magic to gain at the expense of others while the poor would use magic against others.

The Hopi, another North American tribe, had a general rule against bragging because people might steal the property of the boaster or use magic against him out of envy. The Zuni disliked competitive behavior and sacrificed individuality for the collective. The Comanche tribe limited warriors to the ages between twenty and forty-five. An older warrior who failed to leave the warrior society gracefully was suspected of using magic against other members out of envy. The Comanche preferred chiefs who had not distinguished themselves as warriors so they could leave the warrior society gracefully. The Pueblo tribe liquidated specialist skills needed for the tribes' development by destroying the property of anyone suspected of using his skills for personal gain.

In Polynesia, a lucky fisherman had to deal with the potential envy of fellow fishermen in his group. If he caught fish when others failed, he gave his fish to the others for if his kept his catch and allowed the others to go home empty-handed he risked harm from envy.

Hunters of the Siriono tribe in Bolivia ate at night with their wives and children in order to prevent having to share their meat with other members of the tribe. If they dared to eat in the day time, tribal members would gather around and demand a share. The Siriono hoarded food and accused each other of stealing. Females had been known to hide meat in their vagina. A hunter returning from an expedition would often hide his animal outside the village and pretend to have failed then return after dark to recover it and share it only with his immediate family. In Central American tribal cultures, envy was considered a crime. The victim of an illness caused by envy held the right to kill the envious enemy if he could be discovered.

The many proverbs warning against envy among the Azande tribe in Africa advertise their preoccupation with it. They feared that the envy of other tribal members would encourage the envious person to use magic against them. They looked upon every tribal member as a potential enemy and practitioner of magic. If they envied another, they tried to disguise it to prevent the envied person from using magic against them in his own defense. Physically deformed people, the unfriendly, bad-tempered, dirty, quarrelsome and secretive were seen as potential witches. The Azande member knew that others would envy him for his possessions, his lineage, appearance, and skills as a hunter, singer or public speaker and look for ways to destroy him, but he had spells to neutralize the attacks. The tribe had no concept of luck; another tribal member caused every good or bad event.

Members of the Amba tribe in East Africa practiced sorcery in order to deprive other members of something or punish them for possessing wealth or fame earned through heroic deeds. A person could protect himself only by avoiding accomplishments that might attract the attention of envious people.

The Sukuma of East Africa ostracized members suspected of sorcery, sometimes expelling them, because they believed their envy was insatiable. Fear of what harm the envious sorcerer might do has led to lynchings. They accused successful or prosperous members of using sorcery to achieve their success.

> Thus in every society there are at least two possible tendencies and manifestations of envy to be reckoned with: the man who is not well off, or only moderately so, may be seized with envy against relatives or neighbours and practice destructive magic and arson. The victim and other more or less interested persons may attribute to him the motive of envy. As suspicion grows, everyone in the community, whether rich or only fairly prosperous, is driven to fear the incurably envious man. Eventually he may be expelled. The danger to the group lies in the destructive envy of an individual – the sorcerer.

> This situation can also be reversed, in which case social tension arises from the envy felt by several persons against one who may be richer, more popular or more successful than they. The majority then spread the rumour that the happy man owes his success to illicit sorcery. Tanner mentions a notorious case in Sukumaland: A chief was suspected of employing the spirits of dead fellow tribesmen for the cultivation of his fields as the number of people to be seen working there was not enough to explain their excellence and yield.

Anyone known to have been resentful, was unpopular, had an unpleasant face, was unusually old, who reaped better harvests, hunted more successfully or received favor from their European masters was suspected of envy-sorcery among the Lovedu tribe in Africa. The dominating motive in instances of witchcraft was envy. Any technological gadget, such as a sewing machine, elicited envy. Other instigators of envy included the ability to drive a car, find work in town, dance well, enjoy prestige, physical attractiveness, bride prices, acquiring possessions and yields from cattle herds.

In Haiti peasant farmers would disguise their wealth by purchasing several small plots of land and working them by hand instead of one large field in which they could employ machinery to improve productivity. They would not wear good clothes even if they could afford them in order to keep from inflaming envy in others.

A study conducted in a mountain village in Jamaica made up of former slaves revealed that only 3 percent of the adults needed assistance, yet no matter how wealthy a person might have been he believed that everyone else was better off. Inquiring about a person's financial circumstances was intolerable. Nearly everyone in the village thought that his neighbor disliked and was envious of him. Suspicion made it impossible for families to pool resources on large projects or for anyone to take a leading role in village.

Men of the Mambwe tribe of Northern Rhodesia who got an education from a mission school were able to get work in nearby towns. That increased envy in others, especially members of the chief's family, because commoners were able to acquire wealth equal to that of the chief. Successful men often had to leave the village. One was accused of having the power to train crows to steal grain from the bins of neighbors and bring it to his own bins. Villagers suspect successful farmers among the Mambwe of using sorcery, not of using better agricultural methods.

Fear of the envy of others afflicted all decision making in the poor villages of Mexico. People practiced extreme secretiveness and concealed all private matters. Men rarely revealed plans to buy, sell or take a trip. Women did not tell other women outside the immediate family about a pregnancy, a new dress or a special dinner. People could rely only on their immediate family members and community projects were virtually impossible. Few informed the owner of property if something damaged it. If a pig was killed by a bus, the owner would not learn about it until the other villagers had carved the best meat from the carcass. While envy may not have provoked a person to harm another, it often persuaded him to do nothing to avert another's harm. Altruism, generosity, charity, and sharing were absent. People did favors for others only to get favors in the future. Parents scolded children for giving things to friends and for trusting persons outside the family.

Fear of envy existed among the mestizo village of Aritama in North Columbia. The atmosphere of the village exuded suspicion, danger and hostility because of envy. Villagers envied the good health, material assets, prestige, physical appearance, popularity, harmonious family life, new clothes, authority over others and many other things. They used magic as a leveler to reduce inequality by destroying the advantages of others. An envious villager attributed financial loss, a bad harvest, sick cattle, drunkenness, violence, impotence, laziness, unfaithfulness and more to black magic by an another villager. Sellers of property hated the buyer for his perceived superiority. The buyer could expect the seller to seek to damage him as long as he owned the property.

If one artisan in Aritama worked faster or better than the others, he would find a cross marking his work place warning him to conform to the common slower pace. Other workers chanted spells to make the good worker slow down and become tired and thirsty. The good worker might find his tools damaged, while successful hunters and fishermen would discover damage inflicted on his fishing gear, guns or hunting dog. The evil eye (mal ojo) could cause sickness, drought, and decay to houses, crops, animals and fruit trees. The only protection from envy was through not advertising anything that might cause envy in others and pretending to be poor, ill and always in trouble.

The Dobuan of the Western Pacific was one of the most envy plagued tribes studied. Anthropologists found envy between relatives and gardeners. The islanders attributed disease to envy, which provoked recrimination. Their extreme poverty inflamed envy of others.

The Tiv in northern Nigeria admired those of their tribe who could grow rich and keep their health and wealth because they believed such successful people must have had great power not only to accumulate the wealth but to ward off the many spells hurled at them by envious neighbors.

The envy of the Southern Massim, an island people in Melanesia, limited the ability of their chief to work for the improvement of the group. They required their leader to share any goods he obtained in order to prevent being seen as setting himself above others. He could not implement any innovations that might increase economic inequality in the tribe, which applied to all innovations that launch economic development.

Envy inspired the *muru,* or plunder*,* attack among the New Zealand Maori. Equality in material possessions extended to the tribal chief who bore the burden of obligatory hospitality requiring continual expense. Any expression of individuality or deviation from the norm, even if by accident, gave the rest of the tribe sufficient reason to launch a *muru* attack against the offender in which he lost his property, crops and stores of food to the attackers. Maori members watched each other closely looking for an excuse to launch a *muru* attack. Victims of the attack never resisted because that would mean physical harm for him and, worse, disqualify him from participating in attacks on others. The attacks guaranteed that no tribal member could acquire moveable property, so no one tried and that destroyed incentives to work. Durable capital goods, such as a boat, always became public property.

In India, the agent for an economic development organization often suggested to peasants that they try a new type of seed or fertilizer to increase their productivity and thereby their income, but the farmers rarely followed his expert advice. Should the innovation produce an unusually good harvest, the farmer would suffer from *nazar lagna,* the Urdu word for the evil eye. Villagers feared *nazar lagna* if anyone in an Indian village regarded himself as healthier, better-looking, blessed with more children, more prosperous, etc., than his neighbors. The farmer invited danger if he succeeded. On the other hand, he would suffer *schadenfreude* and ridicule if he failed.

The reader should keep in mind that the primitive tribes shot through with envy as revealed by the anthropologists Schoeck presents are among the poorest people on the planet with little in the way of inequality in wealth. Schoeck sums up his survey of primitive people this way:

> There is nothing to be seen here of the close community which allegedly exists among primitive peoples in pre-affluent time – the poorer, it is held, the greater the sense of community. Sociological theory would have avoided many errors if those phenomena had been properly observed and evaluated a century ago. The myth of a golden age, when social harmony prevailed because each man had about as little as the next one, the warm and generous community spirit of simple societies, was indeed for the most part

just a myth, and social scientists should have known better than to fashion out of it a set of utopian standards with which to criticize their own societies.

The myth of harmony and absence of envy among primitive people explains the confusion among Western development experts who scattered out to the far corners of the globe seeking to advise poor countries on how to catch up to the opulent West. The primitives surprised them with what the experts, being linguistically challenged, called a "backward sloping labor supply curve." They meant something like this: workers in in the West work longer hours, or more people joined the workforce, as wages increase. If graphed, the result would show a line sloping upward to the right. But in the West workers continue to respond that way as wages increase. In the developing world workers reach a point at which they supply less labor as wages rise. In other words, the labor supply curve slopes upward to the right until a certain wage is reached, then it bends sharply to the left. This pattern of behavior has buffaloed development experts for decades. They attempted to explain this oddity by claiming the poor people valued leisure more than do Westerners. In fact, the problem of envy avoidance explains it: laborers refuse to earn so much that they attract the envy of others and cause greater harm to themselves and their families.

> Here, perhaps, one may introduce a generalization: Evidently primitive man...considers as the norm a society in which, at any one moment of time, everyone's situation is precisely equal. He is possessed by the same yearning for equality as has for many years been apparent in political trends in our modern societies. But reality is always different. Since he has failed to grasp the empirical causes of factual inequalities, he explains any deviation upwards, or downwards, from the supposedly normal – i.e., emotionally acceptable – society of equals as having been caused by the deliberate and malicious activity of fellow tribesmen. The suspicion increases with the closeness of the relationship.

> It is, however, imperative that primitive man's superstition should not be equated with his chronic state of envy of his fellow tribesmen, or one be used to explain the other. A self-pitying inclination to contemplate another's superiority or advantages, combined with a vague belief in his being the cause of one's own deprivation, is also to be found among educated members of our modern societies who really ought to know better. The primitive people's belief in black magic differs little from modern ideas. Whereas the socialist believes himself robbed by the employer, just as the politician in a developing country believes himself robbed by the industrial countries, so primitive man believes himself robbed by his neighbor, the latter having succeeded by black magic in spiriting away to his own fields part of the former's harvest.

The false premise that one man's gain necessarily involves the others' loss is still indulged in by some modern economic theorists; while these do not make use of black magic, they often have recourse to methods no less absurd, such as, for instance, a special kind of tax which ends up by damaging the very people it was supposed to help.

Politics and envy

In the eighteenth and most of the nineteenth centuries, citizens of Western nations could rely on equality before the law as the foundation for justice. The rule of law required the government to treat all citizens the same; it could not prefer the nobility at the expense of commoners as Europe had done for millennia. The foundation of the rule of law began to crack with the birth of socialism in the middle of the nineteenth century, Schoeck wrote:

> Under a portentous misconception as to what had really happened when, in the West and for the first time in human history, envy had been successfully mastered, socialist thinkers in the nineteenth century again began to popularize concepts on the nature of inequality and, indeed, to make them morally binding. This corresponded exactly to the concepts of primitives. Since then, however, literary left-wing sentimentalists and their ideas of values have taken things to a point where even people who in no way consider themselves socialist, Marxists or ordinary progressives, among them sincere Christians genuinely concerned with ethical imperatives, no longer know how to deal with primitive emotional complexes. Hence they grope desperately and endlessly for 'social' solutions, which in fact solve nothing.

> Apart from a few early chiliastic social-revolutionary sects, no movements save Marxism and some schools of socialism have so far attempted to base their new society on the virtue of envy.

Schoeck found that modern sociology and psychology have succeeded in expunging envy from the common vocabulary, but not from human nature. Envy thrives in politics. Politicians exploit for votes the latent guilty consciences of wealthy groups who suffer from something like survivor's guilt, wondering "why me" or "what have I done to deserve great success when so many fail?" Fundraisers for political campaigns and non-profit organizations push that hot button, too. He discovered envy in the progressive income and inheritance taxes, once considered gross violations of the rule of law.

No longer does justice mean equality before the law. The popular term "social justice" demands the same equality of wealth sought by primitive tribes with its source in envy. Politicians, the media and intellectuals exploit guilt and the fear of envy in the well-off while inflaming the envy of the poorer citizens to attempt to secure greater equality. But to achieve the elusive goal they have had to trample on the sacred right of equality before the law.

Obviously, it is the intellectual elite in any modern society which is especially prone to a naïve and vain, yet politically relevant, form of envy-avoidance behavior. The literature, both of biography and of political science, that testifies to the notable tendency in highly educated people – leading artists and actors, or well-known scientist – to dally with communism is extensive. This permits us to postulate that a man will opt for a philosophically decked-out, long-term communist programme (in contrast to the mob, recruited as a short-term measure for initial acts of intimidation and street fighting) all the more readily, the more unequal, distinguished and exceptional is the position he already holds in society, in so far as he combines his privileged position with a sense of guilt.

Education and envy

In addition to progressive taxation, death taxes, and transfer payments to others by governments, the U.S. and the U.K. have tried to foster equality and dampen envy through education. The U.S. has chosen since WWII to educate all children between the ages of four and eighteen, though from vastly differing classes and abilities, talent and interest, from the mentally handicapped to the genius, using the same curricula. The goal has been to crank out graduates as links of sausage indistinguishable from each other.

However, the effort only pushed back to the college years the age at which individuals can distinguish themselves. Those with money and intellectual ability went to college while the majority went to the military or to work. Parents with money put their graduates in the best schools their academic abilities could justify while poorer parents sent their sons and daughters to state schools. Then the inequality apparent at the college level further enflamed the envy of egalitarians who began to insist that all students should go to college regardless of ability so the federal and state government began subsidizing college education until a majority of people today have spent at least a year on campus. Again, this merely delayed the revelation of inequality as students with the money and skills set themselves apart again by continuing on to graduate school.

In developmental economics the process the U.S. has followed is called "diploma inflation." Similar to the financial principle that excess printing of money devalues currency and causes prices to rise, or "inflate," the excess supply of college graduates has devalued the diploma. Jobs that used to require merely a high school diploma now demand a graduate degree, not because the work has become more difficult, but as a filtering tool to make the human resources function at companies easier. After all, why not hire a ditch digger with a graduate degree if you can pay him no more than you use to pay a high school graduate?

The U.K. took a different approach. It provided the same education to all students regardless of family, social status or ability until the age of eleven. Then students were separated according to ability as demonstrated by a rigorous exam and sent to the appropriate schools. However, egalitarians discovered that few working class students went to grammar schools even when they could. Fear of the envy of less gifted friends or of relatives who did not attend grammar school prevented the best students from improving their opportunities for success by attending the schools and taking advantage of social mobility, Schoeck wrote.

> For in a community or group of people there is no method of social control so loathsomely insidious as that which ensures that no one shall break away from the lower group in order to advance and to "improve" himself. This observation has been made again and again not only in the case of British schoolchildren, but also in that of a number of minority groups in the United States. The inhibition upon progress by social envy within the group that is discriminated against is frequently more marked – and also more verifiable – than the exclusive tendency of the higher group, into which entry would be possible for individuals.

Minorities in the U.S. continue to pressure members through ridicule to fear distinguishing themselves academically. In Oklahoma, tribal children often refer to those who do well in school as "apples," meaning they are red, or tribal only on the outside while being white on the inside. Black students demean successful black students as "Oreos" and Hispanics refer to excellent students as "coconuts."

Kibbutzim – equality on steroids

Schoeck did not consider the old USSR, still a major world power when he wrote his book, or other socialist countries like China, North Korea, or North Vietnam as valid tests of socialist ideas because those nations prevented citizens who disliked the results from leaving and they offered no way for citizens to compare the consequences of socialism with other systems. He discovered the perfect test of socialism in the Israeli kibbutzim. Socialists founded the system of communal living around 1910 to "make communal life feasible in the pure and full sense of Ferdinand Tonnies' famous and influential work of 1887, *Community and Society*." There was no doubt in the minds of the founders, members, friends and supporters that they were conducting an experiment to prove the superiority of a socialist system.

The founders intended to achieve equality in every aspect of life in order to rid the world of envy. In the early decades members could not own even work clothes or underwear. Those were sent to a communal laundry and redistributed to members afterwards. Generally, the kibbutzim were farms and in order to maintain high levels of productivity they used farm machinery invented and produced by capitalists. Of course, that conforms to Marx's theory that capitalism was a necessary predecessor of socialism in order for socialism to have wealth to distribute.

The kibbutzim failed to reduce envy. As just one example, Schoeck described the crisis of authority that the kibbutzim faced due to envy of the person in a position of authority. The kibbutzim did not pay members in leading roles more for the extra work, yet the position left the leader with less time for himself, his family or any hobbies. Other members scrutinized the leader's every move out of suspicion that the he might have taken the role in order to achieve some personal benefit. As a result, most members sought to evade selection to even necessary offices. Eventually, only those members with tough skins and great self-confidence assumed leadership positions. Seeing the same people in the roles over and over again increased suspicion and resentment.

The emphasis on collectivism and equality in the kibbutzim created a climate of anti-intellectualism and animosity toward those talented in the arts. Anyone with gifts in those areas will stand out and authorities cannot collectivize them because they require talent that few have. The individual must exercise his talent according to his own judgment. Socialist experiments have always valued communal work, which usually means physical labor because everyone but the handicapped can do it. Intellectual and artistic workers always offend collectivist, physical laborers. Those with the talent often felt guilty for having something others envied and for taking private time to develop it and not participating in the collective manual labor. From early childhood, members learned to fear any talent that made them stand out by showing some sign of superiority.

Strict equality in collectivist cultures extends to one's time. The state in George Orwell's *Nineteen Eighty-Four* treated privacy as a crime. When all material goods have become equal, and the problem of intellectual or artistic differences settled, the one thing left to envy is time:

> Thus we see how, when the ideal egalitarian condition has been attained, and everything that can be communally owned has long since been collectivized, there will always be something left that will be a cause for envy and hence will constitute a danger to the community; mere time-space *existence* as an individual and private person is enough to irritate. Then there is the reverse situation: in such groups there may be individuals who enjoy exceptional popularity and respect, whose advice, encouragement and company are much sought after. These people may rouse envy in those whom nobody comes to see...It is here, in particular, that the greatest difficulties in the life of the kibbutzim have arisen.

The setting of the kibbutz made it a perfect laboratory experiment for socialist ideas because members could compare life in the kibbutz with life outside and could choose which life they preferred. The results have not been kind to the kibbutz movement. Schoeck found that the kibbutzim obsession with strict equality did not subdue envy; envy fed on it and spread like poison ivy:

> If we pass under review envy's ubiquitous social control of kibbutz members, and see to what revulsion, mockery, resentment and suspicion anyone is exposed who seems to be even slightly different, a little more inventive, creative, gifted, wide-awake or imaginative than the others, one thing becomes clear: the kibbutz culture, prototype of the socialist community and "signpost for the future of mankind," reflects many aspects

of the society of primitive peoples. Displayed, as in a laboratory, we see the degree of the pressure exerted by egalitarianism, the fear of mutual envy, upon the potential inventor, creator or innovator. The ideal of absolute equality, the eschewing of all authority and superior status, of all economic advantage, and the concern for the survival of this system of equality, once established, cannot admit of any individual's success in introducing unforeseen innovations, since he would then, by definition, no longer be equal, even were his invention immediately and selflessly placed at the disposal of the collective.

The problem is not, in fact, so much actual rejection of innovation by the kibbutz community as the fear inculcated from childhood onwards into the individual that he might somehow stop being equal, might show some sign of superiority or in some way become conspicuous.

Judging from what we have seen so far, it is inconceivable that the elimination of all evident difference – even were this practicable – would solve the problem of envy. There would remain countless suspected differences (which already play a major role today), infinitesimal inequalities, disparate performances (even when these are unpaid) and so on.

Hayek and Mises would have disagreed with Schoeck that the kibbutz offered the perfect socialist experiment. First, Schoeck mentioned that the kibbutzim depended on the equipment they purchased from capitalist producers in order to perform their agricultural work. Second, and more important, they benefitted from market prices to help with price calculation problems. Hayek and Mises emphasized for decades that prices coordinate production and reduce waste, but the market requires accurate prices. Entrepreneurs create those prices and bureaucrats cannot. Therefore the kibbutzim escaped this problem of economic calculation without accurate prices because they were surrounded by freer markets and could take advantage of market-determined prices. Bureaucratic attempts to duplicate the work of entrepreneurs caused the USSR to collapse and forced the introduction of freer markets in China.

How the west won

The literature that Schoeck surveyed and the tour of primitive tribes provided convincing evidence that envy and the fear of it preceded Christianity. In spite of this history, many intellectuals and religious leaders mistakenly see the guilt brought on by envy to be a Christian attribute.

In so doing they overlook the New Testament's remarkable religious, psychological and historical achievement in freeing believers from precisely this primitive, pre-religious, irrational sense of guilt, this universal fear of one's neighbour's envy and of the envy of the gods and spirits. For that alone made the modern world emotionally and socially possible. The essence of this idea is already to be found in Max Weber's theory of the role of the Protestant, and more especially the Calvinist, ethic in the development of capitalism.

Schoeck argued that Christianity did not invent envy, but provided the means for breaking through the envy barrier and achieving astonishing economic growth. He observed that nearly all primitive religions contained deities who envied each other and mankind, and as a result ridiculed them. Christianity and Judaism for the first time offered people supernatural beings that experienced no envy and did not ridicule men for their failures.

And it was an astonishing post-Reformation development, and a special feature of Calvinism, which enabled the individual to feel unashamedly superior to others and, what is more, to show it in his works. This was the beginning of the breach in the envy-barrier. Perhaps the development took this course because Christianity had begun by placing man in a new and special relation to the world, and had provided him with a central, logical system of values. When, however, the Reformation placed this spiritual source of power at the disposal of the individual, one consequence was greater immunity from the threat of the evil eye exerted by the less gifted and the less successful...

Most of the achievements which distinguish members of modern, highly developed and diversified societies from members of primitive societies – the development of civilization, in short – are the result of innumerable defeats inflicted on envy, i.e., on man as an envious being. And what Marxists have called the opiate of religion, the ability to provide hope and happiness for believers in widely differing material circumstances, is nothing more than the provision of ideas which liberate the envious person from envy, the person envied from his sense of guilt and his fear of the envious. Correctly though Marxists have identified this function, their doctrines have remained blind and naïve when faced with the solution of the problem of envy in any future society. It is hard to see how the totally secularized and ultimately egalitarian society promised by socialism can ever solve the problem of the residual envy latent in society...

The ethic taught by the New Testament sought to secure differentiated human existence in a world full of envious people and unlikely to evolve into a society of equals. A society from which all cause for envy had disappeared would not need the moral message of Christianity. Again and again we find parables to the tenor of which is quite clearly the immorality, the sin of envy. One should love one's neighbor as oneself – for the very reason that this will protect him against our envy and hostility. Naturally, the avoidance of certain arrogant and ostentatious gestures, such as extravagance – but not of meaningful activity, the feast, excellence of achievement – is essential, if only to appease the envious. In such passages the New Testament nearly always mentions the envious man, exhorting him, in as much as he is mature and a Christian, to come to terms with the inequality of his fellow man.

However, Christianity only won some battles against envy; it did not remove it from human nature and eventually it resurfaced:

In the West, the historical achievement of this Christian ethic is to have encouraged and protected, if not to have been actually responsible for the extent of, the exercise of human creative powers through the control of envy.

Yet the envious succeeded in perverting that ethic by adapting the message to their own ends: kill-joy, ascetic morality whispers persuasively to the joyful, lucky of successful person: "Feel guilty, feel ashamed, for you're envied by those beneath you. Their envy is your fault. Your very existence caused them to sin. What we need is a society of equals, so that no one will be envious." Thus it is no longer the envious who must discipline and control themselves and practise love of their neighbor, it is their victim who must change – and change for the worse, in conformity with envy's own yardstick.

On the eschatological plane the oppressed, the unfortunate and the victims of fate are further told, perhaps in order to help them overcome their envy of more fortunate companions and contemporaries: "After death there is in store for you (maybe) a kingdom of heaven where all (in so far as they manage to get there) will be equal. All men are equal before God, whether kings or beggars when in this world; indeed, the poor have an even better chance of going to heaven."

But here again the envious have succeeded in usurping the New Testament message. The doctrine, progressively secularized, came to mean a mission to establish an egalitarian society, to achieve a leveling-out, a state of uniformity here and now, in this world. This egalitarian utopia is respectably cloaked in the stuff of the New Testament...This doctrine cannot, without chicanery, be read anywhere into the New Testament. Nor should the fact be overlooked that the realization of an egalitarian society would render the context of Christian ethics, for a greater part, superfluous.

How do we know that those who demand equality of wealth and call it social justice are driven by envy? The answer lies in their threats of the disastrous consequences of greater inequality. Marx predicted that capitalism would lead to greater inequalities of wealth until the proletariat starved and revolted. Of course, inequality continued to fall in the West until about 1973 and since has risen mildly. That increase has appalled and excited the left who picture riots, burning buildings and rivers of blood washing the streets. But the rioting and burning that has taken place since 2008, the start of the worst recession since the Great Depression, has all happened in the most socialist countries of Europe where inequality is lowest. Irony aside, the left uses the threat of violent revolution to extort greater transfers of wealth not unlike a mafia operation that demands protection money from small shopkeepers, or as in the threats of violence in primitive tribes against successful members. The rioting in the socialist countries of southern Europe after 2008 proves that equality does not ensure peace.

> What preserves modern democracies from anarchic resentment is not, indeed, the degree of *de jure* or *de facto* equality achieved, but the continued existence of institutions of inherited patterns of experience, of literary and religious ethical ideals, which permit a sufficient number of citizens to remain aware of the limitations set upon mutual comparison, and hence ensure social peace.

Societies have struggled with envy since their beginning. As in Plato's Republic, the solution has almost always been attempts to pacify the envious person by punishing the successful. Attempts at pacifying envy through forced egalitarianism have failed miserably in every instance attempted, whether at the national level as in the USSR or China, or at the commune level in the kibbutzim.

Envy's resurrection day

As Schoeck pointed out, envy never died; Christianity merely suppressed it. Socialism in the mid-nineteenth century released it from its bonds, nourished it and set it loose upon unsuspecting victims across the world. How did socialism free envy? It shot the jailer – traditional Christianity. Atheism flourished in Enlightenment Europe. Sentimental atheists gutted traditional Christianity of all meaning and called themselves deists. In what became known as "liberal" theology, scholars under the guise of searching for the "historical" Jesus cut out of their Bible all of the miracles and recast the histories as myths. They tossed out the virgin birth of Jesus, his sinless life, deity and resurrection. They retained only "Blessed are the poor." Advertising their dishonesty, they clung to the label of Christianity, forcing real Christians to adopt adjectives such as "traditional" or "fundamentalist" in order to distinguish themselves from the liberals and making debate impossible without taking time to redefine all of the theological terms that liberals had changed.

More importantly for economics, they tossed the doctrine of original sin. Judaism and traditional Christianity had always taught that God created mankind perfect and innocent of evil, but the Fall, the rebellion of Adam and Eve in the Garden, had scarred human nature and given it a permanent bent toward evil. As Schoeck noted, no member of a primitive tribe would have been surprised. They suspect all of their neighbors of the worst envy and evil.

In the place of original sin, the atheists and liberal theologians preached the basic goodness of mankind: man is born innocent and turns to evil only because of oppression. Socialism preached its own salvation message: remove the repression and mankind will revert to its natural state of innocence, just as kissing a frog will restore the prince. What was the greatest repressor? Private property. Historian Richard Pipes explained:

> Locke's theory of knowledge, expounded in *The Essay on Human Understanding* (1690), which claimed that human beings have no "innate" ideas but form ideas exclusively from sensory perceptions, remained in England an abstruse epistemological doctrine, devoid of political significance. In France, however, it was applied to politics, providing a theoretical basis for the conviction that by properly shaping the human environment – the exclusive source of all ideas – it was possible so to mold human behavior as to create an ideal society. And the ideal society, much as Plato had envisioned it, was characterized by equality.
>
> The onset of the eighteenth century thus marked a radical break with traditional concepts of human nature. Since the triumph of Christianity thirteen hundred years earlier, man was believed to have lost in the Fall his capacity for perfection and turned into a corrupt being who required discipline to keep him from straying onto the path of depravity. The Christian view was conservative in that it saw human nature as immutable. But now another view emerged and in time came to dominate Western thought: it entailed the outright rejection of the doctrine of Original Sin. It held that there was no such thing as human nature: there was only human conduct, and that was shaped by the social and intellectual environment. The philosopher's task was to design a social system that would make it virtually impossible for humans to be depraved. Once this outlook was accepted – and it became conventional wisdom among both socialists and liberals a century later – there was no theoretical limit to the manipulation of the social and intellectual environment in the quest for human perfectibility.

The prophets of the new faith elected scientists to the priesthood. It seems a bit naïve today with the advances in science made in the past two centuries, but in the eighteenth and nineteenth centuries people viewed the natural sciences as having performed miracles as valid as any Old Testament requirement for the status of a prophet. If the natural sciences could perform such wonders with the material world, what more could they do for human nature. Scientists would create the design for a new society that would perfect human nature;

engineers would build it; artists would persuade the people to follow it. Together they would usher in the golden age of mankind without crime or evil, both of which result from poverty and envy.

Should we wonder that many scientists, engineers and artists are devout socialists? In socialist societies they rule and receive the highest honors. They do not pander to the ignorant masses who do not understand them or their work. In a capitalist world they get respect only if they create something that pleases the paying public. In the socialist system, the elite, the scientists, engineers and artists, lead the masses because the masses are too stupid, evil and religious to know what is best for them. They cling to their God and guns. The elite hold nothing but contempt for the masses. They do not want to pander to them.

Hayek identified the fallacy of the early socialists as "scientism." Scientism (not to be confused with Scientology) is the inappropriate application of the methods of the natural sciences to the social sciences. Austrian economists have pointed out the damage that scientism has done to the field of economics, essentially neutering it and turning mainstream economics into a game played with toy economies. In its extreme form, scientism becomes philosophical materialism which allows for no truth beyond what exists in the natural sciences. Fields considered scientific in the nineteenth century, such as philosophy and theology, were banished to the realms of opinion and superstition. Scientism is behind the frequent claim that economics is not science.

The origins of socialism explain the obsession modern society has with science, and the false history they have written that explains everything good today as a result of scientific achievement. The actual achievements of the natural sciences have been great, but readers need to keep in mind that Nazi Germany and the failed USSR each took pride in having among the world's greatest scientists. Science aids economic development, but cannot cause it.

Historians crown science with much of the honor for giving birth to the industrial revolution and our modern prosperity. But Baumol pointed out that while medieval China, ancient Rome, and other civilizations produced an "astonishing profusion of inventions, virtually none of them possessed a mechanism that induced, let alone rendered mandatory, the cascade of innovation that has characterized free enterprise." The ancient Romans built roads, aqueducts, baths, dams, and coliseums admired today, and in some cases, still used. They constructed sophisticated water wheels and a working steam engine, but not economic development. In fact, Cameron pointed out that science sat on the bench throughout most of the Industrial Revolution:

> In the eighteenth century dawn of modern industry the body of scientific knowledge was too slender and weak to be applied directly to industrial processes, whatever the intentions of its advocates. In fact, it was not until the second half of the nineteenth century, with the flowering of chemical and electrical sciences, that scientific theories provided the foundations for new processes and new industries...Indeed, one of the most remarkable features of technical advance in the eighteenth and early nineteenth

centuries was the large proportion of major innovations made by ingenious tinkers, self-taught mechanics and engineers...

But the former Soviet Union stands out as the most fascinating example in modern times of the impotence of pure science to generate wealth. The Soviets put the first man in space and matched the scientific advances of the free world until the atomization of the USSR. At the same time, the Asian Tiger nations impressed no one with a reputation for world leadership in scientific research, but they have surpassed Russia many times over in per capita income.

Socialist assumptions about the innocence of human nature and the power of science to change it through social engineering have become so pervasive that most Christians subscribe to them. Almost everyone in the West looks to the structure of society to determine the causes of crime and find solutions. Even the temperance movements of the late nineteenth century were nothing more than attempts at social engineering. If Schoeck is correct in his estimation of the role played by Christianity in taming envy in the West, it is not a coincidence that enthusiasm for capitalism faded with a decline of traditional Christianity over the past century. The eclipse of Christianity forecasts a bleak future unless the West experiences an old-fashioned gospel revival.

Individualism domesticated envy

Schoeck argued that Protestant Christianity corralled envy by freeing the individual from the irrational constraints of collectivism based on envy. It did not provide absolute freedom, but enough freedom from envy to unleash the envy-constrained powers of economic growth. Another way to put this is to say that Christianity invented individualism. But why did it take 1,500 years for Christianity to tame envy? First, we need to clarify what we mean by individualism because dishonest people have muddied the pool of ideas with innovative definitions and made discussion of the subject almost impossible.

For example, the English word "sanction," can mean to endorse something or to penalize it. Like sanction, the word "individualism" can mean one thing or the opposite. The context can sometimes clarify the author's intent. Another example is the confusion caused by the word "liberal." In the nineteenth century it meant freedom from government coercion but in the twentieth came to stand for such coercion in the U.S. and U.K., whereas it retained much of its original meaning on the continent of Europe. We can say the same can be true for the term "individualism."

What do we mean by individualism? Clearly it means something more than that humanity is composed of people with their own physical bodies because that is kind of obvious. At its most basic level, individualism is a way of organizing society and that is why Western societies have very different institutions from those of most of the rest of the world. In the same way that Schoeck asserts that societies organize around envy, individualism is the flip side of envy, so societies' views of what it means to be an individual form part of the focus point around which they organize themselves. That is still a little vague I am sure, so let's look at some examples that should clarify the concept.

Larry Siedentop in his book *Inventing the Individual: The Origins of Western Liberalism* writes that the Western view of individuals did not exist in the ancient Greek and Roman world. I would add that it did not exist in ancient China, India, Persia or any other world, either. The ancient Greeks worshipped their ancestors and organized their societies around that worship. The hearth was the center of the home because the flame in it kept the ancestors close to the living and content. Siedentop put it this way:

> Around the family hearth – with the father tending its sacred fire, offering sacrifices, libations and incantations learned from his father – members of the family achieved union with their ancestors and prepared for the future. The fire on the family hearth could not be allowed to die out, for it was deemed to be alive. Its flickering, immaterial flame did not just represent the family's ancestors. It was their ancestors, who were thought to live underground and who had to be provided with food and drink, if they were not to become malevolent spirits...The ancient Greek language has a very significant word to designate a family. It is...a word which signifies, literally, that which is near a hearth.

As the priest and head of the family, the father literally owned all family members and all family property. He could execute any family member or a slave with impunity. The oldest son would inherit the father's role as priest, family head and all of his property, leaving young sons and daughters with no property. Daughters had no choice for survival but to marry, in which case they became members of their husband's family and subject to that family's head. People outside of the family did not share even a common humanity with the family, as evidenced by widespread slavery. Members held no identity or will outside of their family. Siedentop wrote, "Charity, concern for humans as such, was not deemed a virtue, and would probably have been unintelligible. But fulfilling obligations attached to a role in the family was everything." Ancestor worship and the family structure it created survived in Europe as late as the seventh century when pagan families newly introduced to Christianity used the Eucharist to feed ancestors.

Greek and Roman societies evolved as families formed clans then tribes by identifying a common ancestor to worship. Tribes combined in a similar way to build cities. Along the way ancestor worship never waned and the family provided the basic building block of society. Within cities, kings were the high priests and later under a republican form of government the magistrates of the city were the chief priests.

Cities were confederations of families, not of individuals. Only family heads, and later the oldest son, enjoyed citizenship or had any rights within the city. Along the path to full citizenship, the son would go through initiation in the family cult, then the cults of the clan and tribe and finally the cult of the city, each stage involving a ceremonial meal.

Membership in the religions left no space for individuality in conscience or choice. They asserted authority over actions, thought and relationships. "There was no sphere of life into which these rules could not enter – whether it was a matter of dress, deportment, marriage, sport, education, conversation or even ambition," as Siedentop wrote.

To the ancient Greek and Roman, patriotism to one's city was the highest possible virtue because the city protected the ancestors and gave meaning and identity to every citizen and his family. Siedentop wrote, "For the Greeks, to be without patriotism, to be anything less than an active citizen, was to be an 'idiot'. That, indeed, is what the word originally meant, referring to anyone who retreated from the life of the city." Exile from the city was the worst possible punishment; it became a living death. In that world, a person's identity issued from his role in the family and city. A natural hierarchy existed in which some were born to rule because nature had endowed them with superior abilities, others to serve or to fight. "For Plato, everyone is born with an attribute that fits him or her for a particular social role, his or her 'proper' place."

The organization of the cities by tribes and the welfare of the city having the highest priority had enormous consequences. Society was stratified into castes. It allowed no space for personal judgment or will. Individuals could not claim rights that limited the authority of the state or family head. In other words, individualism as we know it in the West did not exist. The next chapter will follow the long difficult birth of the Western idea of individualism. Schoeck explained the history and influence of envy on social organization and how envy crushes individualism. The stamp of ancient Greek and Roman culture is evident in the cultures Schoeck analyzed, even among native tribes in the Americas. Research in cultural anthropology demonstrates that with regard to individualism, most of the world thinks and acts like the ancient Greeks and Romans.

Culture rules

Schoeck insisted that the rise of individuality in Christianity broke the envy barrier in the West and unleashed the productive forces of free markets. To examine the importance of individuality today, let us turn to the field of cross-cultural anthropology and the works of Geert Hofstede, Shalom H. Schwartz and others. In the 1970's and 1980's Hofstede researched the cultural differences across subsidiaries of International Business Machines Corporation in sixty-four countries. As a result of these studies, he identified five dimensions that describe cultural differences. They are power distance, individualism, masculinity, uncertainty avoidance and long-term orientation. The following compares the measures for power distance, individualism and uncertainty with Schoeck's depiction of envy and their impact on economic development.

Societies in which individuals are loosely tied to each other in groups, where everyone is expected to look after himself and his immediate family score high on the individuality index (IDV). The opposite of individuality is collectivism, but not in the Marxist sense. In collectivist societies people belong to strong, cohesive groups, such as extended families and tribes which protect them in exchange for loyalty.

People in collectivist societies are tradition-oriented and hardly think of themselves as individuals. For example, Chinese tradition has no equivalent for the Western concept of personality as a separate entity distinct form society and culture. Hofstede wrote, "The Chinese word for 'man,' (*ren*) includes the person's intimate societal and cultural environment, which makes that person's existence meaningful."

Collectivist societies consider individualism an evil thing. Mao Zedong for example, saw individualism as representing the manifestation of selfishness and an aversion to discipline. Placing the interests of the group ahead of one's own interest is the best way to provide for one's wellbeing. In contrast, an individual in the U.S. who can stand on his own, think for himself, depend on no one and admits to no master is often admired and portrayed as the hero of many films and novels. Hofstede wrote,

> Modern man…is open to new experiences; relatively independent of parental authority; concerned with time, planning, willing to defer gratification; he feels that man can be the master over nature, and that he controls the reinforcements he receives from his environment; he believes in determinism and science; he has a wide, cosmopolitan perspective, he uses broad in-groups; he competes with standards of excellence, and he is optimistic about controlling his environment.

> Traditional man has narrow in-groups, looks at the world with suspicion, believes that good is limited and one obtains a share of it by chance or pleasing the gods; he identifies with his parents and receives direction from them; he considers planning a waste of time, and does not defer gratification; he feels at the mercy of obscure environmental factors, and is prone to mysticism; he sees interpersonal relations as an end, rarely as means to an end; he does not believe that he can control his environment but rather sees himself under the influence of external, mystical powers.

Most countries in Asia earn low scores on the IDV scale, with the important exception of Japan. Five of the six countries that score highest on the IDV scale include the U.K. and her offspring, the U.S., Canada, Australia and New Zealand. The Netherlands is the sixth, with a score between Canada and New Zealand. Cultural attitudes toward individualism have a direct impact on economic development because they structure institutions in ways that encourage and reward innovation or strangle it, and, as noted earlier, innovation is the artesian well that nourishes economic growth. Hofstede's work demonstrates the power of individualism to break the envy barrier in development. As Schoeck wrote:

> *Institutionalized envy*…or the ubiquitous fear of it, means that there is little possibility of individual economic advancement and no contact with the outside world through which the community might hope to progress. No one dares to show anything that might lead people to think he was better off. Innovations are unlikely. Agricultural methods remain traditional and primitive, to the detriment of the whole village, because every deviation from previous practice comes up against the limitations set by envy.

Hofstede's power distance index (PDI) measures the extent to which the less powerful members of society accept the unequal distributions of power in their culture. High scores on power distance suggest that the followers as much as the leaders endorse the society's level of inequality in both material wealth and under the law. Countries with low PDI scores tend to have democratic governments with much discussion and little violence in the political process. The government recruits bureaucrats from a broad cross section of the population. Citizens take ownership of the government, cooperate with it and trust the police. Corruption is relatively low and scandals end political careers. Philosophies and religions tend to emphasize equality before the law and power sharing.

The highest PDI score indicates a dictatorship or monarchy. Leadership changes are sudden and violent. The road to power and wealth leads through loyalty to the leadership. Administrative elites are unrepresentative of the larger population. Citizens trust the press but distrust the police while corruption runs rampant and political scandals are covered up. Citizens wait for the government to make major decisions and rely more on the state for assistance.

In Hofstede's research, nations with the highest PDI scores cluster in Asia, with the exceptions of Japan, South Korea, and Taiwan, and in Africa and Latin America. The English-speaking world, along with Japan, South Korea and Taiwan, take up the middle of the scale, while the lowest scores go to Northern European countries that lean toward socialism, such as Sweden. This seems to suggest that high levels of PDI are worst for economic performance, followed by very low levels with moderate levels encouraging development. This may seem odd, at first, until we remember that too much emphasis on equality of material goods leads to high tax rates and policies which redistribute wealth and discourage productive activity. High levels of PDI encourage corruption and destroy the security that owners of private property need as incentives to invest in plants and equipment. In high PDI countries, those who manage to accumulate wealth tend to keep it by sending it out of the country to safe havens like the U.S. or Switzerland. The optimum is in the middle where the people tolerate higher levels of inequality in wealth but low levels of inequality under the law that holds the elites to the same legal standards as the masses.

The uncertainty avoidance index (UAI) captures a society's tolerance for ambiguity. Extreme uncertainty about the future creates an intolerable anxiety in some cultures. Nations with high scores on the UAI try to minimize novel, unknown, surprising and unusual situations by enforcing strict laws and rules, safety and security measures, and a particular absolute "truth."

Societies have developed a variety of ways to cope with uncertainty through the use of technology, law and religion. They employ technology to defend people against uncertainties caused by nature, while laws protect people from the unpredictable behavior of others. Religion helps people accept the uncertainties that the other two cannot guard against. Societies with low UAI scores in Hofstede's research tend to be more open to innovation, more trusting of others and are more willing to accept foreigners in their midst. Also, they allow more individual decision-making and are more comfortable with competition.

Other characteristics of cultures with a high tolerance for uncertainty (indicated by a low UAI score) include an acceptance of uncertainty as part of life, an openness to change and innovation, willingness to take risks, curiosity about things that are different, comfort with ambiguity, attraction to novelty and convenience and the belief in one's own ability to influence one's life, one's superiors and the world.

On the other hand, societies structured to avoid uncertainty exhibit tendencies toward prejudice, rigidity, dogmatism, intolerance of different opinions, traditionalism, superstition, racism and ethnocentrism. These societies interpret freedom as a threat to the established order, because freedom implies uncertainty in the behavior of oneself and others. Often, citizens accept totalitarian governments in order to avoid uncertainty. Cultures that score high in UAI view uncertainty in life as a threat they must fight. They prefer the *status quo* to change, view things and people that differ from the norm as dangerous, take very few risks, have a strong need for clarity and structure, desire purity, and possess a feeling of powerlessness toward external forces. Hofstede wrote that the authoritarian personality syndrome is related to uncertainty avoidance and is characterized by an

> intolerance of ambiguity, rigidity, dogmatism, intolerance of different opinions, traditionalism, superstition, racism, and ethnocentrism next to pure dependence on authority. Fromm (1965) has suggested that fascism and Nazism were a result of a need to 'escape from freedom,' a response to the anxiety that freedom created in societies with a low tolerance for such anxiety. Freedom implies uncertainty in the behavior of oneself and of others. Totalitarian ideologies try to avoid this uncertainty.

People in uncertainty-avoiding cultures look for structure in their organizations, institutions and relationships that make daily events predictable and easy to interpret. On the other hand, they may take extreme risks in order to reduce ambiguities, such as starting a fight with an opponent instead of waiting for the threat to materialize. Uncertainty avoidance affects the politics of a country. In societies that chafe under ambiguity, the citizens have a low rate of participation in local politics, preferring to leave the decisions to experts. They often feel alienated from the government and social systems that affect their lives.

On the other side, people in cultures that embrace uncertainty feel more competent to direct state policies and consequently reduce the ability of authorities to make fast, autonomous decisions. They demonstrate a lower sense of urgency and an acceptance of familiar and unfamiliar risks, such as changing jobs. Uncertainty avoidance plays an important role in economic development. Aversion to uncertainty produces laws that limit the freedom of markets. For the majority of people in the world, free markets appear chaotic, messy and frightening. Socialists have often advertised their system as offering freedom from the chaos of the market.

Hofstede performed statistical analyses on the relationships between per capita income in countries and the scores of those countries on the power distance index (PDI), uncertainty avoidance index (UAI), and the individualist/collectivist (IDV) indexes. He uncovered strong statistical correlations between them and concluded that PDI and UAI contribute to wealth while wealth causes IND. Schwartz agreed that increases in wealth contribute to individualism, but we will see later that the rise of individualism preceded economic development in the West.

I performed my own analysis on Hofstede's data, but for per capita G.D.P. I used Angus Maddison's data from *The World Economy: A Millennial Perspective*. My results paralleled those of Hofstede, but differed slightly because I used different per capita G.D.P. figures and I included interactions and nonlinear affects. I analyzed the effects of Hofstede's cultural factors on Maddison's per capita data for 1950, 1975 and 1998. The IDV factor dominated as the strongest predictor of per capita G.D.P. for all periods, followed by UAI, with PDI appearing only as it interacted with the other two. For 1950, the model accounted for 67 percent of the variation in per capita G.D.P. among nations; for 1975, 74 percent; and for 1998 54 percent. The p-level for each model was 0.0000, indicating that we can be 99 percent confident that the results of the model are not flukes and that the resonance between wealth and the cultural factors is real. For 1975, the model indicates that we can be 95 percent confident that an increase of one in the IDV scale will raise per capita G.D.P. from $1.00 to $1.78 in a country. Schwartz performed similar analyses using surveys of 15,000 teachers worldwide. He wrote that,

> The first basic issue confronting all societies is to define the nature of the relation between the individual and the group. A large literature suggests that resolutions of this issue give rise to the most critical cultural dimension. This dimension is frequently labeled individualism–collectivism (Hofstede, 1980; Kim et al., 1994). It is also described as contrasting individualism–communalism, independence–interdependence, autonomy–relatedness, and separateness–interdependence...

> For example, in societies where individual ambition and success are highly valued, the organization of the economic and legal systems is likely to be competitive (e.g. capitalist markets and adversarial legal proceedings). In contrast, a cultural emphasis on group well-being is likely to be expressed in more cooperative economic and legal systems (e.g. socialism and mediation).

Development economist William Easterly performed his own calculations by merging Hofstede's and Schwartz's data with that of the World Values Survey and came up with similar results. Easterly arrived at this conclusion:

> To drastically oversimplify, values across different cultures lie along a spectrum between two separate poles: (1) valuing individual autonomy, believing in equal treatment of individuals, reliance on formal law, the same moral standards apply to all, enforcement of morality is between individuals vs. (2) seeing the individual mainly or only as part of the group, different standards of treatment for group insiders and outsiders, morality only applies to interactions within the group, group enforcement of moral standards, reliance on informal rather than formal institutions...So the

bottom line (again drastically oversimplified) could be something like 'the value of individual liberty promotes prosperity.'"

Cultural anthropologists demonstrate that ancient Greek and Roman collectivism still dominates most of the modern world outside of the English-speaking nations and parts of Western Europe. One way it manifests itself is in the different attitudes toward families versus outsiders. For example, I lived in Morocco a few decades ago and needed some furniture for our apartment. A college student I had befriended, Hamid, offered to take my cash and negotiate with the dealer for me while I drank coffee in a nearby *qahwa* because, as he said, the price of the furniture would triple if the merchant glimpsed an American within a block of his store.

I hesitated to take Hamid's offer only because I didn't want to put him to so much trouble, but he mistook my pause for distrust. He assured me that he could not cheat me because I had eaten dinner with him and his family and therefore enjoyed a status similar to that of a family member. No Moroccan can cheat a family member or anyone who has eaten at their table. I gave Hamid my cash and later returned home to find a nice selection of furniture at a good, Moroccan, price.

Later, I met the owner of a construction firm who enlightened me further on business ethics in Morocco. He told me he spent a large part of his time thwarting the efforts of suppliers, customers, and employees to cheat him. The cleverness that went into dreaming up new ways to cheat him surprised me. He confirmed what Hamid had told me: cheating others is not considered unethical at all but a sign of an astute businessman. But cheating family members is immoral. Since then I have read similar stories about the business ethics in Iraq after the war when American companies rebuilt some of the war-torn nation.

This family ethic results in poor countries being dominated by either small, family-owned businesses or giant state-owned, corrupt ones with few private corporations because the owners cannot trust non-family members. In fact, they can trust that family outsiders will cheat them in any way possible. As a consequence, capital is tied up in small, inefficient businesses and cannot be reallocated by investors to more efficient enterprises.

Pseudo-individualism

Why, then, do so many in the West find the concept of individualism repugnant? Part of the answer lies in the deliberate false interpretation of terminology. Adam Smith wrote that self-interest guides the decisions of business people in a free market, but socialists interpreted self-interest to mean selfishness. However, Smith was a moral philosopher first and considered economics a subset of ethics. He was no promoter of selfishness. If self-interest equals selfishness, then the English language has no word for the morality of the activities of the business person to provide food, shelter and financial security for himself and his family, the actions that Smith meant by the term "self-interest." Surely, those activities are not selfish and evil.

Another deliberate misunderstanding comes from socialists twisting the relationship of individuals to associations. Free market individualism opposes forced association, for example the state requiring everyone to join a church. Socialists distort that principle to claim that free markets oppose any kind of association at all and that it advocates an atomistic form of society where every individual is a loner and self-sufficient. However, the division of labor and specialization form the core of free markets, both of which require every person to rely on others for the goods, services or help they cannot provide for themselves. That reliance on others requires associations. Hayek wrote in *Individualism and Economic Order*, "The consistent individualist ought therefore to be an enthusiast for voluntary collaboration – wherever and whenever it does not degenerate into coercion of others or lead to the assumption of exclusive powers."

In addition, Socialist polemics has often used the technique of redefining terms in order to predetermine victory in debates and they accomplished that with the term "individualism." Socialists manufactured a second definition of individualism, which Hayek labeled as false. Unlike Christian, or true, individualism, socialist individualism sprang from the mind of Descartes in the Dutch Republic, as Hayek quoted the philosopher, "There is seldom so much perfection in works composed of many separate parts, upon which different hands had been employed, as in those completed by a single master." He gave as an example the perfection of the building of a bridge by an expert mechanical engineer. Then he applied the same principle to "engineering" society. He wrote, "the past pre-eminence of Sparta was due not to the pre-eminence of each of its laws in particular...but to the circumstance that, originated by a single individual, they all tended to a single end."

Descartes' social engineering took root in eighteenth century France and blossomed in the atheistic Enlightenment. After the French Revolution, its greatest proponent was Rousseau, but the fathers of socialism, the Saint-Simonians, were its greatest promoters. It was rationalistic, meaning the false use of reason, in spite of the fact that the Saint-Simonians insisted that they worshipped Reason as if it were a person. Hayek called Descartes' application of engineering methods to society "scientism" because it was the false application of methods from the natural sciences to the control of human beings.

False individualism asserted that for any principle to be true, the individual must be able personally to understand it and foresee the consequences of implementing it. Otherwise, he need not submit to it. Of course, such individuals suffered from such near-sightedness that all of their analyses concerned only the immediate effects of their principles. False individualism insisted that any organization of society must be consciously designed by a superior human mind. They idolized reason, but did not credit everyone with the ability to reason well. Only an elite group of scientists who reasoned appropriately could engineer society and would organize society according to scientific principles. All non-elites, the "masses," would submit, by force if necessary. They would achieve material equality for the masses, but not allow the masses equality under the law with the elite. Any institution that might stand in the way of the will of the elite scientists would be crushed, especially the church. That resulted in the scrapping of all tradition built up over centuries and all religion. They allowed nothing to interfere with the elite's direction of the masses.

Hayek recognized the Christian origins of what he called true individualism: "To the accepted Christian tradition that man must be free to follow his conscience in moral matters if his actions are to be of any merit, the economists added the further argument that he should be free to make full use of his knowledge and skill, that he must be allowed to be guided by his concern for the particular things of which he knows and for which he cares, if he is to make as great a contribution to the common purposes of society as he is capable of making." But Hayek was only half right. Siedentop demonstrated that Christian individualism was born of a long struggle to institutionalize the Christian concept of the moral equality of individuals. Long before the "Enlightenment," the Dutch Republic had instantiated Hayek's freedom of the "use of his knowledge and skill" in production and in the market because they had regained the Hebrew respect for commerce, work and production.

The Enlightenment definition of individualism morphed into the opposite and spawned collectivism, socialism and totalitarianism because of its insistence that a superior human mind must design and control all social processes. As Hayek wrote, "The concentration of all decisions in the hands of authority itself produces a state of affairs in which what structure society still possesses is imposed upon it by government and in which the individuals have become interchangeable units with no other definite or durable relations to one another than those determined by the all-comprehensive organization. In the jargon of the modern sociologists this type of society has come to be known as 'mass society'."

Both versions of individualism are closely tied to two views of human nature. The traditional Christian view held that mankind enjoys the power to reason, but its rebellion against God had weakened that power and made it less that perfectly reliable in that no individual can foresee all the consequences of policies. Traditional Christian theology labeled this "original sin." It gave mankind a tendency toward evil. Hayek called it antirationalistic and wrote, "The antirationalistic approach, which regards man not as a highly rational and intelligent but as a very irrational and fallible being, whose individual errors are corrected only in the course of a social process, and which aims at making the best of a very imperfect material, is probably the most characteristic feature of English individualism." In other words, the original, Christian individualism included humility about things one knew little and what one could control. "From the awareness of the limitations of individual knowledge and from the fact that no person or small group of persons can know all that is known to somebody, individualism also derives its main practical conclusion: its demand for a strict limitation of all coercive or exclusive power."

False individualism, took an irrational leap of faith, insisting that humans are born innocent and turn toward evil only because of oppression. The state, guided by the rationalism of scientists, can remove oppression and return mankind to its original state of innocence and goodness. What is most relevant to this discussion is the fact that the rationalists of the Enlightenment determined through their vast intellects and powers of reason that the great oppressor of mankind is the unequal distribution of wealth. Equality before the law lost all value and only material equality remained. If Schoeck was correct that the insistence on material equality issues from envy then it becomes clear that envy gave birth to socialism. Socialism elevates envy to a virtue.

To summarize Hayek, here are the main points of disagreement between the true and false versions of individualism:

1.   Rule of law. True individualism requires that general principles of conduct apply, within which people are free to differ. Pseudo-individualism insists on pragmatism; the "right sort of person," that is the socialist, knows the correct course of action in each circumstance and needs no principles to guide him. He labels as ideology any demand that principles be followed.

2.   Equality. True individualism requires that the state treat all people equally without regard for race, gender or status, in other words equality before the law. Pseudo-Individualism abandoned equality before the law in favor of equality of material goods, at least for all but the elite.

3.   Morality. True individualism respected traditional morality and tended to be religious. Pseudo-individualism rejected tradition, especially morality, in favor of variable rules of behavior based on pseudo-reason in which the individual could understand the rationale and see the immediate consequences of his actions.

4.   Envy. Original individualism tamed envy; pseudo-individualism inflamed it.

5.   Government. True individualism required limited government in order for the individual to have room to actualize his abilities. Pseudo-individualism demanded absolute power for the state to mold human nature in its image.

6.   Associations. True individualism allowed people the freedom to choose with whom they would associate. It valued family, church, small communities and other voluntary associations. Pseudo-individualism valued only the state and sought to devalue all other associations.

7.   Religion. True individualism embraced traditional Christianity. False individualism tended to be atheist or deist.

8.   Reason. For true individualism, every person has the power to reason for himself and choose his own goals and means as long as he remains within the borders of general principles, such as not stealing and not committing murder. Pseudo-individualism accorded true reasoning ability only to an elite group, especially scientists headed by mathematicians. Commoners had to relinquish their abilities to reason and blindly follow the elite. On this point, socialism is clearly a regression to the caste system that Siedentop attributed to ancient Greece and Rome in which only an elite group possessed the ability to reason.

True individualism started with the idea that all men are equal before God. God treats the peasant and the king equally and requires both to obey his laws. It encouraged personal salvation instead of corporate salvation. Its emphasis on private property and the condemnation of envy, along with the demand that people be allowed to enjoy the fruits of their own labor subdued envy for the first time.

New Institutional School

Another respected body of academic work that reinforces Schoeck's view of the organizing power of envy and Siedentop's history of individualism is the New Institutional School in economics. Three leaders of the school wrote,

> The fundamental question of economic history can be asked in two ways: how did a handful of countries achieve sustained rates of economic growth and development in the late eighteenth and early nineteenth centuries? or why have most nations failed to achieve sustained economic growth over the last three hundred years? What historical process(es) have generated institutions in a handful of countries capable of sustained economic development in the twentieth century, while most countries still fail to develop thriving markets, competitive and stable politics, and cultures that promote deep human capital accumulation for most of their populations? Economists have thoroughly documented that no one factor explains economic development – not capital accumulation, human capital, resource endowments, international trade, or geographical location to name a few prominent examples. Instead, the complex ways that societies structure human relationships – the institutions that shape economic, political, religious, and other interactions – appear to be the key to understanding why some societies are capable of sustained economic and political development (North 1981, 1990, Acemoglu, Johnson, and Robinson 2002, Greif 2005, Rodrik, Subramian, and Trebbi 2004).

The New Institutional School describes two broad forms of government – limited access and open access, sometimes called extractive and inclusive. Limited access forms of government are those with a single leader supported by an elite ruling over the masses. The single leader can be a pharaoh, king, Caesar, president, secretary of the politburo, military dictator or other term. He and his elite enjoy nearly absolute power.

The elite can be nobility, courtiers, army officers, extended family members or the top group in a political party. The elite give their allegiance to the supreme leader in exchange for his agreement to allow them to plunder the wealth of the masses, although economists use a euphemism for plunder – "extracting rents." The leader needs the elite to keep him in power and the elite need his authority over the masses to allow them to plunder. Throughout history the leader's authority often derived from his assumed relationship to the gods. The elites maintained a gentleman's agreement not to plunder each other most of the time.

The limited access state is the most robust form of government in the history of mankind and for this reason North referred to it as the "natural" state: "We call this the natural state because we believe it is the natural response of human societies to the threat of endemic violence. The natural state first emerged historically about ten thousand years ago and remains the dominant form of human society today." The limitations of natural states versus open states are clear: the need of the leadership to bribe the elite with privileges and power over resources at the expense of the common people increases corruption and restricts competition. Here is North again:

> The difficulty in starting a t-shirt factory in Peru, documented by De Soto, is a classic example of how the natural state not only refuses to support the creation of organized economic activity but actively discourages it for non-elites. The "crony capitalism" common in today's developing world (Campos and Root 1996) represents another manifestation of the natural state's inherent tendency to limit access to organizational forms to members of the dominant elite.

> Second, natural states face impediments to making the credible commitments necessary to protect the rights of non-elites. Non-elites cannot credibly threaten the state or coalition, because a natural state's survival does not depend on the support of non-elites. Independent of what the laws or constitution of a natural state say, non-elites cannot credibly accept promises by the state to protect their rights. Non-elites therefore make significantly smaller investments in physical and human capital than they would if their rights could be credibly guaranteed. This too limits growth in natural states.

> Non-elites also employ what James Scott calls "the weapons of the weak" in order to protect what property and assets they do have. The rational peasant (non-elite) behaves in systematic ways to make it more difficult for the lord (elite) to determine whether the peasant is working hard and using resources effectively. Foot dragging, malingering, dissimulation are the order of the day. As a result, not only are property rights poorly defined conceptually, elites deliberately raise transaction costs.

Transition from a natural state to an open access state is very difficult, as the limited number of countries having made the transition demonstrate. North wrote, "Despite the massive attention to economic development by international donor agencies, only eight countries have made this transformation since WWII...Moreover, none of these countries were the focus of international donor agencies."

The New Institutional School calls the open access system of government "modern," but it has existed a few times in the past in ancient Israel under the judges and in Venice during its earliest centuries. It only gained a degree of permanence with the Dutch Republic. Open access governments are built around the rule of law (general principles) and equality before the law. The courts and police are relatively lacking in corruption and apply the law without prejudice. Those institutions protect private property from confiscation by the government, an elite or any other person. In other words, open access states protect the successful and innovators from the threat of violence by the envious.

Open access nations protect the property of all citizens, not just the elites. As a result, the common people invest in improvements to their property because they know that they will enjoy the fruits of that investment. Investment increases productivity, creates better paying jobs, sparks innovation, reduces the costs of food and clothing and launches nations on the path to economic development.

> In an open access order, economics appears to be independent of politics. This seeming independence is reflected in both the famous classical liberal dictum about limited government and in neoclassic economics' view that markets are antecedent to government and that the government intervenes into markets. A competitive economy requires not only a state that maintains open access, entry, defines property rights, and enforces competition, it also requires a state that is capable of providing the social infrastructure that sustains perpetually lived and extremely sophisticated and complicated organizations.

> Third, our perspective redefines the problem of economic development. In contrast to the perspective in modern economics, our framework suggests that economic development is not an incremental process, such as gaining more education, capital, and making marginal improvements in the rule of law. Each of these can improve a developing limited access order by moving it a bit toward the doorstep conditions, but these incremental changes can take a limited access order only so far: they are not the process of development.

Changing rhetoric

I have already mentioned University of Chicago economist Deirdre McCloskey's series of books explaining the rapid development of the West as a change in values and attitudes toward commerce demonstrated in a change of rhetoric. We will see later that from at least the time of Aristotle until the sixteenth century Europeans held business in low esteem, often lower than prostitution. The culture valued plunder in war, bribery of state officials, kidnapping for ransom and monopolies on trade as the "noble" means toward greater wealth. Commerce was considered worse than prostitution and so evil that it condemned the merchant's soul to hell. As a result of this disdain for their profession, merchants who became wealthy did not reinvest their wealth to expand their businesses but gave much of their wealth to the Church to redeem their souls from hell. They took what was left and bought titles of nobility and land to become members of the plundering class of elite. Innovation does not exist in such a climate.

Then in sixteenth century in the Dutch Republic values changed. Venice produced the first green shoots centuries earlier, but they blossomed into tulips among the Dutch. McCloskey argues that the explosion in innovation that occurred in the Republic could never have happened without the change in values to what she calls the bourgeois values, essentially those of middle class merchants – faith, hope, love, temperance, courage, justice and prudence. McCloskey's first book explains the virtues while the second proves that prudence alone can never explain the explosion of growth that began in the Republic. McCloskey patiently disassembles over a dozen of the most popular materialistic explanations for the industrial revolution, most of which fail because they use factors that existed to a greater degree in other locations, such as China and the Ottoman Empire, empires that did not develop as the West did.

The essence of McCloskey's argument is that a revolution in values had to occur before an industrial revolution would be possible and the lack of the change in values in other nations explains the lack of economic development. A career in business had advertised its material benefits for centuries, yet few people chose it as a career. Jews had no choice. Being barred from positions in the military or government and land ownership, they pursued the only options left – business and banking, which explains most of the animosity toward them by the "Christian" population who despised both fields. Christians who prospered in business abandoned it as quickly as modern entrepreneurs who send their children to law and medical school.

The changes in values in the sixteenth century elevated the bourgeois values and allowed successful merchants to enjoy respect and political power. Instead of hiding their hard won wealth or abandoning their work for a life among the nobility, successful merchants expanded, innovated and grew their businesses, eventually spawning the industrial revolution.

Conclusion

Helmut Schoeck' theory of envy as the driver behind the way societies organize themselves unifies several seemingly unrelated fields – cross-cultural anthropology, New Institutional Economics, McCloskey's bourgeois virtues rhetoric, Siedentop's history of individualism, developmental economics, and Christianity. Schoeck argued that Christianity in the Reformation provided the first brake on envy and Seidentop filled in the detailed history of the slow and painful birth of individualism that accomplished it.

Nations ranking high on Hofstede's power distance index (PDI) scale correspond to Schoeck's depiction of cultures that are organized to appease envy, such as one finds in socialist and economically backward nations. The masses do not envy those in leadership because they see entrance into the group of ruling elites as impossible for them, so they tolerate very large differences in power between the elites and the masses. While demanding strict adherence by their peers to the norm, they overlook abuses, corruption and lawless behavior by the elites.

According to Schoeck, cultures in which envy dominates oppose innovations out of fear that one person will gain at the expense of others. That agrees with Hofstede's individuality index (IDV) and uncertainty avoidance index (UAI). Traditional cultures suppress individualism and reduce uncertainty, both of which crush innovation that leads to economic development.

Open access forms of government described by the New Institutional School of economics are rare and short-lived because they require the subjection of envy to reason and principle. Clearly that is a difficult task. They break through the darkness created by limited access societies like flashes of lightening. The question this arrangement raises is why did the masses put up with millennia of oppression by the elite? History offers many examples of peasant revolts against the elite, even though the resulting government usually substituted one set of elites for another and perpetuated the natural state.

Schoeck answered that question this way: the masses envied each other but not the elite because the ranks of the elite were too far removed from them and access to membership in the elite group was impossible. So the masses ignored the luxury, abuse and corruption of the elite, as Hofstede demonstrated with his power distance index (PDI). On the other hand, the envy of the masses toward each other aided the elite in keeping the masses under control, for if anyone within the masses deviated from the law established for them by the elite, the elite could count on many within the masses to inform on them to the elite. This is the reason that the limited access system of government has been the most robust form of government throughout history. It uses the power of envy against those within the masses who might aspire to joining the ranks of the elite or overthrowing them. Today, politicians continue to use the power of envy to stir up the ranks of voters even in developed nations.

Hofstede's indexes of culture reinforce the new institutional school's concepts of open vs. closed, or natural states. Open states could not occur without changes to the culture measured in the PDI, IDV and UA indexes. Open states did not appear until the Dutch Republic, the nation McCloskey credits with the values revolution that made development possible and enabled the change in cultures that Hofstede found necessary for such development.

The Christianity of the Reformation broke the power of envy, which unleashed McCloskey's values transformation and Hofstede's cultural changes, leading to the birth of individualism, the formation of open states and the institutions to generate sustained economic development through wealth creation instead of expropriation for the first time in human history. From this perspective, socialism is a return to North's closed economy, the natural state, and the ancient Greek and Roman caste system of inequality before the law.

Chapter 3 – The Torah economy

Many Christians who write on economic systems claim that the Bible endorses neither capitalism nor socialism. They think they cut off the heads of both systems with the sword of the Word and install their own system, referred to as a "third way," in which they scavenge through the carcasses for the best parts of each and stitch them together into a new creature. Unfortunately, the creature resembles an economic Frankenstein more than the good doctors care to admit.

Economic systems are nothing but laws concerning how people relate to each other with regard to property. No society has ever existed without an economic system because the things we depend upon to survive are scarce, especially food, clothing, housing as well as the land and resources needed to produce them. They are not like the air which everyone can have as much as they need of it. Because the necessities and pleasures of life are scarce, someone has to decide who controls them and gets to use them.

The Egyptian economy

The Israelis considered themselves blessed to have the law of God and claimed that no other nation enjoyed a system of law as perfect as theirs. To fully appreciate the government and economic system God gave the Israelis, we need to know something about the government and economic system of Egypt, with which the Israelis would have naturally compared their new law.

Pharaoh

To understand the Egyptian economy we must understand the role of the Pharaoh. In ancient Mesopotamian literature, the gods were active on the earth. But in Egypt, according to J. Assmann in *Search for God in Ancient Egypt,* whom John Walton quoted in his *Ancient Near Eastern Thought and the Old Testament,*

> …the gods had withdrawn from their presence among humans to their habitation in the sky. There were important cities (e.g., Thebes or Memphis), but cities were not as central to the identity of the state – rather the state was more directly related to the cult. "The absence of deities made room for a specifically human sphere of activity and responsibility: the state, which – despite or because of its being a divine institution – kept the divine at a distance that had to be bridged by 'sacred signification.' The founding of the state amounted to the same thing as the founding of the cult..."

Walton went on to explain that,

In the ancient world the king stood between the divine and human realms mediating the power of the deity in his city and beyond. He communed with the gods, was privy to their councils, and enjoyed their favor and protection. He was responsible for maintaining justice, for leading in battle, for initiating and accomplishing public building projects from canals to walls to temples, and had ultimate responsibility for the ongoing performance of the cult.

In Egypt the almost total immersion of the persona of the king into the divine realm led inexorably to the conclusion that the acts of Pharaoh were the acts of deity.

In Egypt priests operated only by authority delegated from the king, who had the sole right to perform the rituals of the cult. It was his task "to complete what was unfinished, and to preserve the existent, not as a status quo but in a continuing, dynamic, even revolutionary process of remodeling and improvement." Thus in the ritual observances the order of the cosmos not only was maintained but was transferred to society, resulting in political and social order: "The royal performance of the cult, generally speaking, invoked the sacred power for the preservation of *maat*, the order of the world."

Pharaoh may not have been a god, but he was the closest thing Egyptians had to a god on earth and the primary intercessor between humans and the gods. The pharaoh Sneferu reigned about a thousand years before Moses and took the title *neb maat*. The word *neb* meant not just lord, but owner and keeper. *Maat* was the embodiment of truth, justice, righteousness, and created order, in other words, the divinely ordained pattern of the universe. The Greek word *logos* used by John in his gospel has a similar meaning. The pharaoh brought *maat* to the people through religious rites, government and the construction of sacred monuments and buildings. He repelled foreign enemies, adversity, injustice, and even barrenness through his power in war and his dominion over the earth. As the *Oxford Encyclopedia of Ancient Egypt* explains in the article on the "Economy,"

By placing himself on a level with the gods, the king presents himself as the guarantor of the fertility of the land and the fecundity of the livestock. Thus the king possesses divine powers to confer well-being on the people. He imposes his superiority as victorious warrior; but he also orchestrates feasts that generate prosperity and organizes the country...The king guarantees the subsistence and protection of his people, who in turn owe him obeisance and work.... He has founded domains and constructed towns; in exchange, he can demand total obedience from his subjects, as well as all the fruits of their labor. The sovereign's role as nurturer is proclaimed throughout pharaonic history: he is the provider of Egypt, he gives it an overabundance of provisions…coming from its own land and its neighbors, be they vassals or conquered territories.

As a quasi-god, pharaoh owned all of the land of Egypt, but he granted the use of land and the right to earn income from it, to others in exchange for payment, which would be the equivalent of modern rent or taxes. Some of those grants continued long enough that they resembled modern leases which people could bequeath to descendants or sell, but it was understood that pharaoh owned the land and could give the lease to others at any time.

Pharaoh granted the use of much of the land to temples for growing food and animals for sacrifices to the temple gods and freed them from payment of taxes. At one time temples controlled 300,000 hectares of land. Farmers would sometimes donate their lease to temples if the temple tax was lower than the government tax. Temple taxes could bring in more food or animals than the priests needed for their luxurious lifestyles and offerings to the gods, in which case they would sell the surplus in markets, a common practice for temples throughout the ancient world. However, the only group of people with the disposable income to buy the temple surplus was the nobility. Temples became so wealthy in the ancient world that they became the first banks, loaning vast sums to kings and nobility.

Pharaoh granted land use to military commanders and nobles as a reward for service. In turn, the commanders and nobles would lease the land to peasants to farm. Pharaoh owned the mines from which workers extracted gold, silver, copper and other metals. He owned the quarries that produced the stones for buildings and monuments. And he owned the Nile River which provided fish and rejuvenated the soil during floods. The same principle of rent applied to these as applied to agriculture. In addition to owning everything, pharaoh regulated the flows of goods and services, organized labor and regulated imports and exports.

Pharaoh's bureaucracy collected taxes, or rent, from the various sectors of the economy and redistributed them, some to pay salaries, some as offering to temples, and some stored for future distribution, in the case of drought for example. The Bible describes an episode of such redistribution in Genesis. Four hundred years before the exodus, God gave pharaoh a dream which disturbed the king because none of his advisers could interpret it. Then God gave the interpretation of the dream to Joseph, who was in prison at the time because of his refusal to commit adultery with a former master's wife. The wife had accused him of rape and sent Joseph to prison. Joseph interpreted pharaoh's dream as a prophesy of an approaching seven year famine in which much of the population of Egypt would die if they did not prepare for it. In recognition of Joseph's wisdom, pharaoh made him his vizier, or second in command of all Egypt.

God did not tell Joseph how to prepare for the famine. Joseph may have relied on custom, for he taxed the people's wheat and stored it in preparation for the famine. When crops failed due to the draught, Joseph sold the people's food back to them in exchange for their land, thereby making slaves to pharaoh of the entire population. As the Bible says, "So Joseph bought all the land of Egypt for Pharaoh, for every Egyptian sold his field, because the famine was severe upon them. Thus the land became Pharaoh's." (Genesis 47:20) Technically, pharaoh already owned the land, so the Biblical story must mean that the people gave up even more of their rights to the revenue from the land. The story emphasizes the insecurity of property in Egypt and the absolute control over land and people enjoyed by pharaoh.

The state administrators prepared budgets for the state based on forecasts of the harvest. They had discovered a correlation between the height of the Nile flood and the size of the following harvest to help them make those forecasts. In theory, good pharaohs would live within their means, but like most politicians today, they often lacked such discipline.

Peasants enjoyed little time for themselves. When not working in the fields to plant or harvest, pharaoh drafted them to work on his building projects. The *Oxford Encyclopedia of Ancient Egypt* explains: "In all such efforts – the creation or maintenance of agricultural domains, the organization of expeditions to mines and quarries, the realization of large building projects, or the development of the artisans' class – the central administration, directed by the vizier, acting on behalf of the king, controlled the movements of the population and the use of manpower; through the intermediary of the 'Office of the Vizier' and the 'Office of Manpower.'" The workers on pyramids and other monuments weren't technically slaves, since they received food and wages for their work, but they had no part in the decision to work or not; pharaoh decided for them. "The system of conscription, applicable to the entire working population, excludes by definition the necessity for slavery."

The construction of pyramids was part of the plan of the pharaohs to dominate the Egyptian economy as well as to satiate their enormous egos. Toby Wilkinson wrote in *The Rise and Fall of Ancient Egypt*,

> The monuments were not just *symbols* of the king's authority throughout the country; they were also practical *instruments* of that authority in the central management of the economy. For the local population, the small step pyramid in their midst would have served as a constant reminder of their economic duty to the state: a duty to pay their taxes to support the court and its projects. From the state's point of view, the monuments and their associated administrative buildings – with one facility in each province – made the collection of revenue both easier and more systematic.

> At the end of the Third Dynasty, the monarch and his administration had achieved their ultimate goal: absolute power.

Pharaoh controlled prices directly and indirectly. Taxing and storing surpluses during good harvests and selling the surplus after bad harvests tended to keep prices from rising and falling to reflect supply and demand. He also set prices for many goods. According to the article "Government and Economy" on The Ancient World, Ancient Egypt web site, laborer might earn 5.5 sacks of grain (400 lb.) for a month of work while a foreman might receive 7.5 sacks (550 lb.). A shirt might trade for five copper *deben*, a *deben* being equal to three ounces of copper. A cow could cost 140 *deben*.

The Egyptian economy in light of economic history

The depiction above of the Egyptian economy shows the poverty of our knowledge of the ancient economy and daily life based on primary sources. In addition, court bootlickers wrote most of the ancient texts to glorify the pharaoh and justify to the masses and the gods his theft and murder. However, we can flesh out many details if we assume that human nature has not changed in the past 4,000 years. In that case, the insights distilled from 300 years of economics will apply equally to the ancient Egyptians when adjusted for technology. For example, Egyptian farmers used oxen to plow fields and thresh grain. Oxen continued to be cutting edge farming technology in many parts of the world as late as the 1950's, so we know a great deal about economies based on farming with oxen that would have applied to the ancient Egyptians.

As mentioned earlier in the chapter on capitalism, economic historians have determined that the standards of living of people measured by per capita G.D.P. all over the world remained stagnant from the beginning of written history until about 1600 AD in the Dutch Republic and 1800 AD in Western Europe and the U.S. We will not stray too far from the truth if we assume that people in the seventeenth century lived very much like the ancient Egyptians.

Ancient Egypt likely had a number of beggars equal to at least 20 percent of the population because France and England produced enough food in 1700 for only 80 percent of their people to have the calories needed to perform a normal day of physical labor in spite of vastly improved farming methods according to Nobel Prize winning economic historian Robert Fogel in *The Escape from Hunger and Premature Death, 1700-2100*. The remaining 20 percent could gather only enough calories by begging to manage a short walk, so they could not have lived far from the place in which they practiced their begging. Also, the cycles of drought and famine made famous by the classical economist Robert Malthus would have afflicted Egyptians as well as Europeans and that is what the Bible records in the Book of Genesis. Europe did not escape the vicious cycle until the advent of capitalism in the seventeenth century.

The number of people counted among the non-farm workers, the nobility, craftsmen, miners, soldiers, administrators, priests and temple staff, would have been small because of the low levels of productivity in agriculture. Throughout history, the number of people who could work in non-farming roles depended on agricultural productivity because farmers could grow only enough food for their families plus a small surplus. The surplus fed the non-farm workers and so limited their numbers.

One ancient document, the Papyrus Wilbour, shows that grain was taxed at the rate of one and a half *khar* (20.31 U.S. gallons) of grain per *aroura* (two-thirds of an acre) according to Edward Bleiberg in "Understanding the Ancient Egyptian Economy." At eight gallons per bushel, assuming a maximum of 12 bushels of wheat per acre translates into a tax of 30 percent of the harvest. It is possible that in bad harvests a compassionate Pharaoh would reduce the tax, but it is more likely that he would not if he were ambitious. Wars were very expensive and were the chief cause of the bankruptcy of kings in Europe throughout history. Pharaohs spent huge amounts of wealth conquering and controlling Nubia (Sudan) and

Palestine. And of course their building projects are legendary. It is unlikely that a "god" would scale back his ambitious plans for conquest and building monuments to himself in order to alleviate the suffering of his people.

Today, most farmers in the poorest counties are women whose only tool is a short-handled hoe. Usually the men are busy looking for day labor. Development agencies have tried to give farmers oxen in order to lift their productivity because they can farm about 20 acres of land with a yoke of oxen, far more than is possible with a hoe, so we can assume Egyptian standards of living would have taken a huge leap with the adoption of farming with oxen. But then it stagnated and we know from history that the next advance in farming technology did not appear until a horse collar was invented that did not constrict the horse's ability to breathe, roughly around 1000 AD in Europe. The horse collars used to pull ancient Egyptian and Roman chariots allowed horses to pull light loads, but heavier loads choked the air passages of the animal. The horse collar avoided the wind pipes and allowed the horse to use its full strength to move loads or plows. With horses, farmers could plow twice as much land as with oxen and double their productivity and their wealth.

Along with metal plows, horse shoes and the use of fertilizer, farming productivity first began to rise in Europe in the middle ages. Why did it take farmers so long to discover the horse collar? After all, pharaoh's military used horses to pull chariots. Life in ancient Egypt provides a clue: without secure property rights, farmers have no incentive to innovate and improve their productivity because the people in power will reap the benefits, not the farmers. As with most slaves, Egyptians would have exerted as little effort and thought in their work as possible knowing that they would never get more than just enough to keep them and their families barely alive. Asking Egyptian farmers to invent ways to produce more for the state would have been like asking slaves in the American south to find ways to make their masters richer. As a result, standards of living for the entire world changed little from the beginning of history until the invention of the horse collar.

Scholars have engaged in heated debate over the question of whether ancient Egypt was a command economy or a market economy. The truth seems to be that it was mainly a command economy with a tiny space for markets. To better understand ancient Egypt we need to look to the former USSR or Communist China before the reforms of Deng Xao Ping. Both were command economies in that, being socialist, a small group of elites made all of the decisions about what to produce, who would produce it, and how it would be distributed.

We know from the Soviet and Chinese experiments that command and control economies destroy wealth. Both nations attempted to eliminate markets entirely, even getting rid of currency and banks at one time. Mass death resulted. Over 30 million people starved to death in the USSR in the 1930's and roughly the same starved in China in the 1960's. Neither nation could feed its people in spite of the fact that they enjoyed some of the richest farm land in the world. Not only did farm workers lack incentives to produce, but the transportation systems were so bad that much of the food spoiled before it got to the consumers. The U.S. loaned the Soviets and Chinese the money to buy food through most of the 1970's and 1980's in order to prevent more mass starvation.

After the Bolshevik Revolution of 1917, the Soviet Union abolished private property in land for the most part, but left about 4 percent of the land in private hands. *The New Argument in Economics, The Public versus the Private Sector*, edited by Helmut Schoeck and James W. Wiggins, contains this insight: "In 1959, these little private plots accounted for well over 46 percent of the Soviet Union's production of potatoes and vegetables, 38 percent of the output of beef and veal, 51 percent of the output of pork, 50 percent of the output of milk, and over 80 percent of the output of eggs."

The Pilgrims who founded the Plymouth Colony in 1620 should have served as a warning to the Soviets and Chinese, but they did not know the true story, just as most Americans do not know it. The official story, celebrated by children in thousands of grade schools every November, teaches that the pilgrims faced a rough first winter and many starved. The next year the Indians taught the Europeans how to farm and the next harvest was so abundant that the pilgrims announced a holiday and invited their rescuers, the tribes, to Thanksgiving Dinner.

The truth is far different. Every school child should be familiar with it because the governor of the colony, William Bradford, wrote about it in his *History of Plymouth Plantation*. The colonists practiced a form of command economy. They all worked together on planting and harvesting crops while the leadership distributed the produce according to need. But the pilgrims remained in danger of starvation for years because the harvests were small and "much was stolen both by night and day, before it became scarce eatable." The tribal people could not help them.

Then the harvest of 1623 arrived with abundance undreamed of by the pilgrims. What changed? Tired of the starvation, corruption and crime, Bradford tried a "new" method of organizing production on the farm: he abandoned the command economy, distributed the land to individuals and families and informed them they could eat only what they grew. The energy of the Pilgrims surprised Bradford and seems to have angered him a little.

Another problem with command economies such as Egypt's is waste. The great twentieth century economist Ludwig von Mises in his *Socialism: An Economic a Sociological Analysis* published in 1922 demonstrated that the greatest weakness of command economies is the lack of accurate prices. Prices coordinate market activity by signaling the relative abundance or scarcity of goods. High prices communicate to producers that they should increase production. Low prices tell them to scale back. Without accurate, market-based prices, there is no coordination of production with demand so excess in some goods exists alongside scarcity in others. The excess turns to waste, and if people waste and consume more than they produce, they grow poorer.

The lack of accurate prices plagued the Soviet, Chinese and early Pilgrim economies and caused wide scale starvation. Post-Soviet Russia and post-reform China enjoy an abundance of food, as did the pilgrims when they abandoned communal farming. Ancient Egypt could not have escaped the consequences of a command economy any more than the Soviets, Chinese or pilgrims could. We may not know about the many disasters that must have afflicted the nation over its long history because the records we have left were primarily propaganda for the state. But most of the population would have lived very close to starvation with no hope of achieving a better life.

Egyptians must have suffered greatly from envy, too. Socialists and many Christians have assumed that ridding the world of material differences between people would cure the human race of envy. Envy motivates many crimes and fights, so eliminating it should create a more peaceful and loving society. However, the Bible teaches that evil is part of human nature; only God can cure the human heart, and that takes a miracle. The previous chapter described the work of the great sociologist Helmut Schoeck in his monumental study *Envy: a Theory of Social Behavior* that confirmed the Biblical teachings. After studying history and the anthropology of primitive as well as modern societies, Schoeck discovered that similarity enflames envy. For example, the kibbutzim of Israel eliminated all material differences between members, going as far as prohibiting them from having their own clothing so that every member wore clothing drawn at random. Instead of alleviating envy, the members magnified other differences, especially time spent alone and in leadership positions, and enflamed their envy of each other causing continual conflict. The communes survived, but rarely grew because more people abandoned them than joined.

Envy has kept people poor since the beginning of history. Suppose that a farmer in ancient Egypt overcame the damage that its command economy inflicted on the motivation to work and discovered a technique for growing wheat that produced say 50 percent more output per acre. Envy would have caused his neighbors to charge him with using witchcraft to benefit his acreage or to the harm theirs. They would have insisted that the state prevent him from using the new technique. The United Nations experienced such debilitating envy a few decades ago when attempting to help poor farmers in Uganda. The Ugandan farmers labored with short-handled hoes to scratch crops from the stingy soil. The UN tried to start a pilot program in which it would give oxen to farmers in order to raise their productivity and standard of living to that of the ancient Egyptians. However, the farmers refused the oxen. They told the UN representatives that if they accepted the oxen, their neighbors would be envious and would steal them in the night, butcher and eat them if the farmers did not slaughter them and share the meat with their neighbors. Fear of envy made the farmers prefer poverty to the envious anger of their neighbors.

Another reason the ancient Egyptian people as well as the rest of the world remained in a state of near starvation poverty until the advent of capitalism appears in the reward structure of society. Throughout history, the only paths out of subsistence farming were through service in the military or to the state because of the contempt for commerce in traditional societies. Soldiers could occasionally grow wealthy if their armies won battles and they could loot the wealth of the vanquished. Or if he could get into the bureaucracy, he could accept bribes and use his authority to steal from the masses. Because these were the only means of advancement in society, ambitious people directed all of their energy toward them instead of toward inventing better ways to produce food and clothing.

Finally, the union of religion and state in Egypt resembled the economy of the middle ages in Europe before the separation of church and state. As we learned earlier in the chapter on capitalism, rising standards of living require massive amounts of investment by wealthy people in new processes, technology and businesses. The rich in Europe did not begin to invest in new or expanding businesses until the advent of capitalism. They gave to the Church in order to buy their way into heaven and to share in the Church's political power, and they bought land and titles of nobility in order to protect what wealth they retained. The complete absence of investment guaranteed that the majority of people would remain close to starvation. The same dynamics would have worked in Egypt where the pharaoh spent what little surplus he extracted from the peasants on massive temples, pyramids, monuments, sacrifices and priests for his gods.

The rule of law

Until the modern world, law and religion were closely linked. Being a god was important for creating laws because people understood early in history that no human being has inherent authority over other humans. Only a god could claim authority to determine behaviors that others must follow simply because he told them to. The practice continued as late as the early modern period when European kings claimed divine right to rule.

People look for reason and consistency in law because it makes the future a little more predictable and planning slightly easier. Business people, including farmers, need consistency in the law in order to encourage them to invest for the long term. But law by human gods tended to be capricious, being more human than divine. Pharaohs did not change the law continually, for they had at least the wisdom to understand the chaos it would cause in their kingdom, and too much chaos might cause others who aspired to be the god-king to attempt to murder him and assume the position. Still, the Bible provides several examples of god-kings making capricious laws. Pharaoh enslaved the Hebrew people for no reason but his own insecurities. Israeli kings launched wars to satisfy their egos. David murdered Bathsheba's husband and committed adultery with her. Solomon amassed wealth and bankrupted his kingdom with building programs. Ahab allowed Jezebel to murder Naboth so Ahab could steal his land. Nebuchadnezzar made laws to inflate his ego and would have murdered Daniel and his friends had God not intervened. The King of Persia would have allowed Haman to murder all of the Jews in the kingdom had God not interrupted his plans.

In addition to capriciousness, the law of the Egyptian pharaoh-gods did not apply equally to all people as has been the case with most societies through history. The law usually applied only to the common people. The nobility, who provided the support structure for the pharaoh, followed their own laws.

The common people must have suffered at the hands of the nobility much as they did in Europe during the middle ages. Pieter de la Court, a businessman and economist in the Dutch Republic, offered an example of the oppression of commoners in his book published in 1662, *The True Interest and Political Maxims of the Republic of Holland*. He wrote that before the founding of the republic the nobility searched the land for farmers who attained financial success. Coveting the farmer's land, a nobleman would fabricate criminal charges against the farmer. The nobility employed the judges and sheriffs so the nobleman would bribe a sheriff to arrest the farmer and lock him in jail. He would then bribe the judge to find the farmer guilty of a crime worthy of capital punishment. After the execution, the nobleman would confiscate the farmer's property as part of the punishment for his crime. Two other books by de la Court, *History of the Counts of Holland* and *History of the Stadholders of Holland and West-Friesland* provided more accounts of the crimes of the nobility. The creation of the republic ended the privilege that the nobility enjoyed to steal what they coveted from common people.

To summarize, the ancient Egyptian economy from which the Israelis escaped was typical of all economies throughout history that were controlled by kings so it is reasonable for us to assume that it operated very much like them. The egos of the pharaohs, nobility and priests ensured that all other Egyptians had just barely enough food to keep them alive and working. The Old Testament prophets constantly indicted Israel's kings and nobility for abusing and stealing from the poor. It's unlikely that Egypt's kings and nobility demonstrated greater honesty and compassion. André Dollinger in "The social classes in ancient Egypt" described Egyptian life this way:

> From the unification of the country onward, a diminutive rich upper class ruled with the help of a small scribal administration over the masses of Egyptian workers and peasants living barely above subsistence level, soaking up most of the surplus the labour of the workers produced. This development reached an apex during the beginning of the pyramid age, when the building of the royal tombs and mortuary temples required the effort of the whole nation, setting the pharaoh apart from the other members of the upper class.

By the time Moses led the Israelis out of Egypt the people had been living in such destitution and mutual envy for over 3,000 years. Moses' story provides an example of the absolute rule of pharaoh over his people. God had told Abraham that the descendants of Jacob who had relocated to Egypt because of a famine would become slaves to their hosts. They suffered as slaves for about four centuries, but prospered and multiplied as a result of God's blessings. However, one pharaoh became alarmed at the number of Hebrews and decided to implement population control by murdering all of the baby boys. Pharaohs had the power to murder anyone with impunity.

But Moses' family feared God more than pharaoh and kept baby Moses hid until one day pharaoh's soldiers made a house-to-house search for infants. Moses' sister hid him in a basket floating among the reeds near the river bank where pharaoh's daughter was bathing. Seeing the basket, she had her servants retrieve it and was delighted to find the healthy baby inside. She hired Moses' mother to nurse him and when she weaned him pharaoh's daughter took him to live with her in the palace. There Moses would have attended the school that educated the children of pharaoh, the nobility, and foreign diplomats in the arts, literature, science, religion and governance of the powerful empire.

As an adult, Moses had to escape from Egypt after killing an Egyptian guard who was beating a Hebrew slave. Moses then worked for forty years in the most despised profession in Egypt, a shepherd. One day God appeared to Moses and commanded him to return to Egypt to persuade pharaoh to let the Hebrew slaves go free so they could build their own nation in Palestine.

Employing history and archeology while applying comparative economics to the ancient Egyptian economy we have a good idea of how miserable life must have been for Egyptian peasants. Their lives must have been short, poor, and consumed with the resentment that envy breeds. Many would have starved in famines, just as peasants did in Europe until modern times. Typical of similar societies, the nobility would have extracted any surplus the peasants achieved and spent it on luxurious living or as offerings to the gods who protected them. Now let us look at the Israeli economy that Moses created.

The Israeli economy

Theologians often say that Israel under the judges was unique because it was a theocracy. But that was not the source of Israel's uniqueness because Egypt was a theocracy as well. We know from reading the documents from the ancient regimes in Mesopotamia and Egypt that all empires considered themselves to be ruled by the gods through the king. In fact, we know from the Bible that God has always judged all nations and still does. He does not rule directly, as a king or president might, but then he did not rule directly in ancient Israel under the judges, either. He gave them the law to follow and expected the priests to teach it to the people, the judges to administer it and the people to enforce it. God did not sit as a judge in court cases; people did. Egypt was the same: the gods gave the law to the king who passed it on to the people who administered and enforced it.

Some might protest that Israel was different because God judged the nation by causing pagan nations to conquer it when Israelis succumbed to idolatry. That is true and he did the same thing when Israel had kings, eventually causing the Babylonians to destroy Jerusalem and the temple. But as the prophets make clear, he also judged Babylon and the nations surrounding Israel, but that did not make them theocracies. God judges nations today, but that does not make them theocracies, either. Israel was no more or less a theocracy than any pagan nation in its day, or any nation today for that matter. Israel's uniqueness issued from the structure of its government.

Revelation

Israel was unique among the pagan nations of Moses' day in the fact that it enjoyed direct revelation from God. Pagan nations enjoyed no direct communications from their gods and the many volumes of writing recovered by archeologists provide evidence. John Walton wrote in *Ancient Near Eastern Thought,*

> Historical records in the ancient Near East do not claim to be revelation from deity, but they do show great interest in discerning the activities of the gods. The polytheistic nature of ancient Near Eastern religion impedes the development of any concept of a singular divine plan encompassing all of history. At best the reigning dynasty may identify a divine plan in establishing and sustaining that dynasty. Some documents look back into the distant past to see a pattern that led to the present...These typically concern not what the deity has done, but what has been done to the deity. In Mesopotamia it is assumed that deity plays an active part in the cause-

and-effect process that comprises history. The causation of the gods is understood to be impromptu rather than in accordance with any overarching plan or grand design.

Priests relied on divination for clues to what their gods were up to. "Divinization produced the only divine revelation known in the ancient Near East. Through its mechanisms, the ancients believed not that they could know the deity, but that they could get a glimpse of the designs and will of deity," Walton wrote. Pagan priests compiled catalogues of omens from the heavens made up of movements of the sun, moon and stars and omens from the earth comprising significant events. They tried to match omens in the heavens with those on earth and the more omens that the priest could assemble the more certain he felt about his interpretation of the intentions of the gods.

The closest the gods came to "writing" revelation was on the organs in a sacrificial animal. Priests would prepare an animal such as a goat, sacrifice it to the god then butcher it and remove certain organs, such as the liver, for examination. Different features of the organ served as omens revealing the will of the god. An old Babylonian text offers an example: "If the base of the Presence has a Branch and it (the Branch) has seized the Path to the right of the gall bladder: the prince will expropriate a country which is not his," according to Walton. And, "If a Weapon is placed between the Presence and the Path and it points to the Narrowing to the right: he who is not the occupant of the throne will seize the throne." The Presence is the vertical groove on the left lobe of the liver and acted as the symbol of the god. The Path referred to the horizontal groove and surrounding area and usually symbolized military campaigns. The Weapon was a pointed protrusion of flesh that symbolized armed forces.

Joshua used this pagan obsession with divination to help the Israeli army defeat an enemy as recorded in Joshua chapter 10. Most translations claim that the sun and moon stood still and that translation has caused a great deal of consternation since the rise of modern science. However, Wheaton College's John Walton offers a better translation as a result of his understanding of ancient Near Eastern divination. The ancient world, including Israel, followed a lunar calendar with the first day of the month beginning on the appearance of the new moon. A full moon appeared in the middle of the month and was identified by the fact that it set in the west just minutes after the sun rose in the east, causing both to appear in the sky opposite each other.

According to Walton, the day of the month on which this opposition of the sun and moon occurred served as an important omen for most cultures other than Israel. The opposition happening on the fourteenth day of the month was a good omen and the event was referred to as the sun and moon "waiting," "standing," or "stopping." On such a day, pagan priests determined that "the speech of the land will become reliable; the land will become happy."

But if the opposition of the sun and moon happened a day later, the omen became evil and portended all kinds of calamity, such as "a strong enemy will raise his weapons against the land; the enemy will tear down the city gate." Other predictions of disaster included raging lions and wolves and a diminishing of business.

Walton suggests that Joshua took advantage of his knowledge of pagan divination and, noticing that the opposition of the sun and moon did not happen on the fourteenth day of the month, planned the attack to take place on the fifteenth when the opposition of the sun and moon would become an evil omen for the enemy but not for the Israelis. The omen would strike fear in the hearts of the enemy soldiers and give the Israelis an advantage in battle. Walton suggests the following translation for the key passage of Joshua 10:12-15:

> "O sun, wait over Gibeon and moon over the valley of Aijalon." So the sun waited and the moon stood before the nation took vengeance on its enemies. Is it not written in the book of Jashar, "The sun stood in the midst of the sky and did not hurry to set as on a day of full length?"

Of course, pagans attributed every bad event to the displeasure of the gods and every good one to their pleasure. The problem they faced was in knowing what pleased their gods. Experience and divination provided vague guidelines and often failed to explain why the gods were angry, so worshippers frequently offered sacrifices to appease the gods for unknown sins. Job offered such sacrifices after feasts to cover sins that his children may have committed without knowing it. When the Old Testament prophets made fun of the idols that Israelis worshipped by calling them dumb, they may have been pointing to the obvious lack of revelation from the pagan gods that frustrated worshippers.

The Israelis did not have to resort to the vague methods of divination to guess at God's will as the pagans did. And because of that they rejoiced at the direct revelation of God's will to Moses on Sinai. As Moses wrote in Deuteronomy 4:5-7:

> See, I have taught you statutes and rules, as the LORD my God commanded me that you should do them in the land that you are entering to take possession of it. Keep them and do them, for that will be your wisdom and your understanding in the sight of the peoples, who, when they hear all these statutes, will say, "Surely this great nation is a wise and understanding people. For what great nation is there that has a god so near to it as the LORD our God is to us, whenever we call upon him? And what great nation is there, that has statutes and rules so righteous as all this law that I set before you today?

And unlike the laws of surrounding nations that favored the rulers and powerful, the laws of Israel applied to all people equally. For the first time in history all people stood in equal relationship to the law, as Moses instructed: "You shall do no injustice in judgment; you shall not be partial to the poor nor defer to the great, but you are to judge your neighbor fairly," (Leviticus 19:15) and "nor shall you be partial to a poor man in his lawsuit," (Exodus 23:3).

Image of God

The concept of the "image of god" explains much of the difference between Egyptian and Israeli government and economics. Genesis 1:26-28 relates the story of how God created mankind in his image and gave humanity dominion over the earth:

> Then God said, "Let us make mankind in our image, in our likeness, so that they may rule over the fish in the sea and the birds in the sky, over the livestock and all the wild animals and over all the creatures that move along the ground." So God created mankind in his own image, in the image of God he created them; male and female he created them. God blessed them and said to them, "Be fruitful and increase in number; fill the earth and subdue it. Rule over the fish in the sea and the birds in the sky and over every living creature that moves on the ground."

The image of god referred almost exclusively to the king or the idol in the ancient Near East. In both cases, the image possessed the essence of the deity that empowered the image to carry out the divine functions. The physical features were not important. The emphasis was on the character and attributes of the deity. The image functioned as a mediator of worship of the deity and demonstrated his presence. "Across the ancient world, the image of God did the work of God on earth," Walton wrote.

Moses probably wrote the Torah around 1500 BC. By then, pagan people of the ancient Near East had been making and worshipping silver and gold idols for millennia. The concept of those idols and the king as the images of a god was well established. Moses, under the inspiration of the Holy Spirit, could have chosen any number of concepts to depict the relationship of humanity to God. Most Near East writers preferred the idea of slavery, much as modern Islam does. But Moses wrote that God created mankind in his image. He chose to use the commonly accepted concept of an idol and a king to describe his relationship to all of humanity. In order to prevent the term "image of god" becoming trivialized in our minds, we need to take an in depth look at what it meant to people in Moses' day. Walton wrote,

> An understanding of what it means to be in the image of god in the ancient world can be enhanced by exploring other uses of "image" as well. For instance, in both Egypt and Mesopotamia an idol contained the image of the deity. This allowed the image to possess the attributes of the deity, and serve as an indicator of the presence of the deity. In another reflection, the image of a king was considered to be present in monuments set up in territories he had conquered.

> Across the ancient world, the image of God did the work of God on the earth. In the Israelite context as portrayed in the Hebrew Bible, people are in the image of God in that they embody his qualities and do his work.

They are symbols of his presence and act on his behalf as his representatives...

The foundation of Israel's understanding of human dignity was the democratized image of God passed on generation by generation, beginning from a pair of primordial ancestors. In the large ancient Near East, human dignity was located in the service to the gods as their needs were addressed.

Moses' choice of the concept of the "image of god" to describe humans would have revolutionary implications for all time, but especially for the people in Moses' day. If each individual person was the image of God on earth, then each is a priest and has access to God in much the same way as pagan priests who had exclusive access to their idols. The concept foreshadowed Moses calling the citizens of the new nation a kingdom of priests, as he wrote in Exodus 19:6, "you will be for me a kingdom of priests and a holy nation." Much later, the Apostle John referred to Christians in the same way: "You have made them to be a kingdom and priests to serve our God, and they will reign on the earth." (Rev. 5:10) "and has made us to be a kingdom and priests to serve his God and Father..." (Rev. 1:6)

In terms of government and economics, being the image of God on earth meant that each person enjoyed the same status of a king or pharaoh in terms of owning property and authority. Kings ruled over their subjects in the pagan world because of their unique status as the image of a god. By making each person equal to the king, God is declaring that no man has the right to rule over another just as no king has the right to rule over other kings.

The Bible prohibited the Hebrews from making images of God or any other thing supposed to be divine: "You shall not make for yourself a carved image, or any likeness of anything that is in heaven above, or that is in the earth beneath, or that is in the water under the earth" (Exod. 20:4). God prohibited such artificial images because he had already created a representation of himself on earth in humans. God told Noah and his sons that he will require an accounting for the spilling of human blood, for humankind is made in his image (Gen. 9:6). Through the concept of the image of God, the privileges of the few were transferred to the many.

No king

Philosophers and politicians have debated government for millennia, but God made very clear the type of government he prefers. He created only one system of government in the history of mankind. And, since the form of government and the laws regarding property determine the economic system, God has declared in the Torah the economic system he prefers. What God wants is also what is best for mankind. It will not only encourage godliness and peace, but economic prosperity as well.

The most striking feature of the Torah government is the radical degree to which it differed from that of ancient Egypt. Moses was raised in the pharaonic school and enjoyed an education in the Egyptian wisdom that awed the Greeks. The children of the pharaoh, nobility and foreign vassals attended the boarding school that trained them in the knowledge and skills needed to run the country in the future while indoctrinating them in the worship of the pharaoh and Egyptian philosophy. The curriculum included reading and writing in the Egyptian language and Babylonian cuneiform, mathematics, music, and military strategy. It's likely that Moses lived and went to school with the pharaoh who reigned during the exodus and died in the Red Sea.

Israel could not have been more different from the governments of ancient Egypt and Babylon, or for that matter any government since. Israel's government instantiated the idea of each person bearing the image of God: it had no human king because each person enjoyed the authority of kings over his property. That meant Israel had no executive branch. There was no prime minister or president, no bureaucracies, cabinet heads, or ministers of trade, roads, defense, agriculture, health, environment or the hundreds of other agencies that breed and clog the machinery of modern governments. Israel had no standing army, no police, pentagon, FBI, ATF, NSA, CIA or any other of the alphabet soups of agencies, so Israelis did not have to pay taxes to fund an overbearing bureaucracy as did ancient Egyptians, U.S. citizens and most taxpayers of the world. Family members performed the police work of catching criminals while service in the military was voluntary, except for peer and family pressure. Egypt's executive and legislative powers resided with the pharaoh, according to Walton:

> As individuals who stood between the divine and human worlds, kings were expected to discern the divine will and facilitate its execution. In Egypt the almost total immersion of the persona of the king into the divine realm led inexorably to the conclusion that the acts of Pharaoh were the acts of deity.

Whereas the Sumerians and Egyptians saw their kings as gods or descendants of gods, Israelis had very little good to say about them. Kings are absent in the early chapters of Genesis and when they appear Moses was critical of the violence and arrogance of Lamech and the imperialism of Nimrod. God was very displeased with Israelis for demanding a king in I Samuel 8 and besides David, Hezekiah and Josiah, the rest of the Hebrew Scriptures have very little good to say about any Israeli king.

The Israel created by God had no legislature. God retained Israel's legislative authority and only God could make or change laws. That was necessary since God had created mankind in his image, which made it impossible for one man, or a group of men, to have legislative authority over others. All men were equal in terms of the authority to create legislation, which meant no authority. God gave the first law to Moses on Mount Sinai and again after the forty years of wilderness wanderings just before Moses died and Joshua led the nation to conquer Canaan. The second issue of the law contained some minor additions and changes to the first, but from that point on no man could add to or subtract from the law. Moses needed to be a prophet as well as a judge in order for God to give Israel his laws, but Joshua was no prophet and only one of the judges was a prophet, so no one could add to the law. One of the most important jobs of the priesthood was to teach the people God's laws.

Courts and law

The only branch of modern or ancient government that God instituted in Israel was the court system. The courts of ancient Israel settled disputes between citizens while families and tribes enforced court decisions. The lower courts judged the most common disputes while the more difficult ones filtered up through the system to Moses. Originally, Moses tried to judge all of Israel by himself, but his father-in-law, Jethro, wisely encouraged him to spread the burden among the people. After the conquest of Canaan, the lowest courts convened at the gates of cities large enough to have walls with the elders of the city acting as judges and jury. The people chose respected men as justices who had the wealth necessary to allow them to take time off from work to participate in court.

Israelis paid no taxes to support an executive, legislative or even judicial branch of government. The only tax required was a tithe (10 percent) paid to support the temple and priesthood. God did not give the tribe of Levi land in Canaan for the priesthood, although they could own houses in towns and work at a trade. God intended the tithe to support the priests and provide for the poor. From the perspective of government, the tithe was voluntary: no army, IRS, police or other tax collector would extract payment or throw a citizen in jail for not paying the tithe. As far as we know, no one could take a citizen to court and charge him with a crime for not paying the tithe. Only God enforced the tithe because it served as a test of the people's devotion to God. A godly people would pay the tithes and offerings and cause the temple and priesthood to flourish. But when the people rebelled against God, the priesthood suffered. Such may have been the case in Judges chapter 17 where we read about a priest named Jonathan wandering the countryside looking for a means of support and being taken in as the family priest by Micah. On the other hand, the priest may have been lazy and did not want to submit to the life of a good priest.

Preachers who emphasize tithing today should keep in mind that God instituted the tithe in a government with no taxes, which left believers with more of their own money to live on. U.S. governments - local, state and federal - take close to half of the income of workers in the U.S. and make tithing on gross income much more difficult than it would have been for Israelis under the judges.

According to some Jewish scholars, the Torah law has a mere 613 commandments. Compare that to the tens of thousands of laws regulating American life. The Federal Register publishes only new regulations and has averaged 75,000 pages each year since 1970, totaling over three million pages of new regulations in the past forty years alone. In 1925, all the federal codes could be contained in one four-to-five-inch thick volume. By 1998 the code took 201 volumes on nineteen feet of shelf space but in 2013 it spread out to twenty-five feet. That does not include the tens of thousands of pages of common law created by court decisions or the laws and regulations passed at the state, county and city levels.

Three types of law make up the Torah – religious, moral and civil. Religious law covers the operation of the temple and sacrifices and what God requires of his followers, such as Sabbath observance. Moral law includes responsibilities that people owe others as a result of our relationship to God, such as the requirements to give to the poor, not covet or bear false witness. The failure to perform these duties incurs moral guilt, but does not rise to the level of criminality. The civil law covers criminal activity such as theft, rape, violence, fraud or murder, which the courts adjudicated.

Protestant theologians have maintained the division of the Torah law into moral, religious and civil. For example, John Calvin, quoted by Fred Graham in *The Constructive Revolutionary: John Calvin and His Socio-Economic Impact*, partly based his defense of charging interest on loans to the fact that the prohibitions of usury were part of the civil law: "The law of Moses (Deut. 23:19) was political, and should not influence us beyond what justice and philanthropy will bear." In other words, Calvin believed that God had instituted the political (civil) law of ancient Israel for a particular place and time and did not intend it to apply for all time as he did the moral law. The moral law is universal because it issues from God's character, which never changes.

The courts did not get involved in religious or moral law. They left religious law to the priests and enforcement of moral law to families and God. Joseph Lifshitz wrote in his book *Judaism, Law and the Free Market: an Analysis* that giving to the poor was not a legal obligation:

> For this reason, the Sages defined charity foremost as a moral principle, not a juridical one. Thus, they admonished those who would take money from others in order to give it to the poor: 'Better is he who gives a smaller amount of his own charity than one who steals from others to give a large amount of charity.'

> All the limitations placed by Jewish religious law on property rights are of a moral nature – they have no legal or monetary standing, and there is nothing in them that changes the legal definition of property rights. Hence, any interpretation that claims the existence of distributive justice in Jewish law as separate from the individual's religious identity, and defines individual obligations in legal terms and not in moral ones, must be merely a reduction of Jewish Law's theological principles to an anachronistic political position, and in doing so, also distorts the judicial principle.

A superficial reading of the Torah has convinced many people that all 613 commands in the Torah are civil laws that the courts, the only governmental institution in the nation, must enforce. But Torah scholars have stubbornly disagreed through the ages. Israelis could not take neighbors to court for coveting, for example, or breaking the Sabbath laws. Nor could they sue a neighbor in court for refusing to abide by the poor laws, such as the prohibition of harvesting the corners of a field.

Some scholars will argue that the division of the Mosaic Law into the three divisions is a recent idea, having appeared only in the Reformation. However, judges in ancient Israel must have confronted the issue of whether forced morality and religion are true morality and true religion. They could not have avoided it. If forced by the power of the government, both morality and religion degenerate into ritualism, as often happened anyway in Israel and was one of God's most frequent complaints against them. Considering that the rest of the Hebrew Bible places great importance on Israelis voluntarily following the moral and religious laws, it seems unlikely that the early judges would have been unaware of the problem. Two passages from the ancient Jewish book *Ethics of the Fathers* quoted in Brad H. Young's *Meet the Rabbis: Rabbinic Thought and the Teachings of Jesus* illustrate the limited nature of the Israeli courts:

> (5:11) Seven kinds of punishment enter into the world on account of seven major transgressions. When some people give their tithes and others do not, then famine ensues from drought. Some people suffer hunger while others are full. When they all decide not to give tithes at all, a famine ensues from civil disorder and drought. If they resolve not to give the dough-cake (Numbers 15:20), a deadly famine comes. So a pestilence may come into the world to fulfill those death penalties threatened in the **Torah which is not given over to human court systems**, and for the breaking of the laws regarding the produce of the seventh year. (Leviticus 25:1-7) [Emphasis not in the original]

> (5:12) During four seasons of time pestilence increases: in the fourth year, in the seventh, at the conclusion of the seventh year, and at the conclusion of the Feast of Tabernacles in each year. In the fourth year, it increases on account of failure to give the tithe to the poor in the third year (Deuteronomy 14:28-29). In the seventh year, it increases on account of failure to give the tithe to the poor in the sixth year; at the conclusion of the seventh year, on account of the failure of observing the law regarding the fruits of the seventh years, and at the conclusion of the Feast of Tabernacles in each year, for robbing the poor of the grants that are legally assigned to them.

The last sentence in the first paragraph is bolded for emphasis. Both passages demonstrate that Moses left the enforcement of the moral laws in the Torah to God, not the courts. God would punish violations with drought, famine and pestilence. God used war with Syria and Babylon to punish idolatry, not the courts. Moses specified what types of cases the courts were to adjudicate:

- Purchase and sale (Lev. 25:14).
- Liability of a paid depositary (Ex. 22:9).
- Loss for which a gratuitous borrower is liable (Ex. 22:13-14) .
- Inheritances (Num. 27:8-11).
- Damage caused by an uncovered pit (Ex. 21:33-34) .
- Injuries caused by beasts (Ex. 21:35-36) .
- Damage caused by trespass of cattle (Ex. 22:4) .
- Damage caused by fire (Ex. 22:5) .
- Damage caused by a gratuitous depositary (Ex. 22:6-7) .

- Other cases between a plaintiff and a defendant (Ex. 22:8) .

Property

As God's representative on earth, having been created in his image, mankind exercises dominion over the earth as if he were God and as long as he acts within God's mandates. A quick search through a concordance for other verses using the Hebrew word for dominion, *radah*, reveals the extent of that dominion. Those verses use the word in the context of a king exercising complete control over his realm. Man expresses his dominion over the earth partly by enjoying it. As Lifshitz wrote:

> Man's dominion finds expression, first of all, through his enjoyment of the good of creation…the Jewish sources teach that man is entitled, even obligated, to take pleasure in the world. This is not an endorsement of hedonism; rather, the aim is to enable man to actualize the potential hidden in creation and thereby to bring the work of creation to completion. By benefitting from the world, man infuses it with spiritual content, which serves as a link between the Creator and creation. "If one sees beautiful creatures and beautiful trees," the Talmud teaches, "he says: 'Blessed is he who has such in his world.'" This is not simply an expression of gratitude but an act of elevating the mundane. This is why the Rabbis taught that "man will have to account for all that he sees with his eyes and does not partake of." When we deny ourselves the experiences of this world, even the simplest of pleasures, we cut the creation of God off from its higher source and condemn it to a crude, brutish existence. Judaism insists that man would not limit himself to his bare necessities but instead delight in the goodness of the world as an expression of his dominion over it.

Asceticism did not come from Judaism, but from pagan Greek and Romans. Ultimately, man articulates his dominion through his creativity; one of several traits mankind shares with God and distinguishes him from animals. The church fathers held that the world belongs to God, and man in his state of sinfulness has no right to exercise absolute dominion over it. Judaism, however, insisted that man is required not only to be involved in the world but also to perfect it through creative acts. According to Judaism, man's creative development of the world is the ultimate expression of his unique status.

Judaism anchors property rights to the principles of God having created mankind in His image and having given him dominion over the earth and all other creatures. Only through his property rights can man actualize his role as the image of God with dominion over the earth. And as Lifshitz wrote, "…the right to private property in Judaism is nearly absolute and can be restricted only in the most extreme circumstances."

Of course, one might argue that God may have given mankind as a whole dominion over the earth, but not individuals. In other words, the dominion is corporate. However, the

Torah makes clear that the dominion applies to individuals. God gave the newly conquered land of Canaan to tribes who then divided it among families. The law then specifies how families must relate to each other concerning land and other property. They were

- Not to do wrong in buying or selling (Lev. 25:14).
- Not to remove landmarks (property boundaries) (Deut. 19:14).
- Not to swear falsely in denial of another's property rights (Lev. 19:11).
- Not to deny falsely another's property rights (Lev. 19:11).
- Not to steal personal property (Lev. 19:11).
- To restore that which one took by robbery (Lev. 5:23).
- To return lost property (Deut. 22:1).
- Not to pretend not to have seen lost property, to avoid the obligation to return it (Deut. 22:3)

The Torah holds individual property rights in such high regard that it forbade Israelis in the Tenth Commandment from even thinking about taking the property of others, "You shall not covet your neighbor's house. You shall not covet your neighbor's wife, or his male or female servant, his ox or donkey, or anything that belongs to your neighbor," (Exodus 20:17) which is repeated in Deuteronomy 5:21 as "You shall not covet your neighbor's wife. You shall not set your desire on your neighbor's house or land, his male or female servant, his ox or donkey, or anything that belongs to your neighbor." All of these are negative commands, which if converted to positive statements would say something like, "Respect the private property of others. I have made it sacred."

In the New Testament, Jesus taught that a man who looks at another woman in order to lust after her has committed adultery already in his heart, referring to the seventh commandment, and to hate a brother is the heart attitude of murder, referring to the sixth commandment. Following Jesus' example, one could argue that coveting is the spiritual equivalent of theft.

The state did not issue property rights according to the Torah. That would express property as understood by Egyptians where the pharaoh granted rights to the use of property. In the Torah, God owned everything but gave property rights to humanity through his creation of man in his image and likeness and by giving him dominion over the earth. The Law of Moses further delineates God's vision of property by making it specific to individuals and forbidding even the thought of taking another's property illegally.

Today, people might argue that democracy has given the state the authority to take the property of citizens for whatever use the majority deems necessary. (I realize the U.S. does not have a pure democracy and is a republic instead. Still, I use the term democracy because most writers refer to our system of government as a democracy.) After all, the state gets its legitimacy from the will of the majority of voters in modern political philosophy. But the Bible makes it clear that states can be as guilty of theft as individuals. When the leaders of Israel demanded that the prophet Samuel install a king so that Israel could be like the other nations, including Egypt, God permitted it, not as a blessing, but as punishment. Then he warned them of the consequences:

> These will be the rights of the king who is to reign over you. He will take your sons and assign them to his chariotry and cavalry, and they will run in front of his chariot. He will use them as leaders of a thousand and leaders of fifty; he will make them plough his ploughland and harvest his harvest and make his weapons of war and the gear for his chariots. He will also take your daughters as perfumers, cooks, and bakers. He will take the best of your fields, of your vineyards and olive groves and give them to his officials. He will tithe your crops and vineyards to provide for his eunuchs and his officials. He will take the best of your manservants and maidservants, of your cattle and your donkeys, and make them work for him. He will tithe your flocks, and you yourselves will become his slaves. When that day comes, you will cry out on account of the king you have chosen for yourselves, but on that day God will not answer you. (I Samuel 8:11-18)

God did not give the kings the right to take the people's property. He merely described the vast extent of the theft and violence that kings would commit. God allowed the people of Israel to have the desire of their wicked hearts for a king as punishment, as Paul wrote in Romans 1:28: "Furthermore, just as they did not think it worthwhile to retain the knowledge of God, so God gave them over to a depraved mind, so that they do what ought not to be done." Often, God judged rebellious people by letting them have their way and that is what he did with ancient Israel. He allowed the king to steal the property and the young people of families for his own pleasure. It should not have surprised the Israelis that a king like other nations would act like those other kings and abuse the people in the many ways as kings have done throughout the centuries. In addition to leading the people into idolatry, many of the condemnations by the prophets of the leadership of Israel refer to the abuse of the poor by the nobility who stole their land and enslaved their young people.

God knew that Israel would one day rebel against him and choose a king, so he limited the power of the king in Deuternomy 17: 15-17:

> You shall surely set a king over you whom the Lord your God chooses, one from among your countrymen you shall set as king over yourselves; you may not put a foreigner over yourselves who is not your countryman. Moreover, he shall not multiply horses for himself, nor shall he cause the people to return to Egypt to multiply horses, since the Lord has said to you, "You shall never again return that way." He shall not multiply wives for himself, or else his heart will turn away; nor shall he greatly increase silver and gold for himself....

He forbade the king from collecting horses, because God hated war and wanted his people to be peace loving. He knew that his people would prosper only in peace time and that war destroys wealth as well as killing many young men. The prohibition against wives probably referred to treaties with pagan nations in which the rulers exchanged wives to help guarantee the treaty would be followed. The danger in a king increasing his personal holdings of gold and silver came from the power he had to tax the people that always became oppressive. The fact that God interpreted the demand for a king as rebellion against him and his rule suggests that God anticipated the hard heartedness of the Israeli people and made provision for it, even as he provided for divorce.

In the Gospels, some Pharisees asked Jesus if it was lawful for a man to divorce his wife for any reason (Matthew 19:1-8). Jesus said no, so later his disciples asked him why Moses commanded that husbands give their wives a certificate of divorce. Jesus answered "Moses permitted you to divorce your wives because your hearts were hard. But it was not this way from the beginning." In a similar way, God never intended Israel to have a king, but he knew the rebellious nature of his people and tried to limit the damage that kings could inflict by setting strict boundaries for the actions of a king. But Israeli citizens refused to enforce God's limits on the king just as they had refused God as king.

On the other hand, the king passage in Deuteronomy might be looking forward to the Messiah. After all, David wrote of the Messiah that he would be the Son of God in Psalm 110:1: "The LORD says to my lord: 'Sit at my right hand until I make your enemies a footstool for your feet.'" God was the king of Israel under the judges so only his Son could inherit the throne. The human kings beginning with Saul were impostors and usurpers, which could provide an alternate explanation for God's anger when Israel demanded a king who had no right to the throne.

The kings in Israel ruled with as much legitimacy as today's democracies because God allowed them to rule, yet God never granted kings the right to take the property of others. In the same way, the state created through democracy has no right to violate God's laws any more than private individuals or the kings of Israel. Man may create democracies and have politicians pass laws, but a body of law higher than any man-made laws has always existed, God's law, often referred to as natural law. Man-made law should never contradict God's laws, but it usually does.

Modern Christians should keep in mind that God never created a democracy even though he could have. People created parliaments in order to curb the power of tyrannical kings. Once the people had stripped monarchs of all their power, they gave those same abusive powers to the state in democracies. But democracies can be as tyrannical as kings. Testimony to that can be found in the treatment by the United States of the people who were first slaves then "free" black people until civil rights law; the abuse of native tribal peoples who suffered ethnic cleansing east of the Mississippi River in the nineteenth century and frequently outright murder; and treatment of Japanese citizens during World War II who were imprisoned because of their heritage. Also, consider the income tax rate which has at times reached 90 percent, and the total taxes paid by U.S. citizens, state, local and federal, which consumes about 45 percent of gross domestic product.

God went farther than just general commands about property by giving specific instances of how property should be protected. Stealing can take many forms, and we are commanded to take positive action against it in some cases. God commands the use of fair weights and measures in Deuteronomy 25:15 and elsewhere. We are also told to care for and return found property, in Deuteronomy 22:1-4. Exodus 22 deals with a number of issues, including rules that apply to livestock. The passage requires restitution if an animal wanders off and grazes in someone else's field. This reads more like a penalty rather than a regulation, but the concept here is that private property is to be protected and any extension consistent with that is acceptable. We see the same thing in Exodus 23, where God commanded people to return a lost animal (verse four) and help a struggling animal (verse five) even if belongs to an enemy. Employees are to be paid promptly (Leviticus 19) and fairly (Malachi chapter 3). And God prohibited judges from favoring the poor in Leviticus.

Moses left the general impression that property is sacred. By extension, markets must be free because markets are where people acquire and dispose of property. Without freedom to dispose of property, property doesn't exist. After Israel chose a king, it took about 2,500 years to recover that wisdom.

Jubilee

Jim Wallis, editor-in-chief of Sojourner Magazine and a devout socialist began his lead article, "Seattle: Changing the Rules," in the March-April 2000 issue of *Sojourners* magazine with this:

> From the pulpit, I looked out over the standing room only crowd and could feel the electric excitement in Seattle's St. James Cathedral. It was Sunday night, just before the week of scheduled protests that would rock the World Trade Organization (WTO) meeting and the world. We were all gathered for a religious service organized by Jubilee 2000, the grassroots campaign to cancel the debt of the world's poorest countries. Just before I preached, a text was read from Leviticus 25, which proclaims the biblical Jubilee—a periodic economic redistribution in which slaves are set free, land is returned, and debts are forgiven. Jubilee is a call for a regular "leveling" of things, given the human tendency toward over-accumulation by some while others lose ground. The Bible doesn't propose any blueprint for an economic system, but rather insists that all human economic arrangements be subject to the demands of God's justice, that great gaps be avoided or rectified, and the poor are not left behind. As I listened to the prophetic scripture being read, I marveled at how it was being used that night—as a relevant contribution to a public discussion on the rules of global trade!

Many theologians throughout history have taken the Biblical concept of Jubilee as justification for the state to control markets, ensure an equal distribution of wealth in the nation and provide debt relief. Jubilee 2000 expanded the concept to include debt relief for poor countries who had borrowed from rich nations but were struggling to repay the loans. The fact that the leaders of most of those poor countries were ruthless, corrupt dictators who stole most of the borrowed funds or wasted them on luxurious living did not matter to

Jubilee 2000. Laying aside the undeniable fact that God did not create a state capable of such redistribution of wealth, since all he allowed were courts, and the fact that Jubilee fell under the poor laws that were not enforceable by the courts, any reading of the passages on Jubilee demonstrate that Wallis' interpretation is superficial at best. Let's look closer. Jubilee appears in Leviticus chapter 25, the main points of which are the following:

1)   If an Israeli farmer sold his land at any time, ownership would return to the original owner established by Joshua in the first distribution of land regardless of how many people had owned the land between the sale and Jubilee.

2)   If the owner had donated the land to the temple, it did not return to the original owner and if the temple sold the land it returned to the temple at Jubilee.

3)   Houses on farm land were treated like the land, but houses in towns were not. They could be sold permanently, although the seller had one year to reconsider.

4)   All Jewish slaves were released, but not non-Jewish slaves.

5)   Jubilee occurred every 50 years beginning with the establishment of the Israeli nation, not with the sale of the land.

6)   The seller of farm land prorated the sale price according to the value of the number of harvests remaining until Jubilee.

Now consider the historical context, as any good interpreter should. Banks did not exist. Poor people borrowed from the rich, who usually set interest rates very high. In most poor nations today farmers do not have access to bank credit at market rates and so must borrow from wealthy individuals who act like loan sharks. The interest rate is so high as to make it impossible to pay off the loan and the collateral required for the loan covers far more than the amount of the loan. The unscrupulous rich use such loans to steal land from poor farmers, as did the nobility in Israel under the rule of kings. That is the reason God prohibited usury in the Bible. He required loans to the poor to be made without interest. Competition among banks today keeps interest rates low and people borrow to invest in businesses or buy long term capital goods such as cars and houses. The prohibition of usury today would apply most closely to pay day loans to poor people.

Usually, farmers would have to borrow money from the rich only in the event of a drought, during which they would obviously have no income. Keep in mind that God had promised the land would never have droughts as long as the people followed him. Droughts were one of God's judgments against a rebellious people. For a farmer to be unable to repay a loan, some disaster must have happened as a result of rebellion against God by the nation and forced him to borrow money. Then more disaster happened so that he could not repay the loan. The farm would have served as collateral for the loan, but the lender would not get to keep the farm permanently. He could keep it only until Jubilee.

So the sale of the land was a last resort for a poor farmer to repay his loans. The farmer did not escape from the loan, as Wallis and the supporters of Jubilee 2000 imagined. His sale of the farm land paid the loan. The lender kept the proceeds from the harvests until Jubilee then gave the land back to the farmer, as verses 25-26 prove: "Corresponding to the number of years after the Jubilee you shall buy from your friend; he is to sell to you according to the number of years of crops. In proportion to the extent of the years you shall increase its price and in proportion to the fewness of the years you shall diminish its price; **for it is the number of crops he is selling to you**." [emphasis added] Jubilee was a celebration of the burning of the home mortgage, not the equivalent of modern bankruptcy in which the court frees the borrower of all his debt. The same was true of the seven year limit on slavery for Israelis. The period of enslavement, which was more like the Western practice of indentured servitude than slavery in the U.S. before the civil war, paid off the family's debt, after which the family was free to leave.

The prospect of an approaching Jubilee limited how much a lender could recoup from a farmer for a loan. For example, say ten years remained until Jubilee and the average harvest could be sold for say 2,000 shekels of silver. The lender would realize that he could collect no more in future harvests from the borrower than 20,000 shekels, assuming he would observe the prohibition of charging interest to the poor. In reality, Jubilee set an upper limit on the amount a money lender would loan to the poor and a limit on what the poor could borrow. With forty-nine years to go, a poor farmer could borrow far more than one with just five years left to Jubilee. Jubilee did not remove the burden of debt from borrowers.

What about improvement to the land a purchaser may have made during the intervening years? If those improvements defaulted to the original owner along with the land, Jubilee would discourage new owners from making any improvements and diminish the harvests. The Torah anticipated that problem and requires the original owner to compensate the interim owner who made the improvements for the remaining financial value, not the original cost of improvements.

A closer inspection, Jubilee fails as a tool for wealth redistribution or reductions in income inequality. But a further problem afflicts those who insist it was: even in Moses' day, farmers could not farm without significant investments in capital. The capital necessary for farming in a way that would allow the farmer to support a family included at least a pair of oxen, a yoke and a plow, seed and money to live on until the harvest. Even as late at AD 1600, those amounted to a significant investment for most farmers. Without charity, the farmer would have to borrow the funds to purchase that capital and begin the cycle of land sale followed by Jubilee again.

God promised the Israelis that poverty would not exist among their brothers as long as they followed his laws because he guaranteed the rains necessary for good harvests and he would keep away the locusts. Farmers usually became poor because of droughts or plagues of locusts that destroyed crops as a result of God's judgments. But God also knew that Israelis would rebel against him; Moses told them so in several places. So God provided means of recovery from poverty. If a farmer fell short of what he needed to feed his family or plant a crop he could borrow at no interest or sell a part of his land. A kinsman could help him by redeeming the land, or buying it back.

If he became so poor that he had to sell all of his land, again a kinsman could help him out by repurchasing it or he would get the land back at Jubilee. But he could sell the land for only what the harvests might bring in sales for the number of harvests remaining until Jubilee. If the farmer had incurred so much debt that the harvest would not pay off the debt and he had no close relative to redeem the land, he could sell himself, and or his family as unpaid laborers until Jubilee. At that point any debt that might remain was erased and the family could start all over. The tribulations of Ruth and Naomi probably depict a scenario in which Israel was caught in a judgment from God because of idolatry that forced Naomi's husband to relocate to Moab. The two returned to Israel after the death of her husband and sons, but their only help was the kinsman redeemer, not Jubilee.

The economy under the judges

The book of Judges records mostly the history of the moral and spiritual degradation of the nation of Israel following the death of the conquering generation. Cycles of repentance followed by delivery from oppressive invaders then descent into idolatry and immorality make up most of the book. Those cycles and the phrase "In those days Israel had no king; everyone did as they saw fit," (Judges 21:25) cause many commentators to deduce that the period of Israel under the judges was one of decline and chaos and the glory days of Israel came with the kings. But did Israel benefit from having kings instead of judges? The question suggests that God was wrong about how best to structure the laws of the new nation and that he erred in warning of the tyranny of kings.

However, the record of the kings of Israel demonstrates that God was not wrong. A list of the names of good kings is short with David at the head, but even David kept the nation in continual warfare. God refused to allow him to build the first temple because God saw him as a bloody man. Solomon built the first temple, but he enriched himself at the expense of the people and taxed them so heavily that he caused a civil war that the nation never recovered from. The history of the remaining kings differs little from that of the judges in that most kings led the people into idolatry and immorality followed by God's judgments in the forms of drought, plagues of locusts and invasions by foreign armies. The Israeli leadership may have thought that they could avoid God's judgments of being conquered by foreign armies if they had a king and a standing army, but God proved to them that they could not raise an army large enough to defend Israel without his assistance. He had already proven with Gideon and others that with his assistance they needed only a very small army of volunteers to remain free.

The era of the kings neither protected the nation from invasion nor prevented it from sliding into idolatry, immorality and even child sacrifice. So whatever Samuel, the author of the book, meant by the phrase "In those days there was no king in Israel: every man did that which was right in his own eyes," he certainly could not have meant that Israel was more Godly, prosperous or peaceful under kings. Samuel would never have praised the rule of kings in the way that most theologians think the phrase does. He condemned monarchy.

Samuel's phrase occurs four times in the book of Judges (17:6; 18:1; 19:1; 21:25) and it has led many theologians to assume anarchy reigned the entire time. However, a similar phrase appears in Deuteronomy 12:8 where it refers to Israel under Moses in the wilderness: "There, in the presence of the LORD your God, you and your families shall eat and shall rejoice in everything you have put your hand to, because the LORD your God has blessed you. You are not to do as we do here today, everyone doing as they see fit, since you have not yet reached the resting place and the inheritance the LORD your God is giving you."

Anarchy did not exist under the leadership of Moses with the tabernacle in place and offerings being made. It is possible that Moses meant the people had been free to choose whether to serve God or not without compulsion and many chose to worship idols. Later, kings would determine by decree which gods the people worshipped. In other words, under the judges the people had religious freedom but under the kings they did not. Of course, the history shows that most of the kings led the people into idolatry and child sacrifice. It is possible that Samuel was lamenting the loss of freedom that the tyranny of kings caused.

Under the judges, Israeli families would have been richer than those under the kings because they did not pay taxes to support the royal family, which would have included thousands of princes since David and succeeding kings had hundreds of wives. Nor would they have to pay for the many wars, standing armies and vast array of weapons, especially horses. They would not have paid for the crushing administration and army of bureaucrats required to collect taxes and oversee building projects. And they would not have suffered from the centuries of abuse in which the princes paid corrupt judges to steal the land of common people.

We know from history that the incentives to work hard and produce more, which come from the knowledge that the owner's property is secure, cause enormous increases in wealth. The experiences of the Dutch Republic, the Pilgrims at Plymouth Rock, the former communist nations of Eastern Europe, China and India in the past generation provide overwhelming evidence. The pattern of economic development in history is clear: first productivity increases in the agricultural sector enriches farmers and releases workers to the city. Wealthier farmers then demand more manufactured goods which cause that sector to grow as well as trade with other nations for goods not produced in the home country.

We can assume that ancient Israelis were no different in character and took advantage of their secure property in similar ways. Farmers would have searched for better seeds and farming methods, such as irrigation, better plows and the use of fertilizers. They would have switched to growing higher valued crops, such as grapes, and the production of milk, butter and cheese that earn farmers higher profits than grains while trading for the grains they needed. The farmers would have retained the surpluses they produced instead of losing them to the tax man as in Egypt or Israel under the kings. They would have exchanged some of the surplus for gold and silver to save, but much of it would have gone to buy manufactured goods in the cities. Manufacturing would have increased as well as trading for manufactured goods from other nations. Increases in manufacturing would have led to specialization, which would increase productivity and wealth of workers in manufacturing and raised their demand for better quality farm products. People in the cities and countries would have eaten more meat, milk and cheese and improved their health, further increasing productivity and wealth.

Helmut Schoeck asserts in his book *Envy: a Theory of Social Behavior* that the genius of Christianity lay in its adoption of secure property rights for individuals. Of course, Christians did not create property rights; God did. And God was the first to prohibit envy. God began the Ten Commandments with "I am the Lord your God" and concludes with "You shall not covet your neighbor's house; you shall not covet your neighbor's wife, nor his male servant, nor his female servant, nor his ox, nor his donkey, nor anything that is your neighbor's." Envy, which is related to covetousness, is corrosive to the individual and to those societies that embrace it. Rights to private property blunt the effects of envy by protecting the property owner from the envy of neighbors who want to take his property and distribute it to others. And property rights can redirect envy into productive activity because the envious person realizes that he has a chance at achieving the wealth of the person his envies through hard work and wise decisions, two of the major themes of Proverbs. But he will attempt the hard work and investment necessary to increase his wealth only if he has confidence that the law will not allow his neighbors to vent their envy and take his property and the state will not tax it away.

If envy was controlled, then greed must have run amuck under the judges. But Israel had God's laws preventing theft and fraud, which the courts would have enforced so greed that led to criminal activity would have been kept to a minimum if the people followed God's laws. What about the greed that does not rise to the level of criminality, but is merely immoral? The freedom of entry into businesses that Israelis enjoyed would have increased competition, and as Adam Smith taught us, competition forces the greedy businessman to temper his greed in order to prevent the competition from taking his customers and ruining his business.

More importantly, greedy businessmen work through the state to achieve their ends. Adam Smith warned about that, also. In a free market, businessmen must always worry about their competitors because they cannot force customers to do business with them. Competition forces them to please customers. Unable to get special treatment from customers, greedy businessmen turn to the state and buy the politicians. Only the state has the power to force people to do something they normally would not do. Greedy businessmen lust for that power to free them from the pressures of competition. They get it buy bribing politicians to pass laws that favor them and reduce competition. Today, most business regulations do little more than protect large corporations from competition by smaller companies. Ancient Israel had no politicians to bribe, so greedy businessmen had no relief from the pressures of competition.

Had ancient Israel remained loyal to God, it might have launched the green revolution in agriculture caused by the discovery of the horse collar. After all, horses had pulled chariots for millennia. Then farm productivity would have rocketed and made Israelis extraordinarily wealthy for their times. Or they might have ignited the industrial revolution instead of the Dutch Republic. Israel had the most important elements in place – private property, low taxes, and the rule of law. The Dutch powered their machinery with wind; those quaint wind mills were actually factories. The technology existed for Israelis to use wind power and water wheels in the same way.

Israelis under the judges might have been able to create a steam engine. After all, the Romans understood the power of steam by at least the first century AD, using it to power a primitive steam turbine and open temple doors in order to fool worshippers into thinking that their idols were alive. Hero of Alexandria wrote about the *aeolipile*, but others may have known of the power of steam earlier. Ancient Israelis had access to the technology for mining and smelting iron ore. Wooden pistons used for lifting water are ancient technology, too. They might have easily put together the technologies of pistons, iron and steam to create the steam engine. But the world would have to wait until the nineteenth century for James Watt because Israel kept rebelling against God who responded by allowing pagan nations to conquer them.

The pagan nations stood no chance of sparking something like the industrial revolution because until the Dutch Republic all cultures have despised commerce and manufacturing, preferring war and plunder as means to greater wealth. In addition, slavery was so common that the elite saw no need to invent labor savings equipment like windmills, water wheels and steam engines. Roman and Chinese rulers even banned labor savings inventions out of fear of causing unemployment. As a result, most inventions like the *aeolipile* served no purpose but entertaining the bored nobility or deluding ignorant idol worshippers until the Dutch made private property secure again and labor became scarce.

We often have the idea that God blessed Israelis with wealth because they followed his laws. However, it is more likely that following God's economic principles embodied in the Mosaic Law caused the Israelis to become wealthy. God's laws are not arbitrary like man's laws. God gave us his laws because following them will make us prosper spiritually and materially. This is what the founders of "natural law," God's laws, meant when they wrote that the law is natural because it causes mankind to flourish in every way.

In fact, God's principles make people wealthier even if they do not believe in the one true God. We have seen those principles work for non-Christians in the modern world in the rise of the Asian nations such as Japan, South Korea, Taiwan, Singapore, Hong Kong, India and China. Those nations rose from extreme poverty to become among the wealthiest nations on the planet by simply respecting private property a tiny bit more. And that respect does not have to go as far as prescribed in the Bible to produce results. China has lifted over 300 million people from starvation poverty in a generation by only slightly freeing markets and respecting property.

Israel under the judges may have become the wealthiest nation in the region. We can assume that because of the fact that surrounding nations were so eager to conquer it and steal its wealth. After each incident of liberation by a judge, the nation would have accumulated large amounts of wealth as it followed God's principles. Poorer nations would burn with envy, but Israel would have had the material resources to defend itself as long as it remained loyal to God's principles. When the people began to worship idols they would naturally abandon God's principles as well and become poorer, thereby destroying their ability to finance their defense against invaders.

Like many of God's judgments, national defense may be a built in judgment. For example, God does not have to do anything special to punish people who violate his principle of gravity. The principle enforces itself. And God does not have to enforce his warning about drinking too much alcohol. Drunkenness inflicts its own punishments. In a similar way, abandoning God's principles of economics have built-in consequences that we cannot avoid. For the ancient Israelis, that created cycles. Following God meant following his economic principles, which would increase national wealth and the nation's ability to defend itself from attack. When the people in sufficient numbers abandoned God for idols, they would abandon God's economic principles as well and become poorer, thus destroying their ability to defend their nation and permitting another nation to conquer and loot its wealth. God had to do nothing but intervene to rescue the nation after it had repented, as he did in the case of Gideon and others, because it would not be able to re-establish his economic principles under foreign rule and therefore not have time to build wealth.

The economy under the kings

The rebellion against God and his economic system by the leaders of Israel in the time of Samuel would have caused the Israeli economy to degenerate until it became poor as Egypt. Problems began in the reign of Solomon. His temple was magnificent; his wealth legendary. But Solomon invented no labor saving devices to improve productivity. He got his wealth from taxes and international trade. He was wise enough to avoid war. Israel enjoyed forty years of peace under David's son and that saved the nation an enormous expense. Throughout history, war has bankrupted more kings than any other endeavor, except for maybe pyramid building.

Solomon earned some of his wealth through international trade. His attitude toward commerce stands out because of its stark contrast to the attitude of the pagan kings of nations around Israel who despised business and preferred the old-fashioned way of earning wealth through conquest and looting. For example, Solomon may have encouraged others to follow his example and invest in international shipping in Ecclesiastes 11:1: "Cast your bread upon the waters for you will find it again." Most interpreters think the verse encourages charity because those good deeds will be rewarded in the future. But some theologians think he may be referring to the ships he invested in that engaged in trade as far away as the British Isles. Some translations substitute "grain" for "bread" in the passage.

The second interpretation gets support from the verse that follows: "Give portions to seven, yes to eight, for you do not know what disaster may come upon the land." It appears that Solomon is offering sound investment advice to diversify one's investments among at least seven ships. The attitude of humility towards outcomes of one's ventures is reinforced in verse six: "Sow your seed in the morning, and at evening let not your hands be idle, for you do not know which will succeed, whether this or that, or whether both will do equally well."

The book of Proverbs lent further support to commerce in chapter 31 in which King Lemuel describes his idea of the virtuous wife. The wife in the passage is obviously married to a wealthy man, possibly a prince, and does not need to work. Yet she engages in the type of work and commerce that all wealthy people and especially nobility in the nations surrounding Israel despised, and all cultures until the Dutch Republic held in contempt. Here are verses 10-21:

> 10 An excellent wife who can find?
> She is far more precious than jewels.
> 11 The heart of her husband trusts in her,

and he will have no lack of gain.

12 She does him good, and not harm,
all the days of her life.

13 She seeks wool and flax,
and works with willing hands.

14 She is like the ships of the merchant;
she brings her food from afar.

15 She rises while it is yet night
and provides food for her household
and portions for her maidens.

16 She considers a field and buys it;
with the fruit of her hands she plants a vineyard.

17 She dresses herself with strength
and makes her arms strong.

18 She perceives that her merchandise is profitable.
Her lamp does not go out at night.

19 She puts her hands to the distaff,
and her hands hold the spindle.

20 She opens her hand to the poor
and reaches out her hands to the needy.

21 She is not afraid of snow for her household,
for all her household are clothed in scarlet.

22 She makes bed coverings for herself;
her clothing is fine linen and purple.

23 Her husband is known in the gates
when he sits among the elders of the land.

24 She makes linen garments and sells them;
she delivers sashes to the merchant.

25 Strength and dignity are her clothing,
and she laughs at the time to come.

26 She opens her mouth with wisdom,
and the teaching of kindness is on her tongue.

27 She looks well to the ways of her household
and does not eat the bread of idleness.

28 Her children rise up and call her blessed;
her husband also, and he praises her:

29 "Many women have done excellently,
but you surpass them all."

30 Charm is deceitful, and beauty is vain,
but a woman who fears the LORD is to be praised.

31 Give her of the fruit of her hands,
and let her works praise her in the gates.

But Solomon also got a lot of his wealth from very heavy taxes. They burdened the people so much that they caused a revolt that split the nation in two and resulted in centuries of civil war.

The nation's fiscal situation continued to worsen with each king. Isaiah told the people "Your silver has become dross, your drink diluted with water." (Isaiah 1:22) This could mean several things, but we know it did not mean that silver had literally become dross because silver does not do that. It could mean that production had fallen and as a result prices had risen so much that silver had become as worthless as the slag left over from the refining process. But why had production fallen and created such scarcity. The previous and following verses explain: "How the faithful city has become a harlot, she who was full of justice! Righteousness once lodged in her, but now murderers. Your silver has become dross, your drink diluted with water. Your rulers are rebels and companions of thieves; everyone loves a bribe and chases after rewards. They do not defend the orphan, nor does the widow's plea come before them....."

Corruption had destroyed the incentives to work and produce. As we have seen throughout history, especially in communist nations, people will not work when they are certain that the production from that labor will be taken from them by corrupt officials without compensation. The princes were so greedy that they would not judge cases brought by poor orphans and widows because the poor had nothing of value with which to bribe the judge and the princes who acted as judges wanted bribes. Evil people used the court system to steal from the poor by bribing judges for a decision in their favor.

The mention of wine meant that it was either scarce and Israelis watered it down to make it last longer, or they were cheating people by watering down good wine. Either way, the watered down wine indicates an economy experiencing very high inflation rates and causing enormous suffering. A major reason for the failure of Israel's armies in battle leading up to the exile was the poverty of the kings. They could not buy the weapons and supply the armies as they needed.

In Ezekiel 45:9-12, God indicts merchants for using false weights and calls for the removal of "violence and spoil" and the administration of civil justice. When the Old Testament condemns Israel for violence, it is often because of the adoption of human sacrifices. Then He establishes the exact ratio of the shekel to its lesser and greater weights, as well as dealing with balances and measures of capacity. Abandoning the worship of God for idols led the nation into human sacrifice, violence, and corruption. Agriculture and industry die in such an environment and leave the nation much poorer.

Which economic system?

Combining sound hermeneutic principles in interpreting the Torah with knowledge of economic history creates an image of ancient Israel under the judges that is very different from the one often preached. The golden age of Israel would have taken place under the judges, not under the kings. Israelis would have enjoyed a much higher standard of living and freedom under the judges. Under the kings, Israeli life would have differed from the oppression of Egypt in only minor ways. Kings and princes would have grown wealthier and more powerful at the expense of the people. Faithfulness to God may have been slightly greater under the judges than under the kings because the book of Judges mentions no incidents of child sacrifice, which appears to have been common under the kings.

Preachers may extol the period under the kings because the Bible contains so much more material about them, even though the two periods lasted roughly the same amount of chronological time, about 480 years each. The period of the judges takes up one book. The period of the kings occupies six history books, the Samuels, Kings and Chronicles, which detail the sins of the long series of evil and oppressive kings. Most of the prophetic books also condemn the evil of the kings, nobility and common people.

But consider why so much of the Old Testament is devoted to the period of the kings. Most of the writing about the kings comes from the prophets, but God called prophets in Israel only because the people and the priests had become wicked and idolatrous. No news from God was good news in the case of prophets. When the priesthood had become corrupted, as it had under Eli in the book of first Samuel, so that no one was teaching the people the word of God, God would bypass the system and anoint prophets to warn of impending judgment. The volume of writing by the prophets and the apocalyptic judgments coincided with the period of the kings, which should signal to preachers that Israel under the kings was far more wicked and rebellious than Israel under the judges.

Theologians who claim the Bible does not endorse an economic system have not understood the Torah, or what Christians call the Pentateuch, the first five books of the Bible. Neither Moses nor the elite of Israel wrote the laws that created the economic system. God personally wrote them. And God created a government and economic system verging on what people today call anarchy. The government regulated no part of the economy. It did not set prices, tax land or income, or redistribute wealth. Even if Israelis had wanted to regulate the economy, God provided no state to carry it out. There was no president, prime minister, executive branch, parliament or congress; no department of commerce, securities and exchange commission, federal reserve bank, treasury, federal trade commission or FDIC. No one told Israeli farmers or manufacturers what to produce, when to produce it, how to produce it or how much they could charge.

No nation in history has enjoyed such freedom from state control. Even the system of natural freedom proposed by Adam Smith in his book *An Inquiry into the Nature and the Causes of the Wealth of Nations* never came close to imagining the level of freedom that Israelis enjoyed under the judges. Yet anarchy did not prevail in ancient Israel because the people had the law of God. The courts adjudicated disputes in the light of that law and the people enforced court decisions. As a result, theft, fraud, murder, and other crimes were kept to a minimum.

The Torah makes it clear that God would never have endorsed socialism in any of its forms, whether communism, fascism, democratic or Fabian. The Torah government embodied all of the elements of capitalism described in chapters 1 and 2. Those included respect for property, the rule of law, limited government, relatively honest courts, free markets, veneration of business, the bourgeois virtues and individualism.

Chapter 4 – The dark ages

Israel seemed to prosper under kings David and Solomon, but in reality the nation was coasting on investments made during the reigns of the judges. David wasted the nation's wealth and youth on continual warfare. In spite of his wisdom, Solomon ruled like a pharaoh. He increased his personal wealth through international trade and heavy taxation. He describes his luxurious lifestyle and massive building programs in his Book of Ecclesiastes: "I also tried to find meaning by building huge homes for myself and by planting beautiful vineyards. I made gardens and parks, filling them with all kinds of fruit trees. I built reservoirs to collect the water to irrigate my many flourishing groves" (Ecclesiastes 2:4-6).

In the book of I Kings chapters 5-7, the court historian recorded that Solomon spent seven years building the temple in Jerusalem. The temple was one hundred feet long and made of stone overlaid with imported wood, gold and silver. But he devoted thirteen years to constructing a palace for himself that was larger and far more expensive than the temple of God. Then he built reservoirs to hold water for irrigating his groves and vineyards and supply water to Jerusalem. Groves were often places for worshipping idols. Solomon's conspicuous consumption during his reign lit the fuse that set off an explosion ripping the nation apart and reverberating through centuries of civil war and national decline.

After Solomon's death, the elders of Israel asked his son and heir to the throne, Rehoboam, to reduce the crushing tax burden. A delegation told him, "Your father made our yoke heavy; now therefore, lighten the burdensome service of your father, and his heavy yoke which he put on us, and we will serve you." (I Kings 12:1-5) Rehoboam consulted his father's advisors who counseled him to comply with the demands of the people, but the son had inherited none of his father's wisdom and instead increased the tax burden. As a result, Israel ruptured into the northern and southern kingdoms. Both chased idols and generally grew poorer over time.

The rebellion of Israel against God in their choosing a king snuffed out the light of freedom and prosperity for millennia. As a result, "In the ancient Middle East (Mesopotamia and pharaonic Egypt), the prevalent form of government was the 'patrimonial' regime, under which the monarch owned as well as ruled the land and its inhabitants, treating his realm as a gigantic royal estate," according to prominent historian Richard Pipes. Pipes concluded that "private property in land in the modern sense of the word was not known in any of the ancient societies, whether in Europe or Asia, at least up to the latest period of antiquity."

As the hockey stick graph of per capita G.D.P. in chapter 1 demonstrates, nothing much happened economically for 2,500 years after Israel chose a king to replace God. That statement will throw academics to the floor in convulsions. They will immediately point to their research showing the changing fortunes of each empire. Yes, wealth waxed and waned, but around a very low level. Compared to wealth today, the variance in wealth over the previous two millennia is insignificant.

Empires rose and fell. When they rose, they grew rich through military conquest and plundering the wealth of the vanquished. But when the conquered grew strong enough to resist, the wealth and power of the former victor evaporated. The world's wealth did not grow; it merely sloshed around and pooled in the capital city of conquering armies for a brief time. Standards of living in 1800 AD looked pretty much as they had in 5000 BC. The team of oxen was still cutting edge farming technology and that limited food production, which kept the stream of urban population within narrow banks. Three things kept people poor: government, attitudes toward commerce, and envy permeating and uniting the first two.

As they had wished, the Israeli government and economy became like that of the surrounding nations and that form of government has proven to be the most robust in human history. Society was divided between a small group of elites and the masses. The leader of the elite group, the pharaoh, king, emperor, Caesar, dictator or whatever, gave the elite permission to rape and pillage the masses in exchange for their loyalty. The masses put up with the plunder because they envied their neighbors and wanted a greater power that could use force to prevent any neighbor from succeeding more than others. The masses did not envy the elite, because they saw no possibility of joining their ranks. They avoided innovations that might bring success because they did not want to inflame envy in others.

The masses, mostly farmers, hated businessmen because businessmen refused to accept their status as part of the poor and dared to accumulate wealth. In their minds, the nobility had the right to be wealthy because of their status in society. Merchants were consigned to the lowest status and therefore enjoyed no right to be wealthy. In addition, everyone knew that no man could grow richer except at the expense of another so as merchants grew wealthy people assumed that the merchants had taken wealth that belonged to them. But the merchant's chief sin was rising above his neighbors in material success through good business practices and thereby inflaming their envy.

This form of government, called a closed or extractive society by the New Institutional School of economics is the traditional and most robust form of government in history. It never abolished the notion of private property. Going back even to ancient Egypt, philosophers (except for Plato and the later Stoics), theologians and politicians endorsed private property as either a natural right or a necessary evil to keep the peace. Plato and the Stoics thought that common property would end envy and greed, but twentieth century experiments in the USSR, China and the Kibbutzim of Israel proved them wrong. As Schoeck wrote, equality enrages envy against the most trivial differences.

Roman law provided for strong property rights, as Richard Pipes wrote, "Roman jurists were the first to formulate the concept of absolute private ownership, which they called *dominium* and applied to real estate and slaves...The rights implicit in *dominium* were so absolute that ancient Rome knew nothing of eminent domain." Why, then, did not capitalism spring up in the rocky Italian soil? Why did it have to wait until the sixteenth century? The answer lies in the difference between principles and practice.

While almost all nations endorsed private property and punished theft severely, that principle applied only to the masses. Among themselves, the masses could not steal each other's property or the property of the ruling class, but everyone understood the law did not apply to the elite or the state. In most empires, the ruler was the image of a god and owned everything. He allowed people to use his property as if it was their own and they could not steal from each other, but as the ultimate owner the king could dispose of anyone's property as he wished. In other words, the poor could not steal, but the ruling class could steal all they wanted from the masses. Private property was superficial.

Empires with such a system followed empire. Syria conquered the northern kingdom of Israel and carried off the wealth to Damascus then Nebuchadnezzar overran Judah in the south and took all of the wealth of the temple to Babylon. The Medes and Persians in turn overthrew the Babylonians and stole the wealth of that empire. No one created any wealth; they just stole what others had piled up. Then along came Greece.

Greece

After the failure of Israel, ancient Greece resurrected the institution of private property for a brief time and for a few people. By the end of the sixth century B.C., independent yeoman farmers made up the bulk of Greek citizens. Most owned less than ten acres on which they grew grapes, olives, figs and grains. Ownership of land included the rights of citizenship and participation in government. These farmers were freeman, which meant they were exempt from taxes and providing services to the aristocrats. They labored for themselves and enjoyed the fruits of their labor, much as the ancient Israelis had. In battle they formed the columns of armored infantrymen who fought to defend their cities and farms. The historian of antiquity Sir Moses Finley, quoted in Pipes' *Property and Freedom,* wrote:

> In the Homeric poems, the property regime, in particular, was already fully established...The regime that we see in the poems was, above all, one of private ownership...[T]here was free untrammeled right to dispose of all movable wealth...[T]he transmission of a man's estate by inheritance, the movables and immovable together, was taken for granted as the normal procedure upon his death.

Noncitizens could pursue finance and commerce or lease land and mines, but they could not own land or become citizens. Plato and Aristotle devoted attention to the subject of private property because it was prevalent, and their love of farming may account for the low esteem in which they held finance and commerce. Artisans in Greece were self-employed, unlike their counterparts in the Middle East who worked for the king.

By contrast, Sparta enrolled all adult males in the military and allotted uniform plots of land cultivated by bondsmen but retained only on the condition that they used it well. The state could take the property away and give it to another soldier at any time. The law prevented its citizen-soldiers from engaging in commerce or manufacturing because of the low esteem in which society held those professions. Men shared their wives with other men and turned their children over to the state at the age of seven to begin military training. In exchange for iron coins, the state confiscated all gold and silver. As a result, Pipes reports that the historian Plutarch claimed, "luxury, theft, bribery, and lawsuits disappeared." Of course, if the state allows the people no property, then such problems disappear automatically. However, Schoeck's work on envy proves that the Spartans would have suffered from envy as much as anyone, if not more, over the small remaining differences between people, such as talent.

Sparta defeated Athens in the Peloponnesian war and that event may have inspired Plato's depiction of a similar society as the ideal in his *Republic*. Plato saw property as incompatible with virtue and allowed the rulers of his idyllic republic to have none, neither houses nor land, lest they "tear the city in pieces by differing about 'mine' and 'not mine,'" according to Pipes. In Plato's mind, virtue diminished in proportion to the property one owned. The rulers, whom Plato gave the harmless sounding title of "guardians," shared wives and held children in common. In his next work, the *Laws*, Plato tried to be more realistic by tempering his idealism and allowing the rulers to have families, but insisted that the state have to power to prevent extremes of wealth and poverty. Still, he clung to his utopian dream of a propertyless society as the following excerpt from *The Dialogues of Plato* quoted in Pipes' *Property and Freedom* demonstrate:

> The first and highest form of the State and of the government and of the law is that in which there prevails most widely the ancient saying, that "Friends have all things in common." Whether there is anywhere now, or will ever be, this communion of women and children and of property, in which the private and individual is altogether banished from life, and things which are by nature private, such as eyes and ears and hands, have become common, and in some way see and hear and act in common, and all men express praise and blame and feel joy and sorrow on the same occasions, and whatever laws there are unite the city to the utmost – whether this is possible or not, I say that no man, acting upon any other principle, will ever constitute a state which will be truer or better or more exalted in virtue.

Plato made the same mistake as the Plutarch and all socialists, communists, Nazis, fascists and Fabians. While admitting that the notion of private property is an aspect of mankind's nature, he was under the delusion that changing human nature was such a trivial matter that the elimination of property could perfect it. Aristotle shared Plato's belief that inequality in wealth led to social strife, but argued for creating an enlightened nature through education rather than a propertyless society. He saw the positive force of property and defended it on utilitarian grounds: people take better care of their own property and abuse common property. Because people reap the rewards of private property, they work harder and more efficiently, thereby producing more and creating an abundance of goods. As for social discord, he saw that people fight more over common property than over private property, whereas private property encourages ethical behavior by allowing the owners to be generous through charity.

The real differences between Plato and Aristotle lay in their views of human nature. Plato wanted to change the nature of mankind and so designed the society that he thought could manage it. Aristotle was much wiser, which may be why Christians favored him over Plato for centuries. Aristotle did not try to change human nature but adapted society to it in a way that would allow for the greatest cooperation and least conflict. The ignorance of socialists in the early nineteenth century freed them to imagine they had invented a new way of organizing society and perfecting human nature, but they had done nothing more than resurrect Plato's ancient republic based on Sparta. Capitalism championed Aristotle. There is nothing new under the sun.

The first money was barley for small transactions, such as buying eggs, and cattle for more expensive ones, such as buying a wife. Early in human history people discovered the benefits of silver and rapidly replaced barley and cattle with the metal as money. But barley continued to influence money because prices had been set in terms of the weight of barley grains. So the new money, silver, continued to be measured in barley grains. The Biblical shekel, for example, was the amount of silver that equaled about 28 barley grains.

The Lydians created the first coins around 700 BC, as far as historians know. The coin producer weighed the metal, shaped it into a coin and stamped the actual weight on it along with other symbols to give it authority. The uniform size and stamp informed merchants of the metal's purity and weight of the coins without them having to assay or weigh the metal. Coins reduced transaction costs and offered a major benefit to markets, but it did not take long for states to grasp the power of coined money and grab a monopoly on its issue.

In 594, little more than a century after the invention of coins, Greece conducted one of the first coin debasements known in history. Solon, leader of Athens, figured out that he could reduce the content of the precious metal in each coin by adding base metals to the silver then stamping the coins with the same weight as if they contained the original amount of silver. In other words, the kings committed fraud by stamping a false weight on the coins. Solon reduced the silver content of Athenian coins by 25 percent. Then he forced merchants to accept the coin at face value instead of on the basis of the real weight of the silver in the coins. The king had expanded his money supply and was able to pay off his debts without having gathered any more gold or silver through taxes. Many philosophers at the time considered Solon a genius, but he was nothing more than a gangster and fraud.

Producers and retailers caught on very quickly to the fraud and raised their prices enough to ensure they received the same weight of silver for their goods as they had before the debasement. If the coins had been debased by adding 25 percent base metals, merchants raised prices by at least 25 percent. Price inflations, in turn, tended to anger citizens and spark riots, but the rioters rarely connected higher prices with the monarch's fraud and, instead, blamed businessmen for their greed.

Other Greeks cities imitated Solon's debasement, leading Demosthenes to write, "The majority of states are quite open in using silver coins diluted with copper and lead." Athens learned from the experience and maintained the purity of its currency after Solon. As a result, Athenian coins traded at a premium to others and contributed to the extension of Athenian commercial and political power over the rest of Greece.

In spite of the contempt Aristotle and other Greeks had for commerce, democracy created the fertile ground of freedom in which businesses could grow and people become wealthier. Archeological evidence shows that, due to better nutrition, Greek men in the golden age were taller on average than recruits in the army of Greece in 1949. Even as the

Greek city-states increased their populations, food consumption among peasants probably increased 50 percent according to Baylor University historian Rodney Stark in *How the West Won: The Neglected Story of the Triumph of Modernity*. And the size of housing expanded from fifty-three square meters in the eighth century to 325 square meters in the fifth century. Greeks excelled at games, literature, art, philosophy and government, activities that require enough wealth to give a significant part of the population the leisure to pursue them.

Greek progress lasted only until the Macedonians conquered the Middle East, after which the rulers again adopted the ancient Oriental philosophy that all the land belonged to the king who regulated every detail of the economy. The Hellenistic successors to Alexander the Great perpetuated the absolute rule of monarchs over land and the economy, thereby destroying all of the progress made by Athens in previous centuries.

Though Greece never regained the wealth and status of its golden age, Greek culture lived on as the Romans welcomed and perpetuated it. But its most lasting influence may have come from the impact on Judaism and Christianity from Greek philosophy. Alexander the Great incorporated Palestine into his sprawling empire, which led to the establishment of twenty-nine Greek towns. By 200 BC, six times as many Jews lived in Hellenized cities than in Palestine. The Greek language became so common that scholars translated the Hebrew Scriptures into the language and the book became the family Bible for most Jews even in Palestine. The Israeli King Herod built a Greek theatre, amphitheater and hippodrome near Jerusalem. Stark wrote in *How the West Won* that Jewish theologians beginning with Philo of Alexandria interpreted the Torah through their knowledge of Greek philosophy and corrected philosophy using the Torah.

Since most early Christians were also Jews, the Greek influence flowed into the new sect as well. The Apostle Paul quoted from the Stoic Greek poet Aratus in a sermon at Mars Hill in Athens (Acts 17:28). Several of the Church fathers were trained in Greek philosophy before their conversions and, like Philo, saw parallels between it and Christianity. For example, Stark quoted Clement of Alexandria (150-215) who attributed a similar role to philosophy for gentiles as the role that the apostle Paul gave to the Torah:

> Before the advent of the Lord, philosophy was necessary to the Greeks for righteousness...being a kind of preparatory training...Perchance, too, philosophy was given to the Greeks directly and primarily, till the Lord should call the Greeks. For this was a schoolmaster to bring "the Hellenic mind," as the law, the Hebrews, "to Christ." Philosophy, therefore, was a preparation, paving the way for him who is perfected in Christ.

The Church continued to venerate Aristotle into the early modern period until the advance of science under Church scholars shredded his physics. Theologians did not accept Greek theology or morality, but embraced the culture's commitment to reason and logic, which made Christianity and Judaism unique among the world's religions. Modern atheists insist that Christianity is irrational and unscientific, but that is an invention of their own fevered imaginations because historians and philosophers of science have recognized the uniqueness of reason in Judaism/Christianity. For example, Stark quoted the great British philosopher Alfred North Whitehead in *How the West Won*:

> The greatest contribution of medievalism to the formation of the scientific movement [was] the inexpugnable belief that...there is a secret, a secret which can be unveiled. How has this conviction been so vividly implanted in the European mind? ...It must come from the medieval insistence on the rationality of God, conceived as with the personal energy of Jehovah and with the rationality of a Greek philosopher. Every detail was supervised and ordered: the search into nature could only result in the vindication of the faith in rationality.

The gods of other religions, including the ancient Greek gods, were either too irrational or too remote to inspire confidence in a rational world that could lead to the development of modern science.

While the Greek resurrection of private property for a few helped Greece to prosper above its enemies, it failed to birth capitalism for several reasons, the most important of which was the crushing of individualism. As noted earlier, Siedentop demonstrated that property and freedom existed in Greece only for the patriarchs who owned their sons, daughters and slaves. Sons lived only to please the family heads while daughters were raised to please the patriarchs of their husband's family. Though their status gave them citizenship in the cities, the patriarchs were free only in the sense that they did not pay taxes and could vote, for their lives were dedicated to the common good of the city, which meant they were virtual slaves of the ruling elite. Patriotism meant love of the city and those lacking in it were called idiots. Patriarchs could lose everything if the rest of the city elders considered them a threat or saw them as insufficiently devoted to the cause of the city. Individual rights for the patriarchs against the claims of the city did not exist, just as the rights of sons, daughters, merchants, and slaves did not exist in opposition to the demands of the patriarchs.

Social mobility, becoming something other than a slave, for example, was impossible because everyone was born to their status in life. Philosophers like Plato believed that only a few, trained elites could learn to reason, which is why he promoted the idea of a philosopher king. Aristotle and his followers "did not doubt that the *telos* or 'function' in a hierarchy of being established that some humans were slaves 'by nature,'" according to Siedentop. Benjamin Constant in "The Liberty of the Ancients Compared with that of the Moderns" described the lack of individual freedom this way:

> All private actions were strictly monitored. No room was allowed for individual independence of opinions, or of choice of work, or—especially—of religion. We moderns regard the right to choose one's own religious affiliation as one of the most precious, but to the ancients this would have seemed criminal and sacrilegious. In all the matters that seem to us the most important, the authority of the collective interposed itself and obstructed the will of individuals. The Spartan Therpandrus can't add a

string to his lyre without offending the magistrates. In the most domestic of relations the public authority again intervene: a young Spartan isn't free to visit his new bride whenever he wants to. In Rome, the searching eye of the censors penetrate into family life. The laws regulate *moeurs*, and as *moeurs* touch on everything, there's nothing that the laws don't regulate.

Among the ancients, therefore, the individual is nearly always sovereign in public affairs but a slave in all his private relations. As a citizen he decides on peace and war; as a private individual he is constrained, watched and repressed in all his movements; as a member of the collective body he interrogates, dismisses, condemns, impoverishes, exiles or sentences to death his magistrates and superiors; as a subject of the collective body he can himself be deprived of his status, stripped of his privileges, banished, put to death, by the free choice of the whole of which he is a part.

And capitalism did not rise among the Greeks because of the contempt the patriarchs had for commerce. The primacy of the needs of the city revolved around its defense, so military service and glory in battle were held in the highest esteem. Farming came second. The character traits and skills needed for combat and farming differed a great deal from those needed in the market place. Siedentop wrote,

Thus, commerce became associated with 'giving in' to appetites – with refinements, sensual pleasures and a narcissism that subverted civic spirit. Commerce became the enemy of simplicity. It became almost a synonym for decadence. Commerce, along with the taste for luxury it promoted, turned men into quasi-women.

The market, then, threatened the city's existence by robbing it of warriors. Again, Constant wrote,

I don't mean that amongst the ancients there were no trading peoples. There were, but they were somehow an exception to the general rule...If only I had time I would show you—through the details of the ancient traders' *moeurs*, habits, ways of going about trading with other peoples—that their commerce was so to speak impregnated by the spirit of the age, by the atmosphere of war and hostility surrounding it. Commerce then was a lucky accident...

Rome

Roman law went beyond that of Greece with its establishment of absolute property in land, but that existed only on the Italian peninsula and only for wealthy citizens. Roman law did not recognize the power of eminent domain for the state; such was the respect for property in land for citizens in Rome. As in early Greece, yeoman farmers aided by slaves prevailed, although the emperors and nobility owned vast tracks of land.

Roman law protected property in theory; the practice was very different. The wealthy held all of the power and could bend the law to serve them. As a result, the middle class – the merchants, small farmers and artisans – felt very insecure it what property it held. They considered themselves to be poor even if they enjoyed more wealth than others in their class because they were at the mercy of the powerful rich who could easily ruin them financially. They lived in fear of impoverishment. Patronage decided their fate. Peter Brown in *Through the Eye of a Needle: Wealth, the Fall of Rome, and the Making of Christianity in the West, 350-550 AD* quoted Augustine:

> Brethren, you know how people boast of their patrons. To those who threaten him, the client of a greater patron answers: "By the head of so-and-so, my patron, you can do nothing against me...But perhaps you have been made utterly poor and destitute. You had some little family property that had supported you, which was taken away from you by the tricky dealing of a rival...Yesterday, this person was groaning that he had lost his property. Today, backed by a greater patron, he is grabbing the property of others.

Patrons were the wealthy and politically powerful elite of the town. The middle class enjoyed some security as long as they kept a low profile and had the support of a powerful patron. But if they became an opponent of a more powerful patron, a simple lawsuit from him could cause them to lose everything. Under that level of insecurity, most successful manufacturers and merchants will try to hide their wealth rather than invest it in expanding their businesses or improving productivity.

Rome did not fall because barbarians invaded; barbarian tribes merely took advantage of the military weakness of Rome that followed from its economic weakness and it was economically weak mainly because it had expanded its borders to the limit possible at the time. Rome had conquered and looted as much as it could. The Persians held them off in the east, the German tribes in the north and the desert to the south in Africa. With no new wealth to plunder, Rome consumed the loot from past conquests and grew poorer.

As with all ancient empires, the Roman state controlled the price of food. City officials regularly searched for violators and punished profiteering. Keeping the peace concerned officials the most and nothing would motivate the mob to riot as quickly as rising prices for grain, oil and wine. But officials kept prices too low for farmers to earn a profit comparable to that in other industries so, in addition to low levels of productivity, food supplies were almost always tight. By the fourth century the emperors had pushed taxation beyond the optimum of the Laffer curve for their day so that taxes did not generate enough revenue to meet the need for bread and circuses to pacify the masses while feeding and arming a military of 650,000 men that surrounded the Mediterranean Sea. Farmers in North Africa paid up to two thirds of their harvest in taxes according to Brown. Rather than cut spending, the emperors debased the coins to increase the money supply, the same principle used by

Solon in Greece six centuries earlier and by Ben Bernanke, Chairman of the Federal Reserve after the 2008 crisis, but using different means.

Roman emperors had begun debasing coins as early as the reign of Nero, but rising price inflation, shrinking tax revenue and people hoarding gold and silver made emperors desperate and reckless with the practice in the third and fourth centuries AD. As a result, they collided with city officials who strove to keep food prices at the official maximum. The food merchants lost the battle, but instead of accepting the official price for their goods, they simply abandoned their businesses, as did many farmers who could not sell their produce for enough to cover the costs of production. Eventually, the government refused to accept its own debased coins for tax payments and insisted on payment in kind according to George Reisman in *Capitalism: A Treatise on Economics.*

As a result, city residents became desperate for food. The scarcity became so severe that, to avoid starving they left their homes in the cities for abandoned fields in rural areas in order to grow food for themselves. Untilled land existed in abundance because many farmers had deserted their land for more profitable ventures, such as banditry, begging and piracy. Those who remained restricted their production to just the needs of the family since they could not sell the surplus for a reasonable price. No longer having cash from the sale of their produce in the cities, they could not buy manufactured goods, such as pots, dishes and farming implements, so they made them at home.

Slavery had ceased being profitable, so many farmers freed their slaves. Along with the urban migrants, the free slaves rented land from the large landholders and grew their own food, a portion of which they paid in rent. Ludwig von Mises wrote in *Human Action*, "Italy and the provinces of the empire returned to a less advanced state of the social division of labor. The highly developed economic structure of ancient civilization retrograded to what is now known as the manorial organization of the Middle Ages."

The emperors responded to the deteriorating economy with greater enforcement of the maximum price laws, more debasement of the coins and heavier taxes, but they only accelerated the decay. "To him [Diocletian], and to his successors, only a command economy in which the government regulated nearly every aspect of economic life could provide the resources needed to maintain both the army and a newly expanded bureaucracy. All pretense of a free market was abandoned," wrote Stephen Hause and William Maltby in *Western Civilization: A History of European Society*. The emperors destroyed their monetary system and as a result lost the ability to pay a professional army. They had to replace the army with militias made up of farmers who lived along the frontier. When the Romans had weakened themselves sufficiently, the barbarians invaded. The population of Italy declined from seven million in 200 AD to five million in 400 AD.

After the barbarian invasions in Spain and Gaul, power shifted from Rome to the local German kings and the tax money followed. As Peter Brown wrote, "Once the farms and villages had broken loose from the tight net spread by the villa, it was next to impossible to extract from them the high level of wealth that had supported the affluent residences of the fourth-century age of gold."

The Eastern Roman Empire, known today as the Byzantine, lasted another thousand years, partly because the emperors never resorted to debasing the coins until the later centuries. The Byzantine Empire took great pride in its laws protecting private property, which later influenced the formation of European property laws. Still, property was insecure in the Eastern Empire, as well, for all but the governing elites. As if in imitation of the pharaohs, the Byzantine emperor enjoyed absolute power. He was not as god-like as pharaoh, but he was the next worst thing, the vicar of God on Earth. As such, he controlled the lives and property of his subjects and could punish or confiscate without appeal. Common sense restrained the exercise of this arbitrary power most of the time.

Diocletian constructed a massive bureaucracy to enforce his commands. Succeeding emperors in the Eastern Roman Empire expanded the bureaucracy and regulated every aspect of economic, political, and religious life. It fixed prices and wages while preventing people from leaving their homes or occupations by installing a system of internal passports. Heavy taxes to pay for the bureaucracy, army and navy allowed only a few to rise above the poverty level. Escape from common poverty led through the military or the bureaucracy. In other words, Egyptians living 2,000 years earlier would have been quite at home in the Byzantine Empire.

The immaculate conception of individualism

Four centuries before the sack of Rome by barbarians, a carpenter from Nazareth had already planted the seeds of the destruction of Greek and Roman culture. Larry Siedentop wrote,

> The ancient doctrine of natural law was being revised to take account of belief in the incarnation, the idea that 'God is with us'. For that belief removed the previous radical divide between divine agency (whether in the form of the 'gods' of polytheism or the Old Testament's Yahweh) and human agency. The idea of the incarnation is the root of Christian egalitarianism."

Siedentop credits Paul for developing the idea of Christian liberty, which is a major theme of the books in the New Testament that the Apostle authored and one most fully developed by him. With the incarnation, God became accessible to everyone regardless of social status. As the Apostle John put it in the Book of Revelations, followers of Jesus became a "kingdom of priests." The Emperor, one of whom would become a Christian centuries later, held no greater standing with God than did the lowest slave or poorest field hand. Believers did not have to go through a priest or the patriarch to reach God. And the roles into which they were born no longer limited their identities.

In his letters to the churches, Paul insisted that God sees no difference between Jew and gentile, male and female, slave and freeman, rich and poor in terms of their access to him. All are equal before him. All mankind is God's creation and all believers his children. Roman society had been built on the ancient Greek idea of natural inequality: some were born to rule and others to serve with gradations in between. The patriarch was the priest who provided access to the gods. Women were virtual slaves while slaves were cattle. Aristotle called slaves 'living tools.' Paul's theme of Christian liberty destroyed the foundations which supported that hierarchical structure of society.

Paul and the Apostles taught the ancient Jewish theology of a single God, not a superior god among many, as was Zeus, but the one and only God. Any other creature with the title of god did not actually exist. Monotheism threatened Roman society by erasing the many gods upon which it depended. Christianity threatened the gods that protected the cities and thus survival of the cities. Christians were called atheists not only because they refused to worship the pantheon of gods but because they denied their existence. As a result, pagans not only considered Christians unpatriotic, or idiots, but terrorists as well. Finally, Christians endangered the solidarity and peace of the Roman Empire by refusing to worship Caesar. Siedentop recognizes that few ideas in history have been as subversive to the dominant culture as early Christianity:

> Was Paul the greatest revolutionary in human history? Through its emphasis on human equality, the New Testament stands out against the primary thrust of the ancient world, with its dominant assumption of 'natural' inequality. Indeed, the atmosphere of the New Testament is one of exhilarating detachment from the unthinking constraints of inherited social roles. Hence Paul's frequent references to "Christian liberty".

Luc Ferry teaches philosophy at the Sorbonne in Paris and agrees with Siedentop. Although an atheist, he devotes chapter 3 of his book, *A Brief History of Thought*, to the Christian origins of modern liberty. Here are excerpts from that chapter:

> To explain further: the Greek world is an aristocratic world, one which rests entirely upon the conviction that there exists a natural hierarchy…of plants, of animals, but also of men: some men are born to command, others to obey, which is why Greek political life accommodates itself easily to the notion of slavery.

> It would be obtuse to try and pass from the Greek experience to modern philosophy without any mention of Christian thought.

> But there is more: by resting its case upon a definition of the human person and an unprecedented idea of love, Christianity was to have an incalculable effect upon the history of ideas. To give one example, it is quite clear that, in this Christian re-evaluation of the human person, of the individual as such, the philosophy of human rights to which we subscribe today would never have established itself.

> Christianity was to bring to ethical thought at least three novel ideas, none of which was Greek – or not essentially Greek – and all of which directly linked to the theoretical revolution we have just observed in action. These

new ideas were arresting in their modernity. It is probably impossible for us, no matter how much effort we make, to imagine just how disruptive they must have seemed to contemporaries. The Greek world was fundamentally an aristocratic world, a universe organized as a hierarchy in which those most endowed by nature should in principle be 'at the top', while the less endowed saw themselves occupying inferior ranks. And we should not forget that the Greek city-state was founded on slavery.

In direct contradiction, Christianity was to introduce the notion that humanity was fundamentally identical, that men were equal in dignity – an unprecedented idea at the time, and one to which our world owes its entire democratic inheritance.

At the same time, the idea of the equal dignity of all human beings makes its first appearance: and Christianity was to become the precursor of modern democracy. Although at times hostile to the Church, the French Revolution – and, to some extent, the 1789 Declaration of the Rights of Man – owes to Christianity an essential part of its egalitarian message.

First century Christianity attacked traditional Roman and Greek culture from above by denying the gods that protected the cities and the superior status of the patriarchs. From below it undermined the foundation of that society by intentionally breaking up families. Jesus had said in Luke 14:26 "If anyone comes to me and does not hate father and mother, wife and children, brothers and sisters – yes, even their own life – such a person cannot be my disciple." And the record shows that the new faith did divide families.

Early Christians put the family back together in the Church. In Acts, Christians shared their wealth with each other as if they were family. Paul tapped into the power of family bonds by urging Christians to think of each other as family members. In Romans 12:10 he wrote, "Be devoted to one another in love." The word for love is *philostorgoi*. Most people are familiar with the Greek words for Godly love, *agape*, brotherly love, *philos* or *philadelphia*, and sexual love, *eros*. But Paul used a different word, *philostorgoi*, which refers to the natural love within a family between parents and children. And in I Timothy 5:8 Paul wrote, "Anyone who does not provide for their relatives, and especially for their own household, has denied the faith and is worse than an unbeliever." The process of converting a novel religion into an organizing principle of society would take fifteen centuries. This section includes only the highlights of Siedentop's account.

Christianity had an early impact on society with the response of Christians to persecution and execution by Roman authorities. Pagans paid attention. The martyrs insisted that they were willing to die for a relationship they found more valuable than that of family and that their relationship with God gave them a will of their own, not one dictated to them from the patriarch. Siedentop observed that,

Martyrdom illustrated the exercise of an individual will, founded on conscience. It made that will visible."

In making martyrs of Christians, the ancient world was consecrating what it sought to destroy and destroying what it sought to preserve. For the Christian martyrs gained a hold over the popular imagination. And it is easy to see why that should have been so. The martyrs offered a model of heroism open to all, a democratic model of heroism...Thus an unintended consequence of the persecution of Christians was to render the idea of the individual, or moral equality, more intelligible. The glimpse of a depth of motivation, at once individual and potentially universal, was not easily forgotten.

The next shock to the equilibrium of ancient Greek and Roman culture came from the development of monasticism. The earliest monastics had absorbed some of the Platonic contempt for the material world as well as the heresy of Gnosticism and the pagan mysticism of the cynics. They were mostly individuals who moved to the wilderness on the edge of town and lived as simply as possible, keeping body and soul together. Others joined them and eventually communities developed, but they were voluntary. Siedentop wrote,

The first striking thing about that new identity was that its basis lay in voluntary association, in individual acts of will. This was a radical departure from the beliefs and practices of the ancient world. Family cult, civic status and servitude had been assigned by birth or imposed by force.

Christianity continued to subvert traditional values and the structure of society as people began to see the monastic communities as more spiritual. Still, none of the monks intended to commit suicide. They needed food, water and shelter to live, simple as it might be, so they spent much of their day performing manual labor. Only slaves had done manual labor in the traditional Greek and Roman societies. That status conscious culture did all it could to avoid manual labor in order to prevent being seen as slaves. But monks, many of whom came from wealthy, aristocratic families, embraced manual labor. As a result, they rehabilitated labor according to Siedentop: "Work acquired a new dignity, becoming even a requirement of self-respect." In other words, the Protestant work ethic imagined by Max Weber appeared a millennium before the term "Protestant." Second and third century monks engaged in their own style of protest against materialism, the caste system, and sloth.

Around the year 300 the Emperor Constantine embraced Christianity and ended persecution by the state. The Eastern Church fell under the domination of the emperor and remained subservient to the state until after its conquest by Muslims. As a result, Christian liberty had very little influence on the organization of society in the East where the ancient Greek and Roman structure based on hierarchies of status persisted. But the invasion of the barbarians in the West forced change.

Christianity today in the U.S. is primarily a rural and suburban phenomenon, but for most of its history in Europe it was limited primarily to the cities and the middle class. When barbarians flooded into the weakened Roman Empire and set up their governments, the pagan patriarchs were killed or fled leaving the bishops of the towns as the de facto rulers of the people and intercessors with the conquerors. Bishops had earned their political power over the centuries by representing the common people to the emperor. After the fall of the Roman Empire, they represented the people to the German invaders and earned the respect of the new rulers because of their education, eloquence, and genuine concern to assist the new governors with understanding their conquered people and customs. The new rulers began sending their sons to local monasteries to become educated like the bishops and in the process the descendants were indoctrinated into the egalitarianism of Christian liberty. Gradually, Christian egalitarianism eroded the legitimacy of slavery until it disappeared from Europe except in the east under the Ottoman Empire.

Charlemagne subjected the Church to the state as the Eastern Roman Empire had, but with his death the Church reasserted its sovereignty by inventing the concept of secularism. Kings and nobility had gained increasing control over the Church until they were appointing popes and bishops. The Church fought back after Charlemagne's death by insisting that the Church needed to govern itself and be separate from the state because the Church represented God on earth and needed to be able to criticize kings and governments when they abused their citizens. Siedentop quoted one pope who wrote, "But it may be said, that kings are to be treated differently from others. We, however, know that it is written in the divine law, 'You shall judge the great as well as the little and there shall be no difference of persons'."

Over time, the Church succeeded in achieving its independence from the civil rulers and creating two spheres of control – religion for the Church and all other matters for the civil government. As it has separated the roles of church and state, the Church initiated a revolution in science by exorcising ghosts from the physical world. Science had been chained for centuries to Aristotle's physics in which material objects were categorized by their nobility and intentions. Led primarily by the influence of William of Ockham, church councils began to exorcise demons and demigods that had controlled the movement of objects in Aristotle's world. Modern science began to develop by observing, testing theories, and using inductive reasoning.

The churches had elected their bishops since the end of the period of the apostles and monasteries continued that tradition by having members elect their leadership. Christianity reformed cities as citizens began to see themselves as associations of equal individuals that elected their own government. Historians often credit the growth of cities in Europe for its economic development, but they fail to inform the reader that European cities enjoyed many advantages over cities in any other part of the world due to the Church's long struggle to instantiate Christian individualism.

> That model, with its roots in the church and canon law, promoted egalitarianism by reinforcing the notion that the individual was the fundamental unit of legal subjection...There was a major difference between

European and Islamic cities in that respect. Islamic cities developed, but they were never legally constituted. They grew, but they were never founded as autonomous legal entities.

During the "Dark" Ages, the Church adopted and transformed the Stoic concept of natural rights to fit with Christian liberty. Under the Stoic concept, rights came from the status that nature had assigned different groups and those could not change. Patriarchs held all of the rights with slaves, children and wives having none. The Church reconstructed natural rights along individual lines where they came to mean the sphere of action and belief that neither the state nor the Church could infringe upon. The incarnation "lies behind the transformation of the ancient doctrine of natural law into a theory of natural rights." By 1300, property, consent to government, self-defense, marriage, procedural rights and even the rights of infidels to be left in peace were defended as natural. Eventually, these would be boiled down to the formula of the rights to life, liberty and property.

With the dawn of the fifteenth century, the foundation for what became known as liberalism – "belief in a fundamental equality of status as the proper basis for a legal system; belief that enforcing moral conduct is a contradiction in terms; a defense of individual liberty through the assertion of fundamental or 'natural' rights; and, finally, the conclusion that only a representative form of government is appropriate for a society resting on the assumption of moral equality" – had been firmly established in Europe. Siedentop adds that the words "individual" and "state" first appear commonly in dictionaries in the fifteenth century. The ideas were in place, but Europe still awaited a nation to instantiate them. That would happen in the Dutch Republic.

Pre-industrial Europe

Historians slice and dice European history into many periods - the dark ages, the medieval world, the Renaissance, the late middle ages, the Reformation, the early modern period, etc., but in terms of economic development measured as per capita income, living standards had stagnated for most of human history, as the hockey stick graph discussed in chapter 1 demonstrates. Hause and Maltby wrote in the book *Western Civilization* that in the middle ages, "The basic conditions of material life had changed little since the Neolithic revolution and would remain relatively constant until the industrial revolution." But even as the period came to a close, "For most people in the eighteenth century, life was little changed from the Middle Ages and closer in its essentials to that of ancient Rome than to the early twenty-first century." And Roman life had differed little from that of ancient Egypt.

Historians have often depicted pre-industrial life as an impressionist painting in which contented families lacked nothing because they could raise their own food on their little plots of land beside their huts and make everything they needed at home. If they chose, they could sell excess production at the local market, but they faced no pressures from cutthroat competition, greedy capitalists or low wages. Mises wrote in *Human Action* that historians painted a false, idyllic image of pre-industrial Europe:

The peasants were happy. So also were the industrial workers under the domestic system. They worked in their own cottages and enjoyed a certain economic independence since they owned a garden plot and their tools. But then "the Industrial Revolution fell like a war or a plague" on these people. The factory system reduced the free worker to virtual slavery; it lowered his standard of living to the level of bare subsistence; in cramming women and children into the mills it destroyed family life and sapped the very foundations of society, morality, and public health...

The truth is that economic conditions were highly unsatisfactory on the eve of the Industrial Revolution. The traditional social system was not elastic enough to provide for the needs of a rapidly increasing population. Neither farming nor the guilds had any use for the additional hands. Business was imbued with the inherited spirit of privilege and exclusive monopoly; its institutional foundations were licenses and the grant of a patent of monopoly; its philosophy was restriction and the prohibition of competition both domestic and foreign.

Friedrich Engels perpetuated the myth of the idyllic peasant life before the industrial evolution. He wrote in *The Condition of the Working Classes in England in 1844,* quoted by Hayek in *Capitalism and the Historians,* that before the onslaught of industry,

[T]he workers vegetated throughout a passably comfortable existence, leading a righteous and peaceful life in all piety and probity; and their material condition was far better than that of their successors. They did not need to overwork; they did no more than they chose to do, and yet earned what they needed. They had leisure for healthful work in garden or field, work which in itself, was recreation for them, and they could take part beside in the recreation and games of their neighbors, and all these games – bowling, cricket, football, etc. contributed to their physical health and vigour. They were, for the most part, strong, well-built people, in whose physique little or no difference from that of their peasant neighbours was discoverable. Their children grew up in fresh country air, and, if they could help their parents at work, it was only occasionally; while of eight or twelve hours work for them there was no question.

They were 'respectable' people, good husbands and fathers, led moral lives because they had no temptation to be immoral, there being no groggeries or low houses in their vicinity, and because the host, at whose inn they now and then quenched their thirst, was also a respectable man, usually a large tenant farmer who took pride in his good order, good beer, and early hours. They had their children the whole day at home, and brought them up in obedience and fear of God...The young people grew up in idyllic simplicity and intimacy with their playmates until they married, etc.

Even as excellent an historian as Richard Pipes wrote in his book *Property and Freedom* that, "from the middle of the nineteenth century onward even liberals came to be troubled by the growing disparities in the distribution of wealth." However, it was not possible for the historians to have witnessed increasing inequality in the nineteenth century because the industrial revolution shrank differences in wealth over that century. For example, the Gini ratio measures the concentration of wealth with zero indicating perfectly equal distribution and one representing maximum inequality. The Gini ratio in England stood at 0.65 near the beginning of the eighteenth century, falling to 0.55 near the end of the nineteenth, according to Nobel Prize-winning economist Robert Fogel in his book *The Escape from Hunger and Premature Death, 1700-2100*. The ratio in the U.S. is currently around 0.35. Fogel wrote,

> The relatively generous poverty programs developed in Britain during the second half of the eighteenth century...have given the unwarranted impression that government transfers played a major role in the secular decline in beggary and homelessness. Despite the relative generosity of English poor relief between 1750 and 1834, beggary and homelessness fluctuated between 10 and 20 percent. Despite the substantial reduction in the proportion of national income transferred to the poor as a result of the poor laws of 1834 and later years, homelessness declined sharply during the late nineteenth and early twentieth centuries.

> The fact is that government transfers were incapable of solving the problems of beggary and homelessness during the eighteenth and much of the nineteenth centuries, because the root cause of the problem was chronic malnutrition. Even during the most generous phases of the relief program, the bottom fifth of the English population was so severely malnourished that it lacked the energy for adequate levels of work.

Anti-capitalist writers of the nineteenth century may have been fooled by the upper-class propaganda from the end of the fourteenth century. The disasters that had unfolded in that century caused the upper classes to seek refuge in nostalgia for a fictional past through art and literature which presented idyllic visions of happy peasants toiling near beautiful castles, much as plantation owners in the U.S. South once depicted the happy slaves enjoying their mild labor in the cotton fields. Such visions are found in the *Tres riches heures du Duc du Berry*, an illustrated prayer book from the middle ages.

However, the factory owners in nineteenth century England could not force people to work in their factories. They could only entice laborers with slightly higher wages or better working conditions. By the standards of the upper classes and those of today, the conditions were abysmal, but the fact that people chose to work in those conditions proves that their alternatives were worse, unless we want to portray the working classes are irrational. Hayek explained in *Capitalism and the Historians* that the success of capitalism partly inspired the fantasy portrayals of pre-industrial life:

> The very increase of wealth and well-being which had been achieved raised standards and aspirations. What for ages had seemed a natural and inevitable situation, or even as an improvement upon the past, came to be regarded as incongruous with the opportunities which the new age appeared to offer. Economic suffering both became more conspicuous and seemed less justified, because general wealth was increasing faster than ever before.

However, Hayek added that ideology played a major role as well: "[B]ecause the theoretical preconceptions which guided them postulated that the rise of capitalism must have been detrimental to the working classes, it is not surprising that they found what they were looking for." In other words, many historians were Marxists whose dogma insisted against overwhelming evidence to the contrary that industrialization had enslaved workers and made their lives miserable.

Much of the anti-capitalist writing in England originated in Germany from socialists. What became known as the Historical School dominated history and economics in Germany for the sixty years preceding World War I. Professors took pride in calling themselves "socialists of the chair." They exerted a great deal of influence on historians in the U.K. and U.S. Socialists made up the bulk of members of the "institutional" school in the U.S. "The whole atmosphere of these schools was such that it would have required an exceptional independence of mind for a young scholar not to succumb to the pressure of academic opinion. No reproach was more feared or more fatal to academic prospects than that of being an 'apologist' of the capitalist system," wrote Hayek. Accurate history would have to wait for another generation in which economists would become interested in history.

Some historians assumed that cries for reform proved that industrialization had made worker's lives worse, but another likely explanation reaches back to ubiquitous envy. As Schoeck wrote, people rarely envy those in positions so far above them that they have little chance of lifting themselves to that level. That explains the acceptance for millennia of the vast inequities between the nobility and the masses. Among the masses, everyone was equally destitute, but as soon as one of their own raised his head above the crowd in terms of wealth, envy erupted from his neighbors who lopped it off. Workers in industrializing Europe did not envy the nobility, who had always been wealthy, but their own neighbors who dared to achieve a better life. Peasants would rather all were poor than suffer the envy of seeing another peasant do better.

However, when Ms. Cooke Taylor investigated the conditions of workers in a Lancaster factory, she said, quoted by Hayek, "Now that I have seen the factory people at their work, in their cottages and in their schools, I am totally at a loss to account for the outcry that has been made against them. They are better clothed, better fed, and better conducted than many other classes of working people."

If historians and social reformers got the living conditions of factory workers wrong, they went even farther astray with medieval life. Late medieval reality diverged cruelly from the historian's candy land. In the middle ages, the Malthusian model of economic growth strangled the world in a death grip. Productivity in agriculture improved very slowly, with developments such as the horse collar causing great advances. As a result, the population would often grow until it outstripped the capacity of the land to feed the people. Then famine, soaring prices and mass starvation reduced the number of mouths to feed. The Netherlands experienced its last famine in the middle of the sixteenth century. Much of the rest of Europe would endure this vicious cycle for another two centuries.

Peasants

Most of Europe struggled to survive in villages surrounded by open fields. The village leaders apportioned the available land according to family size, determined the crops to be grown, the farming methods, and which plots were to remain unplowed. Peasants and small farmers worked the land that belonged to the nobility, the state or the Church as sharecroppers, meaning they paid a portion of the crop as rent. A contract from the late eighteenth century France described in Hause and Maltby's *Western Civilization* gave the marquis who owned the land 85 percent of the crop. Peasants paid heavy taxes and mandatory tithes out of their meager revenues. They supplemented their income with small gardens near their homes and livestock such as pigs and chickens. When they slaughtered a pig, they usually bartered the best cuts of pork for items they could not make at home then made soups and stews of the fatty remnants.

Families rarely bought anything at markets. Men made their own tools, furniture, and housing, and wove cloth from the yarn spun by the women, who then sewed the clothing for the family. Children worked alongside their parents at the earliest age because the whole family needed the income from their labor in order to survive.

Robert Fogel estimated that European agriculture in 1700 could produce enough food for only 80 percent of the population to have enough calories to perform labor for a day. The remaining 20 percent were reduced to begging and were able to acquire only enough calories to sustain a short walk each day from where they slept to the place where they begged. Many of the calories people ate provided little nourishment because disease prevented their bodies from absorbing the nutrients according to Hause and Maltby.

The typical peasant family lived in a two-room house; the walls of which they made by weaving limbs together to form a frame and then covering it with mud. For security, they cut no windows. Thatch formed the roof with a hole in the center to let the smoke from cooking fires escape because peasants could not afford fireplaces with chimneys. Packed earth became the floor. Wealthier peasants might build a barn for storing produce, but livestock shared the hut with the family in the winter to provide heat because few families could afford wood for heating.

The law chained peasants to the land and they had to obtain permission from their lords to move to another village, marry, or acquire and dispose of land. Young men who desired to marry had to compensate their lord for his loss of labor when the peasant girl became a wife and mother. Peasants farmed strips of land scattered throughout the fields of the manor and worked together to perform the plowing, sowing and harvesting. The organization of work involved cooperation and coercion, with little room for individual initiative.

Peasants owned a team of oxen that they grazed on common pastureland. Lords required peasants to work three or four days of the week on their property as rent payment and they appropriated most of the peasants' surplus production. By the late medieval period, peasants had begun to pay rent in crops or cash instead of labor. Because the lords did not pay peasants for their labor, peasants took little interest in the tasks assigned them and performed as little work as they could get by with. Peasants knew that no matter how poorly they labored, the lords could not reduce their wages or discharge them. In fact, "they considered it a point of honor to cheat the seignior in the performance of the obligation," Jerome Blum wrote in *The End of the Old Order in Rural Europe*.

Tolstoy described in his novel *Anna Karenina* the frustrating attempts of a nobleman farmer in nineteenth century Russia to persuade his peasants to use new farming techniques that he was convinced would produce higher crop yields. The nobleman ran into the rock wall of resistance that peasants had built up centuries earlier to keep out change. Peasants fought the adoption of new crops that could regenerate the soil, increase yield and provide greater nutrition. They prevented the introduction of new breeds of sheep that offered more meat and better quality wool. Their resistance derived partly from ignorance and superstition, and partly from the certainty that the lord would appropriate the increased output that such innovations might bring. If innovation succeeded, they would fear the envy of other peasants.

Pressure to conform exerted enormous influence on peasants, for farming methods meant more to them than merely techniques for raising food; they represented customs and traditions that had developed over centuries and had woven the fabric and rhythm of village life. "It took a strong will to withstand the criticism, and even the opprobrium, of neighbors that an innovation would bring, and to survive the ridicule if the innovation did not succeed," wrote Baumol. Peasants lived in a culture that valued collectivism, accepted power inequality, and avoided uncertainty. But most of all, they endured intense envy from neighbors that thwarted innovation and any attempt at achieving a standard of living greater than other peasants.

Peasant families might eat three pounds of rye or barley bread (wheat was too expensive) a day in good times, or share a pound in lean ones. Fuel for baking, wood or charcoal, was expensive so many villages baked their bread in large loaves once a month. The loaves would dry out and peasants had to break them with a hammer and soak them in liquid to make them edible. Poor nutrition ensured that their health was bad much of the time.

The nobility

Noblemen who attempted to improve the farming methods of peasants often failed because of peasant resistance, but few concerned themselves with innovations. Blum wrote,

Conspicuous consumption and ostentatious display were matters of great moment to a nobleman. They could determine his social and political status among his peers and affect his own and his family's fortunes. And so the usual noble showed scant interest in investment in improvements to increase the productivity of his property. That would postpone present consumption, and most nobles did not think in those terms. In any event, the many petty seigniors who in the best of times barely managed to make ends meet, and who lived always in fear of ruin, could not afford to invest for future gains.

The nobility not only controlled production, but trade as well. They rarely left surpluses for peasants to sell at markets, but relied upon markets for selling their own surplus and for purchasing goods that they could not produce on their own estates, such as luxury imports. Within the boundaries of their jurisdiction, lord's taxed and regulated the markets. Taxes could substantially enhance a lord's income, but in addition to the regulations, they increased the cost of trade and acted as a major hindrance to economic development. Another roadblock to development rose up in the concepts among the noble classes of what constituted honorable means of achieving wealth. According to Baumol,

> The "preferred" medieval ways to wealth were the public and private wars carried on by kings and nobles alike. Also in line with the orientation of the times were the occupations of the robber barons and of the leaders of private armies whose services were for hire and who undertook aggression on their own initiative when market demand for their services was poor. In the same period, rent-seeking was also a respectable avenue to wealth. The king's friends at court who helped him against his enemies, who entertained him, and who provided him with various forms of amusement could hope for rich rewards in the form of generous grants of land, castles and other privileges...Destructive wars and rent-seeking activities as means to enhance wealth and power, of course, continued through the Renaissance and, indeed, they manifestly continue today.

The Hollander Pieter de la Court would have agreed with this assessment of the nobility. De la Court had served in several government positions in Holland under the leadership of Johan de Witt. The Dutch Republic became a true republic after the assassination of Prince William of Orange, who had led the rebellion against Spain, and the ascension of the Grand Pensionary Johan van Oldenbarnevelt to political leadership. The war for independence lasted eighty years with a twelve year truce in the middle. In spite of continuous war, the republic under the brilliant leadership of Oldenbarnevelt with the help of Hugo Grotius was transformed into one of the wealthiest and most powerful nations in Europe.

Prince Maurice, grandson of the first William, ended the republican government through a coup d' etat in 1618. He had Oldenbarnevelt executed and Grotius jailed. The monarchy lasted until the death of William II and the revival of the power of the Grand Pensionary under Johan de Witt in 1650, whose rule ushered in the zenith of power and wealth for the Dutch. That republic died in another coup by Prince William III who ignited the envy of mobs against the leadership of the Republic, including de la Court. Rioting rabble murdered De Witt and his brother, tore out their hearts and ate them raw, after which the Prince apologized for the sluggishness of his military in coming to the aid of the victims. De la Court fled to France to escape a similar fate. In exile, he wrote *The True Interest and Political Maxims, of the Republic of Holland,* published in 1662.

De la Court identified the source of Holland's wealth as "traffick," shipping, fishing, and manufacturing. By traffick, "I mean the buying of anything to sell again, whether for consumption at home, or to be sold abroad, without altering its property, as buying in foreign countries cheap to sell dearer abroad;" His book compares the growth of those sources of wealth in the republic with their ruin under the monarchs. De la Court used examples from ancient and classical history as well as recent Dutch history to bolster his points. He concluded that the rulers of a republic need to please the people in order to remain in power and so will promote the commercial activities that made Holland wealthy and able to afford a militarily capable of defending its borders.

> It follows then to be the duty of the governours of republicks to seek for great cities, and to make them as populous and strong as possible, that so all rulers and magistrates, and likewise all others that serve the publick either in country or city, may thereby gain the more power, honour and benefit, and more safely possess it, whether in peace or war: and this is the reason why commonly we see that all republicks thrive and flourish far more in arts, manufacture, traffick, populousness and strength, than the dominions and cities of monarchs: for where there is liberty, there will be riches and people.

Monarchs, on the other hand, impoverish cities, destroy trade and burden the nation with debt through long and expensive wars in order to prevent cities from gaining power and challenging the monarch's rule:

> For then it follows as truly from the said general maxims of all rulers, that the next duty of monarchs, and supreme magistrates, is to take special care that their subjects may not be like generous and mettlesome horses, which, when they cannot be commanded by the rider, but are too headstrong, wanton, and powerful for their master, they reduce and keep so tame and manageable, as not to refuse the bit and bridle, I mean taxes and obedience. For which end it is highly necessary to prevent the greatness and power of their cities, that they may not out of their own wealth be able to raise and maintain an army in the field, not only to repel all foreign power, but also to make head against their own lord, or expel him.

De la Court offered as evidence the waste and incompetence of the princes of the Dutch Republic in handling the land wars against Spain and France, which caused the debt burden of the state to explode and the tax burden to become unbearable. His longest attack he saved for the fraud and incompetence the princes practiced in their duties of clearing the seas of pirates. He noted that Holland required a small number of ships to clear the sea lanes when it shouldered the responsibility alone. But under the dictatorship of the princes, vast armadas with budgets that ruined the treasury proved insufficient for the job and allowed pirates to ravage shipping from Amsterdam. He claimed the princes were negligent on purpose in order to weaken the finances of Holland because it opposed monarchical rule most of the time.

De la Court anticipated the political economics championed by Nobel Prize winner Patrick Buchanan known as "public choice theory" almost three centuries in advance. Buchanan argued that selfishness and not the public interest motivates politicians. De la Court warned his countrymen that monarchs often satisfy their selfishness by creating monopolies:

> As concerning the freedom of all inhabitants to set up their trades everywhere in Holland, without molestation from the burgers, select companies, and guilds; this is not at all to be expected under a monarchical government. For everyone knows that at court all favours, privileges and monopolies are to be had by friendship, or else by gifts and contracts, for the king's profit, and that of the favourites and courtiers."

For example, the Dutch had given the East India Company a monopoly on all trade with the Far East, but de la Court pointed out that the revenue to the state from the monopoly was tiny compared to that from the other sectors of the economy:

> For it cannot be denied, that the free Eastern trade alone, the herring-fishing alone, and the French trade alone, produce ten times more profit to the state, and the commonality of Holland, than twelve or sixteen ships which yearly sail from Holland to the East-Indies do now yield to the state, and the inhabitants.

The princes found the support they needed to overthrow the republican government and maintain their power from unscrupulous people and even the clergy:

> For not only officers, courtiers, idle gentry, and soldiery, but also all those that would be such, knowing that under the worst government they use to fare best, because they hope that with impunity they may plunder and rifle the citizens and country people, and so by the corruption of the government enrich themselves, or attain to grandeur, they cry up [promote] monarchical government for their private interest to the very heavens: although God did at first mercifully institute no other but a commonwealth

government, and afterwards in his wrath appointed one sovereign over them. 1 Sam. 1. 8, 12.

Yet for all this, those blood-suckers of the state, and, indeed of mankind, dare to speak of republicks with the utmost contempt, make a mountain of every molehill, discourse of the defects of them at large, and conceal all that is good in them, because they know none will punish them for what they say: wherefore all the rabble (according to the old Latin verse) being void of knowledge and judgment, and therefore inclining to the weather or safer side, and mightily valuing the vain and empty pomp of kings and princes, say amen to it; especially when kept in ignorance, and irritated against the lawful government by preachers, who aim at dominion, or would introduce an independent and arbitrary power of church-government;

For fans of Max Weber's thesis that Calvinism created capitalism, it is ironic that the Calvinists in the Dutch Republic championed the monarchy and opposed free markets. The non-Calvinist Protestants endorsed the republic and free markets. Honest citizens who supported the republic were afraid to discuss the weather let alone express their opinions about the princes out of fear of reprisal from the nobility:

Nay there are few inhabitants of a perfect free state to be found, that are inclinable to instruct and teach others how much better a republick is than a monarchy, or one supreme head, because they know no body will reward them for it; and that on the other side, kings, princes, and great men are so dangerous to be conversed with, that even their friends can scarcely talk with them of the wind and weather, but at the hazard of their lives; and kings with their long arms can give heavy blows.

Another way the nobility had destroyed the foundations of economic growth was by perverting the law. De la Court wrote that before the revolt against Spain, the earls of the Netherlands, called *statholders*, sold the offices of judges and bailiffs to the highest bidders. Appeals of judges' decisions went to the earl himself, who acted as the supreme court. The law demanded that criminals who forfeited their lives also forfeited their estates to the earl. As a result, many innocent people were tried and convicted for the sole purpose of enriching the earl and his partners in crime. De la Court charged that these earls "stood much upon enlarging of their power and profit, and but very little on the welfare of the common people."

The perversion of law mentioned by de la Court was not unique to the Dutch Republic. Throughout Europe the landed aristocracy oversaw the police, judiciary and civil government on their lands, so a noble might preside over the arrest, trial and punishment of peasants under him. Most countries in Europe had separate laws for the nobility exempted them from taxes and many of the laws that applied to commoners. The contempt in which the nobility held business; their obsession with conspicuous consumption; the ignoble means they admired for gaining wealth, and their abuse of power all contributed to making property insecure, regardless of the written law, for anyone who managed to accumulate a little, thereby keeping people poor and preventing economic development. And as Schoeck noted, the nobility suffered from extreme envy of each other, but especially of any commoner who might grow nearly as wealthy as them.

The great German economist, Wilhelm Roepke, summarized the abuses of the people by the nobility in his book, *The Social Crisis of Our Time*:

> All the more, then, must we insist on rekindling the memory of that pre-revolutionary era with its abuse of power, its arbitrariness and oppression, its exploitation and humiliation of the masses held in subjection by State, Nobility and Patriciate: that time of the enslavement of the peasantry in large parts of Europe and its extermination in England, of the cruel suppression of every free and daring thought, of the enthrallment of the middle classes in the small German states, of class justice and class taxation and the most brazen-faced enrichment, of the trading and ill-usage of soldiers and the harsh laws of war, of the negro slave trade and the inhuman cruelties of colonization overseas. In order to prompt our dulled imagination, we add that in the eighteenth century with all its vigorous intellectual ferment a Margrave of Ansbach could still display his marksmanship to his mistress by shooting a tiler from the castle tower for the sheer fun of it and then most graciously hand his widow a florin; a Duke of Mecklenburg could command the Privy Councillor von Wolfrath to be put to death in order to make his widow the ducal mistress; and a Prince of Nassau-Siegen was able to deal with a peasant in the same fashion just to prove that it was within his power; and in Swabia a lawyer could be beheaded because he had quoted Voltaire in a tavern.

Urban life

One to 2 percent of the population belonged to the clergy and another 2 percent to the aristocracy, both of which owned most of the land. The nobility owned between two thirds and 95 percent of the wealth. Peasants made up between 65 percent and 85 percent of the population. The rest lived in towns where about half the urban population was laborers. City life was so unhealthy that as late as 1750 most cities recorded more deaths than births. Towns grew through immigration. Artisans typified the urban resident with a thin veneer of wealthy merchants at the top and a large group of laborers and beggars at the bottom.

As Mises wrote, mass production is a defining characteristic of capitalism and it did not exist in pre-industrial cities. Mass production is production for the masses as well as production of large volumes of cheap, identical goods. The process characterizes capitalism because it reduces the cost of production and therefore prices so that the masses can afford to buy them. The history of capitalism has been the progress in making available to the masses things only the wealthy could afford. For example, the simple marshmallow was so expense when first invented that only the wealthy aristocracy could afford it. Instead of mass production, artisans hand crafted all goods except those made at home in pre-industrial Europe. Each good was unique and intended for sale to the nobility or wealthy merchants because artisans, laborers, beggars and peasants, the vast majority of the population, could not afford it.

After the tenth century, artisans organized into guilds or associations. Social, political, and economic life for artisans revolved around the guilds, which often provided for the welfare of widows, orphans, and those members who could no longer work. In terms of economic growth, guilds filled the same role in Europe as in the Ottoman Empire. They stifled competition, regulated wages, prices and quality standards, blocked entry into their fields and maintained monopolies on their particular industries, all with the power of city governments behind them. Guilds outlawed competition among guild members in order to ensure that members earned the income they deemed appropriate for their status in society. Being very class-conscious and consumed with envy, medieval society ferociously defended gross inequalities in income between classes lest lower classes become uppity and achieve wealth comparable to that of the higher classes. But they refused to tolerate inequality within classes, such as one brewer making more money than another, a clear manifestation of envy.

Often, the city council controlled the local guilds and manipulated their rules to favor local producers. Cities barred non-citizens from starting new businesses and from doing any trading within the city except through the services of local business people. De la Court observed that persecuted Protestants fleeing Antwerp would have preferred settling in England, but the English charged double the taxes on foreigners and excluded them from all guilds, halls of trade and manufacturing. They settled in Holland in spite of the high taxes.

Cities levied heavy duties on goods imported from neighboring towns and forced local farmers to sell their crops to merchants within the city. But with all of these hindrances to economic growth, arguably the most damaging were the tolls charged on the transportation of goods between cities. Hecksher in his book on mercantilism wrote that tolls, "more than any other measure of economic policy, affected the most valuable part of trade, that moving along the chief rivers, which constituted almost the only long-distance natural means of communications before the invention of the compass. Consequently, medieval trade was much more restricted than was warranted by purely technical difficulties."

Travelers could smell cities long before they came into view. Many cities outlawed the dumping of human waste in the streets, but it had to go somewhere so it piled up in courtyards and sometimes close to wells. The engines of transportation left city streets full of horse manure. Pigs consumed the garbage for city residents and left behind their own waste. Traffic pulverized both into a fine powder that hung in the air for residents to breathe. Disease spread rapidly as a result of the congestion, lack of sanitary conditions and pour nutrition.

Life expectancy was low because of infant mortality and childhood diseases, both of which chronic undernourishment made worse. Most people consumed 50 percent to 75 percent of their calories from bread. Urban workers often spent half their wages on food. Two consecutive bad harvests would cause famine and mass starvation. In the 300 years before 1750, Tuscany suffered one hundred years of famine and just sixteen bountiful years.

France endured sixteen years of famine nationally during the eighteenth century and many more local ones due to poor transportation.

The Church

The earlier section described the history of how the Church replaced ancient society and its hierarchical structure of status with one less stratified and organized around individual rights. This section will present the Church's role in the treatment of commerce and property. We have discussed the roles of lords, peasants and cities in the medieval economy. The third major concentration of economic power in the middle ages lay in the hands of the Catholic Church. As difficult as it is for our modern secular society to accept, people throughout history have feared hell and longed for heaven. The Church held the keys to both, and therefore enjoyed enormous power over the hearts and minds of peasants, nobility and merchants.

In spite of the progress of Christianity in many areas, theologians found their minds shackled by pagan economics and unable or unwilling to adapt it to the faith in the same way they had translated Stoic philosophy into Christian individualism. As a result, they uncritically rejected most commerce as evil, except for the long distance transport of goods, while glorifying agriculture. This quote from Cicero provided by Richard Ebeling in his article "Anti-Commerce and Quietism in Ancient Rome" summarizes pagan and Christian economics for centuries:

> Now in regard to trade and other means of livelihood, which ones are to be considered becoming of a gentleman and which ones are vulgar, we have been taught, in general as follows: First those means of livelihood are rejected as undesirable which incur people's ill-will, such as those of tax-gatherers and usurers [money-lenders]. Unbecoming to a gentleman, also, and vulgar, are the means of livelihood of all hired workmen whom we pay for mere manual labor, not for artistic skill; for in this case the very wages they receive is a pledge of their slavery.

> Vulgar we must consider also those who buy from wholesale merchants to retail immediately; for they would get no profits without a great deal of downright lying; and verily there is no action that is meaner than misrepresentation. And all mechanics are engaged in vulgar trades; for no workshop can have anything liberal about it. Least respectable of all are those trades that cater to sensual pleasures: Fishmongers, butchers, cooks, poulterers, and fishermen. Add to these if you please, the perfumers, dancers, and the whole corp of ballet. But the profession in which either a higher degree of intelligence is required or from which no small benefit to society is derived – medicine, and architecture, for example, and teaching – they are proper for those whose social position they become.

> Trade, if it is on a small scale, is to be considered vulgar; but if wholesale and on a large scale, importing large quantities from all parts of the world and distributing to many without misrepresentation, it is not to be greatly disparaged. Nay, it even seems to deserve the highest respect, if those who are engaged in it, are satisfied with the fortunes they have, and make their way from the port to the country estate, as they have often made it from the sea to the port.
>
> But of all the occupations by which gain is secured, none is better than agriculture, none more profitable, none more delightful, and none more becoming to a freeman.

But at the time of the conversion of Constantine, "the main strength of Christianity lay in the lower and middle classes of the towns, the manual workers and clerks, the shop keepers and merchant's," according to Peter Brown in his *Eye of the Needle*. They were engravers, glass makers, candlestick makers, traders, lawyers, merchants and bureaucrats who chose their pastors from among them. Christianity has always been bourgeois, so it is unlikely they would have agreed with Cicero's estimation of their livelihoods. They said of themselves,

> It is good that we are middling persons [*mediocres*]. It is not for us to live in houses sheathed with marble, to be weighed down with gold, in flowing silks and bright scarlet. But all the same we have our little places in gardens and by the sea-side. We have good quality wine, neat little banquets and all that goes with a sprightly old age.

For more than a millennium, theologians condemned commerce as a necessary evil because, "While profits from trade can possibly be made by honest means, it is difficult to avoid the occasion of sin in the process of buying and selling," according to *Business, Banking, and Economic Thought in Late Medieval and Early Modern Europe* edited by Julius Kirshner. Early Church fathers, such as Tertullian (160-240), had judged merchants "as necessarily stamped with the sin of greed, and as almost always accompanied by deceit and fraud," wrote Murray N. Rothbard in *Economic Thought Before Adam Smith*. Jerome (c.340-420) preached, "All riches come from iniquity, and unless one has lost, another cannot gain. Hence that common opinion seems to me to be very true, 'the rich man is unjust, or the heir of an unjust one.'"

How did the church hierarchy turn against the majority of its members and condemn their professions? The answer lies in the fact that the Church fathers learned their economics not from the Bible but from pagan philosophers such as Aristotle, Cicero, Seneca and mystics such as Plotinus. Ambrose (340 - 397), for example, was so impressed with Cicero's concept of the common good that he rewrote the philosopher's *De officiis* with a Christian twist as part of his effort to forge a Christian community along the lines of Cicero's *res publica*. Cicero had valued private property, though he thought most wealth should go to the state. So Ambrose borrowed from Seneca who perpetuated the ancient Roman and Greek belief that a Golden Age had existed in the past in which property did not exist and people lived in peace by sharing nature's bounty equally. Ambrose imported the fiction into his theology according to Peter Brown in *Eye of the Needle* and taught that a Christian Golden Age was possible if the rich renounced property and gave their wealth to the Church and the poor:

> For nature generously supplies everything for everyone in common. God ordained everything to be produced to provide for everyone in common; his plan was that the earth should be, as it were, the common possession of us all. Nature produced common rights, then, it is usurping greed [*usurpatio,* in a negative sense] that has established private rights.

So while the Christian doctrine of salvation promoted individual rights and freedom, many Church fathers undermined them with their promotion of pagan mythology encouraging socialism. The ideal was the common good; anything private was evil. Avarice alone had created property, but it was a necessary evil until the Church could get rid of it. Augustine (354 - 430) in the generation after Ambrose based his *City of God* to a large degree on Cicero. Here is Brown again:

> Augustine had doubtless repeated Cicero's opinions for years on end as a teacher, long before he became a bishop. What Cicero had passed on to him was an acute sense of the tension between the public and private good – between unity around a common goal and disunity caused by individual self-interest.

Augustine saw the private will as always opposed to the common good, but he went beyond Cicero. Drawing from the pagan mystic Plotinus, he denied the monks in his monastery any private property at all. Of course, asceticism in the East had preceded him in that notion, which they had learned from pagan Cynic philosophers and not the Bible. Augustine saw his monasteries to be something like beach heads for a new world. If they could exorcise private desire from their members, that fire might spread to the rest of Christianity and issue in the Kingdom of God. Theologians refer to Augustine's eschatology as amillenialism or post-millenialism, which refers to the thousand year reign of Christ at the end of the age. It taught that the Christian world would continue to grow more Godly, that is, more socialist, until the spiritual kingdom of God became political reality and Christ returned. The doctrine continues to afflict Western society as many theologians insist on using the power of the state to perfect society.

Some historians claim that the monasteries of Europe invented capitalism because they promoted work as being holy, were organized as corporations that produced and sold large quantities of goods, such as wine and used sophisticated accounting techniques. However, all socialist countries have done the same thing. The monasteries stifled Christianity's greatest contribution to economics – individualism. All monks owned nothing and shared everything. The common good of the monastery as defined by the leadership determined the lives of individual monks. Monasteries were bastions of ancient socialism fighting the Christian gift of individualism to promote the common good.

In the ancient Greek and Roman world, the common good meant what was good for the survival of city or the empire, that is, the collective; individuals had no rights. Of course, the elite determined what the common good was and individuals could only comply. The collective was all important. Christian individualism broke down the city walls that protected the collective and established footholds for the rights of individuals, such as equality before the law. It was building a society in which the respect for the rights of individuals as defined by the Bible constituted the common good. But it advanced the least against the section of wall reserved for economics (wealth and commerce). The fathers furiously re-bricked with pagan philosophy as quickly as Christian individualism tore down a section. Pagan collectivism concerning wealth and commerce masquerading as the common good would push economic development into the future for over a thousand years.

Still, Jerome was correct about most cases of how wealth was gained because the "noble" ways to gain it had always been through plunder in war, kidnapping for ransom or taking bribes as a bureaucrat. But he was wrong about commerce unless the merchant defrauded customers. Church fathers had fallen victim to one of Aristotle's errors regarding a just price, as Murray Rothbard wrote:

> Another grave fallacy in the same paragraph in the Ethics did incalculable damage to future centuries of economic thought. There Aristotle says that in order for an exchange (any exchange? a just exchange?) to take place, the diverse goods and services 'must be equated', a phrase Aristotle emphasizes several times. It is this necessary 'equation' that led Aristotle to bring in the mathematics and the equal signs. His reasoning was that for A and B to exchange two products, the value of both products must be equal, otherwise an exchange would not take place. The diverse goods being exchanged for one another must be made equal because only things of equal value will be traded.

The damage in Aristotle's thinking came from his insistence on equality of value in exchange, which led theologians to assume that merchants conducted a just exchange only if the value of the goods exchanged were of equal value. That was the just price. If not equal, then the party that gained had cheated the other. Further confusing matters, Aristotle thought that goods had an intrinsic value based on their nobility or cost of production. Merged with St. Jerome's idea that one person cannot gain except at the expense of another, equality of value in exchange lead to the conclusion that all merchants who earn a profit are cheating their customers.

Today, good economists would say that trade will not happen unless both parties profit. After all, why would a consumer trade one item for another of equal value to him? Consumers trade money for goods because they value the goods more than the money. The profit might not be monetary; it could be psychological satisfaction or simple necessity, the need for food for example. The merchant would make an explicit profit while that of the consumer was more concealed so theologians condemned the visible profit while ignoring the less visible one.

How would merchants know if the value in exchange was equal? Theologians partly followed Roman law and determined that if merchants sold goods at the commonly estimated price, that is, the price in a market with many buyers and sellers and no monopoly or coercion, they had sold at a just price and their profits were legitimately earned. But they added that state-determined prices were also just. Of course, most states throughout the world in the middle ages set prices for food and theologians allowed them that right in spite of their insistence on private property rights.

St. Augustine rescued wholesale merchants from total depravity by insisting on his usefulness in transporting goods from long distances and alleviating scarcity. Therefore such merchants deserved compensation for such labor, but Cicero and other pagan philosophers had already made that concession. To the charge of endemic deceit and fraud, he replied that farmers and shoemakers were capable of the same. The fault lay with the person, not the occupation.

Augustine did not convince every theologian much less the people. Later theologians frequently revived the ancient stigma against commerce. With the exception of Venice, the majority of people never allowed commerce to shake the scarlet letter. It did not help that the hated Jews clustered in the vocation, though not by choice. Success in most nations required entrance into the military or the government but Christians blocked Jews from both while preventing them from owning land. Left only with commerce, Jews excelled at it, but the wealth it brought them inflamed envy and led to many episodes of persecution.

As a result of the wide-spread condemnation of their trade, wealthy merchants often used part of their wealth to buy land and titles to nobility, following Cicero's advice, in order to protect their wealth from taxes and confiscation by aristocrats, while assigning another large portion to the Church in the desperate hope of buying a ticket to heaven and redeeming a life spent in the wicked vocation of commerce. Wealthy merchants rarely invested in expanded production or labor saving equipment that would promote economic development.

In addition to the influence of Aristotle, Cicero and early Church fathers, teaching on commerce flowed naturally from the medieval situation. Peasants did not wander far from their villages and each village usually boasted of a single baker, brewer, cobbler, or moneylender, etc. Each business enjoyed a monopoly on its products or services in its village. R. H. Tawney wrote in *Religion and the Rise of Capitalism*, "Indeed, a great part of medieval industry is a system of organized monopolies, endowed with a public status, which must be watched with jealous [envious] eyes to see that they do not abuse their powers. It is a society of small masters and peasant farmers. Wages are not a burning question...usury is...for loans are made largely for consumption, not for production." Or, loans were made to peasant farmers for seed.

St. Thomas Aquinas advanced Augustine's tolerance for long distance commercial activity in the thirteenth century, adding that in addition to compensating him for his labor and providing for his family, profits repaid the merchant for the risk he had taken to bring goods to sell to the people. Rothbard wrote,

Aquinas referred to the common market price as the normative and just price with which to compare other contracts. Moreover, in the *Summa*, Aquinas notes the influence of supply and demand on prices. A more abundant supply in one place will tend to lower price in that place, and vice versa. Furthermore, St. Thomas described without at all condemning the activities of merchants in making profits by buying goods where they were abundant and cheap, and then transporting and selling them in places where they are dear.

Finally...Aquinas, in his great *Summa*, raised a question that had been discussed by Cicero. A merchant is carrying grain to a famine-stricken area. He knows that soon other merchants are following him with many more supplies of grain. Is the merchant obliged to tell the starving citizenry of the supplies coming soon and thereby suffer a lower price, or is it all right for him to keep silent and reap the rewards of a high price? To Cicero, the merchant was duty-bound to disclose his information and sell at a lower price. But St. Thomas argued differently. Since the arrival of the later merchants was a future event and therefore uncertain, Aquinas declared justice did not require him to tell his customers about the impending arrival of his competitors. He could sell his own grain at the prevailing market price for that area, even though it was extremely high. Of course, Aquinas went on amiably, if the merchant wished to tell his customers anyway, that would be especially virtuous, but justice did not require him to do so. There is no starker example of Aquinas's opting for the just price as the current price, determined by demand and supply, rather than the cost of production (which of course did not change much from the area of abundance to the famine area).

As with Augustine, Aquinas merely reflects Cicero's grudging acceptance of long distance trade. Theologians found it impossible to extricate their minds from the tar pits of pagan economics inherited from Plato, Aristotle and Cicero. But the rise of Venice as a commercial power motivated theologians to investigate business practices more closely. Their quest set scholarship on a path of discovery that would transform economic theory. Several theologians began to endorse commerce as a worthy vocation. By the fifteenth century, the Scholastics had begun to accept trade as a permanent institution, but profits continued to endanger the merchant's soul. Scholars considered profits good if motivated by the need to support one's family, provide relief to the poor, or improve the welfare of the community. But gain for its own sake constituted covetousness and pushed the merchant's soul to the edge of the abyss.

Medieval scholars condemned monopolies (except the monopoly of the state) and gave the term a much broader definition than what we use today by including cartels, guilds, unions, state-sponsored monopolies, and any effort to corner the market or control prices.

They rarely discussed competition, but promoted the freedom of every man to enter the profession of his choice, the goal being to encourage production in the midst of chronic shortages.

The Church controlled an enormous portion of the economy through its ownership of large tracts of land and through the hundreds of thousands of priests, nuns and monks it supported. Also, the Church hired thousands of artisans in the construction of hundreds of churches, abbeys, monasteries and schools. In the Netherlands, the Church employed about 15,000 people, which amounted to more than one percent of the population. Jonathan Israel wrote in *The Dutch Republic, Its Rise, Greatness, and Fall 1477-1806* that the "Church in the Netherlands in the early and mid-sixteenth century was rich and powerful and exerted, as it had for centuries, an immense influence in society."

To curtail monopolies today, economists encourage competition, but competition was anathema to the medieval Church, which pictured society as an organism with the government ensuring that the parts cooperated. Clergy asserted "Every social movement or personal motive which sets group against group, or individual against individual, appears, not the irrepressible energy of life, but the mutterings of chaos," according to Israel. Economic individualism was no less abhorrent than the religious kind, which equaled nonconformity at best, heresy at worst.

In spite of the Church's insistence on private property, Europeans kept alive the ancient myth about property throughout the Middle Ages. As Richard Pipes wrote, they perpetuated the belief in a

> Golden Age when man had been innocent and property unknown. Some believed that even in their own time remote regions existed, often pictured as islands on the edge of the world, where people continued to live in such bliss. Because of Original Sin, most humanity was excluded from these realms, but they were accessible to heroes and saints able to surmount great perils. The church fathers debated for centuries whether an earthly paradise still existed. This may have been one of the factors that inspired Columbus to undertake his voyage of discovery."

When Columbus stumbled upon the natives of the Americas, many people believed he had found one of those remote societies on the edge of the earth still living in the Golden Age without property and envy. That gave rise to the idea of the "noble savage." The myth inspired a body of fictional literature parading as fact, culminating in the writings of Karl Marx.

Unfortunately, the Church inherited its doctrines on property from pagan Greece and Rome instead of the Bible. It adopted Aristotle's utilitarian view that property works better than property held in common. Humans, not God, created property in order to maintain peace. Augustine displayed that spirit when he responded to the Donatist heretics who complained when the emperor confiscated their property in the fifth century, as Lifshitz wrote:

Since every earthly possession can be rightly retained only on the ground either of divine right, according to which all things belong to the Righteous [i.e., God], or of human right, which is in the jurisdiction of the kings of the earth, you are mistaken in calling those things yours which you do not possess.

Augustine used the power of the Roman government to confiscate the property of the rival Donatist churches and give it to the Roman Catholic churches. He limited the right to property to only those possessions which the owner properly used, which for the most part meant that merchants who profited more than they needed to live a modest lifestyle should give the excess to the Church or the poor, inferring that the state had the right to take it from him if he hoarded wealth. According to Lifshitz, Ambrose, Augustine's teacher and an eminent Church father, wrote, "It is no less a crime to take from him that has, than to refuse to succor the needy." Augustine agreed with his mentor in another quote provide by Lifshitz:

> Do we not convict all those who enjoy things they have acquired legitimately and who do not know how to use them, of possessing the property of another? For that certainly is not the property of another which is possessed rightly, but that which is possessed rightly is possessed justly, but that is possessed justly which is possessed well. Therefore, all that which is badly possessed is the property of another, but he possesses badly who uses badly.

Aquinas carried the utilitarian approach to property of Augustine into the thirteenth century, asserting that property comes from practical law, not natural, or God's law. In other words, property is good or bad depending on its use. Proper use involves the pursuit of higher, spiritual, ends. It logically follows that if a wealthy person does not use his wealth properly as defined by the theologians, that is, by giving most of it to the poor or the Church, his improper use nullifies his ownership. Excess wealth retained by the owner became the equivalent of stealing from the poor, as Etienne Gilson wrote in another quote provided by Lifshitz:

> [W]e must not forget that by natural law the use of all things is at the disposal of everyone. This fundamental fact cannot be removed by the progressive establishment of private ownership. That each should possess as his own what is necessary for his own use is quite sound a safeguard against want and neglect. But it is a very different matter when some accumulate more goods than they can use under the title of private property. To assume ownership of what we do not need is to make fundamentally common good our own. The use of such goods should

remain common...the rich man who does not distribute his superfluous wealth is robbing the needy of the goods whose use is theirs by right.

Aquinas had an opponent in John Duns Scotus (1265-1308), professor of theology at Oxford and later at Paris. Scotus held that property was not natural, but a consequence of mankind's sinfulness. In a state of innocence people would own everything in common and no property would exist. The Franciscans championed Scotus' ideas and prompted Pope John XXII to issue his famous bull *Quia vir reprobus* (1329) in which he stated that mankind's God-given dominion over the earth gave him the right to property. With the bull, property rights advanced beyond the utilitarian justification and became rooted in divine law. For the first time, Church doctrine on property approximated that of ancient Israel in the Bible.

In their defense, the Church fathers worried about the poor, and rightly so, for much of the population lived on the edge of starvation. Until long after the advent of capitalism, the only way to help the poor was through charity. Church scholars had no idea that investment in better tools could improve worker productivity, raise wages and rescue most of the poor from their starvation. Even today few theologians understand it and too many economists refuse to acknowledge it. Another two centuries would pass before Adam Smith discovered how the dynamics of his "system of natural freedom" could lift an entire nation to levels of wealth not imagined by the nobility in the late Middle Ages.

Theologians failed the common church members by applying different principles to the nobility and king. While the Church insisted that wealthy merchants should give their excess wealth to the poor, they often justified the conspicuous consumption of the nobility and kings as necessary because of their status in society. They insisted on the sanctity of property between common people, but ignored the theft by the nobility and kings of property owned by commoners. And while preaching the importance of free markets and condemning monopolies, they allowed the state virtually unlimited power over the market. Finally, by allowing just price to be the price set by the state as well as the market price, the states often overruled the market and determined prices by dictate, especially those for food and other necessities. State determined prices were usually set low in order to please consumers and prevent food riots, but were too low to encourage production. Essentially, theologians justified the status quo, whatever it was, instead of preaching against the abuses of power as the great Old Testament prophets had done.

The University of Salamanca

The merchant, despised since ancient Greece, attracted his first great defender in the theologian San Bernardino of Sienna (1380-1444). Bernardino wrote the book *On Contracts and Usury* (1433) that analyzed private property, trade and usury. Other theologians had peppered their writings with economics. Bernardino dedicated his book to the subject. He justified property on the old utilitarian grounds and the sections on usury remained as tangled as the thoughts of earlier theologians, but his treatment of the entrepreneur broke new ground. Bernardino argued that all vocations, even that of a bishop provide opportunities for sin. The participant in any occupation can practice it honestly or not, even merchants.

Bernardino wrote that merchants perform many useful functions. They transport goods from areas of where they are abundant to those where they are scarce. They store and preserve goods until consumers want to buy them. Craftsmen transform raw materials, which no one else can use, into goods which consumers demand. Wholesalers buy goods in bulk which they break down into smaller lots for retailers who sell them in smaller amounts to consumers. Merchants earned profits as compensation for their labor, expenses and risk.

Managerial talent, Bernardino wrote, combined competence and efficiency, the rareness of which justified higher returns. Efficiency meant knowing the prices, costs, and qualities of products, and being astute in assessing risks and opportunities. Managers had to be responsible and keep good accounts. Few businessmen were capable at either. The work involved trouble, toil, hardships and risk and for these the businessman earned compensation in successful ventures.

Bernardino applied just price theory, that the just price is the market price, to wages and insisted that the just wage is the market, or commonly estimated, wage. Wages diverged because of differences in skill, ability, intelligence and scarcity. For example, architects earned more than ditch-diggers because the architect's job required more of those qualities and few men possessed them.

In the sixteenth century, the Reformation erupted and the Counter-Reformation responded. Spain subjugated the Americas, enslaved the native population and stole their gold and silver by the shipload. Spain, Portugal and Italy emerged as European centers of commerce and exploration. Aquinas' natural law theory faded. Most nations had fallen under the spell of absolutism in politics which asserted that the state enjoyed unlimited power and authority, especially over the property of its citizens. Fitting for its leadership role at the time, Spain possessed a university at Salamanca that would challenge the status quo, defy the state and launch modern economic theory. Its scholars inspired the greatest theological support for private property, free markets and limited government since the demise of ancient Israel, though in academia only, at first.

It began with the revival of Aquinas' natural law theory under Francisco de Vitoria (1485–1546), a moral theologian at the University of Salamanca, the queen of Spanish Universities. Salamanca boasted of seventy academic chairs filled by Spain's best scholars teaching the traditional medieval curriculum as well as the new sciences of navigation and the Chaldean language. In reviving natural law, Vitoria reminded students that a law above that of the king existed and could be used to judge the king and his laws. He initiated a long tradition at the school of denouncing the enslavement of the natives of the New World and argued that government interference with trade violated the Golden Rule.

Vitoria produced students in the sixteenth and early seventeenth centuries that advanced economic theory to levels that would not be matched again until the late nineteenth century with the birth of the Austrian school of economics under Karl Menger. Those students included Domingo de Soto (1494–1560), architect of the purchasing power parity of exchange theory; Martin de Azpilcueta Navarrus (1493–1586), famous for opposing state price fixing; Diego de Covarrubias y Leiva (1512–1577), who provided the clearest explanation of subjective value; and Luis de Molina (1535–1601), who wrote that the king was subject to the same law as everyone else. Other great scholars included Juan de Mariana (1536 – 1624), Tomás de Mercado (1525–1575), Juan de Lugo y de Quiroga (1583–1660), and Leonardo Lessius (1554-1623). Lessius is most important for his role in transmitting the economics of Salamanca to the Dutch Republic.

The scholars of Salamanca argued for private property on several grounds. The Bible commanded, "Thou shalt not steal," which assumed the existence of something to steal. In a positive form the commandment might read, "Respect the property of others." Much of the Torah law is concerned with property. And the bull of Pope John XXII anchored property to God having given dominion of the earth to mankind according to Alejandro Chafuen in *Faith and Liberty: The Economic Thought of the Late Scholastics*:

> Whenever man has perfect domain [ownership] over a good, he can use this good as he pleases, even to the extent of destroying it...De Soto specified that the purpose of domain is the use of the thing. Indeed, the Late Scholastics argued that things are better used when they are held in private ownership than when they are held in common. When the Schoolmen said that things were better when used, they were speaking of social, political, economical and, above all, moral use.

And they furthered the utilitarian arguments of Aquinas. They wrote that the institution of private property performs these functions:

1. Private Property helps ensure justice because evil men would take more and produce less in a system of common property.

2. It preserves peace and harmony.

3. Men are more productive with their own goods. Scarcity, especially of food, concerned theologians.

4. It helps maintain order. Under common property people refuse to perform the less pleasant tasks.

5. People are attached to their things because of original sin.

6. It gave mankind an opportunity to demonstrate morality through charity.

Through most of its existence the Church saw private property as ethically neutral although a necessary force to counter the baser nature of humanity, but in the fourteenth century, the Church began to defend private property as an inalienable right according to Pipes.

On the issue of pricing, the scholars considered the scarcity of a product, the popular demand for it, its cost of production, the supply of money, and other factors. They carried forward the ancient concept of a just price established by Augustine in which the common estimation (or the market) determines it. For example, Chafuen quoted San Bernardino who wrote:

> Water is usually cheap where it is abundant. But it can happen that, on a mountain or in another place, water is scarce, not abundant. It may well happen that water is more highly esteemed than gold, because gold is more abundant in this place than water.

The scholars encouraged government officials to fix prices, especially those of food and clothing, but only after having consulted the community for the commonly estimated price because some areas may have too few people for market prices to work. The goal of price fixing by the state was to protect poor people from price gouging during periods of shortages. But they also understood that the just price was too complicated for any one person to calculate and encouraged officials to rely on the commonly estimated, or market, price where they could discover it.

The scholars rejected the idea that goods had an intrinsic price based on their nobility or any other characteristic, or on the labor involved to produce them. The doctors anticipated the subjective-marginalist revolution in economics by three centuries. For example, Chafuen quoted Vitoria who wrote:

> It follows from this principle that wherever there is a marketable good for which there are many buyers and sellers, neither the nature of the good nor the price for which is was bought, that is to say, how expensive it was, nor the toil and trouble it was to get it should be taken into account. When Peter sells wheat, the buyer need not consider the money Peter spent nor his work but, rather, the common estimation of how much wheat is worth...once the price is established in this way, it should be respected.

Juan de Lugo rejected Aristotle's justification of prices according to the "nobility" of the article and wrote that it is not the job of theologians or government officials to protect the uneducated from their ignorance:

> Price fluctuates not because of the intrinsic and substantial perfection of the articles – since mice are more perfect than corn, and yet worth less – but on the account of their utility in respect of human need, and then only on account of estimation; for jewels are much less useful than corn in the house and yet their price is much higher. And we must take into account not only the estimation of prudent men but also of the imprudent, if they are sufficiently numerous in a place. This is why our glass trinkets are in Ethiopia justly exchanged for gold, because they are commonly more

esteemed there. And among the Japanese, old objects made of iron and pottery, which are worth nothing to us, fetch a high price because of their antiquity. Communal estimation, even when foolish, raises the natural price of goods, since price is derived from estimation. The natural price is raised by the abundance of buyers and money, and lowered by the contrary factors.

Following Bernardino, the theologians at Salamanca preached greater respect for merchants, a vital component of economic development as Deirdre McCloskey has proven. For example, Chafuen quoted de Soto who wrote,

> Mankind progresses from imperfection to perfection. For this reason, in the beginning, barter was sufficient as man was rude and ignorant and had few necessities. But afterward, with the development of a more educated, civilized, and distinguished life, the need to create new forms of trade arose. Among them, the most respectable is commerce, despite the fact that human avarice can pervert anything.

Doctor Molina went so far as to defend what people call price "gouging" during shortages caused by natural disasters:

> And it must not be said that this action is correct because it is convenient for the common good that the wheat be sold at the same price in times of scarcity and in time of abundance; and that acting in this way the poor will not be burdened and they will find it easy to buy wheat...I insist that this is not reasonable...They [the poor] must be helped with alms rather than with sales [meaning maximum prices]...It would be unjust to place the burden upon the owners of the wheat only.

The scholars held that the just price theory that had developed over centuries applied to wages for labor as much as to commodities. They focused their greatest concern on helping the poor, and for that reason they rejected the modern idea of a "living" wage for poor workers. Doctor Molina wrote that a just wage reflects the salary usually paid for similar jobs in similar circumstances:

> After considering the service that an individual undertakes and the large or small number of people who, at the same time, are found in similar service, if the wage that is set for him is at least the lowest wage that is customarily set in that region at that time for people in such service, the wage is to be considered just...
>
> This is true even though the servant may barely support himself and live a miserable life with this salary, because the owner is only obliged to pay him

the just wage for his services considering all the attendant circumstances, not what is sufficient for his sustenance and much less for the maintenance of his children and family...and when many are found who willingly undertake this service for the given wage, the wage is not to be considered an unjust payment for that service or task because it is paid to an individual for whom it does not afford a living because he lacks other resources or employment, or because he has many children, or because he wishes to live at a higher standard, or with a large household than he would otherwise live.

Socialists have attacked the theologians of Salamanca for what they perceive as their lack of concern for poor workers, but that accusation merely advertises the ignorance of the socialists, as Chafuen explained:

The Schoolmen's attitude toward low-paid workers was not prompted by a lack of social consciousness. The consumer's and the laborer's welfare was a recurring topic in late-scholastic economic discourse. Their condemnation of monopolies, frauds, force, and high taxes are all directed toward the protections and benefit of the working people. Nevertheless, they never proposed the determination of a minimum wage sufficient to maintain the laborer and his family. In the belief that fixing a wage above the common estimation level would only cause unemployment, they recommended other means...

The protection of private property, the promotion of trade, the encouragement of commerce, the reduction of superfluous government spending and taxes, and a policy of sound money were all destined to improve the condition of the workers. They recommended private charity as a way to alleviate the sufferings of those who could not work.

The Church, through the Scholastic scholars, never accepted the charging of interest on loans, except for international finance between wealthy merchants, or between the Vatican and those merchants. The Church often borrowed large sums from wealthy merchants and paid interest on the loans, but it sought to protect peasants and small craftsmen from unscrupulous moneylenders. It allowed penance for a variety of sins related to greed and avarice, but for usury, it permitted none, unless the offender made restitution. Usury included not only charging interest on loans, "but the raising of prices by a monopolist, the beating down of prices by a keen bargainer, the rack-renting of land by a landlord, the sub-letting of land by a tenant at a rent higher than he himself paid, the cutting of wages and the paying of wages in truck, the refusal of discount to a tardy debtor, the insistence of unreasonably good security for a loan and the excessive profits of a middleman," according to Tawney.

Except for the teaching on usury and profit, the Church doctors espoused essentially capitalist economic doctrines, so the reader may wonder why capitalism did not emerge in Catholic nations. The answer lies in the fact that the scholarship remained an ivory tower industry for the most part and rarely shaped the way kings and princes governed. As we have already seen, state-sanctioned monopolies, guilds, price gouging, warfare and all that the Scholastic fathers abhorred were common features of the medieval economic landscape. Sometimes scholarship became the law of the land, but the state rarely enforced those laws. For example, Church doctrine, and the resulting legislation outlawing monopolies erected no barrier against the powerful international cartels of Antwerp or the guilds. Public opinion against the cartels inspired limited assaults against them until the Dutch Republic crushed them so effectively that they did not revive until the twentieth century in Kirshner's view found in *Business, Banking, and Economic Thought*.

Until the Dutch Republic, governments at all levels suppressed innovation that might ignite economic growth. McCloskey has listed a few instances of such behavior in his *Bourgeois Dignity*:

> Joel Mokyr gives plentiful examples of such shooting-oneself-in-the-foot: In 1299 a law prevented bankers in Florence from adopting Arabic numerals. In the late fifteenth century the scribes of Paris delayed the adoption of the printing press (there) for twenty years. In 1397 the vested interest in Cologne outlawed the making of pins in presses rather than by hand. In 1561 the city council of Nuremburg passed an ordinance imprisoning anyone who would make and sell a new lathe that had been invented by a local man. In 1579 the city council of Danzig secretly ordered the inventor of the ribbon loom to be drowned. And on and on into modern times – since the springs of such anti-innovative activities are prudent, self-interest, not some foolishness unique to primitive times. In the late 1770s the Strasbourg council prohibited a local cotton mill from actually selling its stuffs in town because the merchants who specialized in importing cloth would be disturbed: "It would upset all order in trade if the manufacturer were to become a merchant at the same time." In 1865 the Wiggin's Ferry Company of St. Louis stopped the first attempt to build the Eads Bridge over the Mississippi. The white members of the City Council of Chicago, with the support of the intellectual left this time, stopped WalMart from opening grocery stores in the food deserts of the South Side.

Many of the merchants and all of the scholars in The Netherlands, such as Hugo Grotius, drank from the fountain of knowledge of the University of Salamanca, Spain, and the Dutch could boast of having one of Europe's top schools at Leiden. So the intellectual pool from which the founders of the Dutch Republic drew consisted of more than a millennium of scholarship on matters of money and commerce. Historians refer to these scholars, beginning with Thomas Aquinas and ending with Adam Smith, as the Scholastic school. Where modern economists attempt to explain how economies work, Scholastics viewed economics as a sub-discipline of ethics. They concerned themselves with how wealth was distributed and whether or not individuals made contracts and conducted transactions in a just manner. In the process, they distilled high quality economic theory, which when forgotten took the West another two centuries to recover.

Capitalism is far more than sophisticated commerce as most journalists, historians and anthropologists assume. As mentioned in chapter 1, informal and formal institutions had to be created in order to give birth to capitalism – individualism, the suppression of envy, respect for commerce (the bourgeois values), security of private property, free markets, limited government, the rule of law and equality before the law. All of these institutions overlap. Siedentop might argue that all of them are just subsets of individualism, for respect for property rights gives individuals freedom from the demands of family and tribe for equal distributions of wealth. And property cannot exist without free markets because property requires that the owner be free to use and dispose of it as the owner sees fit.

It took Western Europe over fifteen centuries to craft these institutions and we will see in the next chapter that the ingredients come together first in the Dutch Republic.

Chapter 5 – The Dutch Republic

The Low Lands of Northwestern Europe had escaped the worst aspects of feudalism due to its late colonization and distance from Rome. By 1500, the Church owned about 10 percent of the land in Holland; nobility owned about 5 percent and town-dwellers roughly a third. Peasants possessed 45 percent of the total available land, were free from feudal control and owned their land with few restrictions on how they could dispose of it according to Jonathan Israel in *The Dutch Republic, Its Rise, Greatness, and Fall 1477-1806*. Unless noted, all of the quotes in this chapter come from his book.

The Church and nobility owned the best land. Peasant land was often so poor that the owners had to supplement their income with odd jobs. The most striking feature of the Low Lands "was a sustained intensity, versatility, and higher crop yields than were to be found elsewhere in Europe. This was the only part of Europe which had, thus far, experienced a true 'agricultural revolution' and it was one which was already largely complete in Flanders and South Brabant by 1500."

The nobility was much stronger in the south than in the north so the lack of a strong feudal legacy offered many benefits to northern residents. In the first place, it meant the absence of a society in which each member held a legally fixed position assigned by birth, so that social mobility was possible and found greater acceptance. Also, it diminished the influence of communal institutions and collective behavior while promoting individualism.

A high rate of urbanization also characterized the Netherlands of the early sixteenth century. By 1550, the north had twelve cities with more than ten thousand inhabitants, the largest of which was Amsterdam. The northern states, which later comprised the Dutch Republic, had about twice the ratio of urban to rural inhabitants as the rest of Europe. In Holland, half the people lived in towns. Frequent flooding had forced many rural dwellers to move to the coastal towns and take up fishing for a living, which explains part of the high rate of urbanization. But Amsterdam before the revolt was much smaller than the southern cities of Antwerp, Brussels and Ghent, which would remain a part of Spain. The southern provinces were the richest, most densely populated and most urban in Europe outside of northern Italy. Amsterdam, in contrast, had no important merchants and trade was largely confined to shipping bulk grain, herring and timber to the Baltic States.

A casting of the European economy including the Dutch Republic as the curtain descended on the middle ages would reveal a complex figure. Politically, the era of city states had ended, except for Italy, but economically towns and cities continued to act as sovereigns and protect local merchants, guilds and manufacturers from competition with outsiders while controlling the agricultural production in their vicinity. The rule of law and protection of property, though preached by the Church, could not be found. Kings murdered Protestants with impunity and the encouragement of the Church, but the Church failed to persuade kings to enforce its doctrines on financial matters, with the exception of usury. The nobility remained above the law, and preferred to increase its wealth through extortion, bribery, private wars, state-granted monopolies and outright theft through perversion of the justice system.

Society enforced equality of incomes within classes while tolerating gross inequalities between classes. Peasants suffered the most, living lives that differed little from slavery and starving to death in famines that appeared like clockwork. Merchants and manufacturers remained the outcasts of society who purchased respectability by building cathedrals and buying titles of nobility rather than investing in new or expanding enterprises for production. The Dutch Republic would shatter the Old Regime.

The republic

The Dutch Republic began life as a monarchy under the brilliant leadership of Prince William of Orange. After an assassin's bullet cut him down, the leadership tried to retain a monarchy by offering the head of the nation first to Henry III of France then Queen Elizabeth of England, but both declined the honor partly out of fear of the wrath of Spain. Admirers of a republican form of government under Johan van Oldenbarnevelt took advantage of the vacuum in the ranks of the nobility to establish the new nation as a republic.

However, the Republic did not allow voting for the leadership as happens in modern republics. The political leadership, the regents, in the many states that made up the nation as well as the national government consisted of wealthy brewers, cloth, herring and dairy dealers, Baltic traders, and soap-boilers, in other words, wealthy merchants. New regents were chosen by the existing membership when older ones died, retired, or lost too much wealth. The regents required members to be wealthy enough to be able to devote large blocks of time to government issues because they did not receive a salary from the state.

The choice of a republican government was a revolutionary idea in an age when the dominant political philosophy across Europe endorsed the divine right of kings. As mentioned, circumstances forced the decision to some degree since no monarch accepted the offer to rule. And, as will be shown, the nation flip-flopped from a republican government to a monarchy several times during its two centuries of existence, finally adopting a monarchy after the defeat of Napoleon. Why were so many in the nation determined to keep a republican form of government in an age of absolutism? The answer is important to our search for the roots of modern capitalism because economic historians have achieved a consensus on the idea that economic development, especially the explosive kind registered by the Dutch, required freedom and the rule of law of the sort that only a republic can provide.

Before the middle of the seventeenth century, political theory going back to classical Greece identified three good forms of government - monarchy, aristocracy and a republic. They classified tyranny, oligarchy and democracies as degenerate forms. The consensus held that each of the three good forms of government were appropriate at different times and under varying circumstances. That consensus broke up in the late seventeenth century when republican government became the only legitimate form in the minds of Western European political philosophers. The Dutch Republic led the way.

The tolerance of the Dutch attracted Jews from Portugal in the 1590s and they created a thriving community. The printing press made copies of the Hebrew Bible, the Talmud and the writings of many Jewish scholars, such as Maimonides and Josephus, widely available and inexpensive. The Republic became the "most vital center of Christian Hebraic scholarship in early-modern Europe," according to Eric Nelson in *The Hebrew Republic: Jewish Sources and the Transformation of European Political Thought*. Hugo Grotius learned Hebrew at the University of Leiden and around 1604 wrote *De republic emendanda* which promoted the Hebrew republic in the Torah as the most clear manifestation of God's will concerning government. At the same time, the Dutch began to see their nation as the new Israel. These strands were woven together to produce in the late sixteenth and seventeenth centuries a "truly remarkable burgeoning of Hebrew scholarship across Europe," as Nelson wrote.

The shift in political thought began with the Reformation. Reformers had announced *sola scriptura* as their standard, but realized quickly that although they knew the New Testament well, they were ignorant of the Hebrew Bible or what Christians called the Old Testament. So they turned to the Jewish community for instruction in Hebrew and as guides to interpreting the books according to Nelson.

> Readers began to see in the five books of Moses not just political wisdom, but a political constitution. No longer regarding the Hebrew Bible as the Old Law – a shadowy intimation of the truth, which had been rendered null and void by the New Dispensation – they increasingly came to see it as a set of political laws that God himself had given to the Israelites as their civil sovereign. Moses was now to be understood as a lawgiver, as the founder of a *politeia* in the Greek sense. The consequences of this reorientation were staggering, for if God himself had designed a commonwealth, then the aims of political science would have to be radically reconceived...It became the central ambition of political science to approximate, as closely as possible, the paradigm of what European authors began to call the *respublica Hebraeorum* (republic of the Hebrews)...

Within a short time, monarchies fell from grace and republics ascended to be recognized as the form of government closest to godliness. None were brave enough to suggest abandoning legislatures and executive branches completely, as had Israel under the judges. Many failed to grasp the differences between civil and moral laws and misunderstood the laws providing for debt forgiveness every seven and fifty years, thinking they were an early form of wealth redistribution. That led to calls for the state to redistribute wealth and encouraged early forms of socialism. But as Pieter de la Court explained, the freedom in the Dutch Republic, while it remained a republic, provided the greenhouse atmosphere for commerce to explode.

Leonardus Lessius

Huibrecht Leys intended his nephew, Lenaert Leys, born in Brecht near Antwerp in 1554 and whose uncle was his guardian, to become a businessman like him. But Lenaert won a scholarship to the University of Leuven in 1567 at the age of thirteen. The Latinized version of his name became Leonardus Lessius. In 1572 he joined the Jesuit order and launched his academic career. When he returned to the university to teach, he relied on the works of Thomas Aquinas and the Salamancan scholar Martinus de Azpilcueta, or Dr. Navarrus.

The town of Leuven was in the Spanish Netherlands, the southern part of the region that remained loyal to Spain and did not become part of the Dutch Republic. Nevertheless, Hugo Grotius, the founder of international law and compiler of Dutch law, read Lessius, which serves as an example of the influence of the academics of Salamanca on Dutch academia, including those of the north in the Dutch Republic. Even Protestant scholars, as was Grotius, studied Catholic scholars. The theological split of the Reformation had not yet caused Protestants to abhor all things Catholic or vice versa.

Unlike today when businessmen ignore academia and ridicule ivory tower speculation, (though often for good reasons) academia in Lessius' time exerted greater influence on practical affairs. Known as the "oracle of the Netherlands," Lessius regularly advised businessmen on the ethical aspects of their practices and held weekly debates on controversial issues. "In their universities and colleges across Europe, the future economic, political, and scientific elite was educated, and many a merchant or prince allowed himself a private Jesuit counsellor and confessor. Lessius, in particular, served as an adviser of Albert and Isabel, the Hapsburg archdukes governing the southern Netherlands during the last twenty years of his lifetime," according to Wim Decock in "On Buying and Selling" in the *Journal of Markets & Morality*.

Lessius advised businessmen, as did his mentors at the University of Salamanca, that calculations of the just price must consider the abundance and scarcity of the good, the number of buyers and sellers, the mode of selling, and the money supply, but the particulars of the situation could justify deviations because the just price was actually a range of prices in Decock's words:

> For example, take the following case. A buyer requests me to sell my good on the spot, whereas in fact I intended to sell it not until ten months later, being pretty sure that by that time its price would have doubled. Am I obliged to sell at the current market price, or would it be allowed for me to demand a surplus, given that I am giving up a realistic profit in the future? Alternatively, is it licit for me to deviate from the current just price by virtue of the particular circumstances constituting my specific case?
>
> It is licit indeed, according to Lessius and other sixteenth- through seventeenth century moral theologians, to deviate from the just price in circumstances such as these...

To come back on the merchant who gives up a future profit by selling in advance, his situation can be classified as an instance of the paradigmatic case in which a businessman rightly deviates from the just price by virtue of the extrinsic title cessant gain (*lucrum cessans*). The gradual but steady expansion of these so-called extrinsic titles enabled the scholastics to account for new developments in business practice and escape the merciless rigidity of a general normative framework. Strictly speaking, any deviation from the equality principle, namely, the just price in buying and selling would be illicit, but by virtue of typical circumstances, extrinsic to the contract itself, this deviation may become entirely licit, not to say imperative.

Loopholes had inflicted many fractures on the doctrine of usury that possessed academics for millennia by the time Lessius came along, but the doctor's vigorous trumpeting of exceptions caused the walls to crumble. Previous scholars had insisted that any surplus payment above the contract price amounted to illegal and immoral usury. Later scholastics, including Lessius, found sound reasons for such profits, such as damages incurred, cessant gain, and capital risk. Damages included adverse circumstances that might happen during the term of the loan in which the merchant suffered while being deprived of his money. For example, his house might burn and he would be forced to borrow money for rebuilding.

Cessant gain (*lucrum cessans*), was an early form of opportunity cost, a concept at the heart of modern micro economics: if the lender could not use his money to invest in profitable opportunities he was entitled to compensation by the borrower. Finally, the debtor might go broke and be unable to pay back the loan. The lender was justified in demanding interest in order to compensate for the risk. "By the time Lessius edited his treatise *On Justice and Right*, damage incurred and cessant gain were widely accepted titles by the moral theologians. Yet, it is only with him that the title capital risk starts to gain solid ground," according to Decock.

Lessius undermined traditional dogma on usury even further by adding the principle of the lack of money (*carentia pecuniae*), which essentially defined interest as the price of money and introduced what economists centuries later would call the time value of money. Money became a good like any other commodity which could be bought and sold in the market for a just price determined in the same way as the price for other goods. "In sum, it is very typical of Lessius' analytical genius first to discern the underlying economic mechanisms of a particular business practice and, subsequently, to integrate this insight into his normative judgment," in Decock's view.

Lessius contributed to the growing esteem for commerce among the Dutch. Though he fails to mention him, McCloskey credits the rise of the bourgeois virtues that promoted commerce in the West to the Dutch Republic. McCloskey argues persuasively that the upward sloping blade of the hockey stick in the graph of the per capita G.D.P. time series could never have happened without a reversal of the traditional contempt for commerce that dominated Europe.

Lessius promoted that change by insisting that the work of the merchant, the art of buying and selling goods unchanged, increased the prosperity of the community and improved the relations of people around the world. Therefore, merchants should benefit from their efforts. He could do so because the just price was never fixed but established a range of prices in different places at different times. The merchant bought goods at the low end of the just price range where they were abundant and sold them where they were scarce and more highly valued at the higher end of the just price. Lessius understood that making money in that way required a network of people who could inform the merchant of changes in prices at distant locations. Such a network required experience, intelligence, insight, prudence and industry, so forbidding a merchant to benefit from his work amounted to punishing people for using their best qualities.

Lessius even dealt with the modern argument for government intervention into markets known as asymmetric information. The principle states that the seller of any good, such as a used car, has vastly more information about the product than the buyer and that places the buyer at a disadvantage. In the fevered imaginations of mainstream economists that means the market has failed and justifies government intervention to regulate a merchant's activities. The argument is not new; people made the same demand in the middle ages. But Lessius would have nothing to do with it. Clearly, fraud was immoral and should be illegal, but the merchant should not have to give away for nothing his years of experience and knowledge. Ignorance on the part of the buyer did not justify breaking a contract according to Decock:

> What is more, Lessius would explicitly state that everyone can deceive themselves through imprudent behavior: The professional buyer should blame the ignorance on himself because he has not been virtuous enough to inform himself about the market in which he is taking part. Regularly repeating that, among professionals, the marketplace is not a realm of charity and donation but of commutative justice and inner economic logic, Lessius was not prepared to take on a paternalistic attitude in his moral judgments.

Lessius illustrated the licit nature of asymmetric information (though not fraud) with the story of a merchant who traveled to Rhodes where an acute shortage of grain had led to high prices. The merchant knows that other sellers follow him, but the people of Rhodes do not. Should the merchant inform the people and risk the price of his grain falling? Lessius answered no, according to Decock.

> Thus, even though the common estimation is based on error and ignorance, the just price ensuing from it still prevails. Though we cannot go into details here, Lessius' solution and further elaboration of this case reveals at least three distinctive features of his economic thought: (1) a consistent application of the general just price doctrine to all kinds of cases, (2) a restrictive interpretation of the vices of the will violating contractual

consensualism, and (3) a concept of business as governed by rules of its own that should be recognized by an ethicist who boasts himself on stimulating virtuous and free-market behavior.

Scholastics such as Lessius never intended to invent a new system for organizing the economy. They influenced businessmen, not politicians. The nobility and monarchs ignored the scholastics. However, businessmen ruled the Dutch Republic during much of its history, the economically better years anyway, and they implemented the ideas of scholastics such as Lessius. While the scholastics never put it this way, it is not difficult to connect the Church's teaching on private property with the scholastic notion of the just price to realize that free markets are necessary for property rights to exist. After all, ownership means the right to use one's property as one sees fit, especially to dispose of it. But that right cannot be exercised except in free markets. Free markets instantiate the airy notion of property.

The first modern capitalist nation

The businessman leaders of the Dutch Republic repealed the privileges of the nobility and made all citizens equal before the law. They established relatively honest courts, private property rights and freer markets. They held commercial activity in high esteem and promoted individualism. As a result, they created a new system of economic management without knowing it, intending it or giving it a name, but which Adam Smith would call the natural system of liberty. Followers of Marx would attempt to ridicule it as capitalism.

In his masterpiece, *The Wealth of Nations* Adam Smith held up the Dutch Republic as the nation that had most completely implemented the principles of natural freedom, "a country that had acquired that full complement of riches which the nature of its soils and climate and its situation with respect to other countries allowed it to acquire," according to Jan De Vries in *The First Modern Economy, Success, failure, and perseverance of the Dutch economy, 1500-1815*. In other words, Smith catalogued what the Dutch had accomplished.

For thousands of years before the founding of the Dutch Republic, Europeans had cycled between famine and stingy growth. The sixteenth and seventeenth centuries escorted onstage the first episode of explosive economic growth in the history of mankind, but the drama took place in just one country, the Netherlands. Angus Maddison's estimates of the per capita G.D.P. in The Netherlands in his *The World Economy* stand out: it doubled in the sixteenth and seventeenth centuries while the rest of Europe wallowed in stagnation. Maddison wrote, "They created a modern state, which protected property rights of merchants and entrepreneurs, promoted secular education and practiced religious tolerance."

In another book, *Dynamic Forces in Capitalist Development*, Maddison wrote, "In the past four centuries there have been only three lead countries [defined as the country which operates nearest to the technical frontier, with the highest average labor productivity]. The Netherlands was the top performer until the Napoleonic Wars, when the U.K. took over. The British lead lasted till around 1890, and the USA has been the lead country since then."

Two other prominent economists, Douglass North and Robert Thomas wrote in *The Rise of the Western World*, "In point of fact the Netherlands was the first country to achieve sustained economic growth as we have defined it…" Innovations in finance and trade had evolved for centuries, but institutions had changed little. The Dutch manufactured new institutions as quickly as they did wooden shoes.

> It was in the Netherlands, and Amsterdam specifically, that these diverse innovations and institutions were put together to create the predecessor of the efficient modern set of markets that make possible the growth of exchange and commerce. An open immigration policy attracted businessmen; efficient methods of financing long-distance trade were developed, as were capital markets and discounting methods in financial houses that lowered the costs of underwriting this trade. The development of techniques for spreading risk and transforming uncertainty into actuarial, ascertainable risks, the creation of large-scale markets that allowed for lowering the costs of information, and the development of negotiable government indebtedness all were a part of this story.

North quoted a famous Dutch historian in his *Rise of the Western World* as writing, "Where else was there a civilization that reached its greatest peak so soon after state and nation came into being?" The Netherlands won its independence from Spain in 1640 after eighty years of bloody war. But long before the shooting stopped, the infant state dominated the larger nations of France, Spain and England. For the next two centuries, it would rule much of the continent economically, intellectually, militarily and artistically, but never politically. Its dominance would frustrate England and France so much that the two behemoths would attack again and again in vain attempts to break its hegemony, succeeding only when they resorted to blocking Dutch imports and declaring open warfare on Dutch shipping.

Readers will naturally wonder about the role of the cities of Northern Italy, especially Venice, in birthing free markets. Some historians trace the DNA of capitalism to those cities long before the founding of the Dutch Republic and their reasons are good enough that it would be easy to agree and adopt the Dutch Republic as a more advanced state of capitalism. The Republic owed an enormous debt to the tremendous work of those city states in advancing Scholastic thought about business and elevating the status of commerce, as Rodney Stark illustrates in his book, *The Victory of Reason: How Christianity Led to Freedom, Capitalism, and Western Success*. It was a close call, but I chose the Dutch Republic over the Italian cities for a couple of reasons related to the definition of capitalism outlined in the first chapter.

First, Venice and the other states earned most of their income from international trade and they used their navies to establish monopolies on that trade. Except for the East India Company, which contributed a small part of the Dutch economy as Peiter de la Court argued in the previous chapter, the Dutch used its navy to protect shipping from pirates but not to force others to do business with it. Second, the nobility of cities like Venice kept commerce limited to citizens and primarily the nobility. Entry into the trades was strictly limited, especially by guilds.

Third, manufacturing did not follow the capitalist kind, but the medieval pattern. Capitalistic production is capital intensive mass production for the masses, as stated earlier. The only mass production that took place in Venice was the manufacturing of ships for the navy and commerce, but the state owned that facility. It was not a private company. As for the rest of the manufacturing, it was still carried out by artisans who hand crafted unique items under the guild system for consumption by the wealthy, local and foreign, but not for the masses because they could not afford the products. Most people made what they needed at home.

Finally, Christian individualism had not yet matured in the cities of Northern Italy as it had by the time of the Protestant Reformation. Chapter 2 discussed the differences between the true individualism of capitalism and the false monster that atheists and deists fabricated in the French Enlightenment. The individualism of Christianity and capitalism broke the bonds of envy that had kept civilizations in starvation poverty for millennia.

Pre-tribulation

By the end of the sixteenth century, the tiny nation that would become the Dutch Republic would tutor the rest of Europe in economic development and in the military tactics to defeat the mighty hordes of the Ottoman Empire. "Both the suddenness and the intensity of the Republic's economic prosperity provoke amazement and compel us to search for factors that might help to account for such an achievement," wrote historian Jan de Vries. In response, many economic historians point to the growth of cities. But as we saw earlier, towns and cities erected high barriers to economic growth in the Middle Ages. Besides, great cities had existed since Rome, and other European countries had cities greater than those of the Netherlands, while Instanbul, Alexandria, Damascus and many other cities of the Ottoman Empire made those of Europe appear as backwater villages.

In spite of their size and development, the cities of Europe and the Ottoman Empire demonstrated their utter impotence in siring sustained economic development. Rather than causing economic growth, the high rate of urbanization in the Netherlands was an effect of development, resulting largely from greater agricultural productivity that freed workers for urban labor. Also, the cities in Europe had very different charters than those in the rest of the world. European cities embraced individualism in which all citizens were equal before the law and had a voice in the government. They were cities of refuge from oppression by the nobility in the countryside. In the rest of the world, cities followed the ancient Greek and Roman model in which they existed for the nobility.

Other economists point to improvements in agriculture for the source of growth. Few people would argue against agricultural productivity as necessary for growth, but was it sufficient? Improvements in agricultural techniques could provide the source of the capital that the Dutch needed to invest in other productive ventures. But it seems unlikely that it could spawn the changes in values and institutions that gave birth to this small, remarkable nation and created its dominance over countries many times its size for almost 200 years. And as we learned in previous chapters, values and institutions provide the greenhouse environment for development to take place. It is only reasonable, then, to examine the

Netherlands in greater detail to try to discover in what way its values and institutions demonstrated its uniqueness from the bulk of Europe as well as the Ottoman Empire at the beginning of the sixteenth century. The chief difference lies in its religious beliefs. As the previous chapter demonstrates, the rise of individualism, freedom, equality and respect for property as well as the institutions to protect and encourage those values form the true foundation of capitalism and those originate in religion.

The gestation period for individualism from its inception by the Apostle Paul to its birth in the Dutch Republic was over fourteen centuries. "The identity of the individual – of a status which creates a space for the legitimate exercise of personal judgement and will – had broken through the surface of social life by the fifteenth century," in the words of Siedentop in *Inventing the Individual*. But it was still an abstraction, rarely instantiated outside of a few cities. It had not taken on flesh and blood so that it could slay envy. The doctor who performed the delivery was Desiderius Erasmus Roterodamus, better known as Erasmus. Erasmian Protestantism would produce a form of individualism so radical that its natural parent, the Catholic Church, would stagger at its image and eventually disinherit and repent over it.

Born in Rotterdam, Holland in 1466, Erasmus' parents educated him in monastic schools. He took the vows in 1492, but never seems to have worked as a priest. In 1495 he went to study at the University of Paris where he found life at the university, and scholasticism, distasteful and left. He lived in England for a while and became lifelong friends with the leading thinkers in the days of Henry VIII.

Erasmus' first book, *Dagger of the Christian Gentleman*, published in 1503, sketched the outlines of his image of the normal Christian life. He portrayed formalism, i.e., the veneration of tradition and the concern for what other people think, as being opposed to the true teachings of Christ and as the chief evil of his day. Formalism manifested itself in monasticism, saint-worship, war, and the spirit of class divisions. His remedy for this evil involved searching Scripture to determine what Jesus would do, and then doing it without fear. He would return to this theme and amplify it throughout his life.

Erasmus published his most famous book, *Praise of Folly*, in Paris, 1509, but he considered it a trifle that he had tossed out to relieve the boredom of travel. In it, Folly praises, encourages and justifies foolish activities. The book backhands superstition, uncritical "scientific" theories, and the vanity of Church leaders, peasants, poets, rhetoricians, lawyers, and merchants. Throughout his life, Erasmus attacked the sale of indulgences and got away with it when a similar thrust by Luther a decade later would bring down on Luther the full terror of the Church's wrath. Bishops and popes, he wrote, should imitate the poverty, labor, doctrine, and sacrifice of Christ. Instead, he indicted them for concentrating on financial gain and living like princes.

In 1516 he published the *Institutio Principis Christiani*, in which he advised the young king Charles of Spain on how to be the proper Christian prince, which he understood to be the servant of the people. Erasmus wrote this during a time in which, generally, kings ruled by divine right and considered the people their property, very much in line with the attitudes of Ottoman Sultans.

While in England, Erasmus began the systematic examination of New Testament Greek manuscripts that would result in the publication of a new Latin translation by Froben of Basel in 1516. His translation formed the first attempt by a competent scholar to ascertain what the New Testament writers had actually said. Erasmus considered it his greatest contribution to the cause of Christ and it laid the foundation for most Bible study during the Reformation. His translation diverged from the Church's Vulgate on significant matters, another wounding thrust at the Church's authority. Immediately after publishing the translation, he wrote paraphrases of the New Testament, an early version of a Living Bible, which were translated into Dutch for consumption by the masses and contributed greatly to the spread of Protestantism. For the preface to his Greek New Testament, the volume *A History of Western Society Since 1300* quotes Erasmus as having written,

> Only bring a pious and open heart, imbued above all things with a pure and simple faith...For I utterly dissent from those who are unwilling that the sacred Scriptures should be read by the unlearned translated into their vulgar tongue, as though Christ had taught such subtleties that they can scarcely be understood even by a few theologians. Christ wished his mysteries to be published as openly as possible. I wish that even the weakest woman should read the Gospel—should read the epistles of Paul. And I wish these were translated into all languages, so that they might be read and understood, not only by Scots and Irishmen, but also by Turks and Saracens.… Why do we prefer to study the wisdom of Christ in men's writings rather than in the writing of Christ himself?

Erasmus saw Christendom as an arena in which Christian humanism battled traditional scholasticism. His genius lay in fusing humanist techniques of exegesis with a systematic articulation and a strong commitment to Christianity. At the same time, he saw dangers in scholarship and the humanism of the Italian Renaissance, dangers such as paganism, ceremony and schism. For Erasmus, scholarship should lead the scholar to a deeper commitment to Christ. "I brought it about that humanism, which among the Italians…savored of nothing but pure paganism, began nobly to celebrate Christ," he wrote according to E. H. Harbison in *The Christian Scholar and His Calling in the Age of the Reformation*.

In addition to his translation of Scripture that challenged the official Vulgate, Erasmus taught that the ultimate authority for interpreting Scripture resided in the scholar, thus usurping Church authority once again. He held salvation to be an individual matter, between a person and God, as opposed to the traditional Church view that salvation came through the sacraments and membership in the Church. Erasmus did not invent the concept of personal salvation. He stood on the shoulders of many theologians and martyrs who preceded him. But he proved more gifted, eloquent and persuasive, and he preached it at a time in history when dissatisfaction with the Catholic Church flowed deep and wide across the continent. This subversive doctrine of personal salvation would prove as important to economics as to religion, because it would contribute to the rise of a radical individualism.

Erasmus intended to reform the Church from within through sound scholarship, writing and preaching. He advocated outward submission to Church ritual and authority, but personal devotion to Christ and the scholarly study of Scripture. Those in Europe who could read consumed his writings, but his books especially appealed to middle class merchants and manufacturers in spite of his scorn for their profession. Due to Erasmus' influence many in Europe were already what historian Jonathan Israel calls crypto-Protestants decades before Luther's rupture with the Church.

Erasmus was one of the most prominent scholars of his age, but his greatest concern was for a pure, personal Christianity that imitated Christ. He considered himself a preacher of righteousness above all else, but he struggled to liberalize Church institutions and free scholarship from the rigidity and formalism of medieval traditions. He corresponded with over 500 men of the highest importance in the world of politics and thought, and rulers sought his advice on all kinds of subjects according to *The Internet Encyclopedia of Philosophy* in its "Erasmus" article.

Then, on October 31, 1517, Luther nailed his ninety-five theses to Castle Church door in Wittenberg, Germany, condemning the Church's sale of indulgences to raise money for the construction of St. Peter's in Rome. Luther did not write anything that Erasmus had not already published for decades, but he rushed into battle unarmed with Erasmus' popularity, political contacts, and eloquence. In contrast to the tolerance shown Erasmus, Church authorities demanded that Luther recant. Luther refused and crypto-Protestants throughout Europe burst into flaming Protestants.

Luther and other Protestants appealed to Erasmus to support them, but the scholar refused, fearing schism and the wrath of the authorities. Erasmus thought Luther was wrong to disturb the unity of the Church, but the Church recognized in Erasmus the intellectual power behind the revolt, charging him with having "laid the egg that Luther hatched," according to *The Internet Encyclopedia of Philosophy*. Erasmus pleaded no contest to the paternity charge, but claimed he had expected a different kind of bird. A Dominican theologian remarked, "Luther is pestilential, but Erasmus more so, for Luther sucked all his poison from Erasmus' teats," according to Israel in *The Dutch Republic*. A papal nuncio reported to the Pope in 1521 that "Luther's doctrines were being preached publicly in Holland and that 'all this happens because of the Hollander Erasmus,'" Israel wrote.

The Church pressured Erasmus to break openly with Luther and declare his allegiance to the Church. He resisted as long as he could, but when the pressure became too great, he left the Netherlands in a state of spiritual civil war and migrated to Switzerland where he hoped to reside in peace. He wrote *De libero arbitrio* (1524) in which he laid down both sides of the argument on freedom of the will, and finished with an easy-going semi-Pelagiansism. Then in 1530, while living in the Protestant city of Basel, he tossed the Church another bone by writing a half-hearted endorsement of the Church's interpretation of the Eucharist. He also espoused the position that a man may have two opinions on theology, his true opinion that he keeps between intimate friends and the outward one that conforms to official teaching. Erasmus died in Basel in 1536, ten years before Luther's death and the same year that John Calvin arrived in Geneva.

Erasmus' legacy continued to energize Protestantism in the Netherlands for a century. Nowhere in Europe did Protestantism and public authority clash more explosively, partly because the government there took a harsher line against rebels. As Luther became increasingly confessional minded in the late 1520's, the persecuted clandestine Reformation of the Low Lands developed a "non-dogmatic pluriform crypto-Protestantism and this, by its nature, could more easily draw on the biblical humanism of Erasmus than the theology of Luther."

Erasmus lived to witness the schism he feared. In 1520, Emperor Charles V added Erasmus' commentaries on the New Testament, *Enchiridion*, to the list of banned books. The following year he ordered the burning of all Protestant books in the Netherlands and the peasants of Germany revolted against the nobility, citing as justification Luther's writings. Two years later Charles executed two Augustinian friars for teaching Protestant theology.

The crypto-Protestantism of Erasmus and Luther's outward manifestation appealed to merchants and nobility, but the task of recruiting uneducated peasants and artisans fell to the Anabaptists whom Lutherans, Calvinists and Catholics all persecuted. Their opponents called them Anabaptists because they denied the validity of infant baptism and insisted that new church members be re-baptized. They adopted a congregational, autonomous form of government, opposed state sponsorship and control of churches, and shunned hierarchy. Some adopted a form of communal living in which they abandoned private property. Anabaptist leader Menno Simons was one of the greatest figures of the Dutch Reformation. His *Foundation of Christian Doctrine* emphasized practical holiness, discipline and submission to Christ. He encouraged Christians to lead sober lives based on Scripture, but to submit to no ruler other than Christ.

Anabaptists launched the first political rebellion against Spain in 1534 when they stormed the city of Munster and expelled all who refused baptism. They held the city for eighteen months, but the crypto-Protestants in the rest of the country were not ready for open rebellion and refused to join them. The government retook the city and slaughtered the Anabaptist rebels. From 1530 through 1560, Anabaptists led the charge for Protestantism in the Netherlands. The merchants, regents and nobility preferred to hide their Protestant beliefs behind closed doors, but attendance at Catholic services plunged. Those too roused to keep quiet joined the Anabaptists and suffered the wrath of the state. In 1550, Charles V intensified the Inquisition in the Low Lands with his "eternal edict." Under the edict, a person accused of heresy but refusing to confess was burned alive; men who confessed were beheaded and women buried alive. Between 1523 and 1565, the Spanish king murdered 1,300 people, almost all of them Anabaptists.

Calvinism came to the Netherlands in the late 1550's, mainly from Dutch refugees living in Germany. From 1565 on, Calvinism began to dominate, but not displace the multi-hued Protestantism of the past. For another century, Protestantism would remain split between radical Calvinists on one side and Erasmian Protestants on the other, which included moderate Calvinists, Lutherans and Anabaptists. The two groups would clash many times politically, with radical Calvinists supporting a monarchy, religious conformity and state control of the economy while the Erasmians pushed for a republican form of government, freedom of religion and free markets.

Birth pains

In 1555, Charles V surrendered the throne of Spain to his son, Philip who increased the pressure on the crypto-Protestants of the Netherlands. He appointed William of Orange, also known as William the Silent, as Stadholder, or earl, of Holland, Zeeland and Utrecht as a reward for William's contributions in the Spanish war against France. William would eventually lead the Dutch Republic in rebellion against Spain. His father had strong Lutheran tendencies and William married the daughter of a German Lutheran prince. He confided to friends that he was Protestant at heart, but maintained an outward loyalty to the Church and Spain as Erasmus had modeled while attempting to reach a political compromise between the Protestants and the Church.

Calvinists began preaching openly in the countryside of the Netherlands in 1566, but not in the cities. Then, in August, mobs began ransacking Catholic churches all over the Netherlands and destroying statues and paintings. Israel wrote, "Alienation of a society from its own religious culture, on such a scale, was a phenomenon without precedent or parallel." Historians try to explain the rioting as frustration over the poor economy of the 1560's, but as Israel wrote, "…the iconoclastic outbreaks of 1566 involved no assaults on government officials or town halls, or against tax-farmers, and no plundering of shops and food-stores. In form the *beeldenstorm* was purely and simply an attack on the church and not anything else." Calvinists began to preach openly as they took over some of the Catholic churches.

Protestant nobles took advantage of the situation to lead an armed revolt, but two quick defeats in battle deflated the movement. The state closed Protestant churches and thousands of Protestants converted to Catholicism. William decided that prudence demanded he take his family to visit relatives in Germany. Philip responded to the rebellion by sending his top general, the Duke of Alva to the Netherlands at the head of 10,000 of his best troops. During the five years of Alva's rule, almost 9,000 people were investigated for heresy or treason with more than a thousand being executed and 60,000 refugees fleeing the country. The Duke took William of Orange's fifteen year old son prisoner, condemned William as a heretic and confiscated his lands. William gathered an army of German troops and invaded, but Alva's hardened veterans slaughtered most of them.

William would have to wait until 1572 for the revolt to gain traction. That year, Queen Elizabeth expelled the Sea-Beggars, a small Dutch navy, from England in response to threats from Philip. With no port to call home, the Sea-Beggars decided to capture Brill, a small town on the coast of the Holland. Encouraged by their success, they took the more important cities of Flushing and Veere. Soon, Haarlem and all of North Holland joined the rebel cause. The States of Holland, a congress of representatives from the many states that constituted the province of Holland, met and agreed to fund William's army from taxes and the sale of confiscated Church property. Without consciously deciding to, "the States of Holland had transformed themselves from being an occasional, chiefly advisory body into an embryonic government endeavouring to organize and finance a war while maintaining order and justice and taking over the reins of administration."

The revolt spread to Friesland, but a counter attack on Dokkum by Spanish troops caused its fall and the massacre of many of its citizens. Alva launched a new campaign to crush the revolt and retake the rebel cities. After capturing Mechelen, he allowed his troops to sack the city and murder the inhabitants. Next, he massacred hundreds in the city of Zutphen, but at Naarden, he murdered every man woman and child in the city. Alva surrounded Haarlem, but the citizens fought so well that they exacted a high price from the Spanish troops before abandoning the city.

The Spanish laid siege to Leiden in 1574 and by August the defenders' supplies had run out. William sent a carrier pigeon with a letter promising to relieve the city and had the surrounding dikes cut in hopes of flooding the area and permitting his troops to reach the city by boat. But the water did not rise to a level high enough to force the Spanish out and the rebel forces were stuck short of the city. For weeks they could advance no further. Suddenly heavy rain began to fall; the waters rose and the Spanish retreated. William's forces entered the city and found the citizens so weak that hardly any could stand.

After Leiden, the Spanish left southern Holland and gave the rebels control of most of the province. Philip replaced Alva with Don Luis de Requesens and authorized him to negotiate a settlement with William. Talks began in 1575 with the rebels insisting that they had not rebelled against the Spanish Crown, but against Alva. They demanded a limited monarchy over their country, tolerance for Protestants, and sharing in the government by the States General, all of which went well beyond what Philip would agree to. The next year, the Spanish troops, which had not been paid for months, mutinied and attacked Antwerp. "For several days Europe's greatest commercial and financial centre was subjected to slaughter, pillage, and rape."

Negotiations led to the signing of the Pacification of Ghent in 1576 by most of the states of the Netherlands, but not by the Spanish under Don Juan who withdrew to the south, gathered Spanish troops and launched his re-conquest. The northern states pushed for a closer union and won with the signing of the Union of Utrecht in 1579, which established the Dutch Republic.

That same year, Huguenots (French Protestants) published a tract, *Vindiciae contra Tyrannos*, that became the most celebrated justification for rebellion of the age, asserting that kings and magistrates were subject to laws and ultimately responsible to the people. Its most likely authors, Languet and Duplessis-Mornay, were close friends of William of Orange in the view of Charles Wilson in *The Dutch Republic and the Civilisation of the Seventeenth Century*. Two decades later, the Salamancan scholar Juan de Mariana published a similar defense of tyrannicide in his second most popular work, *De Rege et Regis Institutione*, which appeared in 1599 at Toledo.

William struggled to maintain the unity of the northern and southern states in the rebellion by ensuring toleration for Catholic worship, although he had become a Calvinist. He might have succeeded had not the radical Calvinists in the northern states refused to permit any religion but their own. The predominantly Catholic southern states responded to the northerner's intolerance by surrendering to Don Juan's armies as he marched north.

In 1581, the states repudiated Philip II and his heirs as their sovereign with the Act of Abjuration and offered sovereignty to the Duke of Anjou, younger brother of the French king. Until the Acts, the rebels had paid lip service to the King of Spain. But in 1583, Anjou abandoned the Netherlands and William retreated to Delft in Holland to lead the rebellion.

The States General, the legislative branch of the Republic, transferred their assembly from Antwerp to The Hague. The following year, William died at the hands of an assassin. His last words were, "My God, my God, have pity on me and these poor people."

Desperately seeking an ally that could assist them against Spain, the Dutch offered their tiny nation to Henry III of France. But his own country suffered from a civil war in which the Protestant Huguenots fought to save themselves from the genocide at the hands of the French state. The Saint Bartholomew's Day Massacre of 1572, in which Catholics murdered an estimated 70,000 Protestants in a week's time, including William of Orange's father-in-law, had ignited the war.

Henry declined the offer of sovereignty so the Dutch turned to Queen Elizabeth. She also declined, fearing the wrath of Spain, but she agreed to place the Provinces under her protection and provide military assistance if she could appoint the Republic's military and political head. The Republic agreed and the queen selected the earl of Leicester as the governor-general, dispatching him with 7,350 troops to defend the Republic. The Leicester regime proved disastrous. At one point, English troops mutinied and fought with the Spanish against the Dutch. The English protectorate ended with the earl attempting a coup and when that failed, sailing for home in 1587.

The golden age

From the beginning of the revolt, William and the Holland regents had thwarted the radical Calvinists' efforts to determine the political and religious character of the new republic. The Calvinists in the Dutch Reformed Church disliked the freedom that William and the Holland regents, who favored an Erasmian Protestantism, wanted for other faiths. William had fought to give Catholics equal status and the freedom to worship openly. The regents had suppressed Catholic services in public, but tolerated private gatherings of Catholics, Anabaptists, Lutherans, Jews and other groups. But that was not enough for the Calvinists. They wanted to strengthen Calvinist orthodoxy within the church, rid the nation of other forms of Christianity, and increase the influence of the church in affairs of state, society and the economy. This struggle for power between the radical Calvinists and Erasmian Protestants would outline the political battles for the next century.

In the year of William of Orange's assassination, 1584, Cornelis Hooft, a regent of Amsterdam, urged the Republic not to enthrone William as a monarch, arguing that the people opposed it and that it violated the intent of the revolt to defend their historical freedoms and privileges. But in the power vacuum left by the death of William, radical Calvinists agitated for a strong monarchy and buttressed Leicester's position, while Erasmian Protestants campaigned for a republic with a weak executive. Thomas Wilkes said of the Hollanders in 1590, "They hate to be subject not only to a Spaniard but, tasting the sweetness of their liberty, to any kingly government." The struggle between the moderate Hollanders and radical Calvinists weakened the Republic to the point that Thomas Bodley, wrote in 1589, that he "considered the Dutch state 'weaker at this present than it hath been these many years; and unless by Her majesty's extraordinary assistance, and counsel, it be presently holpen, there is little appearance that they can hold it out long.'" But they did hold out.

In 1588, Philip dispatched the Spanish Armada, with the Pope's blessing, to commit the same genocide against English Protestants that he had perpetrated in the Netherlands and that the French were committing against the Huguenots. Queen Elizabeth desired the help of the Dutch navy against the Armada and so ordered her representatives in the Netherlands to cooperate more with Holland. Due to Leicester's clumsy rein, the Holland regents consolidated their power under the brilliant leadership of Johan van Oldenbarnevelt, the Advocate for the States of Holland. Thus began the golden age of the Dutch under its first republican government.

Military innovations

By 1590, the Dutch Republic had transformed itself. Israel wrote, "Successful state-building on the scale achieved in the 1590's, by the Republic, occurs only rarely in history…" In the midst of war and internal dissention, the Dutch had created new institutions and reformed the military and economy in ways that would make them a world power for almost two centuries.

The Dutch military took the offensive and regained much of the territory they had lost, at the same time setting new, higher standards for the conduct of soldiers. In the past, European soldiers had been free to murder, rape and steal from citizens. In contrast, Dutch generals disciplined their troops so well that villagers around Geertruidenberg felt safe to sell produce to Dutch troops during their siege of the city, and fine ladies would visit the scene of battle. The city capitulated in 1593 after four months. In all of their re-conquests, the Dutch never intentionally killed civilians as the Spanish had. By 1597, "…what initially had been a precarious strip of rebel territory had become one of the great powers of Europe."

The Dutch had the second largest standing army after Spain and one of the largest navies. Innovation became its hallmark. The Dutch military reforms signified a turning point in the history of soldiering and military organization, introducing changes that spread across Europe. Soldiers who committed crimes against civilians could expect a jail sentence for rowdiness and theft, and the death sentence for rape or abduction. The Venetian ambassador was surprised that, unlike elsewhere in Europe, towns in the Dutch Republic competed to have garrisons quartered in them because of the economic benefits. The Brandeburg-Prussia military tradition originated in the Dutch reforms, while the Swedes employed Dutch tight discipline, extended infantry lines, counter-march and mobile field artillery with their most devastating effect in defense of Protestants on the German battlefields of the 1630's and 1640's.

Freedom

Throughout the seventeenth and eighteenth centuries, the Republic gave its citizens greater liberty than any other European society of its time. Based on freedom of conscience, Dutch openness extended much further, creating a "general liberty and ease, not only in point of conscience, but all others that serve to the commodiousness and quiet of life, every man following his own way, minding his own business, and little enquiring into other men's," according to a letter from the English ambassador Sir William Temple in 1672.

An Italian who settled in Amsterdam in 1683 contrasted the freedom of Holland with the "corruption, institutionalized despotism, and lack of respect for the individual, which, in his opinion, characterized the decayed Italian republics of Venice and Genoa." The freedom that Dutch women enjoyed impressed visitors the most. Even young, unmarried women came and went as they pleased unchaperoned. Dutch wives were less subservient to their husbands and less likely to be beaten by them, as were servants.

While foreigners expressed surprise at the extent of Dutch freedoms, they usually responded with criticism, resentment, disdain and outright hostility. Many were appalled with the religious diversity and freedom of discussion. Others disapproved of the liberty of women, servants and Jews, whom other countries confined. The mixing of common folk with nobility as if they were equals outraged gentlemen. The United Provinces "were widely perceived in Europe as a seedbed of theological, intellectual, and social promiscuity which subverted the usual, and proper, relations between men and women, Christians and non-Christians, masters and servants, nobles and non-nobles, soldiers and civilians, perversely refusing to accord the noble, the soldier, and even the husband the honour and status which were their due."

This attitude of distrust toward freedom characterized the responses of much of the rest of the world when they encountered the concept. "The Japanese, when first exposed to Western influences in the nineteenth century, had great difficulty translating 'freedom'; they finally settled on *jiyu,* which means 'licentiousness.' The same held true of China and Korea," according to M. I. Finley in *The Ancient Economy.* Freedom puzzled Muslim writers as well. Bernard Lewis wrote in *Islam in History,* "The first examples in Islamic lands of the use of the term in a clearly defined political sense come from the Ottoman Empire in the late eighteenth and early nineteenth centuries, and are patently due to European influence, sometimes to direct translations from European texts... Early references to freedom in works of Muslim authorship are hostile, and equate it with libertinism, licentiousness, and anarchy."

Yet Dutch society was more prone than other European societies to repress bawdiness, eroticism, undisguised homosexuality, and street prostitution. While women adopted French fashion, "society simply would not tolerate the plunging necklines and flaunting of the bosom prevalent, at the time, in France, England, and Italy." But it was precisely the Dutch emphasis on morality and order that enabled their women to move about freely and unaccompanied without being molested. Solitary males and females could wander, day or night, in town or country with relatively little fear of being robbed, or assaulted. The Dutch invented the first neighborhood watches and gave the world the first public streetlights in order to reduce crime and check wife beating.

Dutch ingenuity

As the rest of Europe, the economy of the Netherlands had remained static until the 1580's. Then it exploded. One reason for the breakaway performance was the productivity of its agriculture. Cameron wrote in *A Concise Economic History*, "In the course of the sixteenth and seventeenth centuries Dutch agriculture underwent a striking transformation that merits its description as the first 'modern' agricultural economy." The Dutch were the first in Europe to cross over from the subsistence farming that had sustained humanity for millennia to specialization and production for the marketplace.

Subsistence farming takes place when farmers try to produce all of the food that their families and animals will eat, as well as wool and cotton for clothing and other necessities. American artists, historians, poets and novelists idolize self-sufficient agriculture, but farmers know well its deficiencies. To achieve self-sufficiency, farmers must become experts in a wide variety of production techniques, from raising sheep, cattle, horses, pigs and chickens, to growing wheat, corn, rye, cotton, flax, and hemp as well as the means to process them. With specialization, a farmer can concentrate on a few commodities and produce higher quality goods for less. As a result, he will need fewer tools. But the most important benefit comes from producing the items most in demand in the market because those products command the highest prices. He can then use some of his profits from the sale of those items to purchase what his family and livestock need at a cost lower that what he could produce them for himself. In some cases, Dutch farmers would grow and sell wheat, which could command a premium price in the cities, and purchase cheaper rye for their families to eat. Dutch agriculture pioneered the formula for success that the great developmental economist Peter Bauer discovered later and wrote about in *From Subsistence to Exchange and other Essays*:

> One general feature of the early stages of economic progress is the replacement of subsistence production by market production for wider exchange. This process is accompanied by certain types of capital formation, important categories of which are incompletely recorded in statistics or altogether unrecorded. This applies to the establishment, extension, and improvement of agricultural properties, for instance the planting of cocoa or rubber trees in plantations on small holdings where the output is collected and distributed by traders. These categories of capital formation are indispensable for the advance from subsistence production. They usually do not require monetary savings or investment, which explains why they often escape statistical record. My experiences in West Africa and Southeast Asia, in which I studied the cocoa industry and the rubber industry, have alerted me to the significance of such categories of capital formation.

Dutch farmers specialized in high-value livestock and dairy products that required large quantities of feed such as hay, clover, and turnips. The intensive agriculture practiced by the

Dutch also demanded high inputs of fertilizer, which animals produced in abundance. Cameron wrote, "So great was the demand for fertilizer that some entrepreneurs found it profitable to specialize in collecting urban night soil and pigeon dung, for example, which they sold by the canal-boatload or cartload—an activity that incidentally kept Dutch cities cleaner and more sanitary than others." Dutch agriculture proved so profitable that entrepreneurs invested substantial capital in reclaiming land from the sea, by draining lakes and marshes, and by planting peat bogs after the peat had been sold as fuel.

The Dutch restructured the financial industry of Europe, too. In 1609 they created the first public bank. De Vries wrote, "The Bank of Amsterdam succeeded instantly in attracting depositors, who became the envy of Europe for their access to deposit, transfer, and payment services that were trustworthy, safe, efficient, and virtually costless." Credit became widespread and interest rates low, about half the rate in England. According to De Vries, Amsterdam's financial institutions offered unparalleled opportunities: "One could trade commodities as well as financial instruments such as company shares and government bonds; one could buy sea insurance, arrange for freight, and get foreign exchange quotations."

Most importantly, however, the bank severely reduced two evils dating from the ancient world – debasing of coins and fractional reserve banking. The previous chapter described the first debasement of coins by Solon in Athens in 594 and the ruin the practice caused there and in Rome during the third and fourth centuries. Monarchs often took on debt they could not afford in order to fight more senseless wars and build monuments to their vanity. Then they would devalue the nation's coins by adding base metals to the silver and gold while stamping the value as if the coins contained pure metal for the purpose of escaping that debt. The practice was fraud, but all monarchs considered it their right and duty. The Bank of Amsterdam ended that practice for merchants who held accounts with it, although smaller banks continued the practice.

The other evil, fractional reserve banking, it much more esoteric and therefore has the potential to cause much more havoc. With coin debasement, people could easily determine how much precious metal coins contained and adjust prices accordingly. Fractional reserve banking has the same effect as coin debasement but is much more subtle and therefore dangerous. As with coin debasement, fractional banking probably began with temples that acted as banks in the early centuries of history. Fractional banking refers to the fact that banks keep only a portion of the money deposited on hand to meet the daily demands of the depositors while loaning out the rest. It refers only to demand deposits in which the depositors think that all of their money remains in the vault and they can withdraw all of it whenever they wish. It does not apply to money that people give to the banker for the purpose of lending it to others for a period of time because in those cases the depositor does not expect to get his money back on demand at any time but must wait for the borrower to repay it.

Fractional banking of demand deposits appears to a few economists as fraud and many scholars have labeled it that. The Roman Empire outlawed the practice without stamping it out. The excellent Spanish economist, Jesus Huerta de Soto has written the definitive history of fractional banking in his *Money, Bank Credit and Economic Cycles* and he considered the practice grossly immoral. De Soto makes excellent points, but several of the Church scholars of the Salamancan school defended it on moral grounds. I will pass on the moral judgment while pointing out that the practice has caused all of the boom-and-bust cycles in history other than those caused by crop failures, war or coin debasement.

Banking started in the third millennium B.C. in temples and probably fractional reserve banking with it. But the first known incident happened in 393 in ancient Greece. Of course, few people knew that bankers or goldsmiths were conducting fractional reserve banking until they went to the bank to withdraw their money and the banker could not deliver. That was how a friend of the philosopher and lawyer Isocrates discovered the practice. Isocrates represented his friend in court and accused the banker of misappropriating his friend's deposit according to Jesus Huerta de Soto in *Money, Bank Credit and Economic Cycles*. The banker had loaned most of the friend's money to others and would have met the friend's demand for his money had his debtors repaid their loans. But the business ventures failed and the debtors could not pay, or could not pay fast enough. As a result, Isocrates' friend lost his deposit.

Bank failures always hurt more than one person and that was most likely the case in Isocrates' situation as well. De Soto recounts the history of many of those bank failures, which would usually cause widespread economic depression as people learned that most of their savings had disappeared. Naturally, people would cut back on consumption in order to rebuild their savings and cause consumer goods businesses to fail. Economists rediscovered the dangers of fractional banking and bank failures in the nineteenth century, but had to wait for the great Austrian economist Ludwig von Mises to explain that credit expansion leads to investments in the wrong businesses in the capital equipment sector followed by the failure of those businesses and the onset of the recession, which has become known as the Austrian business-cycle theory.

The Bank of Amsterdam reduced the threat of boom and bust cycles caused by credit expansion followed by bank failures, but it was incapable of eliminating all credit expansion because fractional banking is very lucrative; it is essentially a license to counterfeit without the burden of having to print paper money. The Dutch suffered through some credit induced booms and busts as a result of the excessive issues of bills of exchange by businesses, which would have worked in much the same way as fractional banking.

One famous episode that may have been the national obsession with the Turkish Tulip that led to the "tulip mania" in 1637 and the financial disaster afterwards. In their defense, the Tulip bubble resulted from an expansion of the money supply, possibly in the form of gold entering the country, but more likely through an expansion of bills of exchange which served as an early form of paper money. Similar bubbles popped in the U.S. with the dot.com bubble of the 1990's and the housing bubble of the first decade of the next century. But we should keep in mind that the Dutch viewed Tulip breeding as a new technology and developed an obsession with it in the same way that the U.S. suffered from an obsession with the internet in the dot.com bubble of the late 1990's.

The Dutch changed the way government finances worked, too. Before the revolt, Holland used tax revenue to retire government bonds and demonstrate the credit worthiness of the government. Afterward, the Republic continued to pay its debts, a rare practice among European governments. More common across the continent was the habit of forcing wealthy citizens to loan money to the state only to have the king default on the loan. Because of its fair treatment of lenders and regular repayment of loans, the Republic could borrow at much lower interest rates. The Dutch created modern international lending in 1688 when they invaded England and enthroned Willem III, the Dutch Stadholder. Willem set in motion constitutional changes, following practices in the Dutch Republic, that made England the first country outside of the Republic "to achieve creditworthiness capable of attracting voluntary, long-term Dutch investment in its public debt and in the English joint-stock companies," according to De Vries. The Bank of England was created in 1694.

The Dutch added a twist to the practice of colonization that the Spanish and Portuguese had pioneered. They devised a joint-stock monopoly company backed by the state but observing policies established by a board of directors. In 1601 they created the United East India Company, which took the Spice Islands from the Portuguese in 1605. The Dutch West India Company emerged in 1621. Shares of both were traded on the stock exchange. Their charters instructed the companies to promote the Dutch Reformed Church as the sole public Church in their colonies, but at the same time allow for a freedom of conscience similar to that enjoyed in the Netherlands. However, the directors saw Catholicism as an enemy so the East India Company expelled all of the Catholics from territories it acquired.

The Dutch did not follow the Spanish practice of forcing natives to convert to Christianity, but they saw a purpose in the companies greater than just financial gain. Willem Usselincx, whom Israel called "the most notable Dutch economic writer of the early seventeenth century," lobbied for the creation of the Dutch West Indies Company in order to take the gospel, along with Christian civilization to the native inhabitants. Usselincx believed that peaceful trade would prove more effective than the forced conversions practiced by the Latins, arguing that "the Indians would become more civilized and become accustomed to labor in order to enjoy the fruits of labor," according to Ruben C. Alvarado in his article "Redeemer Nation" published in *Common Law Review*.

The single feature of the Dutch Republic that impresses historians most is the small country's rapid rise to dominance of international trade and its longevity, almost a century and a half. Before the revolt, Antwerp ruled the economy of Western Europe. By 1590, Amsterdam had wrested control from the old city. Part of the explanation for the transfer of economic power resides in the migration of Protestant merchants from Antwerp after the city fell to the Spanish re-conquest of the southern part of the Netherlands. But the character of trade in Amsterdam differed greatly from that of Antwerp. De Vries wrote, "To put it baldly, the merchants who flocked to Amsterdam brought capital, expertise, and contacts with them, but they now *used* these assets differently than before, as they came into contact with new resources, institutions, and opportunities."

The two cities had important differences: 1) Amsterdam oriented itself to maritime trade, while Antwerp relied on overland trade; 2) Amsterdam practiced continuous and atomistic trade, while Antwerp retained much of the old forms of periodic fairs and the organization of merchants into privileged nations; 3) Amsterdam's merchants actively combined shipping, trade and distribution, while Antwerp's merchants passively traded in goods brought to them by others; 4) Antwerp depended on its relationship with the imperial power of the

Habsburgs, while Amsterdam, enjoying no imperial benefactor, struck out on its own according to De Vries.

How did the Dutch so quickly achieve their primacy in international trade? Certainly the money that accompanied immigrants fleeing Antwerp and Spain contributed a great deal to the capital stock necessary for such rapid growth, but for the most part the Northern Netherlanders lifted their economy by their own boot straps in the view of De Vries:

> But the chief explanation for the growing amounts of capital committed to inventories of trade goods is the profitability of trade conducted from the Republic. The reinvestment of major portions of these profits certainly accounted for most of the new funds expanding year by year the trading capital at the disposal of the Republic's merchants...as it grew, the institutions of the commercial economy (the Bank, *Beurs*, notarial system, consular support, money supply) became more efficient; shipping services benefited from the major technological advances represented by the *fluitschip* and mechanized lumber sawing; and merchants became more specialized. Together, these institutional, technological, and organizational improvements reduced transaction costs further than even the bulk trade traditions of the pre-Revolt commercial system had managed to achieve...."

In stark contrast to the Dutch practice of reinvesting profits in business, merchants in the rest of Europe carried on the ancient tradition of stashing their profits in land, purchasing titles of nobility and giving to the Church in hopes of buying forgiveness for their sins and entrance into heaven. Also, other nations retained the old guilds and government sanctioned monopolies. Dutch merchants initially tried to preserve their monopolies, but the sheer number of new merchants and businesses made it impossible to maintain them for long. As the Republic succumbed to competitive markets, they discovered that competition did not create chaos, as medieval wise men had warned, but sharpened skills, spawned innovations and improved productivity.

Dutch merchants did not restrict their investments to just piling up inventories, either. They invested in every manner of domestic production, especially textiles, fishing and agriculture. These productivity-enhancing investments fueled the rapid rise and long-term dominance of trade by the Dutch by making it a leader in technology. For most of the seventeenth and eighteenth centuries, the nation led the world in total factor productivity, operating nearest to the technological frontier and doing the most to define that frontier according to De Vries. In the seventeenth century, Dutch entrepreneurs introduced innovations into the iron industry and increased their own production as well as that of iron rich Sweden. Sweden had been endowed with almost as much copper as iron. With Dutch capital and expertise, it became Europe's largest supplier.

The Dutch also reformed the shipbuilding industry. Between the beginning of the sixteenth century and the middle of the seventeenth, the Dutch fleet expanded by tenfold, making it the largest fleet in Europe and three times the size of the English fleet. To meet the demand for ships, the Dutch organized their shipyards along elementary mass production techniques using mechanical saws and hoists powered by windmills. They standardized parts and made them interchangeable, whereas previously, parts were custom made in the artisan mode. The Dutch imported most of the wood but produced the sailcloth and cordage locally. With the *fluyt*, or flying ship, a tanker created to carry bulk products such as grain and timber, the Dutch made the most significant contribution to ship design in centuries. Introduced at the end of the sixteenth century, it operated with smaller crews and reduced shipping costs dramatically.

As Bauer and others have pointed out, a lack of natural resources has not barred nations from development and the Dutch were no exception. Having a shortage of coal and mineral ores, they imported what they needed, but mostly they relied on abundant supplies of peat and wind power at home. De Vries wrote,

> Industrial windmill technology experienced a veritable explosion of innovation, chiefly concentrated between 1591 (with the construction of the first mechanical lumber-sawing windmill…) and 1674 (with the introduction of the 'Hollander' to the paper-making windmills, whereby high-quality 'white' paper could be produced by the Zaan paper industry). In between these dates, craftsmen applied the principles of the windmill to the specific motion and striking action needed in pressing oilseeds, shelling kernels, beating hemp, crushing shells, fulling cloth, mixing mustard and paint, grinding tobacco for snuff, and other industrial processes.

The Hollander, a pulverizing machine, could produce more pulp for paper than eight stamping mills. Dutch inventors introduced an array of pumps, steam-machines and cranes, and in "microscopical science, botany, anatomy and medicine, the Dutch Enlightenment may fairly be described as the instructor of Europe, including Britain," according to Israel. The pendulum clock of the Dutch scientist Christian Huygens introduced an age of reliable timekeeping. Accurate watches were important to shipping because it enabled the calculations of lines of longitude for the first time. Sailors determined latitude by the positions of the sun and stars, but calculating longitude had to wait for the arrival of mechanical clocks. The Dutch tried to prevent the loss of their technological secret weapons by passing laws that prohibited their export, but they failed for the most part to prevent entrepreneurs from smuggling their wealth of knowledge to neighboring countries and enriching them as well.

Society – wages, poverty, education and morality

One would expect the migration of 100,000 to 150,000 people into the Dutch Republic, which barely reached a total population of two million at its peak, after the revolt would reduce wages for the working class, but just the opposite happened. Throughout its Golden Age, Dutch employers had to contend with wages that were often twice as high as those in the southern Netherlands or Germany. After 1590, workers in Republic alone out of all of the rest of Europe experienced wages that increased faster than the cost of living. This meant that the standard of living for workers, skilled and unskilled, improved in the Republic while workers elsewhere became poorer. Wages grew much faster than prices until 1660. Afterwards, wages remained static but prices fell, which produced the same effect as before – greater purchasing power and improving standards of living.

In real terms, Dutch laborers earned roughly twice as much as those in England until the late eighteenth century. Unskilled workers saw their wages climb from 55 percent of skilled wages in 1570 to 75 percent in 1650. These real wage increases reduced inequality as well. "A labor force growing rapidly, attaining higher levels of productivity, and earning higher real wages – this is the appealing picture we have of the Dutch labor market from the Revolt to the mid-seventeenth century, and most intensely to 1620," De Vries wrote.

Funds for the relief of poverty rose substantially in the decades after the revolt when the Republic appropriated the assets of the Catholic Church for charitable purposes. The Dutch opened or expanded schools, orphanages, hospitals, homes for the elderly, and workhouses for beggars and criminals. In other European countries, relief consisted mainly in periodic crisis intervention, such as the provision of bread in periods of famine. The deacon's boards and municipal relief agencies of the Republic distributed bread, peat (for heating), and cash to the working poor as well as the cyclically and seasonally unemployed on an ongoing basis. In Amsterdam, as many as 12 percent of all households received temporary help during the winter when jobs were scarce according to De Vries. And 16 percent of the population of the small town of Graft received some kind of aid according to Philip S. Gorski in *The Disciplinary Revolution: Calvinism and the Rise of the State in Early Modern Europe*.

The poor found qualifying for assistance easy and the Reformed deacons turned away few applicants. Residents of a town applied to the head of their ward who directed them to the appropriate church or public agency. After 1650, the Reformed deaconate required that applicants be professing members of the church for at least two years in order to receive assistance. Non-members could apply to municipal agencies for help. Expenditures from the Reformed deaconate rose from 40,000 guilders per year in 1600 to 500,000 guilders in the 1750's at a time when De Vries calculated that a poor family needed a minimum of 200 guilders per year to live. Modern readers might assume that the increase was only nominal and most of it due to price inflation, but price inflation was very limited due to the fact that money was gold and silver and the Bank of Amsterdam kept credit expansion to a minimum. As mentioned above, prices after 1660 fell, which is typical of gold based economies. Adjusted for deflation, the 500,000 guilders would have represented much greater purchasing power than the nominal amount.

Foreign visitors to the Dutch Republic, in Israel's account, marveled at the system of poor relief and charitable institutions and "its superiority over what one then found in neighboring countries…." Sir William Temple wrote that a home for aged seaman he visited was "a retreat stor'd with all the eases and conveniences, that old-age is capable of feeling and enjoying, a fitting retirement for those who had spent their whole lives in the hardships and incommodities of the sea." The resources spent and the orderly, well equipped, and efficient system of care for the elderly, sick and poor amazed visitors. Towns competed to build the most imposing orphanages, old people's homes, hospitals and workhouses for the poor. The quality of a town's hospital was considered a major test of the city's standing and status. An English visitor described an institution for the mentally ill as "…so stately that one would take it to be the house of some lord."

The historian Philip Gorsky wrote that, "Comparatively speaking, the Dutch system of social provision seems to have been very extensive and quite well funded. Such at least was the impression of foreign visitors to the Netherlands, who often commented on the number of almshouses that they encountered during their travels and on the cleanliness of these institutions and the quality of the care they provided."

After the revolt, the northern states widened the education gap between themselves and the Catholic southern states, as well as the rest of Europe. Both sides emphasized teaching the people their religious beliefs, but while Catholics used primarily oral teaching and art, Protestants since Erasmus had insisted on the centrality of understanding the teachings of Christ and the Apostles through personal Bible study, which required the ability to read. So the States, town councils, and Protestant churches established the goal of making cheap, subsidized primary education available to most children and instilling in them the necessary reading, discipline and confessional attitudes.

Schools instructed students in reading skills without charge to the parents, but if they wanted to learn to write or do arithmetic, they had to pay a small additional fee. In time, even that charge was dropped for the poorest children. The States gave the responsibility for licensing schools and appointing teachers to the town councils, or the nobility in rural areas, but to the churches they granted advisory roles concerning teachers and curriculum, and the burden of helping poor children with funds. As a result, by 1630, 57 percent of bridegrooms and 32 percent of brides could sign their names; by 1680, the figures had risen to 70 and 40 percent. In 1780, 87 percent of bridegrooms and 69 percent of brides could sign their names.

While aimed at spreading the faith, the high level of literacy helped diffuse many kinds of technical knowledge, including military and naval drill, and increased opportunities for the poor to move up in society. It also enabled humble men such as sailors and bargemen to read political and religious pamphlets that had become popular campaign tools.

> It is clear that in the Dutch Republic literacy among both men and women attained a level, and a literacy-based culture developed to an extent, which was wholly exceptional in Europe and which did not become normative elsewhere until centuries later. When the great scholar, Scaliger, arrived from France in 1593, he was astonished to find that even servant girls could read.

Education followed a different track in the southern States. The Jesuits took over the task of re-education and produced a new generation of Catholics as militant as the Protestants. While the Protestants in the north taught their children to read the Bible, the Jesuits produced a flood of devotional literature, art and architecture while the common people remained illiterate. The Jesuits, "inculcated a political and social outlook in the sons of the Catholic nobility and merchant class… hostile to toleration and the civic privileges and freedoms around them, an attitude militantly confessional and favourable to the new

Catholic princely absolutism…" As a result, in 1843, 51 per cent of army recruits in Belgium were illiterate while only 26 per cent of recruits in the United Provinces could not read.

Catholics tended to reject all innovations from the Dutch because they were Protestant and, unfortunately, that meant they rejected free markets as well. As a result, Catholic nations in Europe would remain poor and backward much longer than Protestant ones except for France which had abandoned the Church in favor of radical atheism and deism.

The Dutch appeared to have reduced crime in their republic compared to neighboring countries, according to historian Philip Gorski:

> Without exception, contemporary observers agreed that the level of crime in the Northern Netherlands was exceptionally low. In reference to Amsterdam, one English traveler remarked that: "'Tis rare to hear of any Disorders committed here in the Night-time, notwithstanding the great number and variety of Inhabitants and Strangers." A German traveler said much the same about Leiden, Holland's second largest city and the seat of its best-known university. "In Leiden," he claimed, "you can go out without a gun and leave your door unlocked, even If you will be away for days," the implication being that this was not the case in German university towns.

In contrast, John Locke found the level of crime in the south of France shocking. And the behavior of students in Paris was nothing like those of Leiden. Gorski quoted one traveler who wrote, "It is as dangerous at Madrid as at Lisbon…for a stranger to be abroad in the Streets in the Night-time. On the Contrary one may travel Day or Night in Holland, without fear of being robb'd or otherwise molested." The northern Rhineland was "generally regarded as the most dangerous area in all of western Europe. In the eyes of these travelers, and diarists, then, the Dutch Republic appears as an island of order in a sea of violence," according to Gorski.

Gorski provides some limited statistics to back up the claims. Leiden had just one hundred people convicted of murder in the first quarter of the seventeenth century. Amsterdam held 6.6 murder trials per 100,000 people in 1500 and that declined to 0.5 in 1670. However, Stockholm convicted 20 per 100,000 in the mid-sixteenth century and 36 per 100,000 in the last of the sixteenth. The murder rate in Paris in 1643 stood at 75 for each 100,000 people with 14 murdered in a single day in 1643 in Gorski's accounting.

The Dutch excelled at another measure of morality, too, legitimate births. The rate of out-of-wedlock marriages in Holland remained below 1 percent until the late eighteenth century when it rose to 2 percent. In Rotterdam and Maasluis, the rate of illegitimate births reached 3 percent around 1770. But in Paris, 8 percent of children were born to unwed parents in the 1710s and 25 percent in the 1770s. The rate rose from 3 percent to 10 percent in Nantes during the same period. "Moreover, the actual number of out-of-wedlock births was probably around twice as high as these figures suggest because illegitimate children in France were abandoned at about the same rates at which they were baptized, and illegitimacy was a common motive for abandonment," according to Gorski.

Christianity's contributions

Chapter 2 introduced Schoeck's explanation that the rise of capitalism in Western Europe depended upon Christianity's suppression of envy, especially in the admonition to love your neighbor as yourself. Loving your neighbor makes it difficult to envy him because of his accomplishments or success. But the admonition was over 1,500 years old when the Dutch Republic earned its freedom from Spain. Why had the command not produced capitalism in other Christian nations over such a long period of time? The answer lies in Christianity's unique contribution – individualism.

Schoeck demonstrated that individualism rarely exists in traditional cultures. Hofstede added empirical evidence that individualism is rare in poor countries and common in rich ones. Throughout time and across geography most cultures have suppressed those who would stand out in the group. Identity and rights came from the group. Constant, Stark and Siedentop show that the Greeks and Romans had no concept equivalent to the modern Western idea of Christian individualism. The accent for Plato and other philosophers fell on the needs of the city, not the individual, according to Rodney Stark in *Victory of Reason*:

> The notion that individualism was *discovered* seems absurd to the modern mind...Nevertheless, some cultures emphasize feelings of separate individuality while others stress collectivity and suppress the sense of self. In the latter kinds of culture, which seem to be in the great majority, a person's real sense of "being" is quite collective: whatever rights individuals possess are accorded not to them but to their *group* and are, in turn, conferred upon them *by their group*. In such circumstances, no one supposes that "I am the master of my fate." Instead, it is the idea of fatalism that rings true: that one's fate is beyond one's control, being fully determined by great external forces.

Societies need individualism in order for innovative people to achieve their potential to create new tools and processes that will benefit the group. Christian Europe carried the seed of the idea for almost 1,500 years, but it never sprouted in the sphere of economics until planted in the soil of the Dutch Republic. Much of the credit should probably go to Erasmus for his influence and teaching about personal spirituality. Erasmus taught people to obey the group, the Church, outwardly but to care for their own soul through person Bible study, prayer and helping the poor. Individualism, in turn, initiated a greater respect for equality before the law in which the nobility no longer formed an elite group that was above the law. The nobility could not steal the property of common people or start wars to plunder the wealth of others among the nobility.

The United Provinces made common people equal in status to nobility before the law, which shocked other Europeans, and they prohibited confiscation of property by the state without just compensation. They created militias to thwart the efforts of criminals to steal or defraud even the humblest citizen of his property and they enforced contracts. They reduced corruption among the militia and the court systems so that those charged with enforcing the law would do so without partiality. And the Republic respected the property of other nations, for while the Spanish continued to loot and pillage in the Americas, the Dutch traded with the natives.

In Europe outside the Republic, peasants enjoyed few rights to property. The nobility could take what they wanted from peasants, and as William of Orange learned, the king could take a noble's land if he fell out of favor. In contrast, the United Provinces established a legal structure that provided unprecedented protection for private property. Theologians since Thomas Aquinas had defended private property on the grounds that taking it without the consent of the owner violated the eighth commandment as well as the many other prohibitions of theft in the Bible. The Protestants of the Dutch Republic continued to sanctify private property, but while the Catholics wrote about its importance, the Dutch created laws and institutions to protect property.

On that foundation, Church scholars descending from the university at Salamanca, Spain, influenced the Dutch to recover the Biblical attitude of respect toward commerce and wealth. They rediscovered the "bourgeois values," as McCloskey wrote, for even if people have free markets they will not take advantage of them if they do not value commerce. The Dutch elevated business to a position of high esteem in society and church and encouraged profits as a sign of a man's diligence. In fact, Adam Smith wrote that in Holland it is "unfashionable no to be a man of business. Necessity makes it usual for almost every man to be so, and custom everywhere regulates fashion." They permitted the charging of interest on loans on the grounds that interest was nothing more than rent on money and no different than rent on land, which the Bible did not condemn. The result was, as Pieter de la Court wrote,

> And seeing the inhabitants under this free government, hope by lawful means to acquire estates, may sit down peaceably, and use their wealth as they please, without dreading that any indigent or wasteful prince, or his courtiers and gentry, who are generally prodigal, necessitous, and covetous as himself, should on any pretence whatever seize on the wealth of the subject; our inhabitants are therefore much inclined to subsist by the forenamed and other like ways or means, and gain riches for their posterity by frugality and good husbandry.

The preferred methods for gaining wealth throughout the Middle Ages involved war, extortion, ransom, accepting bribes, tax collection and rent-seeking, that is, getting a grant of a monopoly on trade or transportation and charging exorbitant prices. The Dutch made all of these illegal on the grounds that they violated the teachings of Scripture, leaving men with little but business and religion to exhaust their ambitions on. For the first time in European history, business achieved respectability.

Chapter 1 demonstrated that attitudes and institutions provide the greenhouse conditions for the innovation and technological advance that raised per capita income by enabling people to produce more for the same amount of effort, i.e., increased productivity. Many economists have written about the connection between institutions and economic development, as Prak noted in *Early Modern Capitalism*:

> At a basic level growth or stagnation is determined by the constant and self-reinforcing struggle between forces that obstruct or encourage technological progress (the approximate causes of growth). Yet the balance between constraints and stimuli depends on the institutional environment, most notably the system of property rights and the size and efficiency of the market (the ultimate causes of growth)…The transition to modern economic growth involved revolutionary changes in the political and institutional framework as well as the introduction of ground-breaking technologies."

In the United Provinces of the sixteenth and seventeenth centuries, the Dutch overhauled virtually every institution, including church, finance, government, schools and charity. These new institutions created the environment for great leaps in productivity that led to the world's highest standard of living. Such institutions do not spring to life from nothing, but owe their existence to the core values, beliefs and attitudes of the society and those come from their religion. According to Hofstede, the attitudes most important for economic develop are individualism, tolerance for ambiguity, and egalitarianism.

Without a doubt, Protestantism caused the rupture between the states of the Netherlands and the Spanish Empire. Most historians assert that the people rebelled against new taxes imposed by Spain, but they ignore the historical fact that the Dutch people paid much higher taxes under the Republic without bolting. The people of the Netherlands rebelled because they wanted to follow the Protestant faith, and the King of Spain tried to murder them for it. They rebelled not for economic reasons, as Marx and many historians insist, but for self-defense and religious freedom. Devout Protestants, such as William of Orange and Johan van Oldenbarnevelt led the fledgling nation, and its chief economist, Willem Usselincx, intended the Dutch West Indies Company to evangelize the heathen in the Americas. The Dutch may have acquired the necessary courage to break with millennia of precedence, established political theory and theology to establish their new nation without a monarch from the Huguenot (French Protestant) writers who insisted that kings and princes must be subject to the same laws of God as the people and could be deposed if they abused their privileges.

Hugo Grotius, the leading philosopher during the formative years of the United Provinces and founder of international maritime law, was also a Protestant theologian. Grotius and Oldenbarnevelt teamed up to shape a consultative government without a monarchy. Grotius argued in his writings that a consultative government with a strong constitution best preserves liberty, stability, virtue, and prosperity, and compared the Dutch Republic to ancient Judea, Athens and Rome. He venerated Erasmus, defended the Trinity, and fought for tolerance on secondary theological issues in the Dutch Reformed Church against the absolute conformity demanded by the radical Calvinists.

But Grotius also insisted that self-government would never work unless the majority of citizens submitted themselves to God. Gary De Mar in *God and Government* quoted Grotius who wrote, "He knows not how to rule a kingdome, that cannot manage a Province; nor can he wield a Province, that cannot order a City; nor can he order a City, that knows not how to regulate a Village; nor he a Village, that cannot guide a Family; nor can that man govern well a Family that knows not how to govern himselfe; neither can any govern himselfe unless his reason be Lord, Will and Appetite her Vassals: nor can Reason rule unless herselfe be ruled by God, and (wholly) be obedient to Him." In The Netherlands, Grotius is best known as the father of Dutch law. The obsession that the Dutch founding fathers had with the rule of law was their most significant contribution to Dutch economic development, because the rule of law made the Dutch Republic a safe place to invest in new businesses ventures.

The Dutch Protestants established another institution essential for the protection of private property – free markets. Markets implement the right to private property by freeing owners to use and dispose of their property as they desire. The opposite of a free market is a controlled one and control defines ownership. When the state sets prices and regulates the uses of property, it also takes away ownership and appropriates some of its value.

In the medieval economy, the church and state wrested control of property from its owners by regulating wages, prices, content, quality of work, working conditions and interest rates while promoting monopolies in order to block competition. Dutch Protestants freed property owners from most of these regulations. Also, the Dutch had elevated spiritual matters to the position of highest importance; they sacrificed their lives and property throughout an eighty-year war to achieve religious freedom. Economic matters held such a subordinate position to religious ones that the Dutch may have considered giving people more freedom in the market place to be a trivial matter.

Calvin was not the father

It is ironic that Weber and Tawney chose Calvinism as the spiritual father of capitalism when Calvinists, from John Calvin down through the seventeenth century, fought to preserve medieval economics and regulations with its low regard for commerce and property rights. Calvin had removed the stigma of charging interest for loans, but he insisted on the state's obligation to regulate every aspect of finance as well as the prices, wages, etc., of all other markets. Calvin's followers carried forward his emphasis on regulation. For example, Bucer, a disciple of Calvin and professor of divinity at Cambridge, tutored King Edward VI on economic matters. He encouraged the king to nationalize the textile industry, to force landowners to plow pastureland, and to fix the prices of merchants. He held merchants in low esteem, writing of them, "next to the sham priests, no class of men is more pestilential to the Commonwealth," according to Tawney in *Religion and the Rise of Capitalism*.

Calvin's Geneva emphasized order to the exclusion of freedom. Laws regulated what people could wear, eat, how they could entertain themselves and how late they could stay out. They controlled how servant girls could dress in order to maintain distinctions between social ranks according to Graham in *The Constructive Revolutionary*. Geneva fixed interest rates at 5 percent and penalized lenders for exceeding the limit by confiscating the principal and fining them. Eventually, the number of lawbreakers forced the city council to raise the limit to 6.67 percent. Still, many of those with money to lend found the risks too great for a 6.67 percent return and preferred to keep their money idle.

Geneva suffered from the general price inflation that hit Europe in the sixteenth century, and workers responded by demanding higher wages. In 1559, the Council passed maximum wage laws, as Graham wrote:

> Here there was discussion of workers who are so expensive and proud, a strange thing, so that no one can be found who wants to work in the vineyards. Therefore it is ordered to make public edicts that no one may pay masons, hat-makers, nor other workers nor laborers more than six sous per day, and to women ten quarters; and when they are fed, just half that, at a penalty of sixty sous, both for the worker and the master.

The Geneva city council censored the output of the printing industry and prohibited masters and laborers from organizing, requiring that they submit to the judgment of the council members on matters of wages and labor disputes. The law guaranteed job security to journeyman printers until a piece of work was complete, fixed the number of hours that the journeyman could work an apprentice and determined the number and length of holidays. The council abolished copyrights for editions of the Bible, catechisms, prayers and psalms, making them common property after the first impression. Since religious publications were the most popular and profitable, making them common property prevented printers from making up their losses on other topics with new editions of religious materials. The Geneva city council established quality standards and repossessed the licenses of those who failed to meet council standards. Most of the restrictions on commerce in Geneva did not originate with Calvin; many were ancient and part of the traditional attitude toward markets. But Calvin and the Consistory approved of them and expanded many.

Geneva allowed no room for privacy, even in the home according to Graham, for the council hired people to "play peeping tom to catch persons in private peccadilloes," and sent spies to parties in order to discover heresy. Unlike Erasmus, Calvin allowed no freedom of religion, public or private, no freedom in commerce, and stingy freedom in the bedroom. Society in Geneva suppressed the attitudes of individualism, acceptance of uncertainty, bourgeois values and egalitarianism that are necessary for capitalism to take root.

Radical Dutch Calvinists fought to rein in the freedom cherished by the Erasmian Protestants and mold the United Provinces in Geneva's image. Had Oldenbarnevelt, Grotius and others failed to curb the radical Calvinists of their day, the creation of a capitalist society may have been delayed until the establishment of the United States, if then.

Dutch influence

The Dutch perpetuated their economic hegemony for about two centuries. As late as 1720, "Novelty, innovation, cleanliness, prosperity, the magnificence of the towns, and relative absence of poverty compared to neighbouring countries: these were the hallmarks of

Dutch society...." Israel wrote. That year England and France witnessed two manic/depressive episodes, the South Seas bubble in England and the Mississippi bubble in France. Both were financial disasters that would make the earlier tulip bubble in the Dutch Republic wither in comparison.

The United Provinces, not England, "was still the world's technological showcase down to around 1740." Per capita income slipped in the latter part of the eighteenth and early nineteenth centuries, falling from $2,110 in 1700 (calculated in 1990 dollars) to $1,821 in 1820 according to Maddison in *The World Economy*. The rapid rise of protectionism and high tariff rates among all of its trading partners, as well as crushing taxes to pay for the many wars its neighbors had launched against it, were the chief causes of the decline. Other than the pre-emptive strike against England in 1688, the Dutch never initiated a war with its neighbors. With no new markets outside the country and a small domestic market, the Dutch responded by exporting technologies and investing in promising opportunities behind the barriers.

Still, the Dutch lived better than the British who had to get by on just $1,707 in per capita income in 1820. British per capita G.D.P. did not surpass that of the Dutch, which began growing again, until the latter part of the nineteenth century. British per capita income grew faster than that of any other European country from 1688 to 1820, Maddison wrote, due to the "improvement of its banking, financial and fiscal institutions and agriculture on a line which the Dutch had pioneered, and to a surge in industrial productivity at the end of the period." Even the "surge in industrial productivity," also known as the Industrial Revolution, owed a large debt to the improved security of private property and patent laws patterned after the Dutch model as well as transfers of Dutch technology and investment.

How did Dutch success influence the rest of Europe? Heckscher wrote in *Mercantilism*, "The Netherlands were the most hated, and yet the most admired and envied commercial nation of the seventeenth century." The so-called mercantile writers studied the Dutch economy for clues to its power and often cited it as the ideal system. Like the peasant in the Russian tale who did not ask for a goat from a visiting angel but that the angel might kill his neighbor's goat, their chief aim was to find ways to destroy Dutch wealth and power.

For example, the Great Colbert saw economics as a form of war. The Dutch in his opinion increased their trade in order to build their military power, and with sufficient power, the Dutch would dictate policy to the rest of Europe. For Colbert, limiting Dutch power meant destroying Dutch trade in any way possible. Heckscher quoted from a letter he wrote his cousin, the Intendant at the naval base of Rochefort in 1666 that, "Trade is the source of finance and finance is the vital nerve of war." Of the Dutch, according to Heckscher, he wrote that they

> acquire the trade of the whole world into their own hands...and to rob other nations of the same...Upon this they base the principal doctrine of their government, knowing full well that if they but have the mastery of trade, their powers will continually wax on land and sea and will make them so mighty that they will be able to set up as arbiters of peace and war in

Europe and set bounds at their pleasure to the justice and all the plans of princes.

In 1670, Colbert expressed French economic policy in this way according to Heckscher:

> It seems as if Your Majesty, having taken in hand the administration of your finances, has undertaken a monetary war against all European states. Your Majesty has already conquered Spain, Italy, Germany, England and several other countries, and has forced them into great misery and poverty. At their expense Your Majesty has waxed rich and so acquired the means of carrying out the many great works Your Majesty has undertaken and still daily undertakes. There remains only Holland, which still struggles with all its great power...Your Majesty has founded companies which attack them (the Dutch) everywhere like armies.

And in 1679, after one of several wars against the Dutch, Colbert wrote that Marseilles was "a city which must be employed in a constant trading war against all foreign commercial cities," as Heckscher quoted him. And Heckscher cited the English mercantilist Roger Coke who tried to rouse the English against the Dutch with his pamphlets: "…The whole of his work is permeated with bitterness and envy of the Dutch." William Petty aimed much of his work at "besting" the Dutch in the words of Joseph A. Schumpeter in his *History of Economic Analysis*.

Europeans did not hate the Dutch just because they were different and successful. In addition to pure envy, the wellspring of their enmity was a static view of wealth that was universally accepted – the idea that the total amount of wealth in the world is limited, like a pie. If one nation intends to increase the size of its slice of wealth, it can do so only by taking part of the slice of another. Authors from millennia past have expressed the thought that one man (or nation) cannot increase his wealth except at the expense of others. Such "limited wealth" economics dominates the thinking of most people on the planet today, including that of many professional economists and is the reason most poor nations in the world think they are poor because the rich West stole their wealth

Some of the greatest thinkers of the period espoused pie economics, including Roger Bacon according to Heckscher who commented, "Any attempt at economic advance by one's own efforts in one country must therefore have appeared pointless, unless it consisted in robbing other countries of part of their possessions. Scarcely any other element in mercantilist philosophy contributed more to the shaping of economic policy, and even of foreign policy as a whole." In France, Michel de Montaigne wrote in his "Essais" in 1580 that "no profit can be made except at another's expense, and so by this rule we should condemn any sort of gain," as reported by Erik S. Reinhert in "Benchmarking Success: The Dutch Republic (1500-1750)."

Since ancient Israel, the world had never seen a nation grow wealthy without having conquered another empire and looted its wealth as the Spanish were doing to the Stone Age empires in the Americas. So kings assigned their wisest advisors to figure out how the Dutch had done it. The result turned out to be a hodgepodge of mostly bad advice, such as that which Colbert implemented. Historians call it "mercantilism" but there was no unified theory. Had they merely read Pieter de la Courts' excellent book on Holland they would have saved time and inflicted much less misery on their people. Nevertheless, the practice caused people to specialize in the subject of economic development and attempt to discover the Dutch secret. After de la Court, the French physiocrats were the first to see behind the veil, followed by Richard Cantillon and then Adam Smith. Essentially, those economists rediscovered the truths that de la Court had written about and before him what the Salamancan scholars had written.

The next chapter traces the influence of the Dutch on other European powers and how they responded.

Chapter 6 – Fading Empires

The French and English respond

The United Provinces fought Spain for eighty years to reach freedom, finally achieving it in 1647. Capitalism gave the Dutch a competitive advantage in shipping, freight rates, and finance and a wide range of higher quality manufactured goods. As a result, Dutch merchants dominated trade with all other European countries. It did not matter to the English or the French that trading with the Dutch lowered the cost of living for their own citizens; they had eyes only for the gold from the king's treasury sailing for Holland. They allowed the Dutch only a short rest from warfare because of their envy and medieval economic theories.

Rather than learn from the Dutch and improve their own efficiency, the French and English chose to try to conquer and loot their competitor. In 1651, the English passed the Navigation Acts to limit trade with the Dutch. Both England and France passed volumes of protectionist legislation. When those failed to slow Dutch success, the English resorted to violence. Under Cromwell, a Protestant, the English attacked in 1652 and fought until agreeing to a peace settlement in 1654. They attacked again in 1664 but lost the war three years later, although they managed to keep the Dutch colony of New York in North America.

The French chose to combat the Dutch economic juggernaut by having the state control French commerce. King Louis XIV appointed Jean-Baptiste Colbert, revered by the French as the Great Colbert, as Minister of Finances in 1665. Colbert held the position until 1683. He raised tariffs, built state-owned industries to produce a variety of goods, prevented many workers from emigrating, and created monopolies on trade with the Middle East and Africa. He wrote quality standards for many products and imposed severe punishments for producing inferior goods. To protect existing cloth makers, for example, Colbert outlawed calico prints and a few who broke the law paid with their lives.

Colbert did some good for the state by rationalizing the tax collection system and building roads. But after one of his speeches to businessmen advertising all he had done for them, he asked what else he could do. A businessman in the back shouted *"Laissez-nous faire!"* or "leave us alone." The speaker has remained anonymous, but he gave us one of the most important terms in economics: laissez faire. In spite of Colbert's vigorous efforts over two decades, the French economy did not prosper. Apologists for Colbert point to the drain on state finances caused by war, but the truth is that the measures Colbert implemented could never have increased the wealth of the French people but could only impoverish them further. Still, governments continue to imitate Colbert's methods, except for executing offenders of his policies.

In response to the massive failures of Colbert's policies to lift standards of living, the French raised tariffs against Dutch imports to prohibitive levels. Portugal, Sweden, Denmark and Spain followed and inflicted enormous damage on the Dutch economy. But when the smoke of the commercial battle cleared, the Dutch still led the world in trade. French impatience boiled over in 1672 and they teamed with the English to launch a war against the United Provinces again. For the English, this was the third act of aggression against the Dutch in twenty-five years. The French marched up the Rhine with 120,000 troops against a Dutch force one-fourth that size, while the English attacked the smaller Dutch navy. The Dutch navy routed the English in almost every battle and forced Charles II to withdraw from the war in 1674. With the help of Austria and Spain, the Dutch chased the French out of their country, too.

Tensions remained high in Europe after the war, but Dutch trade rebounded. As the French economy withered, Louis XIV again resorted to high tariffs. The Dutch became convinced that France and England were about to join forces to attack again and their military leadership doubted that the little republic could survive another assault by the two leviathans. Their only chance of survival would be a preemptive strike against the weaker partner. So in 1688, one hundred years after the Spanish attempt at invading England, the Dutch launched a fleet of 453 ships, four times the size of the Spanish armada, across the channel. With William III at the head, the Dutch army entered London without firing a shot. William's father-in-law, James II, fled to France.

The combined might of the United Provinces, England, the Habsburg Empire, and Spain proved insufficient to defeat the French and war dragged on for another nine years. The Dutch had planned the invasion of England in order to rescue their nation from certain military defeat, but it proved to have far greater consequences for the world. The English would call the Dutch occupation the Glorious Revolution, for "what occurred in 1688-9 changed Britain fundamentally, creating, for the first time, a stable, and powerful, constitutional monarchy, with parliament increasingly in the ascendant," according to Israel.

The reign of William and Mary in England contrasted sharply with the previous regimes. In the earlier part of the seventeenth century, the Stuarts had initiated repeated fiscal crises that increased their debt, for which the monarchs alone were responsible. To pay expenses, they had forced the nobility to loan them money, sold monopolies, confiscated wealth and trampled on property rights in general. William and Mary arrived armed with the Dutch way of organizing government and finance and a Christian respect for private property. Parliament began meeting regularly, assumed a greater role in governing and introduced excise taxes to fund the public debt, for which parliament shared ownership with the king.

In further imitation of Holland, parliament established the Bank of England in 1694 to manage the debt. These innovations empowered parliament to raise substantially more money at lower interest rates than ever before. The Dutch even gained indirect control of English foreign policy because a significant share of the borrowed funds came from the Netherlands and in order to attract the funds, English foreign policy had to please the Dutch lenders.

In addition, the Dutch-inspired parliament created an organized market for public and private securities, a more rational system of taxation and a smaller bureaucracy. The Dutch could not persuade parliament to allow English businesses the freedom that their Dutch counterparts enjoyed, and parliament continued to insist on state regulation of the economy as in France. Generally, though, parliament lacked the means to enforce regulations so that British entrepreneurs enjoyed a freedom that was rare on the continent outside of the United Provinces. Concerning the Dutch legacy in England, Nobel Prize winning economist Douglas C. North wrote in *Institutions, Institutional Change and Economic Performance*,

> the fundamental changes in the English polity as a consequence of the Glorious Revolution were a critical contributing factor to the development of the English economy…The security of property rights and the development of the public and private capital markets were instrumental factors not only in England's subsequent rapid economic development, but in its political hegemony and ultimate dominance of the world. England could not have beaten France without its financial revolution (Dickson, 1967); the funds made available by the growth in debt from 1688 to 1697 were a necessary condition for England's success in the ongoing war with France as well as in the next one (from 1703 to 1714) from which England emerged the major power in the world.

The civic institutions that protected private property, limited the size of government, and created efficient and sound financial institutions prepared England for the coming industrial revolution, much of which the Dutch financed. Through its influence on England, the Dutch laid the foundations for similar institutions in the thirteen British colonies in North America, also. But they had a more direct influence through the founding of the Dutch colony of New York in 1624, and through their influence on the Pilgrims who had spent twelve years in Holland after leaving England.

Legacy in the British colonies

The Pilgrims who landed at Plymouth Rock were devout Calvinists and tried to build Geneva in the New World by controlling production and prices. From its founding, the colony practiced a form of socialism in which those with the ability worked while the government distributed the food according to need so that "all profits and benefits that are got by trade, traffic, trucking, working, fishing, or any other means" had to be deposited in a common storehouse and "all such persons as are of this colony, are to have their meat, drink, apparel, and all provisions out of the common stock," as Richard Maybury quoted Bradford in "The Great Thanksgiving Hoax."

The consequences were ugly and deadly. Bradford wrote in his book, *History of Plymouth Plantation*, that harvests of 1621 and 1622 were stingy, providing only enough to survive the winter. "The first 'Thanksgiving' was not so much a celebration as it was the last meal of condemned men," Maybury wrote. The harvests were meager because many people refused to work in the fields when others who did not work received the produce. In addition, much of the produce was stolen before it was harvested. As a result, the colony suffered from corruption, confusion and discontent.

During their sojourn in the Dutch Republic, Bradford and the other pilgrims had considered Dutch Christians to be too greedy for material gain, so they left to establish a more spiritually minded society in the New World in which, like the early church in the book of Acts in the Bible, they held all material wealth in common. In his struggle to find a way to increase the food supply, Bradford may have remembered the great wealth of the Dutch Republic, especially the abundance of food, for which the Pilgrims had once held great contempt. Out of desperation, he decided to imitate the Dutch and resurrect the ancient idea of private property. He divided the land among the remaining families and instructed them that they could eat only what they raised for themselves.

The harvest of 1623 was so large that it surprised even the Pilgrims. Bradford wrote, "'instead of famine now God gave them plenty and the face of things was changed, to the rejoicing of the hearts of many, for which they blessed God.' Thereafter, he wrote, 'any general want or famine hath not been amongst them since to this day.'" In 1624 they began to export food.

But the Puritans continued to regulate commerce after the pattern of Calvin's Geneva by setting prices and punishing merchants who earned more than a 5 percent profit in a year, or 5 percent interest on a loan to an individual or 10 percent on commercial loans. For example, in November 1639, a fellow merchant in Boston accused Robert Keayne of selling six-penny nails for ten pence a pound, in other words, of overcharging customers. Others flocked to denounce the merchant for similar crimes, accusing him of earning profits of up to 100 percent. The General Court fined him 200 pounds according to Mark Valeri in *Heavenly Merchandize: How Religion Shaped Commerce in Puritan America*. Keayne had apprenticed in England in the Christian humanist tradition of Erasmian Protestants that originated in the Dutch Republic before immigrating to Boston. Valeri wrote,

> Hostile to religious sectarianism, northern humanists wrote in pragmatic terms about the need for European states to mitigate poverty and political oppression without degenerating into chaos, and they often turned to the new middle class, including its merchants, as agents of social reform. This ideology informed the civic leaders of the seventeenth-century Netherlands. Patriotic, nationalistic, and pragmatic, Dutch magistrates favored commerce, approved of increased personal consumption of luxury goods, and ignored Calvinist clergy who complained of secularism, materialism, and selfishness.

But the Puritan fathers of Boston would not tolerate merchants like Keayne. Sermons criticized every aspect of commerce. They condemned buying goods where they were plentiful, transporting then and selling them where they were scarce; trading in bonds, foreign notes, bills of exchange and other financial innovations; storing surplus goods when prices fell in order to sell them when prices rose; using notaries, lawyers and brokers; and earning any interest on loans. Valeri wrote, "Usury served as a synecdoche for the abuse of nearly any form of credit. Preachers made it synonymous with oppression when goods were sold on credit at unfair prices, with rent racking when lodging was provided on credit at inflated rates, or with unfair labor practices when debtors worked off their loans at low wages."

The great Puritan theologian Cotton Mather preached that merchants should never charge more than the "intrinsic" value of goods or the price set by local custom, meaning the price determined by the town council. He and other Puritan leaders subscribed to a form of fatalism that may have followed logically from the Calvinist doctrine of predestination, which taught that God had chosen who will go to heaven before he created the universe. In a similar way, they believed God was sovereign over who gained wealth or lived in poverty and man had no say in it. Planning carefully in order to do well in business merely advertised one's pride and denied the sovereignty of God.

After a series of sermons on trade by Mather, Keayne's church, the First Church of Boston, formally censured him, "a punishment just short of excommunication," according to Valeri. The government ordered a day of fasting by the public and "lamented the merchant's 'excessive Rates' as a 'Dishonor of Gods Name,' an 'Offence of the Generall Court,' and the 'Publique Scandall of the Cuntry.'" In a later sermon Mather compared Keayne's offense to Judas' betrayal of Jesus for thirty pieces of silver. John Cotton likened merchants to King Herod in the Bible who became infatuated with his step-daughter after she danced for him and ordered the beheading of John the Baptist. The Boston church asserted the right to limit profits, assess the quality of workmanship, and judge the motives of businessmen.

The irony in the Puritan attitude toward commerce is that it did not come from the Bible, as they claimed, but from pagans such as Plato, Aristotle and Cicero. Puritans, following Calvin, took pride in the doctrine of *sola scriptura*, which meant they followed no Pope or tradition but the Bible only as the guide to godly living. They were unaware that the near idolatrous veneration of Aristotle and Cicero by the early church fathers had caused them to adopt the pagan Roman and Greek attitudes toward commerce and baptize them as Christian.

The pagan attitude issued from envy and the false notion that one man can gain only at the expense of another. Puritans expressed their envy in their constant concern for equality of wealth among their members. They preached that businessmen should not pursue profits, should limit commercial ventures, never charge interest and always gives alms on the spot to the needy. Thomas Hooker "condemned all creditors as hypocritical, mendacious, and covetous. The notion of a rich Christian, he claimed in equal excess, was a contradiction in terms," according to Valeri. Puritans held up the example of Christians depicted in the first chapters of the book of Acts in the New Testament who sold all they had and shared their wealth the less fortunate, ignoring the fact that the incident was unique and did not become a pattern for the church in the following years, though Christians always practiced charity. They labeled the practice of raising prices an oppression of others.

The ironworks on the Saugus River exemplify Puritan stubbornness. The colony needed iron in the 1640s so the government built two small foundries at Braintree and Lynn on the river. They employed manual laborers, managers, woodsmen, miners, smelters, transporters and colliers (charcoal makers). After years of failure under Winthrop's management, the government sold out to private investors, including Robert Keayne. But the government set the price of the finished iron and insisted that all of the output be sold in New England. As a result, the investors continually lost money and drove one investor to resort to embezzlement. When the owners complained about their losses, the preachers told them to "trust God to provide the necessary income," according to Valeri.

The Catholic scholars at the University of Salamanca, Spain, had recovered the real Biblical doctrines of commerce. Calvin erred greatly in not investigating that theology and unwittingly promoting a pagan tradition as Christian. Calvin could have prevented decades of grief had he studied the centuries of debate within the church on the just price, which scholars ultimately determined was the market price. Calvinists in the Dutch Republic and Puritans in England and the colonies perpetuated that error while persecuting merchants like Keayne who held the true Biblical doctrines. And the intense opposition to almost all innovations of any kind seems to have come from a longing for an idyllic past that never existed.

Fortunately, Calvin's economics survived only the first generation of Puritans. Merchants earned greater respect when the first economic depression of the 1640s increased their importance to the community. After the Glorious Revolution of 1688, Puritans began to identify more with other Protestants and appreciate the importance of a powerful English military for keeping the dreaded Catholics away. They grasped the fact that commercial success paid the taxes necessary to keep armies in the field. A new charter for the colony forced greater tolerance for other Protestant sects, especially Anglicans, who attracted more merchants with a high regard for commerce. Boston merchants traded more with Dutch merchants in New York who had a similar theology of business. Those merchants began to dominate city councils and restrain the power of the pastors over businesses. Succeeding generations of Puritan theologians began to embrace the respect for commerce that the Dutch and English enjoyed.

From 1690 to 1699, prominent ministers gathered at Harvard for irregular debates on church polity and other topics including business. They criticized lotteries and gambling as vices and discussed usury, which encompassed earning profits from loans to needy debtors, trading in money, mortgages, or other securities, determining interest rates according to the market, and making any other loan that guaranteed a profit. But by the end, the clergy informed New Englanders that they no longer regarded usury as a sin. They abandoned older Puritan readings of Scripture for reliance on economic analysis, patriotism, and practical necessity. The second generation of Boston clergy began to study business instead of continually condemning it. They bought Davenants' *Discourses on the Public Revenues, and on Trade in England* (London, 1698) and *An essay upon the Probable Methods of making a People Gainers in the Balance of Trade* (London, 1699) and Child's *New Discourse on Trade*, (London, 1694).

By the turn of the seventeenth century, Puritan ministers no longer equated commerce with greed, but with "industriousness and prudence, moral reform and Protestantism's interest in the world. They maintained that providence used overseas traders to protect English liberty and spread civilization," in Valeri's account. Isaac Newton, having been a great theologian as well as history's greatest scientist, influenced Puritan pastors. Instead of viewing the hand of God directly causing events in the physical world, Newton described 'nature as a system integrated into a regular pattern by universal physical laws' that God had created. God worked indirectly through natural laws. Soon philosophers began to find similar natural laws working in society to promote prosperity and order as well as to restrain vice. Prosperity no longer resulted from God's favor at a Christian's devotion but from following the natural laws of the market, and financial hardship was not a sign of God's wrath as much as failure to understand and abide by God's natural laws according to Valeri.

> Writers on both sides of the Atlantic probed the meaning of the economy as a subset of this cosmic order. They described commerce as a series of natural exchanges that, by the law of nature, coalesced into a balanced system. This reading prompted pastors and merchants to imagine the natural dynamics of exchange as a divinely sanctioned, moral good. Innate desires brought people together into networks of trade that depended on mutuality, confirming the natural integration of variety into a whole; as Foxcroft put it, nature "impresses men with a deep sense of the bonds and benefits of society; and so excites them to feel the good of others" as they pursued their own economic good, "rendering their work daily more and more natural." God designed the market system that ran by moral laws.

Some of the preachers learned economics well enough to express excellent monetary policy. For example, the great Jonathan Edwards preached a sermon in which he admonished the state to reduce its emissions of paper currency because the excess money caused rising prices, borrowing for speculation, and cheating of lenders by allowing debtors to repay loans in paper money worth much less than when they had taken out the loan.

Puritan Calvinists had finally arrived at the philosophy with which the sociologist Max Weber began his treatise that places the birth of capitalism in Calvinism's doctrine of predestination. But it took Calvinists over a century to get there and when they arrived, they had merely traversed the two centuries that separated them from the scholars of the School of Salamanca and caught up to the other Protestant sects that had embraced those ideas much earlier, such as the Dutch.

During the nineteenth century in the old world, David Ricardo, J. B. Say and other economists divorced economic thought from the theology of the Late Scholastics and Dutch Protestants, ending finally in J. S. Mill's rejection of Christianity and embracing socialism, which he dishonestly called "liberalism." But economics continued to be entwined with theology for most of the century in the U.S., creating what one historian has labeled a school of "clerical laissez-faire." The most influential member of the school was the Reverend Francis Wayland who wrote the most popular economics textbook before the Civil War. Wayland briefly pastored the First Baptist Church of Boston beginning in 1821. In 1827 he became president of the Baptist affiliated Brown University in Rhode Island and remained until his retirement in 1855. He introduced political economy to the school and taught it using Adam Smith and J. B. Say's texts until he wrote his own, first published in 1837.

Wayland and the other clerical economists approached the discipline from a moral perspective much as the Scholars of Salamanca had three centuries before. They saw the science of political economy as laws that mankind must follow in the same way they obeyed the laws of the natural sciences. Those laws reflected human nature as created by God, which was originally good but had a tendency toward evil because of the rebellion in the Garden. Following God's laws meant prosperity for people and disobeying them caused poverty and suffering. Those laws called for individual responsibility, private property, free markets and minimal government intervention in the economy. Wayland thought of himself as a theologian first and then a political economist and presented laissez-faire as Christian economics. He wrote,

> By science, as the word is here used, we mean a systematic arrangement of the laws which God has established, so far as they have been discovered, of any department of human knowledge. It is obvious, upon the slightest reflection, that the Creator has subjected the accumulation of the blessings of this life to some determinate laws. Every one, for instance, knows that no man can grow rich, without industry and frugality. Political Economy, therefore, is a systematic arrangement of the laws by which, under our present constitution, the relations of man, whether individual or social, to the objects of his desire, are governed.

Wayland taught that we are required "so to construct the arrangements of society, as to give free scope to the laws of Divine Providence." We must "give to these rewards and penalties their free and their intended operation." For example, he listed the ways in which God's laws increase the standards of living of nations:

Men will be richer, and therefore may be happier, as the following conditions are complied with:

1. As the laws of nature, designed by our Creator for our benefit, are understood;

2. As the means are devised for availing ourselves, in the most successful manner, of the utility of these laws;

3. As the human labor necessary to be expended, is so arranged as, with a given expenditure, to produce the greatest and most perfect result; and

4. As the inhabitants of the earth, in different localities, devote themselves most exclusively to the production of those objects of desire, for the production of which they have received, either directly or indirectly, from their Creator, the greatest facilities.

Or, still more generally, production will be abundant, that is, man will enjoy the means of physical happiness, in proportion to his individual industry, both of body and mind; and to the degree of harmony and good feeling which exists between the individuals of the same society; and also between the different societies themselves.

Wayland saw all exchanges in the market as exchanges of services whether physical products were involved or not, as Frederick Bastiat would express it in France. Many of God's blessings are free, such as the sun, air and water. Wild fruit and animals such as deer are free for the taking. Those items achieved value in exchange, or in other words someone could charge a price for them only because the seller labored to supply them to others. For example, no one would pay for water that they could get from a nearby stream with little effort. But if someone lived miles from fresh water and did not have the means to travel to it, they would have to pay another for the service of collecting and transporting the water for them. The trading of bread for lumber was at its heart an exchange of the labor of baking the bread for the labor of cutting down a true and sawing it into lumber. "But it is plain, that if a man expend labor in the creation of a value, this labor gives him a right to the exclusive possession of that value; that is, supposing the original elements belonged to no one else," Wayland wrote.

Foreshadowing Hayek, Wayland understood that labor requires capital, if nothing more than a shovel, and the greater the amount of capital the more workers than can be hired. Workers lacking capital are virtually useless, even in such a simple job as cutting grass where the lawn mower is the capital. Capital also requires labor, for equipment without the labor to use it is worthless as well. Mainstream economists would be wiser if they kept that relationship in mind when writing about recessions because recessions result not just from sticky prices and wages. For the most part, long term unemployment happens because of the destruction of the value of the capital that workers had relied upon for their employment.

Wayland attributed the prosperity of the U.S. in the first half of the nineteenth century to the success of following God's economic principles and the accumulation of capital:

> Here distressing poverty, or poverty which shortens life, except it arise from intemperance, or from some form of vice or indolence, is very rare. The common laborer, if industrious, virtuous, and frugal, may not only support himself, but, in a few years, accumulate a valuable little capital. And notwithstanding the great immigration of foreigners, the wages of labor are annually rising. Hence, it is evident, that the increase of capital more than keeps pace with the natural and imported increase of the human race.

> In Ireland, the case is reversed. There, the lowest classes are, and have been for a long period, in the most abject poverty. Multitudes of them are said to die, annually, of famine. He is considered in tolerable circumstances, who is able to furnish his family with a hovel, with one full meal of potatoes a day, and with a sufficient supply of straw to be spread upon the earthy floor for

bedding. The reason I suppose to be, that, in addition to the deplorable ignorance of the people, the land is owned in England; and the rent, collected by rapacious underlings, is annually carried away and spent in England, instead of being turned into fixed capital in Ireland. Hence, the annual increase adds but little to the capital of the country; and the people must starve or emigrate.

Wayland also saw that the government could destroy property and capital:

> But the right of property may be violated by society. It sometimes happens, that society, or government, which is its agent, though it may prevent the infliction of wrong by individuals upon each other, is by no means averse to inflicting wrong or violating the right of individuals itself. This is done, where governments seize upon the property of individuals by mere arbitrary act, a form of tyranny, with which all nations of Europe were, of old, too well acquainted. It is also done, by unjust legislation; that is, when legislators, how well soever chosen, enact unjust laws, by which the property of a part, or of the whole, is unjustly taken away, or what is the same thing subjected to oppressive taxation.

The heart of Wayland's clerical laissez-faire was the harmony it produces in society between capitalists and labor and between producers and consumers. When people specialize in the production of those services they had the greatest skill at, they depend on others to supply them through trade with the necessities and pleasures they desire but cannot make. As a result, everyone grows wealthier and society more peaceful. As he put it,

> We see, in the above remarks, another illustration of the truth, that the benefit of one is the benefit of all, and the injury of one is the injury of all. If a man economize labor and capital, he increases his own wealth, and he also rescues as much as he saves, from actual destruction. The whole of this amount may go to the further increase of production, or to the satisfying of human wants. The more he produces, the greater is his wealth; and the greater is the value which is created for the good of the whole community. Hence, we see, that he who is honestly promoting his own welfare, is also promoting the welfare of the whole society of which he is a member.

Wayland's Christian laissez-faire continued to dominate American economics until Richard Ely returned from Germany as a flaming socialist and established the American Economic Association in 1885 to promote socialism in the U.S.

The Catholic Counter Reformation

Dutch capitalism and technology spread to Sweden and parts of Germany, improving the lives of people in those countries as well. But in Catholic Europe, stagnation reigned until the nineteenth century, in spite of the fact that Spain stole so much gold and silver from the Americas that it tripled Europe's silver supply in the sixteenth and seventeenth centuries and ignited rates of inflation that were high for the times. Taxes in France achieved such levels as to constitute confiscation. Adam Smith pointed out that the French farmer "was afraid to have a good team of horses or oxen, but endeavors to cultivate with the meanest and most wretched instruments of husbandry that he can," so as to appear poor to the tax collector and evade taxes on them according to Stark in *How the West Won*. "Writing to a friend back in France during a visit to England, Voltaire expressed his surprise that the British farmer 'is not afraid to increase the number of his cattle, or to cover his roof with tile, lest his taxes be raised next year." Clearly, Voltaire enjoyed no comparative advantage in economics.

The Catholic Church responded to the Reformation by rejecting the concept of free markets because of its close association with Protestantism. As a result, it kept most of Europe chained to medieval ideas of economics. Michael Novak wrote in The *Spirit of Democratic Capitalism*, "In the nineteenth century, the social structure of Catholic Italy, Spain, and Austro-Hungary was still feudal, monarchical, and mercantilist. In 1864, the, at first, liberal pope, Pius IX… condemned nearly every thesis of a liberal society root and branch in his famous 'Syllabus of Errors.'"

Spanish decline

We should credit the Dutch for at least partially having created the field of economics, although it was not one of their goals. Previous chapters in this book honored Church scholars, especially those of Salamanca, as the first economists because they discovered principles of economics that, once lost, took the West two centuries or more to find again. Among those principles are the subjective theory of value and the quantitative theory of money. But the investigations into the workings of commerce and finance by the scholars always aimed at orienting the ethical status of business practices; economics was a sub discipline of moral philosophy.

The mercantilist writers were the first to consider economics as a separate discipline and as a means to promote development. Of course, their goal was to fill the king's chest with gold so he could go to war more often and for longer periods. Antipathy to Dutch wealth and dominance of trade inspired mercantilism just as opposition to mercantilism gave rise to Adam Smith and classical economics. Not that the Dutch practiced mercantilism; they did not. They practiced free trade until long after their trading partners had shut them out. But the burning question of the age for Europe outside of the Dutch Republic was how could Spain, with its mountains of gold and silver from the Americas, become so poor while the tiny United Provinces, poor in natural resources, had become so rich?

Historians estimate that between 1521 and 1590 Spain extracted three hundred tons of gold and twenty-seven thousand tons of silver from its American colonies according to Stark in *How the West Won*. That tripled the stock of silver in Europe and increased the gold supply by 20 percent. The resulting inflation led the Salamancan scholars to discover the quantity theory of money in which, all other things being equal, an increase in the money stock will cause prices to rise proportionally.

The Spanish empire consisted of far more than the Iberian Peninsula minus Portugal. Charles V inherited the power of Europe's greatest dynasties. As head of the House of Habsburg he ruled over Germany and Austria. From the House of Valois-Bergundy he gained the Netherlands, which at the time included modern Belgium. And with the rule of the House of Trastamara of Castile and Aragon came Spain, Sicily, Sardinia and southern Italy.

But defending and expanding that sprawling empire as well as fending off repeated Ottoman attacks in the east required even more funds than Charles' ships could haul across the ocean so he acquired huge debts. Charles' successor and son, Philip II, inherited that debt and in 1556 Philip declared bankruptcy for the first time. He would declare bankruptcy again in 1596, then in 1607, 1627, 1647, and 1653. Each bankruptcy ruined the lenders.

Had Spain enjoyed the manufacturing base of the Dutch it probably still could not have afforded the expense of such a vast and well supplied military as Charles and Philip maintained. But Spain had virtually no manufacturing and trade followed one path, from other nations to Spain. The small amount of manufacturing Spain had before the conquest of the Americas drowned in the deluge of gold and silver pouring in as the wealthy could afford the higher quality goods from elsewhere, especially from the Dutch where most of the Spanish gold washed ashore.

Nor did Spain develop an indigenous merchant class. Foreigners, mostly Italian, conducted most of the import/export business because the Spanish retained the ancient disdain for commerce. Stark wrote in *How the West Won*, "This was a source of pride among leading Spanish citizens – known as the hidalgos. Manufacturing and commerce were for inferior people and nations, so let others toil for Spain, was how they put it."

Spain had to import a large amount of its food because of its poor soil and an institution known as the *Mesta*. The Spanish raised sheep that produced high quality wool which they exported and provided tax revenue to the king. The tax revenue was so important that the king gave the sheep industry preeminence over the property rights of land owners. The sheep herds migrated seasonally north and south to better pastures across lands the shepherds did not own, but the law required land owners to give the sheep free passage, the *Mesta*. The number of sheep was so large that it prevented farmers from growing crops on the lands in the path of the migrations.

In the armada that sailed for England in 1588, only the soldiers and sailors were Spanish and not all of them. The ships, guns, cannon balls, gunpowder and biscuits were all imported. When a shortage of cannon balls fell on Madrid in 1572, Phillip had to quickly import Italian cannon ball makers because no one in Spain knew how to make them. According to North, quoted in Stark's *How the West Won*, Spain's "economy remained medieval throughout its bid for political dominance. Where it retained political sway, as in the Spanish Netherlands, the economy of the area withered." Like France, Spain chose to cling to traditional, medieval ways rather than learn from the Dutch and prosper. Instead, it withered into insignificance.

The Ottoman Empire

The other super power of the sixteenth and seventeenth centuries was an Islamic caliphate, the Ottoman Empire, which dominated the Middle East, North Africa and Eastern Europe as no other had since the fall of Rome. In 1688 it attacked Vienna. Had the Ottomans won the battle, they probably would have conquered all of Western Europe as well. Europeans cowered in terror of the empire that curved like a scimitar from Austria around the eastern Mediterranean to Algiers. But in the three centuries that followed, Western Europe and the Ottoman Empire danced a slow economic and military pas de deux until the two had traded places in the nineteenth century. How did it happen? Did the Ottoman Empire disintegrate? Why, today, are the nations that descended from the Ottoman Empire considered ignorant, poor and backward, terms the Ottoman's had used for Western Europe in 1500?

The Ottoman Empire lasted from before the Renaissance until World War I. Its influence persists to this day in the Middle Eastern and North African countries that once made up the empire. Many intellectuals in those nations accuse the West, particularly the U.S., of being the rich oppressor of poor nations and the cause of their poverty. But the reality is that, as with France and Spain, neither the Empire nor its descendants developed the principles or institutions that empower economies to grow in the manner that the countries of Western Europe had. Oddly, the Ottoman Empire encouraged free trade with other nations three hundred years before Adam Smith, but within the Empire, the state strangled business with regulations while Sultans exercised arbitrary rule and frequently appropriated private property.

The great obstacle to grasping the cause of the decline in the Ottoman Empire is the myth of the Islamic golden age, very much like the myth of Spain's golden age. Like the Spanish, the Ottoman's held commerce in contempt while depending on conquest to acquire the wealth needed for war.

Istanbul

As the sixteenth century faded, the Ottoman Empire retained its position as the wealthiest, most powerful empire of its day. Its capitol, Istanbul, sheltered 1.2 million people of varying races and religions, far more than any European city. It boasted of having over 7,000 mosques, nine hospitals, 1,900 primary schools, 14,500 public baths, hundreds of mansions, the Sultan's palace, the magnificent Suleymaniye mosque, and the Hagia Sophia church converted into a mosque and an architectural marvel even a millennium after its construction, according to Bernard Lewis' *Istanbul and the Civilization of the Ottoman Empire.*

The heart of a rich and growing empire, Instanbul became a magnet for artists, writers, scholars, soldiers, statesmen, merchants and thousands of Jews fleeing Spain. A seventeenth century poet expressed the pride and love that Ottomans felt for their capitol in a lengthy poem. Here is a small excerpt from Lewis' book:

> May God cause Istanbul to flourish
> For it is the home of all great affairs.
> Birthplace and school of famous men,
> The nursery of many nations,
> Whatever men of merit there may be
> All win their renown in Istanbul.
> The heavens may turn about the earth as they will
> They will find no city like Istanbul.
> Drawing and painting, writing and gilding
> Achieve beauty and grace in Istanbul.
> However many different arts there may be
> All find brilliance and luster in Istanbul.
> Because its beauty is so rare a sight
> The sea has clasped it in an embrace.
> All the arts and all the crafts
> Find honor and glory in Istanbul.

In the early 1700's, the residents of Istanbul consumed 200 tons of grain per day so providing cheap bread for the city's residents burdened the Sultan, who considered this job too important to leave to the market because shortages in the past had caused the troops to revolt and citizens to riot. The Grand Vizier, whose role was similar to that of a Prime Minister, led an army of bureaucrats who inspected the grain and bread supplies and set prices daily according to Halil Inalcik in *An Economic and Social History of the Ottoman Empire*.

Honorable wealth

The Ottoman Empire represented the last great Islamic civilization, reaching the peak of its military power and geographic reach under Sultan Suleyman the Magnificent, who ruled between 1520 and 1566. Though German reformer Martin Luther considered the Turkish victories over the Christian armies of Europe God's punishment for Europe's sins, he wrote a pamphlet in which he praised Ottoman piety and their efficiency as rulers according to Gregory Miller in his article "From Crusades to Homeland Defense."

Outside of the differences in religion and military power, Europeans and Ottomans had more in common with each other in the sixteenth century than either would have with Europeans of today. Feudalism ruled the countryside of much the Ottoman Empire, while monopolistic guilds dominated city life. Ottoman rulers espoused just one theory of economic development: conquer your neighbor and take his gold. Like the Arabs before them, the Ottomans sought to expand the realm of Islam through war, but confiscating the wealth of conquered people and collecting taxes from new subjects motivated sultans as well, as Inalcik wrote. For similar reasons, Spain subjugated Central and South Americas in order to bring Catholicism to the natives and relieve them of the burden of their gold. For both empires, war provided the means to enrich the ruler and his treasury and enable him to launch more wars to expand the empire further.

Citizens of the Ottoman Empire had few choices for gaining wealth if they were not born into it. Plunder in war, ransom, and bribery were the most respectable means of increasing a man's wealth, as Baumol wrote in *The Free Market Innovation Machine*. Only people of the lowest classes lived by commerce. This attitude toward the acquisition of wealth had changed very little by the late Middle Ages in the Ottoman Empire where commerce was viewed, at best, as a neutral vocation according to Inalcik. In Europe, the reputation of commerce continued to rise and ushered in the age of mercantilism as a philosophy of economic development, which was a major improvement over the old theory of government sanctioned plunder. But commerce's image did not improve among the Ottomans in a corresponding way until the late nineteenth century.

Because the kings and sultans allowed their armies to keep a portion of the wealth of conquered subjects, the nobility in Europe and the Middle East relied upon public wars to enrich their personal treasuries. But between wars, funds would run low due to their extravagant lifestyles. So in peacetime, when the demand for their services on the part of rulers fell off, the nobility would exercise their entrepreneurial skills by launching private wars. These wars, public or private, destroyed wealth in three ways: the armies consumed scarce resources; they hindered the work of productive people; they left poverty, disease and misery in their wake.

Ottoman economic mind

As in Europe, the nobility staffed the military leadership in the Ottoman Empire. What Europeans called peasants, Ottomans called the *ra'aya*, a word that can be translated as sheep or as citizens, but which accurately describes the attitude of the government toward the common people. To the Ottoman mind, the citizens existed to feed and clothe the military; the military, with the sultan as the head, protected the citizens like a shepherd and expanded the empire. Consequently, the nobility and military were exempted from taxation. During most of the Ottoman empires long dominance, becoming an officer was difficult and the dream of many young men.

Below the military in status were the *ulema*, or religious leaders, and the government bureaucracy. Ottomans remained ambivalent toward agriculture, the trades and commerce, but considered moneylenders and entertainers as belonging to an evil class of people. Ottoman bureaucrats displayed their disdain for commerce by freely granting trade concessions to Europeans. They usually delegated the negotiations of the concessions to minor officials, some of whom served temporarily. Ottomans prohibited the exportation of gold and silver, the money of the day. Otherwise, they championed free trade three hundred years before Adam Smith, but for different reasons, as Inalcik wrote:

> The idea of an economy as a whole and its protection, in physical or
> economic terms, against competitor nations never seems to have occurred

to the Ottomans before the eighteenth century. Apparently, no concern existed for the protection of home industries against foreign products, not even for the traditionally well-established industries such as the Ottoman silk manufacturers of Bursa...Imports were viewed as beneficial to ensure surplus in the market without any other economic consideration.

The author of this quote considered the lack of a mercantilist doctrine in the Ottoman Empire to be one of its weaknesses and a cause of its decline. But as we shall see later, it actually prolonged the life of the Empire by keeping prices low and thereby improving the standard of living of its people.

Islam, the religion of the Empire, dominated economic thought even more than it does today and Islamic doctrine encouraged the Ottoman Empire to establish an early version of what is called today a welfare state. Inalcik wrote, "After all, in the pure Islamic tradition, the state is considered merely a means to promote Islam...The basic orientation 'is the mutual sharing of the community's income between the affluent and have-nots.'" The Islamic emphasis on redistribution of income required that the state control the economy. Luxury goods, such as silk, escaped a great deal of regulation because the clerics considered them unimportant. But necessities, such as meat and bread, earned the scrutiny of the highest levels of government. In addition to the Islamic influence, traditional societies knew from experience that overproduction led to low prices, and shortages to high prices. So both producers and consumers demanded that the government regulate the market out of fear of each other and envy of anyone who might succeed more than others. In response, the central government shackled the economy with strict controls, resulting in static economies and limited markets.

The Ottomans controlled production in much the same way as the Europeans did, through guilds licensed by the state that filled the role of modern unions. The bureaucracy determined which guilds would produce which products, how much guilds could produce, the content and quality of the products, and the prices they could charge. Production outside of a guild was illegal and subject to heavy penalties. For example, at the end of the fifteenth century, guilds in Bursa defied state regulators and gave in to popular demand by producing cheaper silks for common people. The state reacted by passing new regulations defining the quality and amount of silk and dye that could be used for a variety of cloths. In 1485, Sultan Bayezid II outlawed the printing press, a ban which lasted throughout the empire for the next three centuries. In other words, the Ottomans employed the methods of the Great Colbert a century before him.

Islamic doctrine required a tax on the most productive people in the Empire, Christians and Jews. The Ottomans continued a practice begun in the early days of Islamic expansion under the Arabs of offering conquered people three choices: convert to Islam, die, or pay a heavy tax in order to remain non-Muslim. In 1475, this tax on Christians and Jews contributed 45 percent of the total budget of the Empire according to Inalcik. Non-Muslims paid this tax in addition to the heavy tax burden required of all citizens. Of total state revenue in 1475, 81 percent came from the predominantly Christian Rumeli, or Eastern European provinces of the empire. By 1740, the tax on non-Muslims had fallen to 40 percent of the total as a result of conversions to Islam, Inalcik wrote. The percentage supplied by non-Muslims might have fallen more severely had not the government begun to limit conversions.

Ottoman superiority

Ottomans felt a strong sense of superiority over every other culture they encountered, and for good reason. Their military had recently defeated the remnant of the ancient Byzantine Empire, the Christian standard bearer in the region for over a thousand years, when the Turkish army of eighty thousand overwhelmed the seven thousand defenders of Constantinople. In 1526, the Turks destroyed the entire Hungarian army in a battle lasting just two hours. Suleyman's army laid siege to Vienna in 1529. Though the Austrians forced him to withdraw, they knew the reprieve was temporary.

The Ottoman military defeated their opponents so often that Europeans went into battle expecting to lose. Europeans erupted in jubilant celebration after rare victories. In 1571, when a European navy defeated an Ottoman fleet in the Gulf of Patras in Greece, King James VI of Scotland (later James I of England), wrote a long, ecstatic poem about the victory. All of Europe rejoiced. To the Turks, however, it was a minor affair. When the sultan asked his vizier about the cost of rebuilding the sunken fleet, the vizier commented that the wealth of the sultan's treasury was so vast that he could supply a new navy with silver anchors and silk sails if he wished, Lewis wrote in *What Went Wrong*.

Still, the Turks had lost 210 ships sunk or captured to the Europeans' twenty ships. The defeat revealed a weakness in Ottoman culture that would prove to be an omen of the Empire's decline: several of the captured ships belonged to admirals and European sailors found hidden in them fortunes in gold coins. Fearing confiscation of their wealth at home by powerful enemies in the government, the admirals had no choice but take all of their wealth with them into battle. "The Ottoman sultan, like the emperor of China, claimed ownership of everything; whenever either of them needed funds, 'confiscation of the property of wealthy subjects was entirely in order,' as the economist William K. Baumol observed," Stark wrote in *How the West Won*. If the wealth of admirals was in danger, how much more would the middle class and peasants have suffered from a lack of security for their property?

Ottomans regarded their culture as the definition of civilization and they found little outside it that interested them. They considered their religion to be the final and perfect revelation from God, superseding Judaism and Christianity. They believed that European science had begun by translating the works of Islamic scholars from Arabic while the Ottomans had pushed astronomy, medicine, mathematics, engineering and the arts to loftier levels. As the great historian of the Middle East Bernard Lewis wrote in *What Went Wrong*, Islam "had achieved the highest level so far in human history in the arts and sciences of civilization...medieval Europe was a pupil and in a sense dependent on the Islamic word."

Europeans had studied Arabic for centuries and many merchants learned Turkish as they wandered through the empire in search of business opportunities. But Turks, and Muslims in general, rarely ventured into Europe and few had any knowledge of European languages.

While Europeans imported hundreds of products from Ottomans, the latter purchased mainly slaves from Europe.

In the early seventeenth century, Ottoman officials knew little about the subtleties of diplomacy, for they had never needed to negotiate. Their armies almost always destroyed the enemy, after which, the Ottomans dictated the terms of surrender and the vanquished signed the document. Never recognizing heads of other governments as equals, Ottomans referred to them by lesser Ottoman titles, such as *bey*, or by transliterations of European titles. In a letter to Queen Elizabeth of England, the sultan wrote that he expected her to be "loyal in her vassalage and subservient," Lewis wrote in *What Went Wrong*.

Ottoman agriculture

While Islam condones private property, the Islamic concept diverged from the Western one in important ways. In the Ottoman Empire, as in most of the Middle East today, it meant that a person has the use of property rather than the control. Ottoman farmers retained exclusive use of their land as long as they remained productive and on good terms with the state and local officials, but the state controlled the land. The government obtained the bulk of its income from taxes on agricultural production and regarded that sector of the economy as too important to be left to the control of ignorant peasants. So it regulated every aspect of rural life. Peasants could not harvest unless the military governor was present so that peasants could not hide any of the produce. The governors often did not respect the laws of the central government that attempted to protect peasants and extracted double the official taxes in order to enrich themselves.

The law bound peasants to their land with severe penalties for leaving. But officials had difficulty enforcing the laws, especially because they had a weakness for bribes. Throughout the history of the Ottoman Empire, the central government struggled to keep peasants down on the farm. Peasants abandoned farms for many reasons: taxes became so heavy that farmers faced starvation; price controls prevented farmers from earning enough to save money against bad times at best; at worst they caused farmers to earn less than cost of production; mercenary bands raped and pillaged rural areas with impunity; finally, drought, famine, and war forced many to escape to the cities according to Inalcik.

Sometimes peasants left one farm to farm in a different jurisdiction where the local military governor offered better conditions and lower taxes. Others fled to the cities where they tried to join guilds. Some left to take part in wars in hopes of prying open the door to a military career. As a result, population shifts in the rural areas of the empire were continuous throughout its history. Usually, military governors took over abandoned land and tried to attract sharecroppers.

High taxes, corrupt officials, drought and marauding bands forced peasants to abandon simple things that might have made their lives easier, such as carts. Carts had been familiar in Roman and Byzantine times, but became scarce during Islamic rule and remained so until their reintroduction by Europeans. Peasants in Islamic countries saw carts as poor investments because they were hard to conceal and easy to steal, either by mercenaries, bandits or the government, and they had to pay heavy taxes on them, Lewis wrote in *What*

Went Wrong. If possible, the plight of farmers in the Ottoman Empire was worse than Smith's description of French farmers.

While the sultan's treasury bulged with tax revenues, the dawn of the seventeenth century saw the wealth of his subjects slipping behind that of Europeans. One writer has calculated the average per capita income in Europe to be around $894 in 1600, using 1990 dollars. Eastern Europe, mostly under Ottoman control, managed to get by on just $516 per head. Most of the gains to European standards of living had come from greater security for property, which led to improvements to productivity in agriculture and increases in trade according to Maddison in *The World Economy*.

Seventeenth century

Many historians picture the seventeenth century of the Ottoman Empire as one of relentless decline. Recent research shows that image to be inaccurate. Ottomans finished the century with higher standards of living than when it had begun though growth was slower than in Western Europe. Increased wealth in Europe led to greater revenue for governments and more money to spend on the military. European armies became better organized, equipped and trained. As a result, they began to defeat Ottoman armies in battle on a regular basis.

The Ottoman government found itself in a dilemma in this century. Expansion by military conquest continued to be the reason for the existence of the Ottoman state. Had they not suffered military defeat, they would have finished the century very content. War had become very expensive and to pay for it, they desperately needed the income from taxes on newly conquered people. But those people, primarily Europeans, had become very good at defending themselves. As the century progressed, the Ottomans spent more and earned less profit with each war. In the budget for 1669-70, the state spent 62.5% of its income on war according to Inalcik's history.

In 1683, the Austrians spoiled the Ottoman army's second attempt at establishing a franchise in Vienna with a military defeat that the Ottoman rulers and the people considered calamitous. Later, the Austrians, Venice, Poland and Russia formed a coalition that defeated the Ottoman army again at Carlowitz in 1698. The treaty of Carlowitz marked the first time in the history of the empire that the Ottomans signed as the defeated party.

The military defeats in the late seventeenth century caused Ottoman subjects from the Sultan to the peasants to question what had happened to the great empire. At first, their rulers dismissed their defeats as nothing more than better military strategy or superior weapons. They sought the remedy in imported weapons and advisers, most of who came from Europe. The state had to look for increased revenues to finance these improvements, since they could not conquer new territories, so they increased the tax burden on farmers, merchants and craftsmen. At the same time, the state fixed the prices of goods at artificially low levels in order to reduce military expenses. Then, the state paid for those goods with debased currency much as the Romans had done.

Outside of concern over the military defeats, life in the Ottoman Empire continued as it had for centuries. The government allowed merchants to accumulate wealth to a point, but even mid-level members of the political class were wealthier than the wealthiest merchants according to Inalcik. A long rebellion in Anatolia caused the normal tide of peasant flight to swell to a flood, which reduced tax revenue from farming. The government continued to collect taxes through tax-farming, the ancient Roman technique of selling to the highest bidder the right to collect taxes. The tax farmers were allowed to use any effective method to collect taxes and they usually collected far more than the official levy. As a result, farmers, merchants and craftsmen found it difficult to save money that they could invest in equipment to enhance their productivity. Still, had they managed to save, it is doubtful they would have invested in machinery that would attract the attention of the politically powerful, thieves or tax collectors.

By the end of the century, Muslim clerics, or mullahs, began to object to the trade concessions granted to European merchants during the century because such concessions implied a long-term peace with the infidels. The mullahs admitted that temporary truces with infidels could be permitted, but under the principle of jihad, permanent peace could not be considered.

Eighteenth century

The trends begun in the previous century gained momentum in the eighteenth. European advances in weapons, military discipline, logistics and maneuvers outclassed the Ottomans who were bound up in tradition. The aura of invincibility that once surrounded Ottoman armies faded as they suffered more defeats than victories in the last half of the century.

Improved fiscal management and heavier taxes enabled the government to accumulate significant reserves in the first half-century. But these evaporated with the defeats of the last fifty years. The state continued to collect taxes through tax farming, but even Europeans were shocked by the disparity between what the tax farmers collected and what the government received. In one instance, it was reported that the state received only four million British pounds out of twenty million collected according to Inalcik.

In international trade the Empire pursued free trade policies while Europeans increasingly protected home industries by restricting imports. Occasionally, the Ottoman government would step in to prevent the export of grain or silk when it was in short supply, but it never bothered with imports, which were considered luxuries. Europeans continued to seek capitulations, or lower duties on exports to the Ottoman Empire, and they usually got them. But Ottomans remained indifferent to the rising wall of tariffs imposed on their products in Europe.

Some economists and historians have attributed this lack of concern for international trade to naiveté on the part of the Ottoman's. Instead, it may have been due to the small size of the export market, which was dwarfed by the domestic one. In 1759, France's entire export of textiles to the Ottomans would clothe a mere 800,000 people Inalcik reported. At the end of the eighteenth century, Ottoman exports stood at about the same level of a hundred years earlier in absolute terms, but the empire's share of world trade had declined. As the century passed, Ottomans increasingly exported raw materials and imported manufactured ones. Like the Spanish, they manufactured very few things and those were consumed by the home market. They did not manufacture for export.

In the previous century, the Ottomans had looked to military improvements in order to regain their supremacy. Now they focused on the factories of Europe and decided that they were the secret of Europe's military successes. So the Ottoman government began to experiment with building factories for itself. Private industry could not build the factories because price controls made it impossible for the owners to raise the capital to build them, since investors knew they could never earn enough profit to repay their investment.

With the government still focused on warfare, the new factories produced goods for the military, such as uniforms. The government owned and operated the factories, so the managers cared less about efficiency or quality than for high volumes of production. The same problem would later plague the U.S.S.R. During wartime, the state paid below-market prices to the factories for their goods, which hurt the more efficient factories the most and encouraged inefficiency in the remaining factories. Quality became so poor that soldiers often sold clothing provided by the state and dressed themselves in imported clothes Inalcik said.

To cut costs, the Ottomans decided to populate new, government-owned factories with slaves made up of Christian children from the center of the empire. One Armenian chronicler, reported in Inalcik, described the youth "jobs" program in this way:

> By Royal decree, many [thousands of] Armenian children [from eight to fifteen years of age] from Sebastia [Sivas] and from other towns in Anatolia were assembled in Erzerum and taken to Constantinople for forced labor at the *iplikhane* [spinning mill], the Sultan's shipyard, to manufacture sails for ships and at [the foundry] forging hot iron. They were given bread and clothing, but no salary. And this order is renewed year after year and they collect hundreds of Armenian children from every town, depriving them of their parents and their homeland, and during this thirty-day march [journey] in bare feet and rags, [they] take them to Constantinople. Several die of cold and want on the way and later through the tyranny of their masters, while others convert to Islam, hoping thus to obtain their freedom. None of the Armenian leaders dared protest to the government against this diabolic evil.

Even without large, privately-owned factories, the Ottomans held their own against the onslaught of European manufactured products until about 1770 when severe restrictions on imports began in Europe. Meanwhile, the state supported the concentration of craft production under the control of associations and discouraged production outside of traditional areas.

During this century, the famous Janissary corps deteriorated into a Mafia-like organization. The Janissaries began as an army made up of children torn from the homes of Christian families in the Ottoman territories of Eastern Europe. Every year, beginning in 1326, the Ottoman government had required each Christian village to surrender one-fifth of the males between the ages of fourteen and twenty to the state. (A separate levy of children aged six to ten paralleled this one and lasted two centuries longer, but these served in the sultan's palace.) If parents resisted, they were beaten or killed. Ottoman soldiers raised these young men in harsh conditions, forced them to convert to Islam and trained them as fierce warriors. Then the state unleashed them against their former countrymen. The Janissaries were the shock troops for the bulk of the conquest of Eastern Europe in early centuries according to Bat Ye'or in *The Decline of Eastern Christianity.*

By the eighteenth century, the military importance of the Janissaries had declined to the point that they had become an unpaid militia. However, they still formed part of the elite military class and held enormous political power. They dominated villages as tax-farmers and moneylenders and practiced extortion. The forty thousand Janissaries in Istanbul forced the trade associations to employ them as "consultants." In Cairo, they controlled the guilds and extorted protection money, also.

In the seventeenth and eighteenth centuries, many European governments had reduced taxes and increased the protection of private property. The Ottoman system on the other hand offered little protection for towns, nor could the citizens expect the protection of private property that would encourage investment and experimentation. Instead, the Ottomans implemented more of the policies that stifled progress.

Merchants were tolerated during this century, but not admired. The state taxed them lightly, but they remained vulnerable to extortion and bandits on the road. They invested little in their enterprises because of the volatility of the markets, threat of confiscation and rampant crime. As a result, capital goods in which they had already invested tended to wear out. By the end of the century, the demands of financing wars caused the state to abandon any pretense of respect for private property and confiscate the property of merchants.

The population of the Ottoman Empire grew, but not as fast as that of Europe. Anatolia's population remained about the same, but Syria's and Egypt's declined because of war, fiscal rapacity and crime. Taxes became so heavy for farmers that in Egypt they surrendered two-thirds of their produce to tax-farmers. Farmers got some relief at the end of the century when the state finally freed grain prices, not because of enlightened policy, but because war and disaster had reduced the supply to dangerous levels and threatened the Empire with famine.

Rural residents continued to flee the harsh conditions to neighboring countries and cities and this migration made Ottoman territories more urban than Europe. It is curious that this fact has escaped the many historians who credit the rise of cities in Europe for that continent's economic development. If correct, why did not the larger, richer cities of the Ottoman Empire do the same for it?

During this century, while Protestants in Europe were casting aside the yoke of tyranny and freeing their economies, Ottomans were strengthening the cast iron lock that the state held on its people and economy. The Sultan punished efficient producers by paying prices for their goods that were below the costs of making them; tax farming increased the already heavy burden; and the government protected guild monopolies on craft production and the job market. By the end of the century, the state became so desperate for funds that it required wealthy merchants to pay to equip troops and send them to the front as well as to make loans to the government. Finally, from 1770 to 1810, the state simply confiscated the inheritance of private individuals who were considered rich, wrote Donald Quataert in *Manufacturing in the Ottoman Empire and Turkey: 1500-1950.*

Nineteenth century

For the aging Ottoman Empire, the nineteenth century proved crucial, its last opportunity to restore its former glory and its equality with Christian Europe, if not its former dominance. But the industrial revolution in England was gathering a head of steam and would soon roll over the traditional system to which the Ottomans clung.

Until 1826, sultans had made little progress toward reforming the empire. The pervasive Ottoman bureaucracy continued to regulate every aspect of the economy, emphasizing monopolies in production and restrictions on exports to ensure cheap and plentiful domestic supplies. Many among the leadership of the Empire recognized the need for change, but the obstacles appeared insurmountable. Three principles guided the Empire during this century: 1) Provisionism, which meant keeping a plentiful supply of goods for the government at low prices; 2) Tradition, which emphasized looking to the past for answers to current problems; and 3) Fiscalism, or keeping the tax revenue flowing at all costs, according to Quataert.

The most significant reform of the century took place in 1826 when Sultan Mahmud II broke the power of the Janissaries, who had successfully blocked all previous military and economic improvements. With the Janissaries out of the way, the Sultan was free to proceed with plans for centralizing state power and westernization. He encouraged people to attend western theater productions, listen to western music and adopt western styles of dress. He passed legislation giving non-Muslims equality with Muslims, although the law was generally ignored for religious reasons. A few of the elite called for equality of women and democracy.

From 1826 to 1860, the Ottomans increased freedom of trade and lifted many of the restrictions on the domestic economy. After 1838, the Empire could boast of one of the most liberal regimes of international trade in the world. Imports damaged domestic industries in the early part of the century, but manufacturers adapted. Some sectors recovered and expanded after 1870, achieving record levels of production in the early 1900s. Imports did little damage to small handicraft producers for local markets, and the weaving industry flourished. State built factories that supplied the military proved inefficient and withered. Christians owned and worked the few private factories that existed, which exhibited capitalist efficiency, but rarely had more than ten employees.

Quataert lists three reasons for the lack of growth in manufacturing during this century: 1) War and emigration of non-Muslims to escape high taxes and oppression caused labor shortages. 2) Confiscation by the government, bandits and marauders discouraged manufacturers from investing. And 3) the populace as well as laborers opposed manufacturing out of a fear that factories would create more unemployment. It is curious that Quataert lists labor shortages as a cause for the lack of growth in manufacturing, since labor shortages in England spurred the creation of textile mills. But he may be correct in the Ottoman case in view of the lack of incentives to invest in factories and equipment. Without laborsaving equipment, manufacturers could increase production only by adding more workers.

In spite of its liberal trade policy, the Ottomans fell hopelessly behind the West in economic development. During most of the century, average European per capita G.D.P. grew by 0.9 percent annually, while per capita G.D.P. declined in the Ottoman Empire, Brazil, China, Mexico and India. Maddison estimated the per capita G.D.P. of Western Europe in 1870 at $1,974 in 1990 U.S. dollars. In the richest part of the Ottoman Empire, the European territories, per capita income had grown from $566 in 1820 to just $871 in 1870 Maddison wrote in *The World Economy*.

In spite of the heroic efforts of the Ottoman reformers of the mid-1800s, liberal economic theory remained little more than a coat of new make up on the face of ancient traditionalism. After 1860, the state's Industrial Reform Commission partially restored the monopolies of the old guilds. Ottoman planners turned mercantilist and increased duties on imports while protecting domestic industries. In 1838, the state had charged a 3 percent tax on imports and 12 percent on exports. By 1914, the theory had reversed and the state charged 15 percent on imports and 1 percent on exports in Inalcik's history. The Empire finally adopted mercantile economics long after the West abandoned it.

The Ottomans continued to spend huge sums on warfare in this century, but now they fought for survival, not expansion. The Empire spent fifty-three of 118 years, or 45 percent of the time between 1800 and 1918 at war, which caused labor shortages and left desperately needed crops unplanted. By 1811 the Empire had lost Egypt to Napoleon. Ottoman oppression of Christians in the European provinces boiled over into repeated rebellions until, with the aid of Russia and Austria, Ottomans lost their richest territories.

Russia chipped away at the Empire on its border. French anthropologist Bat Ye'or credits Russian success at defeating the once invincible Ottoman armies for the rise of the myth of Muslim tolerance for Christians and Jews. In fact, news of Muslim atrocities against Christians had energized the Russian armies who fought to bring relief to fellow Christians. But as the nineteenth century aged, European governments began to fear Russian encroachment on the Mediterranean, while memories of the once fierce Ottoman armies had faded. As a result, the British would fight the Crimean War to defend the Ottomans against the Russians, but European governments feared that their citizens would balk at fighting on the side of the Muslim Ottomans if news of atrocities against Christians in the Balkans became widespread. So to safeguard the balance of power in Europe and block the Russian advance toward the Mediterranean, European diplomats manufactured a propaganda machine to convince the public that Turkish rule over Christians in its European provinces was just and lawful; that the Ottoman regime, being Islamic, was naturally "tolerant" and well disposed toward its Christian subjects; that its justice was fair, and that safety for life and goods was guaranteed to Christians by Islamic law. Ottoman rule was brandished as the most suitable regime to rule Christians of the Balkans according to Bat Ye'or in "The Myth of a Tolerant Pluralistic Islamic Society." The European propaganda machine succeeded so well that the myth of Muslim tolerance for non-Muslims persists today.

Factories monopolized the attention of economists and politicians of the Ottoman Empire during the nineteenth century, but four-fifths of the Ottoman population continued to earn their livelihood from the land. Absolute production increased along with the population and the amount of newly plowed land, but farming techniques changed little. A few farmers irrigated and saw increases in production from three to eight times, but due to insecurity from bandits, marauding private armies and greedy governmental officials, few employed the technique. As late as the 1950's, only 24 percent of farms used iron plows in Turkey, the country with the most advanced agriculture in the Middle East. The remainder used wooden plows with iron tips.

Early twentieth century

The twentieth century opened with the Ottoman Empire still considered a military power, though a weak one. The Empire's subjects had become wealthier than at any other time in history, but the growth had not occurred at the rapid rate enjoyed by Europeans. In 1913, the per capita income in the Empire was one-twentieth that of the British, one-tenth that in Europe, one-fifth that of its former provinces, Bulgaria, Serbia and Greece, and one-seventh that of Rumania according to Inalcik.

Manufacturers had survived the flood of European and American imports and continued to expand, although government owned factories had collapsed under the weight of their own inefficiency. Still, the manufacturing sector was small. In 1911, the Ottomans had many spinning mills, but they spun just four thousand tons of cotton yarn per year, which amounted to one-fourth of total domestic consumption. Mills that wove the yarn into clothe made only 2 percent of the Empire's needs, Inalcik wrote.

Then, a disaster struck the manufacturing sector that would take the Turks half a century to recover from. Before the turn of the century, the demand for Islamization of the Empire and the expulsion of non-Muslims had emerged. As a result, Turks murdered 200,000 Armenians in 1896. But the few private factories left in the Empire belonged primarily to Christians of Greek and Armenian descent who were fairly wealthy by Turkish standards. The 1913 census revealed that Christians owned 80 percent of all Turkish enterprises.

As world war approached, the clamor to cleanse the Empire of non-Muslims swelled to a crescendo. In 1915, the government deported the Armenian population from the interior of the country and caused the deaths of hundreds of thousands. Reprisals during World War I led to more deportations and deaths. By the end of the war, it is estimated that over one million Armenians had been killed. Half a million Greeks had fled. By 1924, less than one-tenth of the non-Muslim population of 1908 (2.5 million) remained, Quataert wrote.

Because Christians owned most of the factories in the Empire, their death, deportation and emigration destroyed manufacturing, but no Muslims waited in the wings to take over. The once thriving silk industry provides an example of the devastation. In the Bursa region, Muslims cut down the mulberry trees in which silkworms grew and used them for firewood. Then they planted tobacco in the fields. Cocoon production plummeted from four million kilograms in 1913 to 300,000 in 1922. Though the departing Christian owners had left the silk spinning mills intact, Muslims burned and looted them instead of continuing to operate them. In 1921, the silk weaving industry produced one-fifth of its normal 30,000 kg of raw silk, Quataert wrote. As a result of the atrocities committed against the Christians, Turkey lost all of its export oriented manufacturing, while domestic manufacturing would not reach pre-war levels until long after the end of World War II. Muslims refused to enter manufacturing because of the ancient stigma against it and commerce, which is the reason Christians and Jews dominated it. The path to success lay through the military and government service, as always.

In the 1920s, little had changed in Turkish agriculture since the days of the Ottomans, but a growing population demanded more food. The lack of productivity growth meant that the production of greater quantities of food required more people working on the farm, but agriculture faced a severe labor shortage. Rather than improve productivity on the farm, the state ordered townspeople to the countryside to help, foreshadowing Mao's Cultural Revolution in China during the 1960s.

1929 brought the end of free trade in Turkey with the imposition of high tariffs on imports. The government nationalized the railroads, which the British had paid for and built. As a result, foreign capital that had financed reconstruction fled the country and large manufacturing collapsed. The state adopted a policy of central planning after the Soviet model in the 1930s and built factories, but workers had high rates of absenteeism, high turnover and low work discipline. During World War II, the real income of workers declined 30 to 50 percent and the middle class began to argue for an end to state control of the economy. In the 1950s and beyond, the American example began to grow in importance as American aid and investment invaded the nation.

The myth of Muslim supremacy

Official history, that which dominates other versions because the state crafted it and forced it on citizens Soviet style, or simply popular history because it tells the story most people want to hear, is often myth according to British historian Herbert Butterfield. Official history portrays the Ottoman Empire as a story of the decline of a once great civilization, but it contains myth, as well. The Turks had inherited their advanced science from the Arabs, who inherited it from the scholars of conquered Byzantium, Persia and India. Arab math came from Hindus in India. The legacy of the ancient Greeks passed through the Byzantine Empire and appeared in Arabic as a result of the translations of Christians writing in Arabic, as the historian Rodney Stark noted in *How the West Won*:

> The scholar Mark Dickens pointed out that the Nestorians "soon acquired a reputation with the Arabs for being excellent accountants, architects, astrologers, bankers, doctors, merchants, philosophers, scientists, scribes, and teachers. In fact, prior to the ninth century, nearly all the learned scholars in the [Islamic area] were Nestorian Christians." It was primarily the Nestorian Christian Hunayn ibn Ishaq al-'Ibadi (known in Latin as Johannitius) who "collected, translated, revised, and supervised the translation of Greek manuscripts, especially those of Hippocrates, Galen, Plato, and Aristotle into Syriac and Arabic," in the words of William W. Brickman. As late as the middle of the eleventh century, the Muslim writer Nasir-I Khrusau reported, "Truly, the scribes here in Syria, as is the case of

Egypt, are all Christians...[and] it is most usual for the physicians...to be Christians.

Western scholars continue to refer to the ancient Apostolic Church of the East as "Nestorian" because it embraced Nestorius' views in the debate on the human and divine natures of Christ and opposed those of Cyril of Alexandria. Nestorius, following his mentor, Theodore of Mopsuestia, argued that Christ had two natures, human and divine, united in one person. Cyril argued that the divine and human natures were fused into one nature. Of course, there is no way to settle such a dispute because the Bible does not address it, but theologians in that era thought they could reason their way to absolute certainty on such issues and that their human reasoning was equal to that of the truths of Scripture. Nestorius offered the better logic but lost the debate because Church councils determined "truth" by a vote of the majority and none of Nestorius' supporters were present.

The Council of Ephesus in 431 denounced Nestorius' theology as heresy and with it condemned the Syrian speaking Apostolic Church of the East, which once stretched from Jerusalem to Beijing and from southern India into Russia and shepherded tens of millions of Christians. However, Nestorius did not present his views at the council and only a straw man version fabricated by Cyril was offered. Nestorius was never the "Nestorian" condemned by the council according to Dietmar W. Winkler and Wilhelm Baum in *The Church of the East: A concise history*. The Church of the East did not take part in the Council of Ephesus and felt no obligation to enforce it. The West has ignored this church because the illegal Council of Ephesus declared it to be heretical. The Church of the East allowed the followers of Nestorius to immigrate rather than face death at the hands of their "Christian" brothers.

The Apostolic Church of the East had formed what many scholars consider to be the first universities six centuries ahead of Europe at Nisibis and Gundeshapur in Persia in the fourth century. Those schools were so successful that popes tried to replicate them centuries later. The universities taught theology, philosophy, medicine, astronomy and mathematics and developed most the "Arab" scholars of the Muslim Golden Age. Later, the church created a similar school at Baghdad.

Hunain ibn Ishaq, the most important of the East Syrian translators, was the son of an apothecary from the Arab tribe of Ibad, a lecturer at the medical academy in Baghdad and a deacon of the Apostolic Church of the East. He made great advances in the treatment of eye diseases, which were common at the time. He wrote a *Book of Logic* and a history of the world from Adam to his own time (661). He resisted attempts at converting to Islam in spite of the social and financial benefits, and authored a defense of Christianity. His greatest contribution may have been to the Arab language, according to Winkler and Baum: "Through the development of neologisms and the borrowing of foreign words, he created an academic Arabic terminology and transformed Arabic from the language of the Bedouins into an instrument in which complicated scholarly problems could be expressed. The medical historian Withington referred to Hunain as the 'Erasmus of the Islamic Renaissance.'"

The works of Christian and Jewish scholars had been translated into Arab and Turkish, but "this learning continued to be sustained primarily by the *dhimmi* populations living under

Muslims regimes...as the remarkable historian of Islam Marshall G. S. Hodgson noted, 'those who pursued natural science tended to retain their older religious allegiances as *dhimis*, even when doing their work in Arabic,'" according to Stark in *How the West Won*.

Muslim architecture had been adapted from the Persian and Byzantine, using churches as templates for mosques. Avicenna, an influential Muslim philosopher, was a Persian, as was Omar Khayyam and al-Khwarizmi, the father of algebra. Bakht-Ishu and ibn Ishaq, leaders in Muslim medicine were Christians while physicians were trained at the Christian medical center at Nisibus in Syria. Masha'allah ibn Athari was a Jew. "What may have misled so many historians is that most contributors to 'Arabic science' were given Arabic names and their works were published in Arabic, that being the official language of the land," Stark wrote.

Differences in their approaches to Aristotle emphasize the gap between European and Ottoman cultures. Muslims considered the physics of Aristotle to be authoritative and infallible. If reality refused to comply with Aristotle's teachings, "those observations were either in error or an illusion," Stark wrote. In contrast, European scholars eventually considered Aristotle's works as a good beginning but something they could improve upon. Christian scholars advanced their reputations by finding good reasons to disagree with Aristotle. As a result, European science continued to advance until it gave birth to modern science while the Ottoman Empire descended into dogma and superstition.

Westerner mercantilists had tried for centuries to explain the relative decline of Spain only to learn from economics that Spain never declined because it was never truly great; it was always medieval. Muslims have asked for centuries why the Ottoman Empire declined, yet they continue to refuse to face the glaring truth, as Stark explained:

> What has largely been ignored is that the culture could not keep up with the West because so-called Muslim culture was largely an illusion, resting on a complex mix of *dhimmi* cultures. As soon as the *dhimmis* were repressed as heretical, that culture would be lost. Hence, when Muslims stamped out nearly all religious nonconformity in the fourteenth century, Muslim backwardness came to the fore.

> Waves of anti-Christian and anti-Jewish rioting and murder swept across the Muslim world in the 14th century, by the end of which ...only tiny remnants of Christianity and Judaism remained scattered in the Middle East and North Africa, having been almost completely destroyed by Muslim persecution. And as the *dhimmis* disappeared, they took the "advanced" Muslim culture with them. What they left behind was a culture so backward that it couldn't even copy Western technology but had to buy it and often even had to hire Westerners to use it.

Tamerlane virtually destroyed the Apostolic Church of the East and its universities. Without its Christian and Jewish scholars, the Ottoman Empire remained frozen in its medieval ways while the West advanced. Even the casual reader of the economic history of the Ottoman Empire cannot ignore the major themes of economic policy that changed little throughout four centuries. The military learned too late that conquest had been defeated as a sound economic development policy. The government never trusted control of the economy in the hands of the *ra'aya*, and except for a brief period in the middle of the nineteenth century, strangled the economy with price controls, regulations and monopolies. High taxes, corrupt officials, and the lack of law and order destroyed entrepreneurial effort. A modified form of feudalism persisted into the twentieth century.

But the Ottomans did not invent these policies of economic management; they inherited them. All ancient civilizations had followed the same general principles, including the Chinese and the Japanese, until the late nineteenth century. In broad strokes, the policies constituted the traditional economic policies that empires had followed for millennia. Before the sixteenth century, all of Europe followed the same principles. Afterward, much of Europe and Russia remained stuck in traditional economics until the twentieth century. During those four centuries, Europeans journeyed from a position of cowering in fear of Ottoman assaults to acting as adviser and defender of the crumbling empire. The military power needed to defeat Ottoman armies grew in step with the wealth of nations and individuals. At the same time, individual freedoms flourished in Europe while languishing in the Empire.

A study of the Ottoman Empire's economic history is instructive for several reasons. Many economic historians credit trade and the growth of cities for breaking the chains of the feudal system in Western Europe. Yet, the Ottoman Empire espoused free international trade three hundred years before Adam Smith. Ottoman traded extended from China to Morocco. And the Empire could boast of larger, wealthier, more beautiful cities so advanced in science and art as to shame any in Europe. But these did not transform the Ottoman Empire as historians claim they did Europe. It seems only reasonable to ask of historians who develop grand theories of economic development that their theories apply to more regions of the world than just Western Europe.

Islam itself cannot be blamed because 1) Europe had similar religious institutions until the Reformation and 2) Muslims have done well economically in the West. *Waqf's* in the Middle East played a similar role to that of the Church in that they owned large portions of land. Until the advent of capitalism in the Dutch Republic, the main paths to wealth and prestige in Europe and the Ottoman Empire were the same: through the military or state bureaucracy. And both Ottomans and Europeans held commerce in contempt.

After Dutch and English per capita income began to rise rapidly, Catholic and Orthodox Christendom and the Muslim world remained mired in economic backwardness. The same plagues that afflicted the Ottoman Empire held Catholic and Orthodox Europe back for generations. At the same time, Muslims persecuted, murdered and forced to emigrate the two *dhimmi* groups, Christians and Jews, who had driven the small commercial successes the empire had and produced most of its science. What set Protestant Europe apart was the reformation in values in favor of the bourgeois that accompanied the Reformation.

The economist Timur Kuran in "The Scale of Entrepreneurship in Middle Eastern History" laments the failure to launch corporate structures in Muslim nations as a cause of continuing backwardness because, "Islamic law failed to stimulate the development of organizational forms conducive to pooling and managing resources on a large scale." But that is a sign of the lack of bourgeois values. Businesses in the poorer nations of Europe and the Middle East were small and family-owned for the most part in spite of the adoption of corporate structures in the law because of the ethic of the family. The Middle East was very much as Fukuyama described Mafia culture, quoted in Lawrence E. Harrison and Samuel P. Huntington's *Culture Matters*, "For the rest of Sicilian society, the prevailing norms can be described more as 'take advantage of people outside your immediate family at every occasion because otherwise they will take advantage of you first.'" Most businesses remain family-owned today because the owners can trust only family members to run the businesses.

Living the legacy

The Ottoman elite struggled to catch up to the mounting power of Europe and Russia, first with military reform, next with state-owned factories, then with wholesale westernization. While the continent of the cross waxed stronger, that of the crescent waned. For almost two centuries, the Ottomans positioned the empire as the kingdom of Allah on earth, a lighthouse to guide the rest of the world in the path of civilization, and Islam, the final and perfect revelation from Allah. They credited their military prowess to Allah's desire to protect these treasures and spread their benefits to all mankind. That their conquests of new territories added to the sultan's wealth was a merely a bonus.

The military defeats of the seventeenth century shattered this worldview. For the first time, events forced the elite to search outside the empire, and among modern techniques instead of past traditions, for solutions. They attempted to improve their military by purchasing European weapons and hiring European advisors. When those failed, the state built factories and schools modeled after the ones that ambassadors had toured in the West. Finally, in the late nineteenth century, the government tried to force Western culture on its citizens by encouraging European plays, music and clothing. At times, it made halfhearted attempts at parliamentary democracy. But while the Empire finished each century wealthier than when it began, the West, and Russia, always grew faster in wealth and military power. Bernard Lewis wrote,

> In the course of the twentieth century it became abundantly clear that things had gone badly wrong in the Middle East. And, indeed, in all the lands of Islam. Compared with Christendom, its rival for more than a millennium, the world of Islam had become poor, weak, and ignorant. The primacy and therefore the dominance of the West was clear for all to see, invading every aspect of the Muslim's public and even—more painfully—his private life.

The Ottoman Empire no longer exists, but we can track the progress of the nations that sprang from it through what is known as MENA, or the nations of the Middle East and North Africa. MENA encompasses Turkey, all Arab countries and the old Ottoman enemy, Persia, which followed the same pattern of economic development as its nemesis. Little has changed in the Middle East since the collapse of the Ottoman Empire. The state and agriculture still dominate the economies of the nations of MENA, much as they did in the days of the Empire. Democratic freedoms are scarcer than cash. Productivity runs low. But rather than face these problems, most of the intellectuals in these countries take no responsibility for the miserable conditions in their nations, preferring instead to blame the U.S. and Israel.

Most economic analyses of the region focus on macro variables such as taxes, government spending, monetary policy, etc. Few economists have embraced the recent progress made in social studies concerning the importance of culture, but at least they are paying more attention to institutions. For example Ibrahim A. Elbadawi wrote in "Reviving Growth in the Arab World," a World Bank paper in 2004, "Modern growth literature, along with development experiences in the field, suggests that high growth is associated with certain broad fundamentals: effective institutions for protection of property rights, a stable macroeconomic environment, adequate human capital, structural policies for promoting more open economies and efficient and lean government."

The paper measured institutions using the International Country Risk Guide (ICRG), an index of political, economic, and financial indicators. Arab countries received an ICRG score of seventy on a scale ranging from forty to eighty-five, compared to a score of seventy-five for East Asian nations. However, most of the improvement came from oil exporting nations. Arab countries scored lowest in measure of corruption, rule of law and quality of the bureaucracy. Elbadawi wrote, "In fact, in the 1995-2000 period both groups continue to lag behind all other comparators, including Sub-Saharan Africa."

Another measure of progress is the share of government consumption to G.D.P., called the government burden. Again, Elbadawi wrote,

> Of the three indicators making up the macro-institutional environment, the quality of institutions measured by ICRG and excessive government burden seem to be the most important factors explaining the difference in growth...A large government consumption to GDP ratio is usually associated with a bloated bureaucracy, exorbitant taxes and, as such, constitutes a drag on private sector activities. The evidence suggests that the government burden in the Arab world is a serious problem.

What went wrong?

The explanation that has attracted the greatest following asserts that the failures of the Ottoman armies resulted from apostasy. Religious leaders preached that Muslims had strayed from the true path of Islam and displeased Allah. The clerics sold the Ottoman people on that explanation and began cleansing the Empire of sinful practices and infidels. Subsequent defeats launched periods of intensified cleansing, culminating in the murder of over 200,000 Christians in 1895 and more than a million Christians during the First World War.

The last Islamic Caliphate ended with Turkey's defeat in World War I and soon afterwards Egyptians formed the Muslim Brotherhood to bring it back. The modern radical Muslim groups such as Al Qaeda and the Islamic State (ISIS) are merely splinter groups from the Muslim Brotherhood. Irreligious westerners dismiss religious zeal as a source of radicalism in the Middle East, blaming instead poverty and corrupt, oppressive governments. But religion is the *raison d'etre* for radical Muslims. They find the backwardness, poverty and military weakness of the Muslim world, especially weakness toward Israel, humiliating and the only remedy they will consider is a purification of their countries so that Allah will return them to the hegemony they enjoyed during the Golden Age of Islam when the crescent arched from Vienna through the Middle East and North Africa and into Spain to the French border. The West egregiously underestimates the excitement that the ISIS in Syria and Iraq has caused in the entire Muslim world, not just in the Middle East. ISIS offers the hope of a restored caliphate and with it the likelihood in the minds of Muslims or a return to power under the banner of Allah.

Chapter 7 – The envy barrier resurrected and the decline of capitalism

The reader would be justified in thinking that a chapter on the decline of capitalism should begin with a treatment of Karl Marx. But he would think that only because of the poor state of the U.S. educational system. Marx did not invent socialism or communism and he contributed little to the movement. The first recorded depiction of a socialist society came from Plato's *Republic*, while several quasi-Christian groups had tried communism, and failed, in the 1,800 years after Christ.

According to Hayek, the death of capitalism began with ideas of the philosopher Rene Descartes (1596-1650) who promoted the superiority of things designed by humans, especially institutions, which Hayek called Cartesian rationalization in *The Fatal Conceit*:

> Descending in the modern period from Rene Descartes, this form of rationalism not only discards tradition, but claims that pure reason can directly serve our desires without any such intermediary, and can build a new world, a new morality, a new law, even a new and purified language, from itself alone. Although the theory is plainly false (see also Popper, 1934/1959, and 1945/66), it still dominates the thinking of most scientists, and also of most literati, artists, and intellectuals.

He had written earlier about Descartes in his "Individualism: True and False."

> Descartes argues that "there is seldom so much perfection in works composed of many separate parts, upon which different hands had been employed, as in those completed by a single master." He then goes on to suggest (after, significantly, quoting the instance of the engineer drawing up his plans) that "those nations which, starting from a semi-barbarous state and advancing to civilization by slow degrees, have had their laws successively determined, and, as it were, forced upon them simply by experience of the hurtfulness of particular crimes and disputes, would by this process come to be possessed of less perfect institutions than those which, from the commencement of their association as communities, have followed the appointment of some wise legislator." To drive this point home, Descartes adds that in his opinion "the past pre-eminence of Sparta was due not to the pre-eminence of each of its laws in particular...but to the circumstance that, originated by a single individual, they all tended to a single end." It would be interesting to trace further the development of this social contract individualism or the "design" theories of social institutions, from Descartes through Rousseau and the French Revolution down to

what is still the characteristic attitude of the engineers to social problems. Such a sketch would show how Cartesian rationalism has persistently proved a grave obstacle to an understanding of historical phenomena and that it is largely responsible for the belief in inevitable laws of historical development and the modern fatalism derived from this belief.

The historian Alister McGrath wrote in *The Twilight of Atheism* that "Descartes is a figure of immense importance to our study, as he is widely regarded as laying the foundations for modernity." But as Hayek demonstrated, Descartes is equally important to the problem of the rise of socialism in the West. Nothing characterizes modernity better than the rise of the twin philosophies of atheism and socialism.

Descartes method of investigating the natural world helped give birth to modern science. But Descartes could not control how those who succeeded him would use his insights. Hayek was concerned about the influence of Descartes on the social sciences and the immense damage it caused in the field of economics. Closely allied was the damage done by applying Descartes' methods to the field of theology: it killed God and redefined human nature. The damage to economics required first destroying the God of Christianity and the Christian view of humanity.

Though modest by today's standards, the breakthroughs in the natural sciences of the eighteenth century convinced many people that mankind could achieve mastery over the material world. But some took a leap in logic the size of the Grand Canyon and applied the same thinking to humanity: mankind could use reason to create new institutions, morals, etc., from scratch and build not only a better society but a better humanity. Because modern science had proven wrong much of the old knowledge about the physical world, which consisted primarily of the writings of Aristotle, many assumed that all of the knowledge about humanity and society accumulated through the ages was wrong as well. It would have to be scrapped and the elite scientists would create new and better religions, institutions and morals.

Hayek dealt with that error, which he called "scientism," in his book, *The Counter-Revolution of Science: Studies on the Abuse of Reason*. Scientism was the negative goal of the revolution. It tore down the old structures of society. However, two other fallacies that Hayek did not discuss, atheism and deism, fueled scientism and built up the positive objectives of the new rationalism in which elite scientists would perfect human nature and rid the world of crime, suffering and evil.

There were few atheists in Descartes day. The Dutch Republic where Descartes lived tolerated Catholicism and Protestant sects that differed from the dominant Calvinism, such as Lutherans and Anabaptists. Tolerance inevitably led to an expression of atheism, for atheists have always existed; they just kept quiet. The oldest recorded mention of atheism comes from Israel's King Solomon who wrote that, "The fool has said in his heart, 'There is no god.'" (Psalms 14:1, 53:1) He wrote that around 1000 BC. The fool said it in his heart and not out loud because he knew that advertising his atheism would prove dangerous. Atheists throughout history kept their doubts to themselves for the most part, but they never went away.

Modern science began with devout Christians such as Copernicus, Galileo and others glorifying God by discovering his secrets in the natural world. Alone among the many religions of the world with its emphasis on reason, Christianity had always held that God is rational. The gods of other religions tended to be capricious. Christian theology allowed no room for capriciousness in the Judeo-Christian God. Challenging the conventional wisdom that modern science had to fight the Church to be born, the historian Rodney Stark wrote in *How the West Won*, "The truth is that science arose only because the doctrine of the rational creator of a rational universe made scientific inquiry plausible. Similarly, the idea of progress was inherent in Jewish conceptions of history and was central to Christian thought from very early days." Stark goes on to show that other religions, such as Hinduism, Buddhism and Islam, deny the notion of progress because they worship supreme beings devoid of rationality.

The unique role played by Christianity as the catalyst for modern science was recognized by the great British philosopher Alfred North Whitehead who was quoted in chapter 4. Even though the Christian Byzantine Empire accepted the rationality of its God, it resisted the notion of progress and held ancient philosophy in greater esteem than modern discoveries, which persuaded the government to prohibit innovations such as clocks and pipe organs.

The Christian and Jewish God is rational and has gifted mankind with reason. Reason demanded that God would have followed reason in the creation of the universe, and in the field of astronomy the early scientists found proof. The planets, stars and moons they surveyed moved in such regular patterns that they appeared to obey laws. This knowledge gave medieval Christians the courage to investigate the rest of the natural world to determine if it followed regular patterns that the investigators could distill into laws and that search gave birth to the modern scientific method.

Hayek builds a good case against Descartes for having planted the seed of modern socialism, but the great nineteenth century French economist Frederic Bastiat (1801-1850) proposed that it sprang from the Renaissance and France's veneration of classical Rome and Greece. In his essay "Academic Degrees and Socialism," published in *Selected Essays on Political Economy*, he wrote, "I say that the subversive doctrines called *socialism* or *communism* are the fruit of classical education, whether provided by the clergy or by the university." Greeks and Romans championed the accumulation of wealth by looting in war as well as slavery, promiscuity and absolute submission to the state. Bastiat allowed the leaders of the Revolution to testify to the inspiration they drank from ancient Greece and Rome. He quoted Fenelon, Rollin, Montesquieu, Rousseau, Mably, Mirabeau, Robespierre and others. Here is an excerpt from Montesquieu praising Sparta:

> The ancient Greeks, imbued with the necessity of *training in the virtues* those who were to live under a popular government, designed institutions peculiarly fitted for this end....The laws of Crete served as the model for those of Sparta, and those of Plato corrected the latter.

> I invite the reader's attention to the great genius these lawgivers must have had: in flying in the face of all accepted custom, in confounding all the

virtues, they showed the world *their wisdom*. Lycurgus, in combining larceny with the spirit of justice, the harshest slavery with extreme liberty, the most atrocious sentiments with the greatest moderation, gave stability to his city. He seemed to be depriving it of all its resources, arts, commerce, money, and defenses; there was ambition, but no hope of being better off; there were *natural affections*, and yet no man was either child or husband or father; even chastity was no longer regarded as respectable. *This is the way that Sparta was led to grandeur and glory*; but so infallible were its institutions that nothing was gained in winning battles against it if the victor did not succeed in depriving it of its polity.

Those who would like to have similar institutions will set up a regime in which property is communally owned, as in Plato's republic, and in which there will be the respect that he demanded for the gods and the separation of the natives from foreigners for the preservation of morality, with the state, not the citizens, engaging in commerce;...

In short, all commerce was *ignoble* in the eyes of the Greeks. *It would have required that a citizen render services to a slave, to a tenant, to a stranger, an idea repugnant to the spirit of Greek liberty*. Hence, Plato wants the laws to punish any citizen who engages in commerce...

Although equality of wealth is the very essence of the democratic state, it is, nevertheless, so difficult to establish that it is not always expedient to aim at extreme exactitude in this regard. It suffices to reduce and fix the differences within certain limits, after which it will be the function of particular laws to equalize, so to speak, the remaining inequalities by the taxes that they impose on the rich and the relief they grant to the poor.

Rousseau sired five children and abandoned each to the "foundling hospital" so that he could pretend to regard himself as a member of Plato's republic. He said he did not boast of the act out of compassion for their mother. He praised Sparta as well:

What! Liberty can be preserved only if supported by slavery? The two extremes meet. Everything that is unnatural has its inconveniences, and civil society even more than anything else. There are unfortunate situations in which one man's liberty can be preserved only at the expense of another's, and where the citizen can be perfectly free only on condition that the slave be abjectly a slave. This was the case with Sparta. You nations of the modern world have no slaves, but you yourselves are slaves, etc.

Bastiat condensed his survey of French intellectuals and their worship of classical civilizations to this:

> In citing the absurd and subversive doctrines of men like Fenelon, Rollin, Montesquieu, and Rousseau...what is false in their works is derived from their acceptance of the conventional view of classical antiquity, and what is true is derived from quit another source. My thesis is precisely that exclusive instruction in Greek and Latin literature makes all of us *living contradictions*. It turns us violently towards a past of which it glorifies even the worst horrors...
>
> As true followers of Plato, they openly preached common ownership of property and of women; and they did so, be it noted, by constantly invoking the examples and the precepts of the wonderful age of classical antiquity which everyone agrees is so admirable...
>
> ...What did Robespierre want? "To raise men to the level of republican virtue attained by the nations of antiquity." What did Saint-Just want? "To offer us the happiness of Sparta and of Athens." He wanted, besides, "all citizens to carry on their persons the dagger of Brutus." What did the bloodthirsty Carrier want? "That every youth henceforth contemplate the fire of Scaevola, the hemlock of Socrates, the death of Cicero, and the sword of Cato." What did Rabaut Saint-Etienne want? "That, following the example of the Cretans and the Spartans, the state take charge of every man from his cradle and even from his birth." What did the section of the Quinze-Vingts want? "That a church be consecrated to liberty, by vestal virgins."

By the seventeenth century atheists and deists began to sense that religious tolerance would allow them to speak out and so they did. They discovered each other, formed societies and aggressively challenged all religious sects by denying the existence of the object of their hatred and their common enemy, God. The rise of modern science contributed to their boldness in that the success of the scientific method in helping mankind understand his natural world, and to a small degree control it, made it inevitable that someone would apply the same methods to the study of religion and humanity. Descartes provided the rationale without intending it.

Most of the radical French philosophers of the eighteenth century, such as Denis Diderot (1713-1784), Jean-Jacques Rousseau (1712-1778) were deists instead of atheists. Voltaire (1694-1778) wrote a poem about his supreme being in 1768, which McGrath quoted:

> If the heavens, stripped of their noble imprint,
> Could ever cease to reveal Him,
> If God did not exist, it would be necessary to invent Him,
> Whom the sage proclaims, and whom kings adore.

Most people think the distinction between atheist and deist is important, but the products of the two were hard to distinguish because deists attacked the Bible and Christian theology that gave meaning to the word God. Voltaire referred to god as "Him" in his poem and uses capitalization and poetic sleight of hand to animate his god of reason. But without the content of the Christian God, Voltaire's god became nothing but an abstract idea with no power or personality. As a result, the deist assault on institutions, human nature, sociology and economics differed little from that of the atheist. Deists were just sentimental atheists.

Whereas the greatest scientist of all time, Isaac Newton (1642-1727) argued that the regular motions of the planets testified to their divine design and governance, atheists such as Paul-Henri-Dietrich d'Holbach (1723-1789) denied any reason to employ a god to explain the order of nature. Human imagination not science had invented God. Therefore the scientific method should lead to atheism. McGrath quoted another colorful person from the period, Baron Anacharsis Cloots who "debaptised" himself and wrote,

> We shall, in turn, see the heavenly royalty condemned by the revolutionary tribunal of victorious Reason; for the Truth, seated on the throne of Nature, is supremely intolerant. The star of the day [Reason] will make the meteors and all the flickering lights of the night [religion] disappear.

Of course, he followed the example of Voltaire by capitalizing his deities in order to deceive the reader into imagining them as persons and therefore substitutes for a personal God, even though he would deny they were anything more than mere forces or ideas.

Atheist and deist evangelists relied on the ancient question of evil to win converts: if God is good, why do pain and suffering exist? The question assumes that God controls people as marionettes and implies that evil exists because God is either evil or does not exist. And who wants to believe in an evil god? Of course, atheists and deists ignored the Biblical answer that God had created everything good, including humans, but gave them the gift of a free will. Humans used the gift to rebel against God and employ for evil what God had intended for good. That rebellion created in human nature the tendency toward evil. It occurred only to the atheists of the late nineteenth century, such as Nietzsche, that without God humans cannot know what is good and evil so the atheist answer to the problem of evil not only destroys God but morality and all that distinguishes humans from animals. In the end, atheism destroyed man as well as God, which goes a long way toward explaining the mass deaths at the hands of atheists such as Hitler, Stalin and Mao.

Adam Smith was a Christian

Atheists and deists used the scientific method to fracture Western thought in a way that had not happened since the rise of Christianity in the Roman Empire: they changed the way people thought about human nature. Christian theology had refined the definition of human nature and in the process that took 1,700 years had invented individualism, as described in chapter 2. In addition to individualism, Christianity taught the Biblical story of Adam and

Eve whom God created as good, moral beings without any tendency toward evil. But their rebellion changed their nature, which they bequeathed to all of the children born from them, or all of mankind. God expelled them from the Garden of Eden and humanity began its struggle for survival mired in deep poverty and battling a scarcity of resources. Mankind's fallen nature included a mixture of good and evil with a strong tendency toward evil. Discipline in childhood and instruction by parents could civilize most people, but it could never change human nature. Only God had the power to do that and God offered redemption for mankind from his fallen state only through the death and resurrection of the God-man, Jesus Christ. Theologians summarized these ideas as the doctrine of original sin.

The Christian doctrine offered a bleak outlook on mankind's future. Left to himself, man would naturally gravitate toward evil. Return to the Garden was impossible, as were the utopias dreamed by Plato, Thomas Moore and many others throughout millennia. Becoming a Christian through belief in the death, burial and resurrection of Christ would start the process of changing one's fallen nature, which theologians called sanctification, but it was not guaranteed because the fallen nature could reassert itself if the Christian succumbed to the many temptations to rebel that life offered.

The doctrine of original sin formed the ocean through which philosophers such as Adam Smith swam. They took it for granted as folks do when something is commonly understood. Because of his belief in the doctrine, Smith's "system of natural liberty," which morphed into capitalism, was a very conservative system. It did not attempt to optimize the benefits that good and brilliant men could accomplish, but sought to limit the damage that evil men could inflict. It was a humble system without the pretension of rebuilding the Garden of Eden on earth. Essentially, it said that human nature will get no better or worse than it is, though we can be wealthier than we are if we follow the system of natural liberty.

In Smith's system, government was necessary to protect people from the worst among us, such as thieves, murders and con men. The scholars of Salamanca, Spain, in the sixteenth century had also insisted that the government had the duty to protect the citizen's life, liberty and property. But for the lesser evils such as greed, Smith believed competition would provide the most effective restraint. Citizens could not rely on the government to restrain greed because unscrupulous businessmen would buy the votes of politicians to pass legislation that would favor them. Today, Smith's pessimistic view of government is called the "public choice" school of political economics, which was recently revived by the Nobel Prize winning economist James Buchanan. Competition would restrain greed because greedy businessmen who abused their customers would soon lose them to businessmen who treated them better. In some ways the market is like romance: producers must woo customers and treat them well in order to keep them.

However, unlike competition no mechanism in the market can restrain envy. The task of restraining envy must fall to religion. Competitive businessmen could see the short term damage of their greed on sales, but envious people could reap short term profits and make others bear the long term costs. As Hayek wrote in *The Fatal Conceit*, religion was the only power that could persuade men to ignore their short term envy in favor of longer term goals. Hayek quoted Adam Smith: "Religion, even in its crudest form, gave a sanction to the rules of morality long before the age of artificial reasoning and philosophy." Hayek also observed,

We owe it partly to mystical and religious beliefs, and, I believe, particularly to the main monotheistic ones, that beneficial traditions have been preserved and transmitted at least long enough to enable those groups following them to grow, and to have the opportunity to spread by natural or cultural selection. This means that, like it or not, we owe the persistence of certain practices, and the civilisation that resulted from them, in part to support from beliefs which are not true - or verifiable or testable - in the same sense as are scientific statements, and which are certainly not the result of rational argumentation. I sometimes think that it might be appropriate to call at least some of them, at least as a gesture of appreciation, "symbolic truths", since they did help their adherents to "be fruitful and multiply and replenish the earth and subdue it" (Genesis 1:28).

Atheism and human nature

Atheists of the eighteenth century denied original sin and insisted that the scientific elite could re-create human nature in their image. For them, humans have no tendency toward evil but are born good or innocent at worst. People turn to evil only when forced by oppression. Remove oppression and their natural goodness will reassert itself. Crime and evil of all kinds will disappear. The scientific method will show the way. Just apply the methods of the natural sciences to the study of human beings the scientist will solve all problems. Scientism substituted for the Christian Gospel of redemption through faith in Christ a gospel of redemption of mankind through science and social engineering.

A debate over human nature may seem esoteric and as important as determining the number of angels that can dance on the head of a pin. It is not, as Arthur C. Brooks and Peter Wehner wrote in "Human Nature and Capitalism":

> The model of human nature one embraces will guide and shape everything else, from the economic system one prefers to the political system one supports. At the core of every social, political, and economic system is a picture of human nature (to paraphrase 20th-century columnist Walter Lippmann). The suppositions we begin with—the ways in which that picture is developed—determine the lives we lead, the institutions we build, and the civilizations we create. They are the foundation stone.

Early socialists created a journal in France, the *Producteur*, as Hayek wrote in *Counter-Revolution*, "to develop and expand the principles of a philosophy of human nature..." The atheists and deists of the French Enlightenment such as Jean-Jacques Rousseau believed that science and rationalism could perfect human nature and aimed for the regeneration of mankind. They influenced the original socialists, Robert Owen, Charles Fourier, Henri de Saint-Simon and August Comte who "believed that human nature can be as easily reshaped as hot wax. They considered human nature plastic and malleable, to the point that no fixed human nature existed to speak of; architects of a social system could, therefore, mold it into anything they imagined," according to Brooks and Wehner.

The great scourge of mankind that inflicted all of the evil on society, according to the socialists, was private property. Property forced upon mankind great and unnatural inequalities of wealth and poverty. Poverty and inequality aroused envy, which led to theft, murder, revolution and all kinds of evils. All one had to do was eliminate property, divide all things equally and the new, good man would emerge as a butterfly from the constraints of its cocoon.

Along with the doctrine of the natural goodness of mankind, the atheists and deists who became the early socialists believed that all people are equal, not in the sense of equality before God and the law as Adam Smith and his contemporaries understood it, but equal in abilities. Mises explained in *Money, Method, and the Market Process*:

> Since all men are equal, every individual participates in the genius that enlightened and stimulated the greatest heroes of mankind's intellectual, artistic, and political history. Only adverse postnatal influences prevented the proletarians from equaling the brilliance and the exploits of the greatest men. Therefore, as Trotsky told us, once this abominable system of capitalism will have given way to socialism, "the average human being will rise to the heights of an Aristotle, a Goethe, or a Marx."

And that led to the deification of the masses, Mises wrote:

> The doctrine of the inborn biological equality of all men begot in the nineteenth century a quasi-religious mysticism of the "people" that finally converted it into the dogma of the "common man's" superiority. All men are born equal. But the members of the upper classes have unfortunately been corrupted by the temptation of power and by indulgence in the luxuries they secured for themselves. The evils plaguing mankind are caused by the misdeeds of this foul minority. Once these mischief makers are dispossessed, the inbred nobility of the common man will control human affairs. It will be a delight to live in a world in which the infinite goodness and the congenital genius of the people will be supreme. Never-dreamt-of happiness for everyone is in store for mankind. For the Russian Social Revolutionaries this mystique was a substitute for the devotional practices of Russian Orthodoxy.

Traditional Christianity had taught people to believe in God, and Jesus as his son, but to endure hardships in this world as preparation for a better world in eternity. The conversion of large numbers of Europeans to atheism and deism demolished the old ways of thinking about the nature of man and evil. The new gospel told people that modern science applied to the deliberate design of institutions could perfect human nature, rid the world of all evil and return man to the Garden. This was the *mise en scene* for the drama of the spawning of socialism.

As part of the attack on Christianity, Atheists and deists also assaulted the Christian notion of individualism that had taken 1,800 years to perfect and implement. They replaced it with what Hayek called pseudo-rationalism in his essay "Individualism: True and False." The new, false individualism empowered the individual to demolish traditions and institutions he could not personally understand or foresee the consequences of them. Finally, atheists and deists unleashed envy and elevated it to a virtue through the insistence on redistribution of wealth and calling it social justice.

Mises summarized the dramatic change in the perspective on human nature in his book *Theory and History* this way:

> Christian theology discerns three stages in human history: the bliss of the age preceding the fall of man, the age of secular depravity, and finally the coming of the Kingdom of Heaven. If left alone, man would not be able to expiate the original sin and to attain salvation. But God in his mercy leads him to eternal life. In spite of all the frustrations and adversities of man's temporal pilgrimage, there is hope for a blessed future.

> The Enlightenment altered this scheme in order to make it agree with its scientific outlook. God endowed man with reason that leads him on the road toward perfection. In the dark past superstition and sinister machinations of tyrants and priests restrained the exercise of this most precious gift bestowed upon man. But at last reason has burst its chains and a new age has been inaugurated. Henceforth every generation will surpass its predecessors in wisdom, virtue, and success in improving earthly conditions. Progress toward perfection will continue forever. Reason, now emancipated and put in its right place, will never again be relegated to the unseemly position the dark ages assigned to it. All "reactionary" ventures of obscurantists are doomed to failure. The trend toward progress is irresistible.

Saint-Simon – father of modern socialism

Hayek started part two of his book *The Counter-Revolution in Science* with this depiction of the spirit of the age:

> Never will man penetrate deeper into error than when he is continuing on a road which has led him to great success. And never can pride in the achievements of the natural sciences and confidence in the omnipotence of their methods have been more justified than at the turn of the eighteenth and nineteenth centuries, and nowhere more so than at Paris where almost all the great scientists of the age congregated. If it is true, therefore, that the

new attitude of man towards social affairs in the nineteenth century is due to the new mental habits acquired in the intellectual and material conquest of nature, we should expect it to appear where modern science celebrated its greatest triumphs. In this we shall not be disappointed. Both the two great intellectual forces which in the course of the nineteenth century transformed social thought - modern socialism and that species of modern positivism, which we prefer to call scientism, spring directly from this body of professional scientists and engineers which grew up in Paris, and more particularly from the new institution which embodied the new spirit as no other, the *Ecole polytechnique.*

Hayek wrote that the French Enlightenment embodied an unprecedented enthusiasm for the natural sciences, and rightly so. The great scientists of the seventeenth and eighteenth centuries made enormous advances in their fields. However, scientists began to err when they applied the methods of the natural sciences to the study of man and society. Condorcet, Hayek wrote, "repeatedly exhorts the scholars 'to introduce into the moral sciences the philosophy and the method of the natural sciences.'" Hayek quoted from Condorcet's *Sketch of a Historical Picture of the Progress of the Human Mind*:

> The only foundation for the knowledge of the natural sciences is the idea that the general laws, known or unknown, which regulate the phenomena of the Universe, are necessary and constant; and why should that principle be less true for the intellectual and moral faculties of man than for the other actions of nature?

Hayek wrote that Condorcet had laid the foundation for the collectivist view of history and scientism that remain with us today. The French Revolution took Condorcet's life while taking his philosophy as its guide. The violent destruction of the revolution scraped the ground clean of the ancient institutions and left a barren plain on which the revolutionaries built new ones using the best scientific knowledge of the time. Hayek wrote,

> As one of the new scientific journals which sprang up at the end of the Terror expressed it: "The Revolution has razed everything to the ground. Government, morals, habits, everything has to be rebuilt. What a magnificent site for the architects! What a grand opportunity of making use of all the fine and excellent ideas that had remained speculative, of employing so many materials that could not be used before, of rejecting so many others that had been obstructions for centuries and which one had been forced to use."

And so they did. Like engineers building a bridge, or another tower of Babel, they would construct a new mankind. To aid them, they built a new school, the *Ecole Polytechnique,* with an innovative curriculum. In 1812, the year the French burned Moscow and the British torched Washington, Henri de Saint-Simon wrote about a small flame that a century later would consume the world in its own fire. Hayek quoted him:

> Such is the difference in this respect between the state of...even thirty years ago and that of today that while in those not distant days, if one wanted to know whether a person had received a distinguished education, one asked: "Does he know his Greek and Latin authors well?," today one asks: "Is he good at mathematics? Is he familiar with the achievements of physics, of chemistry, of natural history, in short, of the positive sciences and those of observation?

The graduates of the new French system "prided themselves on having more precise and more satisfactory solutions than anyone else for all political, religious and social questions," and "ventured to create a religion as one learns at the Ecole to build a bridge or a road," according to Hayek.

Henri de Saint-Simon did not attend the *Ecole Polytechnique*. Raised in an aristocratic family, like Karl Marx, he spent his early manhood as a soldier fighting with Lafayette in the U.S. war for independence. After the French Revolution he abandoned his aristocratic title and began speculating with borrowed money on real estate, focusing on the sales of confiscated Church land. He spent some time in prison during the "terror." Out of prison, he worked on a variety of business ideas using borrowed money, such as organizing a stage coach service, selling wine, manufacturing textiles and playing cards, and banking. His entrepreneurial phase ended when his silent partner discovered that Saint-Simon had spent most of the funds on a lavish lifestyle instead of paying the bills of the business.

Saint-Simon still had a modest inheritance to live on and used it to write philosophy. In 1803 he wrote the *Lettres d'un habitant de Geneve a ses contemporains* in which he proposed that a Supreme Council of Newton be formed consisting of three scholars each from seven fields, mathematics, physics, chemistry, physiology, literature, painting and music. The people should elect the members and the mathematician who received the most votes would preside over it. As Hayek wrote, the council would,

> become in their collective capacity the representatives of God on earth, who would deprive the Pope, the cardinals, bishops and the priests of their office because they do not understand the divine science which God has entrusted to them and which some day will again turn earth into paradise...It is necessary that the physiologists chase from their company the philosophers, moralists and metaphysicians just as the astronomers have chased out the astrologers and the chemists have chased out the alchemists.

In other words, the people would elect their dictators and submit to them, while the dictators would use science to restructure society. Saint-Simon even included a religion in which people would worship science in temples of Newton. One of the main jobs of the council was to reconcile property owners with the majority of people who did not own property in order to prevent the struggle that naturally happens between the two classes. Hayek quoted him:

> All men will work; they will regard themselves as laborers attached to one workshop whose efforts will be directed to guide human intelligence according to my divine foresight. The supreme Council of Newton will direct their works...Anybody who does not obey the orders will be treated by the others as a quadruped.

At the pamphlet's publication, Saint-Simon's inheritance ran out and that made him homeless. He became weak and ill until a former valet took him in and supported him for four years. Then the former servant died, tossing Saint-Simon back onto the street. Through the intermediation of an admirer, Saint-Simon obtained a small annual pension in exchange for giving up any claims to an inheritance. With that income, he began again writing about his plan for society.

Before long Saint-Simon attracted a small following of young, gullible men who absorbed and refined his philosophy. Augustin Thierry, then nineteen years old, developed the theory of class conflict that later kidnapped Marx's imagination. Saint-Simon attracted a circle of young bankers and industrialists and, finding praise of industry more profitable than science in attracting donations he became an enthusiast of manufacturing and banking. A governor of the Banque de France gave him 1,000 francs per month to start a new journal on science and industry. The journal raised Saint-Simon's appeal among young artists, bankers and industrialists who formed a larger group of admirers around him.

But his love of planning, and control soon alienated most of those. Among the many things that offended readers, Hayek wrote, were his statements such as, "the principle respect for production and the producers is infinitely more fruitful than the principle respect for property and the proprietors..." and "Politics, therefore, to sum up in two words, is the science of production, that is, the science which has for its object the order of things most favorable to all sorts of production."

Eventually, Saint-Simon lost most of his pupils who advocated liberty and he would likely have died in obscurity had he not attracted his most intelligent follower, a young engineer named Auguste Comte. The *Ecole Polytechnique* had kicked out Comte just before his final exam for being the ring leader in an insubordination. Afterward, he tutored students in math and translated from English a textbook on geometry. Comte worked as Saint-Simon's secretary for three months, during which he absorbed, distilled and advanced his boss' ideas. He summed up his development of moral philosophy, according to Hayek, with this: "There is nothing good and nothing bad absolutely speaking; everything is relative, this is the only absolute statement."

He insisted that property "is the real basis of the social edifice," more so than parliamentary government and suggested changing that edifice by rewriting property laws. With that turn against liberty and property, Saint-Simon and Comte lost all of their support from bankers and industrialists and were forced to shut down the journal. Over the next few years Comte collaborated with Saint-Simon on several publications with untarnished enthusiasm for his old boss, referring to him as the most excellent man he knew and pledging eternal friendship to him.

Most of the complaints about the publications came from those attached to individual liberty and property, which caused Saint-Simon to turn more antagonistic toward the two institutions. He wrote, "The vague and metaphysical idea of liberty...impedes the action of the masses on the individual" and is "contrary to the development of civilization and to the organization of a well-ordered system." Of course, the chief proponents of individual liberty and property were the political economists, or what modern economics calls the classical economists such as David Ricardo and J. B. Say, which shows that the antipathy between socialism and economics arose long before Marx.

Following Descartes' insistence that design by an elite group trumps design by the many, Saint-Simon and Comte insisted that a society consciously designed and enforced by the most intelligent people would prove far superior to the existing system that Christianity had created. Saint-Simon and Comte gave artists the role of suggesting ideas that engineers would implement in the latest iteration of his plan, but an elite group of scientists would guide the process from above. The elite could establish Saint-Simon's perfectly designed social order only if they could in all cases "assign to every individual or nation that precise kind of activity for which they are respectively fitted," according to Hayek. That order presupposed a moral order, but not the existing one which had grown up undirected with Christianity. Comte could endorse only a morality designed by an elite group he called a Government of Opinion which would determine "the entire system of ideas and habits necessary for initiating individuals into the social order under which they must live."

Another financial crisis hit Saint-Simon in 1823 and left him destitute again. He tried to blow his brains out with a gun, but succeeded only in destroying one eye. The incident again attracted sympathy and a financial benefactor, this time until his death at age sixty-five in 1825. He left behind a small group of devoted disciples who would spread his ideas worldwide. The disciples held a series of lectures in 1828 and 1829 on Saint-Simons' ideas as refined by them. Those reached printed form as *Doctrine de Saint-Simon, Exposition* which Hayek called the most important document produced by Saint-Simon or his students:

> If it is not the Bible of Socialism, as it has been called by a French scholar, it deserves at least to be regarded as its Old Testament. And in some respects it did indeed carry socialist thought further than was done for nearly a hundred years after its publication.

The *Exposition* constructed a comprehensive system of Saint-Simon and Comte's original ideas, but his disciples advanced important concepts of their own. Among those were the laws of history that deluded them into thinking they could predict a future state of mankind in which all antagonism between men caused by the exploitation of one group by another will end in a state of harmony. In the past, exploitation took the form of cannibalism, slavery, and serfdom. But in the minds of Saint-Simon's disciples, exploitation existed in the form of work for wages because the business owners, the bourgeoisie, took the products of the wage earners and disposed of them as they wished. Marx would later call this divorce of the laborer from his production "alienation." The scientifically designed society would end this exploitation by terminating private property and transferring it to the state.

The disciples found inheritance particularly irritating. The new order would make the workers the inheritors and thereby destroy the privileges of birth. Hayek wrote of the *Exposition*,

> The main points given will suffice to show that in their description of the organization of a planned society they went much further than later socialists until quite recent times, and also how heavily later socialists have drawn on their ideas. Till the modern discussion of the problem of calculation in a socialist community this description of its working has not been further advanced. There was very little justification for dubbing this very realistic picture of a planned society "Utopian." Marx, characteristically, added to it...the "objective" or labor theory of value.

> But in so far as that general socialism which today is common property is concerned, little had to be added to Saint-Simonian thought. As a further indication of how profoundly the Saint-Simonians have influenced modern thought, it need only be mentioned to what a great extent all European languages have drawn from their vocabulary. "Individualism," "industrialist," "positivism," and the "organization of labor" all occur first in the *Exposition*. [Hayek was mistaken about individualism. See chapter 2] The concept of the "class struggle" and the contrast between the "bourgeoisie" and the "proletariat" in the special technical sense of the terms are Saint-Simonian creations. The word "socialism" itself, although it does not yet appear in the *Exposition* (which uses "association" in very much the same sense), appears in its modern meaning for the first time a little later in the Saint-Simonian Globe.

Saint-Simon's disciples retreated to a commune outside Paris where they practiced and taught their philosophies. They disbanded after charges of outraging public morality were brought against the leaders, resulting in them spending a year in jail. But their influence spread far and wide through literature. Saint-Simonians had preached that art should be contentious and show life in all its ugliness in order to prepare the people for the coming revolution. Many artists took the challenge seriously. Some writers were followers of Saint-Simon while others, such as H. de Balzac, Victor Hugo, and Eugene Sue absorbed and help spread the ideas. Others applied the concepts to music. Thomas Carlyle, who minted the term "dismal science" to disparage economics because he supported slavery when the classical economists opposed it, spread Saint-Simon's ideas in England where the movement bagged its grandest trophy in the capture of J. S. Mill. Hayek quoted Mill who wrote that Comte's *System of Positive Policy*, harmonized well with my existing notions to which it seemed to give a scientific shape. I already regarded the methods of physical science as the proper models for political. But the chief benefit which I derived at this time from the trains of thought suggested by the Saint-Simonians and by Comte, was, that I obtained a clearer conception than ever before of the peculiarities of an era of transition in opinion, and ceased to mistake the moral and intellectual characteristics of such an era, for the normal attributes of humanity.

...[my] eyes were opened to the very limited and temporary value of the old political economy, which assumes private property and inheritance as indefeasible facts and freedom of production and exchange as the *dernier mot* of social improvement."

Mill embraced Saint-Simon and Comte's ideas for 20 years, but they finally so revolted him that he called them "the completest system of spiritual and temporal despotism which ever yet emanated from a human brain, unless possibly that of Ignatius Loyola," as Hayek quoted him.

Saint-Simonians failed to gain the political power they desired, but undeterred, they set about transforming the structure of economies across Europe by creating large companies and promoting public works, especially railroads and canals. Hayek wrote, "One might almost say that after the Saint-Simonians had failed to bring about the reforms they desired through a political movement, or after they had grown older and more worldly, they undertook to transform the capitalist system from within and thus to apply as much of their doctrines as they could by individual effort." They created the European pattern of industrial organization in which large banks financed and owned stock in corporations that built railways, canals, and utilities. They originated the concept of town planning, which evolved into zoning laws in the U.S. "Enfantin, looking back late in life at the works of the Saint-Simonians, was well entitled to say that they had 'covered the earth with a net-work of railways, gold, silver, and electricity,'" Hayek wrote. Finally, they provided the arguments for cartels and the form of socialism that would be known as fascism.

Socialism's success in Germany

In the first quarter of the nineteenth century classical liberal philosophy invaded and captured the hearts of German intellectuals. The ideas had come from England, Ludwig von Mises wrote in *Omnipotent Government*:

But German intellectuals welcomed Western ideas of freedom and the rights of man with enthusiasm. German classical literature is imbued with them, and the great German composers set to music verses singing the praises of liberty. The poems, plays, and other writings of Frederick Schiller are from beginning to end a hymn to liberty. Every word written by Schiller was a blow to the old political system of Germany; his works were fervently greeted by nearly all Germans who read books or frequented the theater...

Whoever rose from misery and joined the community of civilized men became a liberal. Except for the small group of princes and their aristocratic retainers practically everyone interested in political issues was liberal. There were in Germany in those days only liberal men and indifferent men; but the ranks of the indifferent continually shrank, while the ranks of the liberals swelled.

The rising tide of liberalism threatened to drown the absolute rule of the king and nobility who responded by using the military to crush the revolution of 1848 that might have introduced freedom and an industrial revolution to Germany. Only the educated had embraced classical liberalism, whereas the shock troops of the army tended to be illiterate peasants who submitted to the will of the nobility as they had for centuries. The leaders of classical liberalism understood they would have to wait for change until they had educated more citizens and soldiers in the ideas of freedom. As Mises wrote,

> These much-abused German liberals of the 1860's, these men of studious habits, these readers of philosophical treatises, these lovers of music and poetry, understood very well why the upheaval of 1848 had failed. They knew that they could not establish popular government within a nation where many millions were still caught in the bonds of superstition, boorishness, and illiteracy. The political problem was essentially a problem of education. The final success of liberalism and democracy was beyond doubt. The trend toward parliamentary rule was irresistible. But the victory of liberalism could be achieved only when those strata of the population from which the King drew his reliable soldiers should have become enlightened and thereby transformed into supporters of liberal ideas. Then the King would be forced to surrender, and the Parliament would obtain supremacy without bloodshed.

But the liberals did not have the time to educate the population as they had thought, for the doctrines of Saint-Simon achieved their greatest reception in Germany. After the July Revolution of 1830 in France, Paris sucked in intellectuals and revolutionaries like a vacuum from all over, but especially Germany. The Saint-Simonians were at the height of their influence and in the autumn articles on them and translations of some of their writings swept across Germany. Hayek wrote in *The Counter-Revolution*, "The whole German literary world seems to have been agog for news about the novel French ideas and to some, as Rahel von Varnhagen describes it, the Saint-Simonian Globe became the indispensable intellectual daily bread."

The philosophy of Hegel plowed the ground in Germany for the seeds of Saint-Simonianism as John the Baptist had prepared Israel for Jesus. The Young Hegelians found it trivial to merge the two philosophies, Karl Marx and Friedrich Engels being the most notorious members of that group. By 1840, Saint-Simon's ideas had "come to form the basis of all the socialist movements. And the socialism of 1848 apart from the strong democratic and anarchistic elements which by then had been carried into it as new and alien elements was in doctrine and personnel still largely Saint-Simonian," according to Hayek. The failed revolution of 1848 gave the liberals an impotent parliament in which to publicly vent their grievances, but time was not on their side. Before they could achieve their goals through education, socialism rushed in and stole the hearts of the majority and then filled parliament. By the middle of the 1860s, the leading academics were evangelizing the nation for Saint-Simon's socialism. Mises wrote in *Omnipotent Government*,

> Very soon the economic, philosophical, historical, and juridical university lectures were representing liberalism in caricature. The social scientists outdid each other in emotional criticism of British free trade and laissez faire; the philosophers disparaged the "stock-jobber" ethics of utilitarianism, the superficiality of enlightenment, and the negativity of the notion of liberty; the lawyers demonstrated the paradox of democratic and parliamentary institutions; and the historians dealt with the moral and political decay of France and of Great Britain. On the other hand, the students were taught to admire the "social kingdom of the Hohenzollerns" from Frederick William I, the "noble socialist," to William I, the great Kaiser of social security and labor legislation. The Social Democrats despised Western "plutodemocracy" and "pseudo-liberty" and ridiculed the teachings of "bourgeois economics."

Otto von Bismarck, the Chancellor of Germany from 1871 to 1890, viewed the rise of socialism as an ally against the liberals he hated so much. But neither he nor the nobility welcomed a socialist overthrow of the absolute rule of the monarch. Bismarck defeated both threats by co-opting most of the socialist policies, such as old age pensions, accident insurance, medical care and unemployment insurance and by nationalizing key industries. The leaders of the socialist parties opposed Bismarck's reforms because they kept the monarchy in power, appeased the ignorant masses and prevented the approach of the revolution and rule of the proletariat. But the common socialists saw the immediate benefits of Bismarck's reforms and embraced them.

Socialists were justified in their skepticism of Bismarck's plan. The Chancellor revealed his true motives in an interview: "My idea was to bribe the working classes, or shall I say, to win them over, to regard the state as a social institution existing for their sake and interested in their welfare," according to Richard Ebeling in "Marching to Bismarck's Drummer: The Origins of the Modern Welfare State." Bismarck understood that a majority of Germans depending on the state for income would be much less likely to revolt as it had in 1848. In public, Bismarck referred to his policies as "practical Christianity," in the words Frederic B. M. Hollyday in "Bismarck,"

The real grievance of the worker is the insecurity of his existence; he is not sure that he will always have work, he is not sure that he will always be healthy, and he foresees that he will one day be old and unfit to work. If he falls into poverty, even if only through a prolonged illness, he is then completely helpless, left to his own devices, and society does not currently recognize any real obligation towards him beyond the usual help for the poor, even if he has been working all the time ever so faithfully and diligently. The usual help for the poor, however, leaves a lot to be desired, especially in large cities, where it is very much worse than in the country.

Bismarck's fusion of socialism and absolute monarchy became known as *Sozialpolitik* and aimed at raising the standard of living of workers through legislation. But the pro-labor legislation, minimum wage laws and union strikes succeeded only in raising the costs of production, which increasingly made German exports of manufactured goods uncompetitive in the international marketplace. Had Germany been blessed with ample and fertile farmland, the state might have used tariffs to protect manufacturers who would produce for the domestic market alone. But Germany needed to export manufactured goods to pay for desperately needed food and raw materials. Bismarck responded to the problem by allowing manufacturers to create cartels that gave them monopolies on their products inside Germany. Without competition the cartels raised prices at home enough to subsidize the exports they sold overseas at competitive prices. Higher nominal wages fooled the wage-earners into believing they were better off when in truth the higher monopoly prices Germans paid for manufactured goods took back what the higher wages gave.

Bismarck's socialism caused prices to rise but bureaucrats ran the nationalized industries so poorly that they required increasing subsidies from the state. The state had to raise taxes to pay the subsidies while the public found the services unsatisfactory. Higher taxes and wages made German manufacturing unable to compete against imported goods, so the state raised tariffs. The monopolies given to the cartels allowed companies to charge high prices in Germany while selling their products overseas at the lower market prices. In other words, German consumers subsidized exports by paying higher prices at home as well as higher taxes to subsidize inefficient manufacturers.

The German people hated the cartels and monopolies, but Marxists convinced them that residual capitalism and greedy capitalists caused them not socialism. The people saw no connection between the cartels and the government's intervention in the economy to implement its socialist policies. Germany's socialist system would later be called the welfare state and fascism. Unlike communism in Russia which ended private property in favor of state ownership, fascism removed all control of property from the owners while leaving them with the paper title. Of course, without control property no longer exists, but leaving the owners with a meaningless paper title fooled most people, especially journalists and historians, into thinking that Germany had a capitalist system.

The ruse worked so well that when Friedrich Hayek grasped that most British citizens considered Nazi Germany to be a capitalist nation he wrote his most famous book, *The Road to Serfdom*, to attack that delusion. Hayek wrote to his fellow British citizens and did not expect the book to appeal to other nationalities. But when the book crossed the Atlantic, it infuriated members of the Democrat party who thought Hayek had targeted the policies of President Roosevelt because they were so much like those of Nazi Germany and fascist Italy. Roosevelt admired Mussolini and modeled many of his policies after him.

Eventually the "money illusion" evaporated in Germany as workers began to slowly understand that price inflation made them poorer. By the time of the disaster of the first world war had ended and the socialists enjoyed the opportunity to form their first truly socialist government, economic reality had boiled away infatuation with *Sozialpolitik*. Socialist parties faced a dilemma when they formed their government in 1918 according to Mises in *Money, Method, and the Market*:

> At the beginning of the twentieth century, one could no longer deny the obvious fact that the public authorities had scandalously failed in their attempts to administer the various business organizations they had acquired in the conduct of their "state socialism"...Socialism was in their opinion the great panacea, but it seemed that nobody knew what it really meant and how to bring it about properly. Thus, the victorious socialist leaders did what all governments do when they do not know what to do. They appointed a committee of professors and other people considered to be experts. For more than fifty years the Marxians had fanatically advocated socialization as the focal point of their program, as the nostrum to heal all earthly evils and to lead mankind forward into the new Garden of Eden. Now they had seized power and all of the people expected that they would redeem their promise. Now they had to socialize. But at once they had to confess that they did not know what to do and they were asking professors what socialization meant and how it could be put into practice.
>
> It was the greatest intellectual fiasco history has ever known and it put in the eyes of all reasonable people an inglorious end to all the teachings of Marx and hosts of lesser-known Utopians...
>
> And, of course, this committee whose best known members were Doctor Hilferding and Professor [Josheph] Schumpeter, produced a collection of volumes dealing with various subjects, but did not solve the insoluble problem for the solution of which it had been established. It did not indicate a method for a reasonable and successful conduct of business operated by other principles than those of capitalistic profit-seeking.

Socialists have never allowed failure to deter them and always blamed residual capitalism for those failures. In spite of massive failure, Germany retained the policies of Bismarck's welfare state as if they had no other options. Those policies immigrated to the U.S. with German union workers sailing to the New World, with students returning from their indoctrination at German universities, and with intellectuals enamored with the power of the

German state. For example, Richard Ely, a professor of economics at the University of Wisconsin, studied in Germany then returned to the U.S. to launch the American Economic Association in 1885 with the purpose of promoting Bismarck's welfare-state. According to Richard Ebeling in "Marching to Bismarck's Drummer," Ely later wrote,

> Looking into the future we may contemplate a society with real, not merely nominal freedom, to pursue the best; a society in which men shall work together for the common purposes, and in which the wholesale cooperation shall take place largely through the government...We have reason to believe that we shall yet see great national undertakings with the property of the nation, and managed by the nation, through agents who appreciate the glory of true public service, and feel that it is God's work they are doing, because church and state are as one.

One of many admirers from the U.S., Frederic Howe, wrote a book in 1915 that preached the virtues of the socialism called *Socialized Germany*. Ebeling quoted Howe who wrote,

> The state has its finger on the pulse of the worker from the cradle to the grave. His education, his health, and his working efficiency are matters of constant concern. He is carefully protected from accident by laws and regulation governing factories. He is trained in his hand and in his brain to be a good workman and is insured against accident, sickness, and old age. While idle through no fault of his own, work is frequently found for him. When homeless, a lodging is offered so that he will not easily pass into the vagrant class...

> This paternalism does not necessarily mean less freedom to the individual than that which prevails in America or England...[T]he German enjoys a freedom far greater than that which prevails in America or England. This freedom is of an economic sort...It protects the defenseless classes from exploitation and abuse. It safeguards the weak...

> In the mind of the Germans the functions of the state are not susceptible to abstract, a priori deductions. Each proposal must be decided by the time and the conditions. If it seems advisable for the state to own an industry, it should proceed to own it; if it is wise to curb any class or interest, it should be curbed. Expediency or opportunism is the rule of statesmanship, not abstraction as to the philosophical nature of the state.

In other words, no principles guided the German government, only pragmatism, which became a code word for increased socialism. As Mises wrote in *Omnipotent Government*, "And it was Lassalle who spoke the words which characterize best the spirit of the age to come:

'The state is God.'" Bismarck's state socialism inspired Fabian socialism in Great Britain and the Progressive movement in the U.S., neither of which examined the failed outcomes of his policies.

With their growing success, socialists began to change the definitions of words. For example, justice became material equality instead of due process. And the term "liberal," which had referred to individual freedom from the state, socialists re-invented to mean freedom from poverty and insecurity, thereby instantiating the wise words of Confucius, "When words lose their meaning people will lose their liberty." Hayek wrote in *Fatal Conceit*,

> There are of course many other ambiguities and confusions, some of them of greater importance. For instance, there was the deliberate deception practiced by American socialists in their appropriation of the term "liberalism". As Joseph A. Schumpeter rightly put it (1954:394): "As a supreme if unintended compliment, the enemies of the system of private enterprise have thought it wise to appropriate its label."

The failure of socialism with the resulting impoverishment of the working class did not cause intellectuals to divorce the ideology, and that revealed a great deal about socialists' motives. As Schoeck pointed out in his book, the prime mover of socialism is envy. The never ending love of socialism in spite of the misery it has caused exposes the true motive behind it as Mises wrote:

> Granted, many of them replied, that socialism may not result in riches for all but rather in a smaller production of wealth; nevertheless the masses will be happier under socialism, because they will share their worries with all their fellow citizens, and there will not be wealthier classes to be envied by poorer ones. The starving and ragged workers of Soviet Russia, they tell us, are a thousand times more joyful than the workers of the West who live under conditions which are luxurious compared to Russian standards; equality in poverty is a more satisfactory state than well-being where there are people who can flaunt more luxuries than the average man.

Twilight of freedom

Why did Saint-Simon's socialism sweep Europe as it did? How did the classical liberal economists, the arch enemies of socialism, fail to persuade the people? As noted earlier, Schoeck determined that Christianity had catalyzed economic progress by restraining envy, the chief opponent of innovation, individualism and development through most of human history. Apparently, Christianity had never penetrated very deeply into French and German societies because the French Revolution easily sand blasted away the veneer.

By the middle of the nineteenth century, German theologians began to deny the basic truths of traditional Christianity such as the virgin birth of Jesus, his deity, death and physical resurrection. They claimed that Jesus never suggested that he was God and that the Apostle

Paul had hijacked the movement, created a new religion by mixing his Judaism with Greek philosophy and sold it to the eleven Apostles who had been left rudderless by Jesus' death. They denied all of the miracles in the four Gospels and expunged them of any reference to Jesus' deity. Once they had emaciated the New Testament, they attacked the Old, or the Hebrew Bible, again dismissing all miracles and claiming that most of it had been written after the return of the exiles from Babylon.

Of course, the critics never offered any evidence for their ideas. Their "science" consisted of nothing more than asserting that science has proved that miracles are impossible. And they never explained how the Apostles had convinced themselves to die for a cause they knew they had fabricated and was a lie. People often die for false causes, such as communism, if they think they are true, but it was impossible for the Apostles to imagine that the new religion made up by Paul was true.

German theologians who denied the validity of traditional Christianity continued to call themselves Christians and even claimed to represent true Christianity because they had used "science" to chip away centuries of human corruption of Jesus' teachings to reveal the "historical," or true, Christianity. In response, traditional Christians began to refer to themselves as "fundamentalists," because they insisted that followers must belief certain fundamental truths in order to be Christians. Those included the deity of Jesus, his virgin birth, physical death and bodily resurrection. They referred to the new German theologians as "liberals."

Traditional Christianity had the goal of spreading the Gospel, which it saw as the good news of personal salvation by Jesus' death, and converting the world. The Kingdom of God would not come until Christ returned in fulfillment of his own prophesies. But the liberal theologians no longer believed any of that and so were left dangling in the wind without a purpose. Socialism rescued them. It taught them that mankind did not need personal salvation, since people are born innocent. They turn to evil only because of oppression from society and the worst oppression came from private property, so liberal Christianity redefined salvation to mean the equal distribution of wealth and the Kingdom of God to mean a socialist society that would end oppression and restore humanity to its natural state of innocence.

One of the chief ambassadors of German liberalism and socialism to the U.S. and a founder of the "social gospel" movement was Walter Rauschenbusch. His father had been a devout German Baptist fundamentalist who pastored German-speaking churches in the U.S. and loved all things German. But Walter inherited his father's love of Germany without a love for the Gospel, for when his father sent Walter, his two sisters and mother to Germany for four years to complete the children's education, Walter uncritically consumed Germany's liberal theology and socialism. In the U.S., he was influenced by two other socialists, Henry George and Richard Ely, who founded the American Economic Association.

Stanley Hauerwas wrote in his *A Better Hope: Resources for a Church Confronting Capitalism, Democracy, and Postmodernity* that "Rauschenbusch, perhaps somewhat disingenuously, argues that the social gospel effected no significant change to any fundamental Christian doctrine" in his 1917 Taylor Lectures at Yale Divinity School. But Hauerwas' sympathy for Rauschenbush's socialism caused him to pull his punch. The "social gospel" constituted a radical rewriting of church history and a redefining of all of its most important doctrines. For example, like the atheists/deists of the French Revolution and Saint-Simon, Rauschenbush insisted that society, not God, makes people good and society, not human nature, makes them bad:

> An unchristian social order can be known by the fact that it makes good men do bad things. It tempts, defeats, drains, and degrades and leaves men stunted, cowed, and shamed in their manhood. A Christian social order makes bad men do good things. It sets high aims, steadies the vagrant impulses of the weak, trains the powers of the young, and is felt by all as an uplifting force which leaves them with the consciousness of a broader and noble humanity as their years go on.

In other words, real sin was not personal, as theologians had taught for two thousand years, but something society causes. Society played the same role in Rauschenbush's theology as Satan had in traditional Christianity: change the structure of society and humanity would change. Also, historic Christianity taught that it would create the Kingdom of God on earth as the world became more Christian, but Rauschenbush rejected that in favor of a "law of gradual growth" of the kingdom. Mankind did not need God to achieve perfection. We would accomplish it through our own efforts. Though he was not God, Christ initiated the kingdom through the force of his personality. Instantiating the kingdom depends upon socialists. Rauschenbush taught that democracy has saved politics in the U.S.: "The challenge before the church is to secure for the economic realm the same kind of cooperative life that had been achieved in American politics." In other words, all wealth needed to be owned democratically, or equally, in order to complete the task of bringing the kingdom of God to earth.

The social gospel took over the old mainline Protestant denominations, the Lutheran, Episcopal, Presbyterian and Methodist churches. Today, only about 10 percent of the churches in those organizations cling to traditional Christianity. Of the major denominations that existed at the turn of the last century, only Baptists have managed to maintain fundamentalist Christianity in a majority of churches. As people abandoned traditional fundamentalist Christianity for the liberal version, they broke the chains that constrained envy. Socialism made envy not only acceptable, it elevated envy to a virtue by redefining justice to mean equality of material goods, and as Schoeck made clear the demand for material equality has been the chief manifestation of envy through history.

Christianity's vital role

Many academics recoil at the thought of attributing any good outcomes at all to religion, but there is growing evidence of the important role Christianity played in economics and science. Alfred North Whitehead and Rodney Stark, quoted earlier, attributed the rise of science in Western Europe to Christianity. Helmut Schoeck, Rodney Stark and Larry Siedentop, also quoted, ascribed Western individualism (Hayek's true individualism), which was an absolute necessity for economic development, to Christianity. In addition, Hayek wrote about the vital role of religion for transferring vital institutions across generations in his last book, *Fatal Conceit*. Hayek launched the chapter "Religion and the Guardians of Tradition," of that book with the earlier quote from Adam Smith on the importance of religion. And Hayek was quoted earlier on the role of religion in preserving values such as respect for private property, saving, exchange, honesty, truthfulness and contract. Hayek understood that his endorsement of religion would arouse opposition in many academic circles. He wrote the following in *Fatal Conceit*:

> In closing this work, I would like to make a few informal remarks – they are intended as no more than that - about the connection between the argument of this book and the role of religious belief. These remarks may be unpalatable to some intellectuals because they suggest that, in their own long-standing conflict with religion, they were partly mistaken - and very much lacking in appreciation...

> Even those among us, like myself, who are not prepared to accept the anthropomorphic conception of a personal divinity ought to admit that the premature loss of what we regard as nonfactual beliefs would have deprived mankind of a powerful support in the long development of the extended order that we now enjoy, and that even now the loss of these beliefs, whether true or false, creates great difficulties.

> ...even an agnostic ought to concede that we owe our morals, and the tradition that has provided not only our civilisation but our very lives, to the acceptance of such scientifically unacceptable factual claims.

Hayek argued that the pseudo-reasoning springing from the French Revolution with its false individualism jettisoned the traditions of property, saving, exchange, and contract because they could see no immediate benefit in them, whereas the short term profit of abandoning them and redistributing wealth was obvious to most people. Religion had kept those long-term values alive, not because of their reasonableness but because of fear of God and his "thou shalt not" commands.

As an agnostic, Hayek had little interest in religion so he can be forgiven for thinking that religion in general perpetuated the values that advanced freedom and created wealth. But the fact is that the explosive growth in wealth catalogued by McCloskey, Maddison and others did not exist for most of human history. It did not happen in the Greco-Roman world of the Greek gods. It did not happen in cultures dominated by Hinduism, Buddhism or Islam, or for that matter Eastern Orthodox Christianity. And it did not happen in Western Europe during the first fifteen centuries in which Christianity dominated. The hockey stick launch of per capita income took off only in the seventeenth century and only in the Dutch Republic. For the next 200 years it spread only to Western Europe and the U.S. So religion in general provides a necessary but insufficient cause of the transmission of the values necessary for development. As Rodney Stark and Larry Siedentop point out, Western Christianity was unique in its emphasis on free will, reason, individualism, freedom, property, savings, commerce and contract.

Hayek appreciated the work of the scholars of the University of Salamanca, Spain, in the sixteenth century and praised them as proto-Austrian economists. He insisted on having one of the meetings of the Mont Pelerin Society, which he had created, in Salamanca, Spain, in honor of those theologians. But it seems to have escaped Hayek that those scholars had built their economics on the foundation of the Bible's teachings on the sanctity of life, liberty and property. Those principles did not exist in other religions and cultures. Hayek hoped that agnostics such as him could personify abstract traditions and "worship" them as a kind of god. He wrote in *Fatal Conceit*, "Yet perhaps most people can conceive of abstract tradition only as a personal Will. If so, will they not be inclined to find this will in 'society' in an age in which more overt supernaturalisms are ruled out as superstitions? On that question may rest the survival of our civilisation."

Hayek's last sentence punctuated the end of the chapter on religion and exudes an air of desperation. But in a way, Hayek was guilty of the scientism that he had attributed to Saint-Simon and against which he had fought for decades. Hayek vehemently opposed scientism in economics, but by trying to create a new religion based on science he committed the same error of invading theology with scientism. And Hayek's statement about "such scientifically unacceptable factual claims" is another fallacy of scientism because the natural sciences have no tools for examining theology. Trying to use the natural sciences or economics to investigate theological truths would be like dressing a camel in a tutu and expecting it to dance ballet; it would be irrational.

In spite of his hopes, Western atheists and deists did not even try to personify the values that Hayek esteemed; they abandoned them utterly and completely. And in proportion to the degree that the West has shaken off traditional Christianity it has embraced greater socialism, as Hayek feared.

Chapter 1 introduced the work of economist Deirdre McCloskey arguing for the importance of the bourgeois values to the explosive growth of the West over the past three centuries. McCloskey masterfully destroys the reasoning of competing theories. Other scholars also have trouble with the roundup of the usual suspects as causes of development. For example, Lawrence Harrison of the Harvard Academy for International and Area Studies wrote in the book *Culture Matters: How Values Shape Human Progress* that,

> If colonialism and dependency are unsatisfactory explanations for poverty and authoritarianism overseas…and if there are too many exceptions…to geographic/climatological explanations, how else can the unsatisfactory progress of humankind toward prosperity and political pluralism during the past half century be explained?

> A growing number of scholars, journalists, politicians, and development practitioners are focusing on the role of cultural values and attitudes as facilitators of, or obstacles to, progress.

Of course, the next question is where do people get their values? The answer in *Culture Matters* is from religion, as the following quotes illustrate: "Religious traditions seem to have had an enduring impact on the contemporary value systems of sixty-five societies, as Weber, Huntington, and others have argued," according to Ronald Inglehart, professor of political science and program director at the Institute for Social Research at the University of Michigan.

Seymour Martin Lipset, the Hazel professor of Public Policy at George Mason University, and Gabriel Salman Lenz, George Mason University and the Woodrow Wilson International Center for Scholars wrote,

> In the preceding discussion we showed that cultural variables help explain and predict levels of corruption. But what explains culture? Dealing with this complex question is far beyond the limits of this chapter. However, the social science consensus that religion is an important determinant of variations in larger secular cultures offers some helpful suggestions. Countries dominated by Protestants are less corrupt than others.

"Throughout history, religion has been the richest source of values..." wrote Mariano Grondona, professor of government and law at the National University of Buenos Aires, who added,

> It was the Protestant Reformation that first produced economic development in northern Europe and North America. Until the Reformation, the leaders of Europe were France, Spain (allied with Catholic Austria), the north of Italy (the cradle of the Renaissance), and the Vatican. The Protestant cultural revolution changed all that as heretofore second-rank nations – Holland, Switzerland, Great Britain, the Scandinavian countries, Prussia, and the former British colonies in North America – took over the reins of leadership.

Lawrence E. Harrison is a senior fellow at the Harvard Academy for International and Area Studies. He coedited the book *Culture Matters* with Samuel P. Huntington, author of *The Clash of Civilizations and the Remaking of World Order* and director of the John M. Olin Institute for Strategic Studies and chairman of the Academy for International and Area Studies. Harrison wrote,

> In 1968, Gunnar Myrdal [Nobel Prize-winning economist] published *Asian Dreams: An Inquiry into the Poverty of Nations* after ten years of study of South Asia. He concluded that cultural factors, profoundly influenced by religion, are the principal obstacles to modernization. It is not just that they get in the way of entrepreneurial activity but that they permeate, rigidify, and dominate political, economic, and social behavior.

There is a complex interplay of cause and effect between culture and progress, but the power of culture is demonstrable. It is observable in those countries where the economic achievement of ethnic minorities far exceeds that of the majorities, as is the case of the Chinese in Thailand, Indonesia, Malaysia, and the Philippines.

The last quote does not mention religion, but it is well known that the ethnic Chinese minorities who dominate commerce in South East Asia tend to be Christians, many of whom fled China after the Communist takeover and slaughter of Chinese Christians. The recurring attacks on Chinese in Indonesia are partly due to their greater wealth, but mostly a result a Christian minority living among radical Muslims. Some of the amazing economic growth in China can be attributed to those Christian Chinese minorities investing in the mainland after the opening of its markets. Over eighty percent of foreign direct investment in China during the early years of the opening up under Deng Xia Peng came from overseas Chinese businesses in Southeast Asia. As late as 1997, foreign direct investment from Europe and North America amounted to only $8.4 billion while that from Hong Kong alone totaled $21.6 billion.

Of course, cynics will respond with the exceptions of Japan, South Korea, Hong Kong and Taiwan. However, all but Japan have significant numbers of Christians. In Japan's case, it's possible to force economic development in nations that do not support the bourgeois values and do not have large Christian minorities as MIT economics professor Daron Acemoglu and Harvard political scientist and economist James A. Robinson concede in their *Why Nations Fail*. States can buy Western technology to replace traditional methods of farming and manufacturing and force some economic growth through greater efficiency. But as Acemoglu and Robinson point out, those nations will hit a brick wall that limits development if they refuse to continue to reform their institutions. However, the authors fail to grasp that culture builds institutions; values create culture; and religion instills values. The cause and effect relationship does not run sequentially through time, but happens at the same time, as in a building: religion is the foundation; values and culture are the walls and economic development the roof.

In addition, lacking a Christian minority does not mean that Christianity had no impact on a nation. In the nineteenth and early twentieth centuries European and American church organizations sent thousands of missionaries to poor countries around the globe to convert people to the kingdom of God. But in the process they did much more: they built hospitals and schools, established newspapers and fought for the rights of the natives against oppression by colonial leaders. As Robert D. Woodberry wrote in the abstract to his paper "The Missionary Roots of Liberal Democracy,"

> This article demonstrates historically and statistically that conversionary Protestants (CPs) heavily influenced the rise and spread of stable democracy around the world. It argues that CPs were a crucial catalyst initiating the development and spread of religious liberty, mass education, mass printing,

newspapers, voluntary organizations, and colonial reforms, thereby creating the conditions that made stable democracy more likely. Statistically, the historic prevalence of Protestant missionaries explains about half the variation in democracy in Africa, Asia, Latin America and Oceania and removes the impact of most variables that dominate current statistical research about democracy. The association between Protestant missions and democracy is consistent in different continents and subsamples, and it is robust to more than 50 controls and to instrumental variable analysis.

Woodberry proposes a recursive structural model in which missionaries directly encouraged democracy in some cases but worked mostly through economic development, mass education, printing and civil society to create an environment favorable to democracy. Those were the unintended consequences of Protestant missionaries wanting new converts to be able to read the Bible in their own languages as their ancestors in Europe had done for generations. Until the missionaries arrived, only the ruling elites could read, and as happened in Europe before the Reformation, the elites tried to prevent the common people from learning to read out of fear that education would make them unhappy and lead to unrest. The missionaries created alphabets for non-written languages, translated the Bible into hundreds of native languages, printed the Bibles, tracts and textbooks for schools and established schools to teach natives to read as well as train teachers. Their success motivated native elites who did not convert to build competing schools and publishing houses.

Missionaries fostered the rule of law by defending natives against abuse by colonial rulers and forcing the rulers to treat locals by the same procedures and laws as the rulers enjoyed. They accomplished much of that through the regular newsletters to churches back home who provided their financial support. If a colonial ruler oppressed the people, the missionaries let the folks back home know about it and those folks assaulted parliament, demanding reforms.

The efforts of the missionaries distributed power from the elites to educated commoners. "This dispersion of power and resources increased G.D.P., expanded the middle class, and forced most 'Protestant' colonizers to devolve power to non-Europeans via elections earlier than 'Catholic' colonizers had to." As a result, "Protestant missions are also associated with high newspaper circulation…, more organizational civil society…, greater economic development…, stronger protection of private property, greater rule of law, and lower levels of corruption…"

Of course, many atheists in the West have embraced free markets and libertarian ideas, but those tend to be economists who came to their philosophy through utilitarianism. They are small in numbers. A democracy needs a majority of voters to share the same confidence in freedom and markets, but few of those have the mental ability to understand the economic questions, let alone the answers. Another large portion simply is not interested in economics, while a third group have been weaned on socialism from grade school where they learned "milk cow" economics (e.g., I have two milk cows and my neighbor has none; in socialism I give one cow to my neighbor.) that poisoned their outlook on capitalism.

Even ignoring those problems, the universality of envy predisposes most people to adopt some form of socialism. Socialism offers the promise of a nearly perfect society, the elimination of most evil, by evenly distributing wealth and assuaging envy. That is a much more powerful seduction for the average man than utilitarianism or freedom offers. As the socialists in Germany in the nineteenth century revealed, most people would rather everyone be poor and equal than for the average to be wealthy with some inequality. In their minds, freedom matters little if some can use that freedom to amass more material goods than others.

Economic education will not change peoples' minds, especially when mainstream economics itself encourages state intervention in the economy because of its fetishes such as equilibrium, perfect competition and market failures. Remember that the classical liberals of Germany in the second half of the nineteenth century thought they could educate enough people in the ways of freedom to bring about a revolution and they failed. Socialism swept the nation like a flash flood on the American plains with little effort.

Echoing Hayek, Mariano Grondona wrote in *Culture Matters*, "In the struggle between the short and long term, the former will win unless a value intervenes in the decision making process. This is the function of values: to serve as a bridge between short-term and long-term expectations, decisively reinforcing distant goals in their otherwise hopeless struggle against instant gratification." Envy powerfully supports the desire for instant gratification.

But readers might ask, "Isn't the U.S. a Christian nation?" The answer depends on how one defines Christianity. Of course, we have Eastern Orthodox and Roman Catholic Christianity with Protestantism dominating. All three agreed on the definition of God, the deity of Christ and his resurrection. Then in early 19th century Germany a group of theologians who denied all of those doctrines continued to call themselves Christian. They denied the historical validity of most of the Bible, especially all accounts of miracles. In their search for the "historical" Jesus demythologized, they determined that the stories of the virgin birth, all of Jesus' miracles, any claims he made to being God and his resurrection were inventions of later Christians, mostly Paul. They offered no evidence or justification for those views; they simply did not like what the Gospels contain and so dismissed most of them as myths. Those "liberal" theologians make up most of mainline Protestantism. They dominate in universities and are socialists.

Fundamentalist, traditional Christianity gave the world its first taste of freedom and the values to sustain it. It is unlikely that anything as powerful as religion will come along to rescue us. The surest way to a renaissance of liberty in the West is a good old fashioned Christian revival. To employ Hayek again, on that question may rest the survival of our civilization.

Chapter 8 – Christian Capitalism

Readers may wonder how to make sense of a term like "Christian capitalism." How can a field of science be Christian? After all, most would not look for a Christian physics because the principles of physics are the same for Christians as well as non-Christians; those principles do not change because of one's religion. From another perspective, all modern science is Christian because, as has been discussed, monks and clergy in the middle ages had the idea and got the courage to investigate the natural world because of the Christian doctrine that God is rational and distinct from his creation. Neither God nor spirits animate the natural world directly, but the material world responds to laws that God created. Many scientists may be atheists, but the irony is that they assume a unique Christian cosmology in order to practice their discipline.

Of course, those who subscribe to the fallacious philosophy of logical positivism do not consider economics to be a science. They have arbitrarily determined that only the material world exists. For the best defense of economics against logical positivism see Mises' brilliant book *The Ultimate Foundation of Economic Science: An Essay on Method.*

Human nature

Critics of mainstream economics often accuse the discipline of being out of touch with reality and in many cases that criticism is justified. But if we want to have economic theories that accurately depict reality then we must have a correct understanding of human nature and how humans act. Mises and Hayek regularly pointed out the obvious fact that the subjects of economics are vastly different from those of physics because humans reason and learn while electrons do not. Economist John E. Anderson made that point in his article, "Economics and the Evangelical Mind:"

> Since appropriate models and suitable policy can only flow from a correct understanding of human nature, and we are sure that the evangelical mind is well grounded in a biblical understanding of that nature, there is reason to hope that evangelical economists can make additional important contributions to the discipline of economics as they apply their minds and hearts to the work to which God has called them.

That may sound obvious, but it is not obvious to most economists and the failure to understand this has done great damage to the field.

For most of its short history, economics enjoyed a Biblical view of human nature because the early crypto-economists at the University of Salamanca, Spain, were theologians and economics was a subset of moral philosophy. The great Adam Smith taught moral philosophy, not economics. He had more in common with the scholars of Salamanca than with what became the field of economics. One might see his book, *The Wealth of Nations*, as an application of the principles developed in his earlier book, *The Theory of Moral Sentiments*, to the field of economics. Smith followed in the tradition of the scholars of Salamanca who studied markets in order to determine the morality of business practices. The centuries-long quest for a theory of a just price led scholars to break with Aristotle on the idea that a just exchange required items of objective, equal value. The Salamancan scholars determined that any exchange conducted without fraud or coercion was a just exchange, thereby establishing the grounds for free markets.

The theologians who investigated the morality of markets for centuries operated with a traditional Christian view of human nature known as the doctrine of original sin that was based on the Biblical account of Adam and Eve in the Garden of Eden. God had created moral beings without a tendency toward evil, but when they rebelled against God they changed human nature by giving it an affinity for evil. As a result, mankind has within it the capacity for great good but even greater evil, and a tendency toward the latter. Of the seven deadly sins to which mankind has the strongest attraction, envy is the deadliest, most pervasive and most relevant to economics. As Schoeck wrote in his book *Envy: A Theory of Social Behavior*, mankind cannot achieve a utopian society because of that inborn tendency toward envy.

As noted in chapter 7, Adam Smith subscribed to the traditional Christian view of a fallen human nature. He assumed that people are naturally greedy and power hungry. His solution to greed was competitive markets. Society could not trust politicians to restrain greed because businessmen would merely buy the politicians and get laws passed that favored their businesses. But when businessmen had to compete with each other for customers, they would battle to see who satisfied customers the best, and that was all we needed to restrain greed. Smith sought to channel fallen human nature for the improvement of society, not change human nature, which he would have considered impossible except by an act of God. Economics was founded on a Christian understanding of human nature.

The atheist and deist founders of socialism in the early nineteenth century jettisoned the traditional Christian view of human nature and replaced it with their own fabrication: mankind is born innocent and turns to evil only because of oppression. Socialism can save mankind and create the kingdom of god on earth by having the government end oppression through abolishing private property, redistributing wealth, and increasing market regulation and education. This is one reason a Christian cannot be a socialist; it is inconsistent with Christian doctrine of human nature.

But it is also the reason socialism has maintained a strong allure for most non-Christians and many Christians. Capitalism offers an improved standard of living and has delivered that by making the people of most nations in the West at least thirty times wealthier than their ancestors three centuries ago, but modern societies are far from perfect. Socialism promises to perfect society through the elimination of evil in mankind. It competes as a counter gospel to the Gospel of the New Testament, except that it promises salvation on earth, now, instead of having to wait for a distant future when Christ returns.

Divergent views on human nature distinguish Christians and socialists, but they also direct Christians in navigating the many schools of macroeconomics. Under the umbrella of mainstream economists I lump together what are called the neoclassical, New Keynesian, paleo-Keynesian, real business cycle, and monetarist schools. The neoclassical school has dominated mainstream for the past thirty years, but the others still have influence. For example, the Nobel Prize-winning economist and columnist for the New York Times, Paul Krugman, is a paleo-Keynesian who advocates greater government spending in order to rescue the economy from recessions. Recently, the neoclassical, real business cycle and New Keynesian schools have found common ground in what they call the New Neoclassical Synthesis, but the foundational assumptions remain the same.

The core of mainstream economics is the assumption that the economy operates in equilibrium most of the time and spins out of control only due to random shocks. Applied to business cycles, I like to call it the "crap happens" school. But the assumption of equilibrium requires presuppositions about human nature that most mainstream economists never think about: it assumes omniscience on the part of the humans involved in the market.

Hayek criticized the assumption of equilibrium as early as 1936 in his presidential address delivered to the London Economic Club and later published as "Economics and Kowledge." He reminded members that the equilibrium is possible only when the plans of producers who rely on each other mesh and all of their plans match those of consumers. Such coordination requires relevant knowledge of the expectations of suppliers and customers. However, to achieve equilibrium as defined in economics, that knowledge must be perfect. "Correct foresight is then not, as it has sometimes been understood, a precondition which must exist in order that equilibrium may be arrived at. It is rather the defining characteristic of a state of equilibrium."

Hayek illustrated his point with the analogy of building a house. Brick makers, plumbers and others might produce the materials necessary for constructing a certain number of houses. At the same time, prospective buyers will accumulate the savings necessary to buy the houses. If the number of houses for which people saved corresponds to the number of houses the construction industry intends to build, then we have equilibrium in that industry because both builders and buyers will be able to carry out their plans as they intended. However, natural disasters or accidents may destroy some of the building materials or weather may make construction impossible. Then equilibrium is not possible. But there is no reason to assume that the plans would have matched in the beginning, either. So for equilibrium to exist,

> the whole economic system must be assumed to be one perfect market in which everybody knows everything. The assumption of a perfect market, then, means nothing less than that all the members of the community even if they are not supposed to be strictly omniscient, are at least supposed to know automatically all that is relevant for their decisions. It seems that that skeleton in our cupboard, the 'economic man,' whom we have exorcised with prayer and fasting, has returned through the back door in the form of a quasi-omniscient individual.

Mainstream economics adopted the assumption of equilibrium after World War II because it makes it easier for economists to create mathematical models of the economy. But the goal of describing economies with math models began in the nineteenth century as the definition of science began to change. It is hard to imagine today, but theology was considered the "queen" of sciences in the middle of the nineteenth century because science was defined loosely as rational, systemic thought about a subject. Again, the influence of socialists can be seen. In the last chapter, we saw that Saint-Simon considered mathematics to be the most advanced and important science. His Supreme Council of Newton would dictate a new structure for society and in it the top mathematician would head a committee of the best representatives of the natural sciences. It would not include theologians, historians or philosophers.

As socialists gained greater influence, science became defined as the natural sciences only and those were deemed more or less scientific to the degree they could use math to describe phenomena in their fields. Physics became the "hard" science because of its extensive use of math and biology a "soft" science for its lack of math models. Socialists could then dismiss the social sciences, especially economics, as metaphysics and not have to deal with the onslaught of opposition from economists.

Naturally, economists wanted to be included in the club of science and so began to search for ways to imitate physics by mathematizing economics. Leon Walras showed that, with the assumption of equilibrium based on nineteenth century mechanics, the dream became reality. That is why the great economist Axel Leijonhufvud could quip in his humorous essay "Life among the Econ" that,

> The Math-Econ [tribe] make exquisite models finely carved from bones of Walras. Specimens made by their best masters are judged unequalled in both workmanship and raw material by a unanimous Econographic opinion. If some of these are "useful" – and even Econ testimony is divided on this point – it is clear that this is purely coincidental in the motivation for their manufacture.

And Mises wrote in *Human Action*, "The mathematical economist, blinded by the prepossession that economics must be constructed according to the pattern of Newtonian mechanics and is open to treatment by mathematical methods, misconstrues entirely the subject matter of his investigations."

But the assumption of equilibrium causes even more damage. It eliminates time; prices respond instantly to changes in plans and data, and people can accurately predict all relevant future events. It compresses all of the different types of capital, from trucks to trampolines into one homogenous, self-perpetuating blob and eliminates the need for coordination among producers who depend upon supplies of crucial equipment or materials. Finally, and possibly the worst, it euthanizes the entrepreneur. Market participants, consumers and producers, become mere automatons mechanically responding to price signals without thinking. With such a large number of unrealistic assumptions underpinning mainstream economics, it is no wonder they could not see the devastating recession of 2008 coming.

The lack of realism in mainstream economics shocked physicists in 1987 and led to the creation of a new branch of the mainstream labeled "complexity economics." That year, the economist Kenneth Arrow invited a group of top physicists and economists to gather at the Santa Fe Institute in New Mexico to talk about their fields for ten days. The economists' obsession with equilibrium disturbed the physicists. Brian Arthur wrote in the preface to his book *Complexity and the Economy* that,

> I'd summed up my earlier understanding in a 1999 article in Science, and the editor insisted I give this different approach a name. I called it "complexity economics." Looking back now, the features of complexity economics are clear. The economy is not necessarily in equilibrium; in fact it is usually in nonequilibrium. Agents are not all knowing and perfectly rational; they must make sense of the situations they are in and explore strategies as they do this.

Arthur seemed to be unaware that Mises wrote in *Human Action*, "The experience with which the sciences of human action have to deal is always an experience of complex phenomena" in 1949. And Hayek had written about the economy as a complex system twenty years before Arthur in 1967 in his paper "The Theory of Complex Phenomena." Unfortunately, Arthur and his colleagues in complexity economics attempted to re-invent the wheel instead of building on the outstanding accomplishments of Austrian economists and as a result have produced meager results. For example, the researchers created an artificial stock market in which agents randomly generate and test methods for forecasting the stock market. Those that worked were retained and failures discarded. Prices formed from the bids and offers of the computer agents. The results, published in "Complexity Economics: A Different Framework for Economic Thought," showed episodes of bubbles and crashes as well as clusters of high and low volatility. Arthur seems unaware that in the Austrian business-cycle theory savings act as a brake on new investment that would dampen if not eliminate booms and busts if allowed to work by the government. Also, other economists have shown that similar patterns appear in a randomly generated time series. In essence, Arthur has merely fallen victim to the mainstream financial myth that the stock market is nothing but a collection of random events.

So why would intelligent people, as Ph.D. economists are, cling to a method has failed so spectacularly in foreseeing the 2008 "Great Recession" and has such unrealistic foundations? Part of the answer is that because economics is a relatively new field, economists have always suffered from physics envy. But the error persists because most mainstream economics are closet socialists. Socialists need to murder the entrepreneur in order for the state to have credibility in planning and directing the economy. Again, in *Human Action* Mises wrote,

> He no longer deals with human action but with a soulless mechanism mysteriously actuated by forces not open to further analysis. In the imaginary construction of the evenly rotating economy [equilibrium] there is, of course, no room for the entrepreneurial function. Thus the mathematical economist eliminates the entrepreneur from his thought. He has no need for this mover and shaker whose never ceasing intervention

prevents the imaginary system from reaching the state of perfect equilibrium and static conditions. He hates the entrepreneur as a disturbing element. The prices of the factors of production, as the mathematical economist sees it, are determined by the intersection of two curves, not by human action...

The result is that from the writings of the mathematical economists the imaginary construction of a socialist commonwealth emerges as a realizable system of cooperation under the division of labor, as a full-fledged alternative to the economic system based on private control of the means of production. The director of the socialist community will be in a position to allocate the various factors of production in a rational way, i.e., on the ground of calculation. Men can have both socialist cooperation under the division of labor and rational employment of the factors of production. They are free to adopt socialism without abandoning economy in the choice of means.

As a result, many mainstream economists who championed free markets opened the back gate for socialism through their obsession with equilibrium. Milton Friedman was one. Socialists could hear his plea for less state intervention in the economy, but his equilibrium economics shouted louder.

Economics was born with a Biblical view of human nature, but as socialists, mathematicians, atheists and deists began to dominate the field, economics embraced a non-Christian human nature with disastrous results. Nazi Germany had the goal of creating the super race through socialism. The old Soviet Union and China under Mao were primarily experiments in shaping human nature and returning mankind to its original innocence. The Nazis caused the deaths of tens of millions in World War II while Stalin and Mao murdered over thirty million each of their own citizens trying to perfect them.

The mainstream economics view of humans as automatons is strikingly similar to Marx's concept of ideology. Marx taught that except for socialists all people are the slaves of their social and economic conditions and their ideas on any subject merely defended the existing power structure. In other words, only socialists can actually think; others can only respond to the prevailing structure of production and economic conditions, just as mainstream economics casts humans in equilibrium analysis.

Only one school of economics treats humans as they really are, rational but with warts and ignorance, and that is the Austrian school of economics. The differences among the mainstream schools are minor compared to the vast disagreements with the Austrian school. Founded by Karl Menger, one of the three who discovered the marginal theory of value, in nineteenth century Vienna, it was championed by Mises and Hayek in the twentieth. Some recent Austrians have made a close connection between the school from Vienna and the school of Salamanca, Spain, in the sixteenth century, as Jesus Huerta de Soto wrote in "New Light on the Prehistory of the Theory of Banking and the School of Salamanca."

Hayek, Mises and other Austrian economists insisted that the methods of physics cannot be used to study economics because the subjects of study are vastly different: economics studies humans; physics studies matter. For example, electrons do not choose whether they have a negative charge or how they orbit a nucleus. Apples do not debate whether or not to obey gravity. But human beings decide, learn from mistakes and have the gifts of reason and limited foresight. Controlled experiments in physics are easy to set up but extremely difficult in economics. Because of these major differences in the subjects under investigation, Austrian economists insisted that economists must use different tools for analysis.

Instead of a mechanical man responding to stimuli and lacking free will, or an animal that obeys only instincts, the human in Austrian economics is a real human being that can reason, learn and choose. He possesses a free will. Mainstream economics assumes rational agents, but the rationality in Austrian economics bears no resemblance to it. In mainstream, rationality means that every person has the omniscience of a Ph.D. economist. Austrians mean by rationality and reason that entrepreneurs adopt goals and choose the best means to achieve them, although within the range of their limited knowledge.

A student of Mises, Israel Kirzner, devoted much of his career to analyzing the contributions of the entrepreneur to the functioning of an economy because mainstream economics had dismissed the entrepreneur with its assumption of equilibrium. He provided an apt analogy to describe the differences between mainstream and Austrian economics in *The Economic Point of View*:

> The Purposefulness of human action – a category to which nothing in physical science corresponds – is the unique element that invests economic science with its individuality. The propositions of economics relate to the effective execution of the purpose willed by the actor.
>
> Stones dislodged from a hillside by the elements and hurtling down on the unsuspecting traveler in the valley are part of a different "event" than stones hurled with intent by men waiting in ambush. The latter are hurled with purpose; they are – in this case literally – aimed by human beings.

Christian economics should deal with real human nature, as Mises wrote in *Human Action* concerning Austrian economics: "Economics deals with the real actions of real men. Its theorems refer neither to ideal nor to perfect men, neither to the phantom of a fabulous economic man (*homo oeconomicus*) nor to the statistical notion of an average man (homme moyen). Man with all his weaknesses and limitations, every man as he lives and acts, is the subject matter of catallactics. Every human action is a theme of praxeology."

Poverty

The issue of poverty is so laced with myths that it would be impossible to write enough books to untangle the truth from all of them. But one myth tends to be the dragon's head for many others, so if we can kill it then many others will die. The arch myth is that one man cannot grow wealthier except at the expense of others. However, that is a difficult myth to kill because for most of human history it has been true. It has only been a myth for the past three centuries since the advent of capitalism.

As detailed in chapter 4, through most of history people held commerce in contempt. The "honorable" ways to gain wealth, if someone did not inherit it, were through looting in war, kidnapping for ransom, bribing state bureaucrats or accepting bribes as a bureaucrat. In other words, most people who accumulated wealth did so by making someone else poorer. With the birth of capitalism in the sixteenth century, that changed. Only criminals and politicians in the West have accumulated their wealth in the old manner since then. However, some of those methods are still common in other regions of the world. For the most part, the West did not take its vast wealth from others; business people manufactured it by creating new products or services that people wanted to buy or through making popular products cheaper. And they created new wealth by taking unused resources, such as coal and oil, and turning them into something useful.

Poverty was not the original state of mankind. In the Biblical account, Adam and Eve lived in a garden that produced extraordinary abundance. Of course, they were naked and probably did not require housing. God expelled them from the garden after their rebellion and cursed the earth so that humans faced a scarcity of food, clothing and shelter. God blueprinted prosperity in his design of a government for Israel in the Torah, but even the Hebrews refused to follow it after a while. As a result, poverty dominated and standards of living for every human that followed remained static at near-starvation levels for millennia, except for the nobility. No one considered progress possible; everyone saw life as revolving in endless cycles. Empires rose and stole the wealth of others then declined when upstart empires stole their wealth.

Even though a Torah-style government would have increased the prosperity of the Hebrews dramatically, God understood that they would not follow his plan and poverty would continue to exist. So God promoted charity as a means to alleviate poverty in Israel. When confronted with the problem of poverty, Christians understood only one solution: give to the poor.

Then the most important event in economic history happened, the sudden explosive growth in standards of living in the West beginning with the Dutch Republic in the sixteenth century. For the first time in history the middle class made up the majority of the population. Even those considered poor by the relative standards of the middle class enjoyed greater wealth than their poor ancestors. It took a few centuries for economists to catch on, but a new solution to poverty had appeared – economic growth through capitalism.

Charity helps, a little

Still, most Christians continue to cling to the idea of charity as the cure for poverty. There are two problems with that approach. First, it is not too difficult to calculate the total wealth of the world and divide it by the total number of people to come up with an amount of wealth that each person would have. The West has created enough wealth to improve the standards of living of the rest of the world, but not to eliminate poverty. Second, most of the wealth of the West is tied up in businesses. But the left assumes that the wealth of the rich today is like that of the rich in the Middle Ages that consisted of land and stacks of gold coins gathering dust in a warehouse. Centuries ago it would have been trivial to divide up the gold and land among the world's poor. Today it would be almost impossible.

Many Christians live in a world that is more fantasy than even that of mainstream economics. They assume that people in the West are rich because they have stolen the wealth of poor nations and a simple redistribution of wealth would solve all poverty problems. Some, such as Jim Wallis, have called for a rejection of the "gospel of scarcity," by which they mean the science of economics, and an embracing of the "gospel of abundance," by which they mean socialism. But God calls Christians to live in the real world of scarcity and not a fantasy world, and to do that we have to analyze real world data using sound economics. Also, socialists do their best to keep the discussion focused on the short run effects of redistribution while the good economists want to analyze the long term as well.

In 2014, the bank Credit Suisse Research Institute issued its *Global Wealth Report 2014*, one of the most comprehensive compilations of world wealth. It reported that total world wealth added up to $263 trillion, or $56,000 per person in the world. That figure assumes a planet population of 4.7 billion, when in fact it is closer to 7 billion, which would reduce the per capita wealth to about $38,000, but let us stick with the report's figures. Clearly, if wealth was perfectly distributed, the majority of people in the world who have no wealth would be much better off. A family of four would own assets worth $224,000. If we stop our analysis at that point, we can fantasize about a world without poverty and everyone doing well and that is what socialists want us to do. But we must push the analysis into the real world.

The report states that most of the wealth consists of real estate and financial assets such as stocks and bonds. That wealth changes a lot over the course of business cycles. The year 2014 was close to the peak of the latest cycle when asset prices are highest. In fact, the report mentions that high asset valuations usually indicate the beginning of the next recession when asset prices collapse. So asset prices are unusually high at this point in the business cycle, but let us retain them for analysis.

Regarding real estate, the rich in the West do not necessarily own more land per person than people in other countries; real estate merely costs more in the West so the owners are wealthier only on paper. For example, someone in Ghana may own five acres valued at $500 while in the United States five similar acres might sell for $5 million. Since we cannot physically redistribute land, we would have to give ownership of much of the land in the West to people in poor countries who might collect a rent from it. Shares of stock and bonds could be physically transferred and redistributed.

Suppose we could redistribute the wealth of the world as described. What would happen next? A reasonable income to expect from those assets would be a yield of 5 percent, or $11,200 per year for a family of four. If nothing changed, that would be a great improvement in income for the world's poor, but nothing remains the same. One change causes another. In the case of the poor countries, citizens will have much larger incomes but will not have increased production so more money will chase a fixed amount of output and land. That means prices will soar like rockets in poor countries and eat away at the purchasing power of the new income. If incomes rise by a factor of ten, prices will rise close to that amount and real living standards will have improved little. At the same time, incomes in the West will have fallen and that will lead to less spending and investment so that the assets located in the West, but owned by people in poor countries, will fall in value as well. In turn, that will reduce the annual income for poor people who depended on the yields from those assets.

In other words, nothing much will have changed in the long run except that the West will be much poorer while the poor in the rest of the world will be in the same situation as before. That highlights an important economic principle: wealth issues from production, not charity.

Other socialists fixate on redistributing incomes rather than wealth. Some have estimated that if all income was distributed perfectly then the average person would get about $8,000 per year or $32,000 for a family of four. Initially, that looks a lot better than trying to redistribute wealth. But keep in mind that, according to good economic principles, income is a factor of labor productivity. Workers in poor countries earn low wages because their productivity is low. Productivity is a factor of culture, training, intelligence and having the right equipment to work with. Redistributing income will not magically make workers in poor countries more productive.

Meanwhile, will the high income workers in the West continue to be as productive as they have been without the incentives to do so? The experiences of the old Soviet Union and China under Mao prove that they will not. Russians used to quip that the state pretends to pay them and they pretend to work. The whole point of the Soviet Union and Communist China was to change human nature and create people who would work for the common good, who needed no personal incentives. Both failed miserably. They could not change human nature. Therefore, when the productivity of high paid Western workers collapses, there will be no more income to redistribute to the poor. Again, nothing would change for the poor, but the West would join them in their poverty.

However, a problem even more devastating to wealth than a lack of incentive to work happens when wealth gets redistributed as in the Soviet Union and Communist China, and that is the destruction of the system that coordinates market activity – prices. Markets work relatively well because of effective coordination between producers and between producers and consumers. Accurate prices coordinate market activity. Higher prices signal producers to manufacture more goods and consumers to buy fewer. Lower prices have the opposite effect. When wealth is redistributed according to a socialist plan, the prices of labor (wages) fail to accurately reflect supply and demand. Prices send false signals that permeate the economy and distort all other prices. Mises discovered that principle first and wrote about it in his book *Socialism*, published in 1922. The Soviet Union and Communist China lived it. Only extreme ignorance of that history or the arrogance that we can make it work today because we are smarter causes people to want to continually make the same mistakes again. Without accurate price signals to coordinate market activity, waste increases at an exponential rate. Economies grow and make people wealthier by producing more than the people consume and waste. Waste destroys wealth.

The world has found only one way to reduce poverty in the long rung and that has been through more capitalism. The poor world has witnessed it work as it cut extreme poverty, defined as a per capita income of less than $1.25 a day, in half. Here are some bullet points from The Apr 06, 2015 World Bank report, "Poverty Overview":

- East Asia saw the most dramatic reduction in extreme poverty, from 78 percent in 1981 to 8 percent in 2011.

- In South Asia, the share of the population living in extreme poverty is now the lowest since 1981, dropping from 61 percent in 1981 to 25 percent in 2011.

- Sub-Saharan Africa reduced its extreme poverty rate from 53 percent in 1981 to 47 percent in 2011.

- China alone accounted for most of the decline in extreme poverty over the past three decades. Between 1981 and 2011, 753 million people moved above the $1.25-a-day threshold.

- During the same time, the developing world as a whole saw a reduction in poverty of 942 million souls.

In fact, China and India account for almost all of the poverty reduction and they accomplished it by freeing their markets only slightly at first, not through charity, foreign aid or forced redistribution. China's long march to prosperity began after the disaster of Mao's Cultural Revolution that starved to death over 30 million Chinese. In the late 1970's, farmers in a remote region formed a secret organization and divided the state-owned land that they farmed into private plots. Each agreed to live from the produce he raised on his plot and promised to take care of the family members left behind, knowing they would be executed if state officials discovered their conspiracy.

After a couple of years, the enormous increase in crops arrested the attention of everyone, not just state officials. The news climbed up the Communist chain of command to the man who had succeeded Mao, Chairman Deng Xiaoping. Deng had spent decades desperately searching for a way to lift China out of starvation poverty when the news reached him. He is reported to have said that he did not care about the color of a cat as long as it would catch mice. Instead of punishing the farmers, he rewarded them and portrayed them as a model for China's future. Gradually, Deng opened up China's agriculture to private farming and small markets. Each success encouraged him to open other sectors to greater freedom. Eventually, expatriate Chinese who had come to dominate business in Taiwan, Thailand, Indonesia, Malaysia, Singapore and the Philippines discovered that they could invest in their homeland and make a good profit. China suddenly became the favorite destination of foreign direct investment. The economy has not stopped growing since.

India's story is not as dramatic, but it, too, freed markets. From independence until the 1990s India tried to imitate the Soviet Union in economics but with a democracy. As a result, India remained as poor in 1990 as it had been in 1947. Forty years of foreign aid had produced only insignificant results. Then China's success made it jealous and India began to slowly open its markets to private ownership and freer markets. The World Bank report summarizes the nation's success in reducing poverty through freer markets.

Though aware of the near miraculous reductions in poverty in Asia, many still cling to charity as the only way to help the poor. Economics has more in common with the medical world than with physics and an analogy from medicine is instructive. Biblical medicine consisted of little more than having elders of the church lay their hands on the sick, praying for them and anointing them with oil. The parable of the Good Samaritan depicts the level of medical knowledge at the time. The Samaritan poured wine into the wounds of the victim to sanitize them then added oil to soothe them. After the Bible was written, herbal medicine grew in sophistication then modern medicine developed with the rise of science in the West. When Christians get cancer today, few think of limiting their medical options to only the Biblical methods of wine, oil and prayer. Instead, they take advantage of chemo therapy, radiation and any other advancement in treatment available to modern medicine.

In a similar way, the advent of capitalism and the growth of the science of economics introduced new methods of poverty alleviation not described in the Bible, though outlined in the Torah. Why, then, should Christians limit poverty relief to just charity? Do they believe the knowledge of economics, especially Austrian, did not come from God? Unfortunately, that is exactly what many Christians think. They are stuck in the medieval mentality in which all commerce and profit are evil, ignorant of the historical facts that contempt for commerce came from pagans, especially Greeks and Romans, not from the Bible. The church inflicted fifteen centuries of suffering by promoting pagan attitudes toward commerce and wealth, much of which some of Christianity's most beloved saints endorsed. Christians who look to those saints for spiritual guidance find it difficult to admit that those saints were wrong about economics. But in the same way that almost all Christians have embraced modern medicine, they now need to adopt the best of modern economics where it is founded on Biblical assumptions about human nature.

But the Bible condemns the rich

What about the numerous condemnations of the wealthy in the Bible? Here are some examples:

> Why do the wicked live on, growing old and increasing in power? Job 21:7.

> For I was envious of the arrogant when I saw the prosperity of the wicked. For they have no pangs until death; their bodies are fat and sleek. They are not in trouble as others are; they are not stricken like the rest of mankind. Therefore pride is their necklace; violence covers them as a garment. Their eyes swell out through fatness; their hearts overflow with follies. They scoff and speak with malice; loftily they threaten oppression. They set their mouths against the heavens, and their tongue struts through the earth. Therefore his people turn back to them, and find no fault in them. And

they say, 'How can God know? Is there knowledge in the Most High?' Behold, these are the wicked; always at ease, they increase in riches. Psalm 73:3.

There is a vanity that takes place on earth, that there are righteous people to whom it happens according to the deeds of the wicked, and there are wicked people to whom it happens according to the deeds of the righteous. I said that this also is vanity. Ecclesiastes 8:14.

Why does the way of the wicked prosper? Why do all who are treacherous thrive? You plant them, and they take root; they grow and produce fruit; you are near in their mouth and far from their heart. Jeremiah 12:1.

And now we call the arrogant blessed. Evildoers not only prosper but they put God to the test and they escape. Malachi 3:15.

Come now, you rich, weep and howl for the miseries that are coming upon you. Your riches have rotted and your garments are moth-eaten. Your gold and silver have rusted, and their rust will be evidence against you and will eat your flesh like fire. You have laid up treasure for the last days. James 5:1-3.

The Bible seems to advertise the close connection between wickedness and wealth. The left claims those verses prove that God opposes the rich because they oppressed the poor by refusing to share with the poor and equalizing the distribution of wealth in the land. But that would indicate a superficial reading of the Bible. After all, God had blessed Abraham, Isaac, Jacob, Joseph and Job with great wealth. The Torah promised material wealth to the Israelis as long as they respected God's laws. David, the "man after God's own heart," and Solomon were extremely wealthy. Did God change his mind about wealthy people, or did wealthy people change. The latter is the correct answer.

Except for the quote in Job, the link in the Bible between wealth and wickedness begins with the prophets after Israel had rebelled against God by demanding a king like the kings of the pagan nations around them. Even during the great reign of David, the king himself complained that the wicked prosper at the expense of the poor. After Solomon the nobility of Israel began to steal the wealth of the poor. Consider these verses:

Woe to those who enact evil statues and those who constantly record unjust decisions, so as to deprive the needy of justice and rob the poor of my people of their rights. So that the widows may be their spoil and that they may plunder the orphans. Isaiah 10:1-3.

Thus says the Lord, "For three transgressions of Israel and for four I will not revoke its punishment, because they sell the righteous for money and the needy for a pair of sandals. Amos 2:6.

Therefore because you impose heavy rent on the poor and exact a tribute of grain from them, though you have built houses of well-hewn stone, yet you will not live in them. You have planted pleasant vineyards, yet you will not drink their wine. Amos 5:11.

Woe to those who scheme iniquity, who work out evil on their beds! When morning comes, they do it, for it is in the power of their hands. They covet fields and then seize them, and houses, and take them away. They rob a man and his house, a man and his inheritance. Micah 2:1-3.

Behold, the wages of the laborers who mowed your fields, which you kept back by fraud, cry out; and the cries of the harvesters have reached the ears of the Lord of hosts. You have lived on the earth in luxury and in pleasure; you have fattened your hearts in a day of slaughter. You have condemned, you have killed the righteous man; he does not resist you. James 5:4-6.

Clearly, the wealthy were committing worse crimes than merely withholding charity from the poor. They murdered people and they used the justice system to steal from the poor by bribing judges to rule in their favor on indictments fabricated against the poor. And they charged exorbitant interest rates on loans to the poor as well as high rents on land. But God had warned the Israelis that those things would happen when they demanded from Samuel that he give them a king like the pagan nations around them. God told them that a king would act like pagan kings. His sons and daughters, the nobility, would use their political power to steal and murder with impunity.

The Bible illustrates the insights from Douglass North and the New Institutional School of economics discussed in chapter 1. To recap, North discovered that the most robust form of government in human history is the traditional system in which a monarch supported by the nobility oppresses the masses. The monarch gives the nobility permission to steal from and murder members of the masses in exchange for their support. The masses put up with that oppression because it keeps other members of the masses from rising above the rest in wealth. In Schoeck's words, it slakes their envy. The Bible and economics join wickedness and wealth in a common-law marriage and through most of history the union held firm. The wealthy patriarchs were an exception, but an important one. They demonstrate that wealth does not necessarily have to come from evil or cause the wealthy to become evil. The advent of capitalism demonstrated a better way to wealth for all, not just for the nobility.

The Biblical attitude to wealth

What is God's attitude toward wealth for Christians? It has not changed since he blessed Job, Abraham and the other patriarchs. God promised wealth to the Israelis under the Torah government if they remained faithful to him and his laws. Christians have tended to see the fulfillment of that promise as a miracle; God blessed them materially if they were faithful regardless of how wisely or hard they worked. But the condemnation of laziness in Proverbs should have dispelled that idea. And when Christians developed modern science they began to see God working in the natural world through the laws of physics that he had created and not directly. In other words, rain was not a miracle, but the natural world working as God had designed it. In a similar way, it is likely that the material wealth God promised the Israelis would also result from them obeying the principles of economics embedded in the Torah law in the same way they worked in the West after the launch of capitalism. After the initial conquest, the Israelis got their wealth through farming, manufacturing and trade, not through war and looting as the pagan nations did.

God intends for people to get their wealth through honest work. Solomon held up the ant as an example to mankind:

> Go to the ant, O sluggard; consider her ways, and be wise. Without having any chief, officer, or ruler, she prepares her bread in summer and gathers her food in harvest. Proverbs 6:6.

A few Christians think they signal their spirituality through living by "faith," that is, without working but depending on God to feed them miraculously. Or they refuse to save and instead give away all of their surplus income above that needed for a basic lifestyle while depending upon God to provide for them in emergencies such as illnesses or job losses. However, that appears to be the sin of "temple leaping" as described by Jesus in his temptation. Satan encouraged Jesus to leap from the highest part of the temple to prove the truth of the scripture. He said, "If you are the Son of God, throw yourself down from here, for it is written, 'He will command his angels concerning you, to guard you,' and 'On their hands they will bear you up, lest you strike your foot against a stone," Luke 4:9-11. Satan was quoting Psalms 91:11, 12. But Jesus responded, "It is said, 'You shall not put the Lord your God to the test,'" quoting Deuteronomy 6:16. In other words, God does not perform circus tricks for our amusement.

God intends for people to gain wealth through honest work in agriculture, commerce and trade. Adam worked in the garden before the fall and God expects people to work today, though conditions are more difficult. God wants us to work to provide for ourselves and our families, as Paul wrote in I Timothy 5:8: "But if anyone does not provide for his relatives, and especially for members of his household, he has denied the faith and is worse than an unbeliever." And we are to work enough that we have a surplus to help out those less fortunate: "Let the thief no longer steal, but rather let him labor, doing honest work with his own hands, so that he may have something to share with anyone in need," Ephesians 4:28.

God does provide for us in emergencies, but he usually does so by giving us a surplus income to save ahead of an emergency or by persuading others who have saved a surplus to give some of it to us. In God's economy, someone has to save wealth. In addition, God wants us to save in order to leave an inheritance to our children. He wrote through Solomon in Proverbs 13:22, "A good man leaves an inheritance to his children's children, but the sinner's wealth is laid up for the righteous." The American rugged individualism that dictates we cast our children on their own when they reach the age of eighteen and let them make it by themselves is a pagan idea, closer to the way Spartans raised their children. Finally, raising the funds to start a business today is extremely difficult. Friends and family provide almost all of the initial money young entrepreneurs need to launch, which provides another good reason for Christians to save.

Today, the government has stacked the financial world against young people. Taxes for Social Security and Medicare transfer wealth from young people to the elderly. Health insurance taxes the young and healthy with higher premiums than their health justifies in order to reduce premiums for sick elderly members. Add welfare payments and military spending and young people pay so much of their income in taxes that saving is much more difficult than in the past. In addition, very few young people, even with a college degree, will get ahead in life by working for wages because the inflationary policies (discussed later) of the Federal Reserve ensures that the purchasing power of wages do not keep up with price inflation.

When we save, we have to put that savings some place. People in Bible times would hoard gold in a safe place, but God encourages his people to invest in productive enterprises. A popular verse from Solomon says, "Cast your bread upon the waters, for you will find it after many days," Ecclesiastes 10:1. Traditionally, people have interpreted that verse to refer to giving charity and that God will reward the giver in the future in some way that he cannot see today. While the sentiment is certainly true, that may not be the best interpretation of the passage. The quotation above came from the English Standard Version which is similar to the King James. But the New International Version reads, "Send your grain across the seas, and in time, profits will flow back to you."

The ESV is the more literal translation while the NIV offers an interpretation. The NIV may be closer to Solomon's intent in light of the verse that follows: "Give a portion to seven, or even to eight, for you know not what disaster may happen on earth," in the ESV and "Invest in seven ventures, yes, in eight; you do not know what disaster may come upon the land," in the NIV. Verse two appears to be about investing, not charity, for why would one giving charity care what the risks might be? It seems that God through Solomon is giving investment advice. Solomon earned a great deal of his wealth by investing in international trade through shipping, but he kept his investment diversified because he could never tell which ventures would be disasters and which would earn a good return. Following Solomon's example, Christians should diversify their investments.

Finally, God calls some Christians to be self-employed. Paul encourages slaves to gain their freedom if they can: "Were you a bondservant when called? Do not be concerned about it. But if you can gain your freedom, avail yourself of the opportunity," I Corinthians 7:21. Working for wages is not slavery, but wage earners have much less freedom to respond to opportunities than do those who own their own businesses. Also, most wealthy people in the United States earned their wealth by growing a business over twenty to thirty years. Not only do the wealthy pay most of the taxes, but they contribute the most to charities and churches.

Peter, Andrew, James and John worked in family-owned fishing businesses. Matthew was a tax collector, but he did not work for the state. Tax collecting until very recently was a business, called today "tax farming," in which the owner bid in competition with others for the right to collect taxes. His profit came from the amount above the bid that he could collect from citizens. Paul was a self-employed tent maker. Joseph was not just a carpenter, as tradition suggests. The Greek word for Joseph's profession indicates that he was more like a construction contractor and that included carpentry. As the oldest son, Jesus would have worked in the family business and become the chief executive after Joseph died. Jesus' use of the construction business and finance in parables to illustrate aspects of the Kingdom of God suggest that he approved of the market process because it is unlikely he would have depicted the kingdom using examples of things he disapproved of.

Biblical government

Many Christians think the government should be the primary tool with few limits for shaping culture. For example, the temperance movement in the late nineteenth century that produced prohibition in the 1930s sincerely thought that by making the sale of alcoholic drinks illegal they could rid the nation of the evils caused by alcoholism, such as poverty and abuse of women and children. Prohibition was an effort to change human nature through the law very much as socialism but on a smaller scale. It did not produce the intended results and created more problems as it rewarded organized crime for supplying the booze people wanted. But proponents of that philosophy of the state never give up. The war on drugs is a descendant of prohibition. It is over forty years old and has failed to even curb drug use in the United States, but it has succeeded in ruining entire nations, such as Columbia and Mexico, where U.S. purchases of illegal drugs finance the private armies of drug lords. But through most of history people did not have such faith in the power of the state to do good things.

Almost all monarchs, from ancient Egypt through Rome and Spain until the Dutch Republic, insisted that the gods, or God, had given them unlimited power and the people accepted those claims. The Church was the first institution that sought to limit the state by insisting on individual rights. Beginning with the Magna Carta, people fought long and bloody battles to limit the power of the state. The people of the Dutch Republic of the sixteenth century, followed by the United States, then Great Britain enjoyed the greatest freedom from state power and coercion in the history of mankind. So how did the West transition from a centuries-old fight against the state, to freedom then back again to unlimited state power? The details are in chapter 7, but essentially, it happened through the decline of traditional Christianity and its replacement by socialism.

But God had much more limited ambitions for human government. Theologians claim that God created human government in the covenant with Noah recorded in Genesis chapters eight and nine, in which he instructed that anyone who murders another should be executed for his crime. Next, God showed in his Torah constitution that the role of the government was to settle disputes between people through the courts and to protect the life and property of the citizens. Paul affirmed that in Romans chapter 13 where he limits state authority to the punishment evil doers. As mentioned in chapter 4 of this book, the scholars at the University of Salamanca in Spain distilled the state's role to the protection of life, liberty and property. Some refer to that as the "night watchman" state. Thomas Jefferson's formula in the Declaration of Independence, "life, liberty, and the pursuit of happiness" was a variation on the Salamancan theme, although his substitution of happiness for property has caused endless confusion.

The United States was born with a night watchman government under the Articles of Confederation then created a more powerful state with the Constitution, but still very limited by the standards of today. The Constitution limited the federal government to the powers designated within it. But history makes it clear that the document was unloved from the beginning. Jefferson noted that he had no power under the Constitution to buy Louisiana from France, but since no one opposed it he went through with it.

Andrew Jackson violated the Constitution when he conducted ethnic cleansing by forcing most of the tribal people to relocate to Indian Territory, which became the state of Oklahoma. The Supreme Court ruled that Jackson did not have the authority for the removal of the tribes, but Jackson merely challenged the Court to enforce its decision without him. Lincoln virtually shredded the Constitution in order to punish the southern states for rebelling. Wilson turned the country into a police state in order to force the nation into World War I. Still, the country remained close to the Biblical form of government until the election of Franklin D. Roosevelt. The Supreme Court rolled back on some of FDR's policies until the President threatened to expand the size of the court and pack it with his appointees. The Court capitulated and the size and power of the federal government exploded.

In each case, presidents could get away with violating the law of the Constitution only because the majority of people approved of their policies. Just as dictators must not stray too far from the will of the majority or face revolt, even more so in democracies must the leadership respond to the majority. And if the majority wants the state to violate its own laws it will. In the 1930s under Roosevelt, the American people committed essentially the same rebellion as the ancient Israelis when they demanded a king like the nations around them. The majority wanted a powerful central government because it had embraced socialist ideas to replace the traditional Christian ones it had abandoned, ideas that had taken millennia to discover and instantiate.

Today Americans have become so accustomed to an overbearing government that talk about restricting any of its power frightens them. Of course, politicians give the highest priority to keeping the public frightened about something so they can ride to the rescue, for which the people will erect a monument to the valiant politician who saved them from imaginary evils. And the media plays its role as courtesans by amplifying the imaginary villains sewn together by politicians, often fabricating the devils themselves. As a result, most

Americans insist the state must protect us from the evils of monopolies, pollution, child labor, old age, illness, inequality and many others aspects of life.

Corporations have been a popular villain for socialists since the nineteenth century. The growth of Standard Oil under John D. Rockefeller, Andrew Carnegie's steel company and Cornelius Vanderbilt's railroads and shipping business convinced many that Marx had been a true prophet when he foresaw capitalism degenerating into monopolies in every industry that raised prices and starved workers. Those companies, which were organized as trusts, inspired the anti-trust legislation designed to protect the nation from monopolies.

The fact that those companies lowered the prices of their oil, steel and transportation did not affect the popular imagination at all. In fact, the press considered lower prices the greatest evil of all because they drove out of business competitors who lacked the skills to produce at the lower prices. Once they achieved monopolies, the press argued, they would raise prices to the heavens and reap immoral profits. The fact that high profits always lured competitors to enter a free market, reduce prices and destroy monopolies did not sway them. Neither did the fact that no monopoly has ever lasted in a relatively free market without the power of the state behind it. The disastrous history of the monopolies given to railroads by the state should have taught people some basic economics in the opinion of historian Thomas DiLorenzo in *How Capitalism Saved America: The Untold History of Our Country, from the Pilgrims to the Present.*

The trusts came close to achieving monopolies in their industries, but we need to keep in mind that they sold new technologies and had small markets. It is easy to achieve a monopoly on a new technology. Today, the federal government grants a patent, which is a monopoly on the production of a new product for decades. However, as soon as the patent expires competitors rush into the market and reduce prices. Most extraordinary of all is the fact that people can look around them and see the longstanding fact that no monopolies exist that result from competitive markets; governments have created all of the monopolies that exist – the electric power, water, sewer and cable television companies and corporations with patents.

Another frightening evil that socialists proclaim will destroy the nation without government intervention is pollution. They credit the Environmental Protection Agency for cleaning up the country after large corporations dumped their waste in our rivers and clouded our cities with smog. Mainstream economics teaches in introductory classes that pollution is an inescapable externality that requires state action to resolve. Pollution was not a problem before the middle of the twentieth century because the population was smaller so nature could clean itself up. Pollution only became a problem when the population grew large enough that industry could pollute more than nature could clean up, and the population could grow only because capitalism increased food production. But protecting property rights is a function of the government, not the markets, and pollution is nothing but the harming of someone's property. Pollution is an example of government failure, not market failure. Before the EPA, courts adjudicated conflicts between property owners and polluters with the property owners getting the penalties assessed by judges. Under the EPA, the property owners get nothing and the government gets the penalty fees.

But courts can resolve only those pollution issues related to property rights. If no one owns something, such as rivers, the ocean and the atmosphere, courts cannot find a solution. The states and federal government own the lakes and rivers and control the air, so those became the most polluted parts of the country. Those governments needed to enforce their property rights against the polluters but refused to do so. A simpler and more just solution would have been to give property rights over waterways and the atmosphere to private groups and let them fight for protection in the courts. Instead, they created an enormous bureaucracy in the EPA and expanded the powers of the federal government. States soon followed with their own environmental protection agencies. Today, the EPA has grown into a monster that takes property from citizens without compensation when it finds any endangered species or water on private property.

Did not the government end the cruelty of child labor? Actually, no, it did not. After all, most parents did not force their children to work outside the home because the parents were evil; they needed their children to work to help put food in their mouths. Had the state outlawed child labor before parents could feed their children, many would have starved to death. Higher wages for workers through rapidly increasing productivity brought about by "evil" corporations investing in better tools for workers made most Americans wealthy enough that they no longer needed their children to work to help buy food. Higher standards of living for the poor killed child labor, not the state. The true motivation for ending child labor through law was to relieve competition by children for adult males for jobs that socialist saw as scarce.

Mainstream economists promote state intervention in the economy to remedy market "failures." They set up an idyllic market they call "perfect competition," measure the real world market against it and find it lacking. Because the real world does not match up to their fictional utopia, they claim the real market fails. But the market never had the purpose of achieving the fantasies of Ph.D. economists. Free markets exist to instantiate property, because property requires that the owner be able to dispose of it as he sees fit and only free markets make that possible.

Behind the market failure argument lurks the unspoken assumption that bureaucrats can do what the market cannot. For that to be the case, bureaucrats and the politicians who appoint them must be wiser, technically more proficient and have better morals than the public from which they are chosen and the businesses they regulate. Most Americans cling to that irrational faith in government and mainstream economists encourage it. But Hayek and Mises have demonstrated that, even supposing the superiority of bureaucrats, they could never assemble the tacit knowledge necessary to perform better than entrepreneurs at making the market work. Bureaucrats are always working blind compared to entrepreneurs.

As mentioned earlier, economics must have a Biblical perspective on human nature for it to be consistent with Christianity, and Christians know that no one can be as perfect as mainstream economists and the public assume bureaucrats to be. Economist James Buchanan won the Nobel Prize for creating a competing vision of the nature of bureaucrats known as the Public Choice School of political economy. Buchanan taught that politicians and bureaucrats are exactly like the voters who put them in office: they are self-interested. In other words, politicians campaign on promises to put aside ambition and work selflessly for the common good, but when they get into office they work to advance their own careers and personal wealth. That is one reason so many politicians enter office as middle class and leave as millionaires.

Getting elected requires spending millions of dollars on campaign organizations and advertising. Few politicians have the money needed or want to spend it if they do, so all politicians are deeply indebted to campaign donors, especially large corporations. Of course, corporations do not contribute to campaigns out of patriotism; they want something from politicians. Maybe the corporation is a defense contractor and needs an edge getting the next contract. Or the donor owns land next to a freeway and needs an exit ramp to give it value. Or the politician sets on the committee that appoints regulators to the agency that oversees the contributor's industry.

The latter leads to what the public choice school calls regulatory capture. It works like this: voters give power over industries to politicians who set up regulatory agencies to do the day-to-day work of monitoring and enforcing. But who will politicians choose to staff the agencies? There are so many good people to choose from. Corporations simplify the decision by suggesting people from their industry. After all, who knows the industry better? Very quickly the industry being regulated has captured the regulatory agency, which then creates regulations that benefit the largest members. Although always promoted as serving and protecting public health and safety, a great deal of new regulations does little more than reduce competition for the largest corporations. All agencies have been captured, but it is most visible in finance where much of the staff of the Federal Reserve banks, the Treasury Department and the Securities and Exchange Commission comes from the top levels of the largest banks. Also, many government employees who started out as bureaucrats look forward to high paying jobs in the industries they regulated as bureaucrats, but only if they help out the corporations they oversee why still a bureaucrat.

In addition to the conflicts of interest inherent in campaign contributions, politicians succumb to the pressure of lobbyists, for which corporations spend hundreds of millions of dollars each year. A study by the University of Mississippi's Robert Van Ness and Matthew Hill, along with Mississippi State's G. Wayne Kelly discovered that each dollar spent on lobbying Congressmen, "can increase shareholder wealth by roughly $253 million per year. That equates to a 22,000 percent return on the investment in lobbying," according to Aaron Kiersh in "Lobbying is a Lucrative Investment, Researchers Find Using CRP Data."

Christians must firmly plant their perspective of politicians on a Biblical view of human nature without exempting politicians. The Public Choice School is closest to the reality of human nature described in Scripture. But when confronted with reality, the reflex is to try to reform the campaign contribution system and limit the influence of lobbyists. We have tried that for decades with no success because only the naïve follow the laws for campaign finance and there are hundreds of ways to get around them. For example, a potential donor might sell a piece of land to the target politician for half the market price while a buddy buys it from him for twice the going rate. It is completely legal and the politician can claim to merely be good at real estate deals. Other donors will act as investment advisors and pool the politician's own money with that of others in a risky investment scheme in which the politician makes a 200 percent return on his investment while the others lose the nest eggs.

Or donors will give book deals with exorbitant advances or pay outrageous speaking fees to politicians.

The monster socialists fear most is inequality, but regulatory capture by large corporations increases income inequality in the country. Economists call the process "rent seeking." When they capture an agency, corporations get special treatment and regulations that protect the largest from competition by smaller competitors. Less competition increases the profits of large corporations because they can charge higher prices at the expense of consumers and pay higher salaries to executives.

Regulatory capture and public choice theories have been summarized in Adam Smith and in Bruce Yandle's *Bootleggers and Baptists: How Economic Forces and Moral Persuasion Interact to Shape Regulatory Politics*. Baptists want liquor sales prohibited by law on Sunday for religious reasons. But they have unlikely allies in the bootleggers who also want liquor sales banned on Sunday so they will become the only suppliers of alcohol. Applied to politics, the Baptists are environmentalists and advocates for consumer health and safety; corporations play the role of bootleggers.

As long as politicians hold the enormous power over the economy that voters have given them, they will always sell that power to the highest bidder in exchange for campaign contributions or just greater wealth. To paraphrase the great P.J. O'Rourke, when politicians are put in charge of the market, the first thing sold are the politicians. Christians must recognize that sinful people do not become saints simply by winning elections. Politicians are no more honest or altruistic than the people who vote for them. Voters who do not like the politicians in Washington, D.C. have only themselves to blame because people get the government they deserve. The only solution is to take power over the economy from politicians and free the market. Christians need to repent of the socialist fallacy that the state can improve human nature through laws, regulations and education. It cannot. The state cannot change society; it merely reflects the society of the majority of voters.

The only government God ever created, and which shows what a Christian government should be like, is the one in the Torah described in chapter 3.

Christian money

The Apostle Paul wrote that the love of money is the root of all kinds of evil, and certainly Christians must have a proper attitude toward accumulating it. But there is a moral aspect to money far more dangerous than mere greed and most mainstream economists have no knowledge of. It is the damage the manipulation of money supply can cause: it transfers wealth from wage earners to the wealthiest, impoverishes retirees on fixed incomes, bankrupts pension funds and increases income inequality by rewarding the wealthiest for gaming the system. To understand the danger, we need to review the history of money.

There never seems to have been a time when people did not use money. Grains of barley and cattle were among the earliest forms. Barley grains were used for purchasing everyday goods, such as eggs and milk, while cattle served well for buying land and wives. But why did people invent money? Barley and cattle fulfilled the three uses of money: a store of value, a medium of exchange and measuring tool to compare the market values of different goods, or a common denominator. Barley and cattle served those purposes because they retained their value over time relatively well, so people could use them as savings; they were in high demand so almost everyone would accept them in exchange; and people could use them to compare the exchange value, or prices, of other goods. For example, if a large jar would sell for a quart of barley and an axe for a gallon, consumers could see that most people valued the axe about four times as much as the jar in terms of barley.

Keep in mind the foundation of economic thought from prehistory and until recently that wealth is limited and one man can profit only at the expense of another. So if a businessman sells a clay jar to a farmer, neither the businessman nor the farmer can increase his wealth, or profit from the exchange, otherwise the exchange becomes unjust. That is why Aristotle wrote that the items exchanged in trade must be of equal value. And how do we know that the items exchanged had equal value? Aristotle wrote that objects have an intrinsic value, much of which depended on the honor attached to each item. A related theory was that something manufactured should sell for a price close to its cost of production. But the general thought was that the exchange was unjust if one person made a profit from it. The ancient ideas about limited wealth and objective value lead logically to the condemnation of commerce because it was clear that businessmen earned profits from their exchanges, making commerce appear extremely immoral since the businessmen impoverished their customers according to pagan economics.

People continued to think in those ways about business until the theologians of Salamanca discovered the subjective theory of value that says nothing has an intrinsic value; each person values things according to the usefulness for them. Related to it is the quantity theory of how people change their valuation of something: the value of an item in the market will change in proportion to the volume of that item offered for sale. For example, suppose farmers are in the habit of exchanging a bushel of barley for a lamb, but one year the barley farmers discover that irrigating and fertilizing their fields will double their harvest. The farmers might discover that as they bid for the lambs the exchange value of their barley will decline until the price of a lamb becomes two bushels, if the number of lambs for sale has not changed.

The opposite would happen if the barley harvest produced half as many bushels, due to a drought during the growing season, for example. As a result, farmers could buy a lamb for half a bushel. Changing values based on changes in supply and demand are important for coordinating market activity because higher prices signal that a shortage exists and for producers to increase production. Lower prices tell producers to cut back.

Salamancan scholars discovered that the quantity theory of value applies to money as well, because money functions like any commodity in the market. Originally, money was just another commodity. So if the quantity of money increases, the value of that money in exchange for other goods will lose value proportionally, all other things remaining equal. Barley worked well as money because, within a small geographic area, the volume of barley probably remained relatively constant and its value in exchange did not change much. The same applied to cattle.

But barley and cattle had problems as money. Barley can rot and rats can eat it while disease can ruin entire crops. Lions and wolves can eat cattle and illnesses can kill herds. People gradually abandoned those forms of money for silver as mining technology improved, but they measured silver by its weight in barley grains so that the transition to the new money went smoothly. The shekel in the Bible, one of the oldest forms of silver money, equaled the weight of 180 barley grains. For many years people carried silver in bags and used scales to weigh the appropriate amount of silver for a purchase, just as they had with barley. For example, Abraham paid for a cave to bury Sarah in by weighing so many shekels of silver. Eventually, Egyptians began to cast silver into large rings with consistent weights and purity of silver, which made payment easier. Finally in about the eighth century B.C. the Lydians made coins of silver with the weight stamped on them.

Silver worked well as money for centuries because it met all of the requirements for money mentioned above, but was easier to transport and was more durable than barley and cattle. It only became a problem when governments gave themselves a monopoly in the production of coins. As mentioned in chapter 4, Solon, a leader of Athens in the sixth century B.C., discovered that he could cheat people by mixing a base metal, like copper, with the silver. The coins contained less silver but were stamped with the original weight, which is unadulterated fraud. Philosophers considered him a genius instead of a criminal because the new dishonest money allowed Solon to pay off his debts. But when people tried to spend the new money, it did not impress merchants. They ignored the weight stamped on the coins and raised the prices of goods to match the true amount of silver in the devalued coins. Historians call the merchants greedy. Solon had violated the Biblical command to keep honest weights and measures. "You shall not have in your bag differing weights, a large and a small. You shall not have in your house differing measures, a large and a small. You shall have a full and just weight; you shall have a full and just measure, that your days may be prolonged in the land which the LORD your God gives you," Deuteronomy 25:13-16. Using false weights is as much theft as burglary, but governments usually receive praise for it.

Money began to cause the most trouble with the invention of a practice known as fractional reserve banking. The Spanish economist Jesus Huerta de Soto tells the history in his incredible book, *Money, Bank Credit and Economic Cycles*. The original fractional bankers may have been goldsmiths who warehoused for a fee the gold and silver people had saved. Since all of the gold coins looked alike, people did not require that the goldsmith give them the exact coins they had deposited when they asked for them as long as he gave them coins with the same weight and purity.

Goldsmiths noticed that people rarely asked for their savings. Staring at a warehouse full of gold coins for years gave some goldsmith the idea of loaning the gold to merchants who wanted to invest it, say to ship a load of Greek wine to Egypt. The owners of the gold would never know and the borrower would repay the loan with interest, which the goldsmith would keep as his profit. Greed lured the goldsmith into loaning out all of the warehoused gold except for around 10 percent, which he kept on hand to meet the daily withdrawals of the owners.

The process worked well until some of the borrowers defaulted on loans because their business ventures had failed. Then the 10 percent reserves began to run out and the goldsmith had to deny some customers their savings. Word spread quickly; people panicked, and all of his customers showed up to demand their money at once. Of course, he could not pay, but usually he had skipped town before that happened. If not, he often paid with his life. Their life savings gone, the people quit spending in order to rebuild their savings and the economy collapsed as poverty spread.

Similar crises happened enough that Rome outlawed the practice of fractional reserve banking, but did not eliminate it. They merely drove it underground. Fractional banking revived in the middle ages with the growth of banks in Italy. Church theologians debated the practice but split on the issue of its morality. Some considered it immoral, since the bankers were loaning out money that belonged to depositors without their knowledge. Others decided that the practice was permissible because people understood when they deposited their money that the bank might lend it. Governments settled the issue by selling the right to establish a bank and making fractional banking legal in exchange for the banks making large loans to the kings.

The economic problems caused by loaning out depositors' money did not end because it was legal. Banking crises and recessions became common features of life. Theologians who approved of the practice urged bankers to keep more reserves and to take fewer risks, but the crises continued. The Bank of Amsterdam in the Dutch Republic operated on the 100 percent reserve principle, meaning it did not loan depositors' money, in the seventeenth century as was mentioned in chapter 5. But the economy still experienced booms and busts, as the tulip mania episode illustrates. That happened for the most part because of a financial instrument known as bills of exchange, which were nothing more than IOU's. A merchant who had been paid by such a bill could present it at the seller's bank and get his money in gold or silver. Bills made hauling loads of gold and silver coins around the country unnecessary and the holder received interest on his loan.

Businessmen used the bills as an early form of paper money by paying off their debts with bills they had received from customers. The system worked well until businessmen began to abuse it by issuing more notes than they could redeem. They could do that because a bill might pass through a dozen hands before someone presented it to the bank for redemption, so the float between issuance and redemption could be long. The value of bills of exchange in circulation could reach as high as twenty times the amount of gold in banks. As happened with fractional banking, a few defaults would cause the whole stack of bills to come tumbling down and plunge the local economy into a depression.

By the middle of the nineteenth century, economists had begun to understand the connection between the expansion of the money supply through fractional reserve banking and the recurring cycle of expansions followed by depressions. Ludwig von Mises was the first to develop a comprehensive theory in his 1912 book, *The Theory of Money and Credit*. Friedrich Hayek followed in 1933 with his *Monetary Theory and the Trade Cycle*. The theory became known as the Austrian business-cycle theory (ABCT) because both economists were from Vienna.

Introductory macroeconomics courses teach students the process that the banking system uses to expand the money supply through loans. The Federal Reserve controls that process by changing the interest rate banks can charge other banks for loans and by purchasing or selling bonds to banks, both of which change the market interest rates that banks charge customers. The higher the interest rate, the fewer loans banks will make and the slower the money supply will grow. Mainstream economists insist that such money creation has no bad effects on the economy, but the Austrian business-cycle theory (ABCT) disagrees. Essentially, the ABCT insists that credit expansion causes unsustainable expansions of the economy that end in recessions. Mainstream economists deny that the process causes boom and bust cycles, attributing cycles to supply or demand "shocks." The evidence for the ABCT is extraordinarily good so the most likely reason for mainstream economists' rejection is that it neutralizes their theories of market failures that they use to justify government intervention in the economy.

Mainstream economists will admit that in the long run increases in the money supply will cause price inflation, all other things being equal. But rising prices hurt retired people living on pensions and social security because it destroys the purchasing power of their savings. Even 2 percent inflation, the typical goal of central banks, will cut the value of money in half in thirty-five years. And safe government bonds earn almost no real return on investment.

Pension funds suffer as the purchasing power of their funds erode, but in addition, those funds grow at a much slower rate because of the low interest rates the Fed causes in order to boost the money supply. Wage earners suffer annual declines in the purchasing power of their wages because employers make cost of living wage adjustments the year following inflation, so wage increases never keep up. Finally, inflation damages capital intensive industries such as manufacturing because depreciation funds rarely consider future price inflation, so when the time comes to buy new equipment companies find they have saved too little.

The boom and bust cycles the Fed causes by its manipulation of money hurts the working poor the most because they lose their jobs in recessions. But the wealthy can take advantage of Fed policy by borrowing the new money first and buying assets, like stocks, bonds and real estate, before prices rise. Wage earners get the new money last, after prices have risen. That process is one of the major causes of rising income inequality in the United States as it transfers wealth from the poor and middle class to the rich.

The ideal money would be absolutely fixed. It could neither be increased nor shrunk. Under such a system, prices would accurately reflect supply and demand and coordinate economic activity as well as is humanly possible. Prices would rise as the population increased if production did not increase at the same rate. Prices would fall if productivity increased and production outpaced population growth. It would fulfill the Biblical command to use just weights and measures.

But such a system is impossible with humanity. The best system ever devised was the gold standard. Under it, prices in 1900 were roughly the same as those in 1800. The gold system worked because, as long as people could redeem paper money in gold at a fixed rate, banks soon reached a limit on how far they could expand credit. Still, countries under the gold standard suffered many recessions and banking crises because of state intervention into the business. The state's demand for loans to conduct war destroyed the gold standard system, beginning with World War I and ending with President Nixon's taking the United States off the gold standard in 1971.

Governments love price inflation because they survive on debt, and inflation reduces the real value of that debt, accomplishing the same fraud that Solon perpetrated on Athens, but in a subtler way that most people are unaware of. Mainstream economists enable the state's addiction to debt because they have convinced themselves with their little math models that money printing, technically credit expansion, is the only way to save the country from a recession. They honestly believe that without credit expansion, the economy would spiral down into never ending depression and poverty.

But that elasticity of money causes severe problems internationally as well as domestically. When large economies like the U.S. expand credit, much of that new money flows out of the country and into emerging market nations for investment. The sudden flood of new money ignites an artificial boom followed by high rates of inflation. That forces the central banks of the flooded countries to raise interest rates. Eventually, the same "hot" money rushes out of the country when recessions hit in the U.S. and causes economic devastation.

The closest we can come to Biblical money is a gold standard, but mainstream economics and worship of the state by the people will always prevent that. The next best thing would be a central bank that understood Austrian economics and the value of sound money. But that is unlikely to happen for decades because mainstream economists insist on the need for an elastic currency, which in plain English means they want to expand the money supply as much as possible whenever they want. Thriving financially in this world is difficult enough for the average person and the poor without the government making it harder for them through inflation and high taxes, but there are a few strategies that can help. The most important is to pay attention to the business cycle. My book, *Financial Bull Riding*, introduces readers to the Austrian business-cycle theory and gives advice on how to take advantage of that knowledge for business and investing.

Business owners have a slight advantage over wage earners because they can often raise the prices of their products and services and thereby neutralize the effects of Fed-induced price inflation. But businessmen need to pay close attention to the business cycle. Too many entrepreneurs launch new businesses or expand with debt at the peak of the business-cycle expansion when prices and profits are high. But interest rates, the costs of inputs and labor are also at their highest levels, too, making new ventures expensive at that point of the cycle. Then the recession hits and the cost structure of the business is too high for the owner to make the debt payments let alone earn a profit at lower prices. Businessmen need to develop the discipline to pile up cash during the good years of the expansion and start new ventures or expand during recessions when others will not because of fear. Many wealthy people accumulated their wealth by using the cash they saved during the good times to buy businesses that had failed in recessions.

Investors need to follow the business cycle in order to time investments. As with business owners, investors need to do most of their buying in the stock market and real estate market during recessions and the early phases of expansions. As the expansion ages, investors need to quit buying, or buy bonds, and consider selling real estate and stocks in favor of cash, gold/silver, or bonds while they wait for the next crash. Asset markets, especially the stock market, follow the business cycle closely because profits drive the prices of stocks and profits follow the cycle.

Inequality

There has never been a period in recorded history in which people did not dream of a past golden age when all people were equal in wealth and there was no crime or war. Mises quoted the ancient poet Ovid in his book *Socialism* who expressed such a vision:

> The first golden age flourished, which begat truth and justice spontaneously; No laws of formal guarantees were needed. Punishment and fear were unheard of; no savage, restrictive decrees were carved on bronze tablets.

Plato portrayed such a society in his *Republic*: all material wealth as well as wives was shared equally. The great goal of socialism has been to reduce inequality, but as shown in chapter 2, inequality has always been highest in socialist countries because the people at the top of the socialist parties live like emperors while the masses wallow in terrible poverty. Socialism is nothing but a return to what Nobel Prize-winning economist Douglass North described as the traditional, closed society in which a political elite enjoys great wealth while keeping the masses poor but equal.

Equality of wealth might have lasted in the Garden of Eden had Adam and Eve not rebelled and been forced out. But other than that period, mankind has never known a period of equality of wealth because it is impossible as long as people have different abilities. Socialists are loath to admit it, but smarter people will always be richer than average even in a society without crime, fraud or theft. But in a world of fallen people with a tendency toward evil, people who are willing to steal, murder and defraud others will become rich along with the smart ones.

A Biblical society, such as that established in the Torah, will minimize the wealth that wicked people can gain while giving the smarter people, those gifted in business, and hard workers the opportunity to reap the rewards of their efforts. Then those who achieve wealth will help the less fortunate through voluntary charity. That is not a vision of a utopia, but a realistic one of what mankind can actually achieve. Capitalism and classical liberalism never promised equality of wealth, but only equality before the law. The Bible never insists on equality in wealth, either, but on equality before the law because every human being stands equal before God. As Siedentop wrote in *Inventing the Individual*, equality before God gave birth to Western individualism without which capitalism would have been impossible.

Inequality before the advent of capitalism was high because of the nature of traditional societies that allowed an elite political group to extract wealth from the masses. Capitalism reduced extreme inequality for the first time in human history. Chapter 4 quoted Nobel Prize-winning economist Robert Fogel writing that Great Britain cut inequality in half from the beginning of the eighteenth century until the middle of the twentieth century. The United States accomplished similar reductions until roughly 1970.

Inequality in the West has been rising for the past generation. But we need to distinguish between natural and unnatural inequality in order to be wise and Biblical about it. Natural inequality results from the fact that people have different abilities. Some have a greater ability to serve others and thereby make money through their higher intelligence, education, hard work, business insight or other traits. Older people will have much more wealth than younger ones because of their greater experience and the length of time they have worked and saved. Married couples, if both work, will have greater wealth than single mothers. Citizens will have more than recent poor immigrants. As long as wealthy people accumulate their wealth legally and morally, Christians should encourage them.

However, some means of achieving wealth are legal though immoral and unnatural. As mentioned in the section above on money, those who receive first the new money minted by the Federal Reserve benefit unfairly since they can purchase assets before prices rise. That inflationary process produces unnatural inequality because a quasi-governmental agency is giving preference to a few banks and failing to treat all citizens equally. The odd thing is that mainstream economists assume that new money reaches all of the people at the same time as if the Fed had literally printed new money and dropped it from helicopters over the entire nation at the same time. Austrian economics teaches the real process in which the Fed makes loans to preferred large banks first who then loan the funds to other banks or large corporations. As a result, the employees, and especially upper management, at those banks earn much higher salaries than their counterparts in other industries. Earning higher salaries and buying assets before prices rise in the expansion phase of the business cycle helps them to accumulate much more wealth than others because of their government connections.

Another way that unnatural inequality grows is through what economists call rent seeking, an issue addressed above under the subtitle of "Christian government." Rent seeking happens when businesses use their contacts in government to get regulations passed to favor their business at the expense of others. This happens in many forms, all of which are legal, and include subsidies for exports as happens with the Import-Export Bank; tariffs and quotas on imports; regulations that punish small competitors as occurs through regulatory capture; and campaign contributions that persuade Congressmen to direct government business to companies owned by contributors. One economist has estimated that the return on campaign contributions from corporations is about 2,000 percent.

Take one example of rent seeking, import quotas on sugar. A generation ago U.S. sugar beet growers suffered from competition from cheaper imports, so they lobbied Congress for protection. Major agricultural business that grew corn joined them in persuading Congress to restrict the importation of sugar through quotas. The resulting shortage of sugar motivated food makers to turn to cheaper corn syrup as a sweetener. Corn and sugar beet growers benefitted at the expense of food makers and consumers who had to pay more for products containing sugar or settle for corn syrup.

Schoeck emphasized that the obsession with equality of material possessions is one of the hallmarks of envy. Of course, Christians do not want to participate in envy or encourage it, so we should not embrace any policies that merely punish the wealthy and insist on forced income redistribution. At the same time Christians should encourage charity, and we should fight against unnatural inequality that violates the principle of equality before the law.

Progressive taxation

Many people had promoted progressive taxation, in which the wealthy pay a higher rate in taxes, from the beginning of the United States, but Congress rejected the idea on the moral grounds that the government must treat all citizens alike, emphasizing the Christian notion of equality before the law. No one succeeded in defeating the moral argument, but after World War I, people simply ignored it and progressive taxation became the law.

Thomas Piketty, a French socialist economist who wrote the bestselling economics book of 2014, *Capital in the Twenty-First Century*, provides damning evidence of the envy motive behind the demand for equality of income: "A rate of 80 percent applied to incomes above $500,000 or $1 million a year would not bring the government much in the way of revenue, because it would quickly fulfill its objective: to drastically reduce remuneration at this level," and, "The primary purpose of the capital tax is not to finance the social state but to regulate capitalism." Piketty reads no differently than the peasant without a goat in the old Eastern European tale recounted in chapter 2 in which the peasant demands that the angel kill his neighbor's goat instead of giving the peasant one. But Piketty's greatest sin, especially since he holds an advanced degree in economics, is his resurrecting and parading as new the ancient notion that wealth is limited so the wealthy can have gained their wealth only at the expense of workers.

The rich should pay more taxes in absolute dollars, than others because one of the primary reasons for the existence of government is the protection of property, and to whom much is given much is required. But the rich will pay more in taxes than the middle class or poor, even with a flat tax. For a crude example, consider two people, one earning $100 million per year and the other earning $10,000. With a 10 percent flat tax, the rich guy will pay $10 million in taxes and the poor guy will pay $1,000.

The Torah government did not treat rich people differently from the poor. The rich paid the same 10 percent tithe, or a flat tax, just like everyone else. In fact, Moses commanded, "You shall do no injustice in court. You shall not be partial to the poor or defer to the great, but in righteousness shall you judge your neighbor, (Leviticus 19:15), and "nor shall you be partial to a poor man in his lawsuit," (Exodus 23:3).

Christians can never embrace an immoral policy such as progressive taxation.

Libertarianism and conservatism

If Christians cannot be socialists because the principles of socialism contradict Biblical principles, should they become libertarians or conservatives? My answer is neither, for the following reasons. Friedrich Hayek outlined the differences between conservatives and classical liberals in the chapter "Why I Am Not a Conservative" of his book *The Constitution of Liberty* published in 1960. Hayek had in mind the conservatism of the U.K., his adopted home, which differs from that found in the U.S. Still, the similarities are worrisome. For example, Hayek complained about the tendency of conservatives to compromise too easily with socialists:

> But, as the socialists have for a long time been able to pull harder, the conservatives have tended to follow the socialist rather than the liberal direction and have adopted at appropriate intervals of time those ideas made respectable by radical propaganda. It has been regularly the conservatives who have compromised with socialism and stolen its thunder.

We have witnessed conservatives in the U.S. practice something similar. Socialists, under the names of liberals or progressives or others, continually press for small changes toward greater socialism, usually taking advantage of a temporary crisis that the state has caused through its intervention in the economy. Both the socialists and conservatives flee to the state to rescue the nation from the crisis and so promote greater state control of the economy. Conservatives then defend the status quo as if they had arrived at it through a plan of their own. Another point of irritation for Hayek was the conservative love of a powerful state:

> Let me return, however, to the main point, which is the characteristic complacency of the conservative toward the action of established authority and his prime concern that this authority be not weakened rather than that its power be kept within bounds. This is difficult to reconcile with the preservation of liberty. In general, it can probably be said that the conservative does not object to coercion or arbitrary power so long as it is used for what he regards as the right purposes. He believes that if government is in the hands of decent men, it ought not to be too much restricted by rigid rules. Since he is essentially opportunist and lacks principles, his main hope must be that the wise and the good will rule - not merely by example, as we all must wish, but by authority given to them and enforced by them. Like the socialist, he is less concerned with the problem of how the powers of government should be limited than with that of who wields them; and, like the socialist, he regards himself as entitled to force the value he holds on other people.

For example, conservatives want to maintain a large, powerful military that they can use to intervene in any country in the world and force the will of U.S. politicians on them. They may complain about the costs of welfare programs, but few have ever griped about the costs, human or financial, of invading Korea, Vietnam, Afghanistan or Iraq. Conservatives today want a larger, more powerful state to secure the borders, fight the war on drugs, define marriage, educate young people and reduce crime through more and better armed police forces. Conservatives never talk about limiting the size, scope or power of the state except in the matter of helping the poor. Some of this conservative attitude toward the state issues from insecurity in Hayek's view:

> The conservative feels safe and content only if he is assured that some higher wisdom watches and supervises change, only if he knows that some authority is charged with keeping the change "orderly."

> This fear of trusting uncontrolled social forces is closely related to two other characteristics of conservatism: its fondness for authority and its lack of understanding of economic forces. Since it distrusts both abstract theories and general principles, it neither understands those spontaneous forces on which a policy of freedom relies nor possesses a basis for formulating principles of policy. Order appears to the conservative as the result of the continuous attention of authority, which, for this purpose, must be allowed to do what is required by the particular circumstances and not be tied to rigid rule.

Conservatives view themselves as pragmatists. They follow no ideology but judge situations individually according to the specific circumstances, so they claim. Such pragmatism tends to have a short term orientation and what seems best in the short run often results in disaster in the long run. Whether we focus on the long run or not, it always shows up and it is often ugly because of the many expedient decisions made considering the short term consequences only.

Finally, Hayek criticized the nationalism that conservatism promotes. Nationalism is not patriotism, or love of country, but an outlook that demands politicians formulate policies that benefit only the narrow interests that conservatives can understand.

> Connected with the conservative distrust of the new and the strange is its hostility to internationalism and its proneness to a strident nationalism...it is this nationalistic bias which frequently provides the bridge from conservatism to collectivism: to think in terms of "our" industry or resource is only a short step away from demanding that these national assets be directed in the national interest.

That bias leads to calls for protection of U.S. businesses from foreign competition, promotion of exports, limits to imports and businesses investing in other countries, often referred to as "outsourcing" U.S. job or "sending" jobs overseas. And it motivates conservatives to demand limits to immigration in order to "protect" jobs for U.S. citizens. Conservatives need to keep history in mind. Immigrants poured into the country at the greatest rate in the late nineteenth and early twentieth centuries at a time when the U.S. economy grew at one of its fastest rates. Unemployment remained low in spite of massive immigration because the economy was freer from state intervention and entrepreneurs could create jobs faster than immigrants could fill them.

Germans invented modern nationalism in the late 19th century because the country had embraced socialism in the middle of the century and socialist policies destroyed the power of free markets to create jobs. Instead of blaming socialist policies, Germans blamed immigrants for taking jobs from German citizens. Today's opposition to immigration in the U.S. has the same roots: socialism has destroyed the American businessman's ability to create new jobs.

If Christians cannot be consistent conservatives, then surely they can be libertarians. After all, the Torah government would have been a libertarian's dream. I think libertarianism is the closest to a Biblical philosophy of government in most respects because of its emphasis on limited government. Libertarians sometimes refer to their philosophy as anarcho-capitalism to show that its ideal society has no state, but it is not lawless. It provides government in the form of private judges who decide cases according to natural law, their decisions becoming common law. It has no legislature to create positive law. Private insurance companies protect members through private security agencies that capture criminals and bring them to trial. Rich people provide national security through private armies.

Murray Rothbard, the great Austrian economist, created the libertarian movement in the 1950's based largely on the political ideas that one can draw from sound economics, and if he had stopped there, he would have carved a place for himself in history and found good company with his teacher, Ludwig von Mises, and another great student of Mises', Hayek. But Rothbard was an atheist and that emboldened him to join forces for a while with another atheist, Ayn Rand, who promoted a variation on the theme of libertarianism. Rothbard thought it necessary to construct an atheist system of morality and considered himself capable of creating one. Claiming to build on natural law theory, which was a Christian discipline launched by Thomas Aquinas, Rothbard jettisoned most of the political thought of natural law theorists and invented a new morality based on nonaggression that defined the state as inherently evil and, therefore, anything it does is evil. Police and fire work, war, building highways or parks, are all evil because the state takes taxes by force to pay for them.

Obviously, Christians should never take their morals from atheists. Even the great atheist philosophers of the past, beginning with Nietzsche, understood that true morality can only come from God. The Christian stance on the state and taxes must be more nuanced than that of libertarians and be Biblically based. The next chapter deals with the subject in more detail. It is clear from the Torah that God intended Israel to have a libertarian form of government without a state. However, God did not allow Israel to keep that government when the people rebelled against him, which shows that God intended such a state of freedom only for those who followed him. When Israel committed the ultimate act of treason by demanding a king like those of the surrounding pagan nations, God first warned them of the oppression they would suffer then gave them what they asked for, which is one of God's most common punishments. Clearly, the state is God's wrath against a rebellious humanity.

When God tired of Israel's rebellion, he sent the Babylonian army under Nebuchadnezzar to destroy Jerusalem with the temple and deport most Israelis to Babylon. God encouraged them to live peaceful lives there and pay taxes to the state, one of the most ruthless in history. Here is the passage from Jeremiah 29:4-11:

> Thus says the LORD of hosts, the God of Israel, to all who were carried away captive, whom I have caused to be carried away from Jerusalem to Babylon: Build houses and dwell in them; plant gardens and eat their fruit. Take wives and beget sons and daughters; and take wives for your sons and give your daughters to husbands, so that they may bear sons and daughters – that you may be increased there, and not diminished. And seek the peace of the city where I have caused you to be carried away captive, and pray to the LORD for it; for in its peace you will have peace.

Then God placed several Israelis in prominent political positions within the state. Daniel, one of the greatest prophets, served as a minister under Nebuchadnezzar, his son and Cyrus in the Persian kingdom. Esther married the Persian emperor and rescued Jews in Babylon from genocide. In the first century, Israelis lived under the brutal Roman boot and Jesus encouraged his followers to pay taxes to Rome (Matthew 17:27, Mark 12:17). Later, the Apostle Paul encouraged Christians to pay taxes (Romans 13:6).

So while Christians live in predominantly non-Christian societies, we will suffer the same oppression that others suffer from the existence of a powerful state, but we should still follow the laws, respect the authorities and pay taxes as long as the state does not require us to violate Biblical principles. And although the state is God's wrath against rebellious people, God mixes mercy with all of his judgments and uses the state to suppress the criminals that afflict society and thereby establish a kind of peace. So Christians cannot consider the state to be inherently evil as libertarians do.

If Christians achieve a majority in any society, then they are free to establish a state-less, Torah-like, government and God would bless it. First the Dutch Republic then England and the United States came very close to achieving that for about two centuries each. But as each nation rebelled against traditional Christianity, the citizens demanded a "king," or a more powerful state like the nations around them and each became increasingly socialist.

Libertarians should understand that a libertarian society can exist only as long as the majority of citizens subscribe to libertarian principles. But the only instances in history in which the majority of people in a country followed libertarian principles were when they were Christians. Quite a few libertarians are atheists, but most atheists are hard-core socialists. As Hayek demonstrated, atheism gave birth to socialism. The two are natural companions.

Immigration

Illegal immigration terrifies many conservatives, many of whom think it will destroy the nation. The issue has become the defining policy of the Tea Party movement, which wants to build a Great Wall of China on the southern border of the U.S. to keep out the hordes, or its modern version, the fence and wall that separates Israel from the West Bank. Any potential candidate for the Presidency in 2015 had to impugn illegal immigration loudly and often or he had no chance of wooing the conservative vote.

276

Of course the Tea Party and its groupies do not oppose legal immigration. Tea Partiers obey the laws of the land and expect others to do the same. There is an element of the slippery slope argument in their opposition to illegal immigration: it violates U.S. laws and runs the risk of instigating greater anarchy. Then there is the fear that illegal immigrants are either taking jobs that citizens might work or are reducing wages below what workers would earn without massive illegal immigration. And many conservatives fear that illegal immigrants bring crime with them as well as burden schools, medical facilities and the welfare rolls. All of the objections to illegal immigration are true, but they are only half true and half-truths are the worst kind of lies. Before we untangle the threads we need to ask, what does the Bible say about immigration? Many Tea Partiers are Christian and know the relevant verses well:

"You shall not wrong a sojourner or oppress him, for you were sojourners in the land of Egypt," (Exodus 22:21). "When a stranger sojourns with you in your land, you shall not do him wrong. You shall treat the stranger who sojourns with you as the native among you, and you shall love him as yourself, for you were strangers in the land of Egypt: I am the LORD your God," (Leviticus 19:33,34). "When you reap the harvest of your land, you shall not reap to the very edges of your field, or gather the gleanings of your harvest; you shall leave them for the poor and for the alien: I am the Lord your God," (Leviticus 23:22). "You shall have one law for the alien and for the citizen: for I am the Lord your God," (Leviticus 24:22). "Love the sojourner, therefore, for you were sojourners in the land of Egypt," (Deuteronomy 10:19). "When you beat your olive trees, do not strip what is left; it shall be for the alien, the orphan, and the widow. When you gather the grapes of your vineyard, do not glean what is left; it shall be for the alien, the orphan, and the widow," (Deuteronomy 24:20, 21). "Cursed be anyone who deprives the alien, the orphan, and the widow of justice," (Deuteronomy 27:19).

In summary, God requires in the Torah that Israelis treat foreigners in their midst well, almost as if they were Israelis. Of course, foreigners could become Israelis simply by rejecting false gods and having their males circumcised. Caleb and his extended family, the Kennites, were such converts and were given a portion of the land as if they had been born Hebrew. God reminds the Israelis that they had been foreigners in a strange land and knew abuse at the hands of the locals. What principles can we distill from such a small amount of evidence?

If God had wanted to restrict immigration into Israel he would have done so. He does not mention it. He assumes that foreigners will come into the land looking for economic opportunities or to unite in the worship of the true God instead of idols. He makes no distinction between legal or illegal foreigners in the land, but treats them all the same. In the same way that the U.S. Constitution gives the federal government only designated powers, God does not give Israel the authority to limit immigration.

The Bible has more to say on immigration than just what is in the law. Equally important are the many episodes in which servants of God became foreigners in another land as they fled famine, war or persecution. Abraham left Ur for the land of Canaan because of the religious corruption in his birthplace. He immigrated to Egypt during famines, as did Jacob. Moses retreated to the Sinai after killing an Egyptian. Ruth and Naomi migrated to Israel in order to survive. Joseph fled with Jesus and Mary to Egypt to escape Herod's mass murder of baby boys. In the book of Acts, Christians left Israel for other parts of the Roman Empire to escape Jewish persecution. Christians fled the Roman destruction of Jerusalem for safety in Pella. Throughout history, persecuted Christians have fled to foreign countries, especially during the long dark night of the reign of Islam. The principle we can derive from these examples is that God often provides a safe haven for people when tyrants become unbearable and rescues them by having them migrate. It seems that God wants people to be free to escape from hardships, famine and persecution to the sanctuaries he created. We might consider it a natural right.

God has made the U.S. a world sanctuary. Have we forgotten the words inscribed on the Statue of Liberty? Most immigrants have come for religious freedom or economic opportunity, much as the foreign immigrants to Israel did. Lately, the U.S. "war" on drugs has driven many in Central America to the north. General John F. Kelly, commander of U.S. Southern Command in Miami, wrote the following in "Central America drug war a dire threat to U.S. national security" in 2014:

> Drug cartels and associated street gang activity in Honduras, El Salvador and Guatemala, which respectively have the world's number one, four and five highest homicide rates, have left near-broken societies in their wake...

> All this corruption and violence is directly or indirectly due to the insatiable U.S. demand for drugs, particularly cocaine, heroin and now methamphetamines, all produced in Latin America and smuggled into the U.S. along an incredibly efficient network along which anything — hundreds of tons of drugs, people, terrorists, potentially weapons of mass destruction or children — can travel so long as they can pay the fare...

> More to the point, however, it has been the malignant effects of immense drug trafficking through these nonconsumer nations that is responsible for accelerating the breakdown in their national institutions of human rights, law enforcement, courts, and eventually their entire society as evidenced today by the flow of children north and out of the conflictive transit zone. The human rights groups I deal with tell me young women and even the little girls sent north by hopeful parents are molested and raped by traffickers. Many in these same age groups join the 17,500 the U.N. reports come into the U.S. every year to work in the sex trade.

Conservatives are willingly blind to the vast destruction that the war on drugs is causing south of our border. Trillions of dollars spent trying to stop the flow of drugs has accomplished nothing but to so enrich the drug cartels that they can corrupt and take over large sections of entire nations. Much of the recent immigration comes from families trying to escape the violence that the drug cartels introduce as a result of their providing the drugs to quench the cravings of Americans. While the war devastates whole nations in Latin

America, it has not succeeded in making it the least bit difficult for Americans to get any drugs they want. Drug legalization would take away the vast revenues of the drug cartels and help end their crime spree across the south. In turn, that would reduce illegal immigration. But conservatives neither want to legalize drugs nor face the devastating consequences on others of their irrational fight against drugs.

Finally, from the Biblical perspective, Christians need to remember the second of the two great commandments: Love your neighbor as yourself, or do unto others as you would have them do unto you. All people living in the U.S. came from somewhere else. Even the tribes came from China at one point, but all citizens of European descent are much more recent immigrants. Those who subscribe to traditional Christianity are a minority in the U.S. and may face persecution just as most fellow Christians in Muslim and Hindu nations suffer. Fleeing to a safer place may be our only option. Let us hope one exists that will accept us.

Again, conservatives do not oppose legal immigration, only illegal immigration. They are for law and order, sometimes referred to as the "rule of law." But two kinds of law exist – God's laws and manmade laws. God's laws, revealed in the Bible, never change and apply equally to everyone for all time. Manmade law, whether coming from pharaohs, Caesars, kings, parliaments or congresses, is arbitrary and capricious. Laws coming from a congress in a democracy are just as manmade and as arbitrary as those coming from a dictator or king. There is nothing sacred or holy about them. Many things that are legal today may be illegal tomorrow and vice versa. For example, President Reagan converted millions of people who were considered illegal immigrants one day into legal residents with the stroke of a pen. Things that were illegal for centuries, such as divorce or same-sex marriage, can suddenly be made legal. Manmade law does not have the authority of God's law, at least for Christians and Jews, and it has even less authority if it contradicts God's laws, as immigration restrictions do.

The great economist Bruno Leoni wrote in his book, *Freedom and Law*, about the weaknesses in manmade law: "History evidences the fact that legislation does not constitute an appropriate alternative to arbitrariness, but that it often ranks alongside the vexatious orders of tyrants or of arrogant majorities against all kinds of spontaneous processes of forming a common will...From the point of view of the supporters of individual freedom it is not only a question of being suspicious of officials and rulers, but also of legislators."

So one must ask who gave Congress the authority to make the distinction between legal and illegal immigrants? The Bible does not give anyone that authority. It is not part of God's law. Of course, conservatives might quote Romans chapter 13 about obeying the laws of the land, but who gave rulers the authority to invent laws that God did not legislate and even oppose God's intent of providing sanctuaries for oppressed people?

In the same way that manmade law must be subordinate to God's laws, legislation passed by Congress must follow the supreme manmade law of the U.S., the Constitution, which does not give Congress the power to restrict immigration. Article one, section eight says this on the issue: "The Congress shall have Power To...establish an uniform Rule of Naturalization, and uniform Laws on the subject of Bankruptcies throughout the United States;" It gives Congress the authority to determine criteria for citizenship, but says nothing about immigration. Conservatives are supposed to hold to originalism in interpreting the

Constitution and they do so when it is convenient. The document clearly states that any power not spelled out in the Constitution is forbidden to the federal government and reserved for the states. But conservatives fall back on Supreme Court decisions regarding immigration that violate the principle of originalism. Of course, if the only legitimate interpretation of the Constitution is found through originalism, then almost all laws passed since George Washington left office are illegitimate because they violate the prime law of the land. Congressmen, presidents and Supreme Court justices who approved those laws are the greatest criminals in the history of the nation.

The Apostles Peter and Paul admonish Christians to follow the legislation of the land as long as it does not contradict God's laws and U.S. immigration laws come very close to violating God's intent to provide safe havens for oppressed people. Conservatives are very upset with "sanctuary" cities, such as San Francisco, that ignore federal immigration laws. But those cities are merely responding to what are clearly unconstitutional and illegitimate laws.

But the U.S. is a sovereign nation and sovereign nations have the right to control their borders, many conservatives assert. However, the U.S. is sovereign only with respect to other nations; its sovereignty ends where God's begins. Christians need to be concerned that legislation does not violate God's laws or principles. At the same time, legislators need to obey the law in the Constitution when passing their own laws.

What about the practical issues of crime, jobs, and welfare? Obviously, some undocumented residents are criminals and should be prosecuted, but Christians should not exaggerate the crime rate among them. The vast majority of them are quiet, law-abiding people. We should not commit the injustice of punishing all undocumented immigrants because a few are criminals. The crime rate among citizens is at least as high and we do not deport entire cities or racial groups because of it. In addition, classifying undocumented residents as illegal increases crime among them because the good people among them are afraid to go to the police out of fear of being deported. Sanctuary cities have offered crime reduction as one of their reasons for not deporting undocumented workers. Much of the criminal activity involves the drug trade, which U.S. drug laws make enormously lucrative. Legalizing drugs and converting "illegal" residents to legal ones will help fight crime among immigrants.

Most conservatives oppose undocumented workers because some of them use the nation's generous welfare programs. Still, we should not resort to unjust group punishment. Undocumented residents on welfare programs form a minority and should not be used as an excuse to take away the natural right of people to move to a safe haven where they can flourish as God intended. The obvious solution is to end the use of socialist programs by undocumented residents, or better yet, get rid of them altogether and let private charity to the work more efficiently.

It is true, all other things being equal, that undocumented workers compete with citizens for scarce jobs, but that is only half the truth. It considers the supply side of labor. What about the demand side? With free immigration, the supply side of labor can be greater than the demand and cause wages to fall. But that does not have to be the case. Wages rose in the U.S. from the Civil War until the Great Depression in spite of massive immigration, far greater than the undocumented immigration of today. For modern citizens that must sound like a miracle from God, but the fact that it seems miraculous demonstrates how accustomed to socialism we have become. The U.S. is very socialistic and socialism destroys jobs. The U.S. economy was much freer during the decades of the nation's highest immigration, so entrepreneurs could create good jobs faster than immigrants could fill them. After World War I the nation turned increasingly socialist and demanded greater regulation of business by the state. As a result, job creation collapsed. The Great Depression lasted longer and went deeper in the U.S. than any other nation in the West because of the interventions of Hoover and Roosevelt.

Today, net job creation in the U.S. has plateaued and unemployment remains low only because so many workers have become discouraged and quit looking for work. As a result, the government does not include them in the unemployment figures. If they were counted, the unemployment rate would be closer to 15 percent, so jobs are scarce. The solution to scarce jobs is not to punish undocumented immigrants, but to return to freer markets that unleash the job creating power of free people so that companies are again competing for workers, undocumented or not.

The distinction between legal and illegal immigrants is arbitrary and capricious. If it wanted, Congress could immediately transform all "illegal" immigrants into legal ones overnight. Restricting immigration by labeling some of it illegal violates mankind's natural right to seek refuge from oppression in a location where families can flourish as God intended. Most of the fear of undocumented immigrants comes from the devastation of the U.S. economy that socialism causes. Get rid of the socialism and undocumented immigrants present no problem.

Christians should follow sound, Biblical principles even if they appear to work against their short term interests because doing so keeps them from committing errors that no reasonable person could foresee at the time. No opponent of immigration in the 1930's knew that Hitler would murder six million Jews in the next decade. U.S. citizens opposed immigration at that time for the same reasons they do today, with the addition of anti-Semitism of the past brought on by Progressivism's eugenics. In spite of the limits, 200,000 Jews managed to escape the Nazis and flea to the safety of the U.S. as reported in "The United States and the Holocaust," an article in the *Holocaust Encyclopedia* on the internet, but we should wonder how many more might have been saved had the U.S. not feared immigration so much. After the U.S. cut off Jewish immigration from Germany, a ship loaded with Jewish refugees tried to dock at a Florida port, but were sent back to Germany.

Immigration opponents might argue that there was no way they could have foreseen Hitler's genocide, but lack of foresight is the point. We follow Godly principles because we lack perfect foresight and cannot see all of the unintended consequences of our policies. Those principles reduce the occurrences of bad unintended consequences. Hayek reminds us in F*atal Conceit* that only socialists demand to know all of the future consequences of policies before they embrace them.

International trade

As the Israelis of the Torah period understood, and the theologians of the University of Salamanca rediscovered, property requires freedom, otherwise it is a sham. But free markets do not end at the boundaries of a nation. If a property owner is free to trade with anyone within his national boundaries, why should he be forbidden to trade with people across the border? The right to property is the foundation of the Christian insistence on free international trade.

We have already seen that Solomon engaged in international trade and encouraged others to invest in it as well. During his reign (c.971-931 BC) Solomon teamed with King Hiram of Tyre to launch expeditions to the east coast of Africa. He built a fleet of cargo ships at Ezion Geber on the Gulf of Aqaba while Hiram provided experienced sailors because the Phoenicians had been exploring and trading with the people of the far western Mediterranean and possibly the British Isles for centuries. Three years later the ships returned with gold, silver, ivory, apes and monkeys (1 Kings 9 and 10). Solomon traded with Hiram for the wood, gold and precious stones used to build the Temple and his larger, more elaborate palace. He also traded with the Queen of Sheba and bought horses from Egypt and Kue (southeast Turkey) for his chariots. Of course, Solomon would have paid for those with exports of Israel's production, probably wine, grain and some manufactured goods.

While pagan philosophers often condemned bourgeois commerce, and the church adopted their position, both praised the large merchants who imported goods across long distances because they took things from places where they were abundant to where they were scarce, especially food. Theologians have always understood that God in his providence had blessed the nations of the earth with different forms of wealth so that the nations would have to trade with each other to get what each needed to prosper and thereby increase peace and build international community.

Opposition to international trade arose after the Dutch Republic came to dominate trade and the kings of surrounding nations saw their gold sailing to the Republic. Kings needed gold to pay their armies to fight their endless, senseless wars and they needed their people to have gold so the king could confiscate it. What became known as mercantilism was the efforts of courtesans to figure out ways to keep gold in country. The ancient idea that one nation cannot grow rich except by impoverishing another motivated them. And they saw international trade as a cold form of war. Therefore, they sought to block imports and subsidize exports.

Of course, it did not work. De la Court and Richard Cantillon explained why it did not work, but no one listened until Adam Smith lectured them. The nineteenth century witnessed a return to sanity and an explosion of freer international trade that helped enrich Western Europe and the Anglo nations. But bad economic ideas never die because they are based on ignorance and envy; they merely hibernate for a while. Opposition to trade sprouted again and overtook Germany with the failure of socialism under the regime of Bismarck. Rather than accept failure, socialists blamed foreigners – immigrants and nations exporting to Germany. Germany began to block imports and subsidize exports. Then recession hit the West and protectionism exploded in popularity in the U.S. Hoover signed the Smoot-Hawley tariff bill that put high tariffs on manufactured goods. Trading partners followed the U.S.'s example and international trade shut down, turning what should have been a normal recession into the Great Depression, the worst economic crisis in the history of the West.

Austrian economists fight with the mainstream on most areas of macroeconomics, but not on the subject of international trade. David Ricardo's distillation of the concept of comparative advantage in the early nineteenth century is the most confirmed principle in all of economics. In essence it says that every nation should do what they do best and trade with other nations for the things they cannot produce or produce cheaply. It applies to individuals as well as nations. For example, few Americans will go out to their garage and attempt to make a set of tires for their Ford Fusion when the original ones go bald. Instead, they will work at what they do best and buy tires from a company with the expertise to make tires well. Nations should do the same. Centuries of experience have proven Ricardo to be right.

Critics of trade will point out that the U.S. taxed imports for most of its history and did better economically than it has in the more recent decades when it has embraced freer trade. But that argument is an example of the *post hoc* fallacy. Yes, the U.S. has always been plagued with mercantilists in high places and until the income tax of Wilson, tariffs were the main source of revenue for a tiny federal government. But readers must ask if the U.S. economy grew because of those tariffs or in spite of them? All historical evidence shows that standards of living grew in spite of tariffs. And tariffs were relatively low until Smoot-Hawley because the federal government was small. So why has freer trade since the Reagan administration not boosted economic growth? The answer is that trade is not magical or all powerful. It is one factor among many others that can overwhelm the benefits of free trade. The U.S. has become increasingly socialist since the election of F.D.R. as president and that massive increase in socialism destroys the good that free trade can accomplish.

Others criticize the loss of jobs that go with freer trade. And of course when domestic producers encounter competition from abroad with better and cheaper products they tend to fail and their workers lose their jobs. No one can deny that. So why do all good economists continue to support free trade? They do so because they can see the long run. Those job losses are the immediate, short run consequences of freer trade. However, in the long run cheaper and better products free income from consumers and producers to buy other goods that they could not afford before free trade and that creates more jobs than were lost in the short run. Anyway, that is how trade will work in a free market. If we do not see that happening today, and we do not, then we should assume we no longer have a free market, which we do not. We are socialist.

War

A common fallacy held by most historians and the public says that World War II rescued the U.S. economy from the great depression. The idea has its roots in Keynesian economics, which was a resurrection of ancient mercantilism. In Keynesian economics, people saving money take it out of circulation and cause recessions. Money must circulate for the economy to keep growing. It is related to the trickledown economics of the Middle Ages in which wealthy people assumed that their spending on conspicuous consumption enriched the lower classes by providing them with income. Wealthy people often thought their vast consumption was necessary for the benefit of others. Readers will find the same concept in economic textbooks described as the circular flow model. It is also integral to the Modern Monetary Theory.

But Keynes was wrong. Adam Smith had written about savings 150 years before Keynes and anticipated Keynes' mistake: producers borrow the savings of people and use the money to pay workers and buy materials so savings always circulate in the economy as if the money had been spent on consumption. The only time money goes out of circulation is if the owner puts it under his mattress instead of in the bank.

War in the Bible is almost always a judgment of God, except for the early days of Israel when Joshua conquered the land. After that, God used war as punishment for Israel's rebellion. Throughout history, empires used war to steal the wealth of conquered nations but it was a zero sum game; the conquered nation lost as much as the winner gained. That was one of the cases in which the old idea was true that one nation cannot grow except at the expense of another. Mercantilists like Keynes turned war into a source of prosperity. After all, the state at war takes the savings of the people and makes it circulate in spending on ships, tanks and aircraft. But does such spending enrich people as Keynesians claim?

Killing people does not make people wealthier, except in the sense that there are fewer mouths to feed. Some historians argue that the Black Death raised wages in the middle ages because there were fewer people to hire for work. However, after such massive death, as much as a third of Europe, demand had fallen proportionally. The intersection of the supply and demand curves has merely shifted to the left because G.D.P. has fallen.

Nevertheless, we can accomplish the same thing as war without the death. All we have to do is produce Jeeps, tanks, ships and aircraft as if we were at war, then shoot down the planes ourselves, blow up the Jeeps and tanks and sink the ships in the depths of the Pacific and Atlantic oceans. What would we have accomplished? Well the workers would have more cash to spend, but since production of food, clothing, consumer goods and housing will have declined while the country labored to make weapons, they will be in short supply. As a result, prices of all of those goods will soar to match the new amount of spending. In real terms, that is, discounting price increases, people will be able to buy no more after the fake war than before.

Little will have changed. Wages will be higher, but so will prices. And workers will be worse off because now they face higher taxes to pay off the debt the state accumulated to build weapons. Even without the killing, war impoverishes the winners. That is what really happened in WWII, but most people could not see it because rationing kept prices from increasing. So instead of price inflation making people poorer, rationing made them poorer.

Another way to look at war is through the tradeoff between investment and consumption. The two comprise the whole economy; all spending is either investment or consumption and investment comes from savings. In the short run, the economy can increase investment only by reducing consumption, which is another way of describing savings, and providing funds for investment. Greater investment adds jobs and cuts the costs of consumer goods, such as cars, so that consumers in the long run can consume more. Into which category does war fall? Tanks, ships and airplanes do not produce other goods, so they fall into the category of greater consumption. Defense is always consumption. But in order to consume more we have to invest less. Fewer savings means less investment because of war and that means fewer jobs and higher prices for consumer goods.

What about a war for oil, as many socialists claimed was the motive for the second war against Iraq under President George W. Bush? Socialists insisted that we fought the war in order to take Iraq's oil. There are at least two problems with that scenario, which demonstrate the severe lack of reasoning skills among socialists. 1) The U.S. has never received a barrel of free oil from Iraq. U.S. oil companies refused to enter the market for oil exploration in Iraq after the war because of the danger from terrorism. Any oil we got we paid market prices for it. 2) Even if Iraq agreed to give us oil without a charge, or we simply stole it, we would have to figure the cost of the war as the price of the oil. It still would not be free and the price per barrel would have been much higher than the market price.

But we had to prevent Saddam Hussein, the former president of Iraq, from taking over the oil of Saudi Arabia and other Gulf states in the first Gulf war, did we not? There might have been other reasons for defending the Gulf states, but economics and oil were not among them because if Hussein had conquered the entire Saudi peninsula and controlled their oil, he would still have to sell it to someone or it would be no good to him. No one can eat oil and it has no uses until it is refined. If the Iraqis refined the oil they would still have to sell the products because their country had too small a population to use it all. The only thing that would have changed would be that we bought oil from the dictator Hussein instead of the dictators of Saudi Arabia and the Gulf states. Americans are too eager to go to war. Economically, even the victors are losers. And because of its humanitarian ideals the U.S. loses more since it insists on paying to rebuild whatever nation it has conquered.

Another reason Christians should be especially cautious is that war always has unforeseen, unintended and undesirable consequences. WWI defeated Germany, Italy, the Austro-Hungarian Empire and Turkey, and broke up the Austro Hungarian Empire into many tiny nations based on ethnicity. But it also helped the Bolsheviks install communism in Russia. Reparations impoverished Germany and helped Hitler launch World War II. And the tiny nations that had once made up the Austro-Hungarian Empire were too small to defend themselves against Germany when in the late 1930's Hitler began to pick them off one at a time.

WWII saved China from Imperial Japan, but opened the door for Mao and communism to take over. Communism was far deadlier and more brutal than even the worst of the Japanese atrocities, including the "rape" of Nanking. More than 30 million people starved to death, some reduced to cannibalism during Mao's Cultural Revolution. Germany lost the war in Europe only to be replaced by the communist U.S.S.R., which took half of Germany and all of Eastern Europe. But Lenin and Stalin had murdered more than three times as many people as Hitler. The U.S. paid to rebuild Western Europe and the Cold War further impoverished the victors.

During the Cold War, many French people said that if the U.S.S.R. conquered them as Germany had, please do not rescue them. That irritates Americans who think the French should be grateful for defeating the Nazis. The French have a point. By surrendering to Hitler they lost their sovereignty but kept the Germans from destroying their country. The U.S. and U.K. destroyed nearly every town between the coast and Germany on their long march to liberate German occupied Europe.

A lot of fiction has been written about what might have happened had Germany won WWII and the plots make compelling motion pictures. But Germany was never in a position to conquer the U.S. It could not have held Western Europe for much longer. The fallacy that it could lies in the belief that National Socialism was a viable system. It was not. Ludwig von Mises explained why in his 1922 book *Socialism*. For an economy to grow and enrich its people, it needs accurate prices so that producers know what to produce, how much and when. Waste increases without accurate prices and people grow poorer. Germany was as socialist as the U.S.S.R. and its economy would have collapsed even without war within a short time. Besides, Germany was spending over half its G.D.P. on war while the people tried to fend off starvation. The collapse of the Soviet Union proved Mises right.

Republicans in the U.S. credit President Ronald Reagan for having brought down the great Red Bear. The rationale goes something like this: Reagan increased U.S. military spending and forced the Soviet Union to keep up, spending over half of G.D.P. on the military in its last decade. Growing hunger and impoverishment caused the Communist Party to lose support and the whole thing just fell apart. The truth as reported by Yegor Gaidar, the lead economist under Boris Yeltsin after the fall of the U.S.S.R., in his book *Collapse of an Empire: Lessons for Modern Russia* tells a much more realistic story.

The Soviet people were far from starving in the late 1980's because the U.S. had guaranteed loans to the Soviets to buy food from the West. Then the Poles began to rebel against their Soviet masters. When the Hungarians did that in 1956 and the Czechs in 1968, the Soviets had crushed the rebellions with tanks. This time was different. The Soviets asked the U.S. what it would do if Soviet tanks rolled into Poland to put down the current rebellion. The U.S. said that the American people would no longer allow Washington to guarantee loans to the U.S.S.R. to buy food. Without loans the Soviets could not feed its people. So the leadership decided to try other means to quash the revolt and those failed. When the many tiny nations of Eastern Europe saw that the Soviets could not use tanks against them, more of them rebelled. The break up in Eastern Europe caused panic in the Soviet Union and a group of communists tried to pull off a coup. They failed and Yelstin took over Russia while the other states of the U.S.S.R. also went their own ways.

The Soviet Union lasted much longer than it should have. U.S. military and humanitarian aid kept it alive during the war. Afterward, the Soviets stole most of the factories that Eastern Europe had built and that boosted Soviet wealth for a while. High oil prices after 1973 enabled the communists to export oil in exchange for food until the collapse in prices in 1986. Then U.S. loan guarantees kept the empire on life support. The serene death of the empire of the Soviet Union would have happened much earlier without repeated help from the U.S. The same thing would have happened to Hitler's Germany had the U.S. stayed out of the war. And something similar might have happened to Japan had the U.S. not provoked it into attacking Pearl Harbor.

There is nothing good about war. An honest historian could argue that every war the U.S. has fought since the war for independence was unnecessary and based on very faulty economics. Every one of them was avoidable, even the Civil War, which was not civil at all. The explosion of manufacturing from the Civil War until WWI and competition from better farming methods outside of the South would have ended slavery peacefully within a few decades. All of those wars greatly impoverished the U.S. How much wealthier would we be today if we had avoided so many wars? And how many young men would have lived?

Chapter 9 – Romans thirteen

"Every person is to be in subjection to the governing authorities. For there is no authority except from God, and those which exist are established by God. Therefore whoever resists authority has opposed the ordinance of God; and they who have opposed will receive condemnation upon themselves. For rulers are not a cause of fear for good behavior, but for evil. Do you want to have no fear of authority? Do what is good and you will have praise from the same; for it is a minister of God to you for good. But if you do what is evil, be afraid; for it does not bear the sword for nothing; for it is a minister of God, an avenger who brings wrath on the one who practices evil. Therefore it is necessary to be in subjection, not only because of wrath, but also for conscience' sake. For because of this you also pay taxes, for rulers are servants of God, devoting themselves to this very thing. Render to all what is due them: tax to whom tax is due; custom to whom custom; fear to whom fear; honor to whom honor," Romans 13:1-7.

In this passage God tells the Roman Christians through the Apostle Paul to submit to the Roman authorities because God has established those authorities and they are the servants God uses to punish evil people. Many Christians have taken the passage to mean that Christians can never oppose government authorities even when they are unjust or pass unjust laws. Citizens are supposed to endure the abuse. Relief can come only from God's miraculous intervention. Others take a slightly less absolutist approach and claim that Christians must obey all the laws of a state, fair or unjust, but may use nonviolent means to protest unjust legislation or court rulings in the hopes of changing them. The passage has caused some Christians to condemn the colonial rebellion against England that created the United States as a violation of the commands in Romans. But what does the passage actually say?

- God has established all authority.
- Rebellion against that authority is rebellion against God.
- The ruling authorities act as servants of God to punish evil doers.
- Taxes support those servants.

What does Paul not say?

- Submit to evil rulers. Paul does not mention evil rulers, only those who do God's work by punishing evil people, in other words, ideal rulers.
- Ruling authorities can do anything they want with impunity.

- God approves of everything that leaders do.
- God approves of every law that politicians pass.
- Human law is equal to God's law.
- Rulers are not subject to God's laws.
- Who will punish evil rulers.
- What should we do about unjust laws.
- Rulers can charge as much tax as they want.

Those who insist this passage requires Christians to submit absolutely to evil rulers are guilty of eisegesis, that is, reading their own ideas into the passage. Paul refers only to ideal rulers, those who punish evil doers. But who are evildoers? In God's mind they would be people who break his laws, not necessarily those who break manmade laws.

What does Paul mean by submit?

On first look, Paul's command seems to be absolute; there are no exceptions. However, the command is similar to the one he gave to women: "Wives, be subject to your own husbands, as to the Lord. For the husband is the head of the wife, as Christ also is the head of the church, He Himself being the Savior of the body." (Ephesians 5:22-23) Few theologians would argue that Paul commanded wives to do whatever their husbands demand regardless of how evil it might be. And at the end of the passage Paul shades his meaning in verse 33: "Nevertheless, each individual among you also is to love his own wife even as himself, and the wife must see to it that she respects her husband." Paul softens his command to one of showing respect. Paul has a habit of making statements that appear to be absolutes when closer investigation shows that he did not intend them to be.

More evidence that Paul did not mean his command to submit to rulers as absolute comes from Paul's own behavior. In Acts chapter 9, the Jews in Damascus plotted to kill him. We may assume that they had the authority to do so from the high priest just as Paul had the authority to arrest or kill Christians before his conversion. He had supervised the murder of Stephen under the authority of the same rulers. Paul discovered the plot to kill him, but instead of submitting to that authority, and knowing the Jews were watching the city gates, he allowed other disciples to put him in a basket and lower him through a window in the outer wall so he could escape. Near the end of his career, Paul appeared before the Sanhedrin in Jerusalem to answer charges of having defiled the temple but rather than submitting to the council, Paul caused a riot by pitting the Pharisees against the Sadducees over the reality of the resurrection. The Roman commander had to deploy troops to rescue Paul. He submitted to the Roman authorities only because they could prevent the Jewish authorities from killing him.

Paul is not the only example of believers who refused to submit to the authorities. When Herod the Great decided to murder all of the baby boys two years of age and younger in the nation, God warned Joseph through an angel to flee to Egypt. The angel did not tell Joseph to submit to the ruling authority. John the Baptist, whom Jesus called the greatest prophet of all time, publicly criticized the marriage of Herod. That was not submission and he lost his head for it.

Jesus never submitted to the authorities who sought to kill him until his time to die had come, a few times using his divine powers to escape hostile authorities. When the fever to kill him in Judea became too intense, he fled to Galilee. And he warned the disciples not to submit to authorities when they saw Jerusalem surrounded by the Roman armies but to flee to the mountains. Jesus launched his ministry by cleansing the temple of the money changers and sellers of sacrificial animals and closed it with the same event. Both were radical acts of rebellion against the highest ruling authorities at the time in Jerusalem.

Most theologians recognize one exception to Paul's command to submit to authorities – when they order Christians to stop preaching the gospel. They point to the episode in Act 5:17-42 when the high priest had the apostles arrested and imprisoned. An angel appeared to the apostles in the night and rather than tell them to submit to the authorities, opened the prison gates and organized a major jail break. The officers found the apostles preaching in the temple, arrested them again and took them back to the Council, which ordered them to stop preaching about Jesus. Peter responded, "We must obey God rather than men."

Interpreters who admit this exception insist it is the only exception to Paul's command to submit to authorities. But let us not forget that it is an exception and destroys the idea that Paul's command is absolute. However, there is no reason to think that is the only exception. Later, Herod arrested Peter and put in him in prison. An angel appeared to him in prison, but instead of instructing him to submit to the authorities, the angel launched another jail break. Christians in Israel faced persecution after the murder of Stephen, but instead of submitting they left for safer parts of the empire.

The pattern is clear. The Apostles and Christians did not submit to the authorities when told to stop preaching about Jesus, nor did they submit when the authorities intended to persecute, jail or kill them. But neither did they fight. They simply relocated to safer territories.

The only examples of rebellion against established authorities are in the Old Testament and mostly in the book of the Judges. Each time Israel succumbed to idol worship, God would punish the people by having a pagan power conquer and oppress them. God had ordained that judgment so any rebellion against those pagan rulers was disobedience to God. Yet God each time prepared a leader who successfully rebelled and restored Israel's independence. Some theologians argue that we can no longer rebel as the Israelis did unless God gives us direct revelation to do so as he did to Gideon, for example.

However, consider how God spoke to his people at that time. They did not have the Holy Spirit and they only had the Torah as permanent revelation so direct revelation was God's only option. How does God speak to Christians today? Direct revelation is still possible, but we have the Holy Spirit living in us and speaking to us on a regular basis. And we have God's complete, permanent revelation in the Bible from which God expects us to study and distill theology and principles for godly living and governance. Since the Torah is clear that God wants freedom, justice and independence for his people when they are in a right relationship to him, it is not a logical leap to assume that Christians can rebel against tyrannical rulers much as the Israelis did.

As an example, most the leaders of the American Revolution against Great Britain were extremely godly men. It is highly likely that the desire for freedom from tyranny that burned in their hearts came from the Holy Spirit residing in them.

What authority do rulers have?

Most theologians focus on the word "submit" in the passage, but the word "authority" is more important. Paul wrote that God had established all authority that exists. That does not mean that God approved of everything the emperors and governors did or imply that God has given authorities the right to commit any crimes they wanted to against citizens with impunity. That would be tantamount to the theory of the divine right of kings. If accurate, that would make God complicit in the many crimes of rulers over the centuries. Clearly that was not Paul's intent. The Old Testament is full of God's condemnations through the prophets of rulers for their crimes against the people.

When interpreting Romans 13, it is important to keep in mind that "All authority in heaven and earth has been given to me," (Matt. 28:18) according to Jesus. Paul declared that God has "disarmed the principalities and powers and made a public show of them in Christ's triumphal procession," (Col. 2:15). Commenting on these verses, Oliver O'Donovan, Regis professor of moral and pastoral theology at the University of Oxford and Canon of Christ Church wrote in *The Desire of the Nations: Rediscovering the roots of political theology*, "That must be the primary eschatological assertion about the authorities, political and demonic, which govern the world: they have been made subject to God's sovereignty in the Exaltation of Christ. The second, qualifying assertion is that this awaits a final universal presence of Christ to become fully apparent." Paul employed the imagery of a conquering general who paraded his captured enemies before crowds of citizens to show his victory and authority over the defeated authorities. If humans have any authority, it is derived from Christ. They have authority only to do what Christ allows them.

What authority did God give rulers? According to Paul, God gave them the authority to punish evildoers. Clearly, rulers have the authority to enforce God's laws, especially the civil laws that forbid theft, murder, fraud, kidnapping, rape, etc. Governmental authority is not opened ended or a blank check. But what about rulers who want to commit those same crimes against the people, either directly or through laws? Did God give them that authority? Clearly, the answer is no.

Paul's delineation of the role of ruling authorities, to punish evil doers, limits state authority because of Christ's exaltation. Paul's statement, then, would be one of the first declarations of limited government since the Torah. Paul is telling rulers they have no authority to do anything but punish evil doers who violate God's laws, the same authority that he gave the judges and people in the Torah government. O'Donovan wrote,

> No government has the right to exist; no nation has a right to defend itself. Such claims are overwhelmed by the immediate claim of the Kingdom.

There remains simply the rump of political authority which cannot be dispensed with yet, the exercise of judgment.

Paying taxes

Paul and Peter instructed believers to pay their taxes, but Jesus had set the example for his followers and in doing so clarified his attitude toward the existing government authorities. In Matt.17:24-7, Peter is asked to pay the temple tax. Most theologians grasp that this was a religious tax, but it was also a state tax because the authorities who collected it were political rulers as well. Jesus taught Peter that the sons of the king were exempt from the taxes of the subjects. Technically, the fish that Peter caught paid the tax for Jesus and his Apostles with the coin in his mouth. O'Donovan wrote the following about the incident:

> To recognise the coming of God's Kingdom is to be a son of the Kingdom, and so emancipated from the order in which God's rule was mediated through such alienating institutions as taxation. But purely as a concession Jesus and his disciples will pay taxes 'to create no scandal', i.e. lest they be misunderstood as mere rebels, who refuse God's mediated rule as such. As it were to emphasize the purely peripheral character of this compliance, their payment is provided for them by the almost comic intervention of a miracle.

The episode of the temple tax helps clarify the earlier incident in which Pharisees and Herodians tried to trap Jesus into either offending half the crowd or inciting rebellion against Rome (Mark 12:17ff). They asked Jesus if it was right for Israelis to pay the Roman census tax. Jesus responded by asking for a Roman coin. Someone in the crowd produced a coin with the head of Caesar on it. Alfred Edersheim wrote in *Life and Times of Jesus the Messiah* that such coins were rare in Israel at the time because the Romans respected the Jewish hatred of idolatry and images that might be worshipped, so they used coins in Israel without representations of people or animals. He added that the rabbis taught the people that the right to mint coins implied the right of the state to tax the people.

Without doubt, Jesus instructed his followers to pay taxes to Rome when he said, "Render unto to Caesar what is Caesar's and unto God what is God's." He was not dodging the issue or cleverly disguising his answer as some libertarians want to read the passage. The libertarian assumes that Jesus disapproved of paying taxes to Rome. The best interpretation says that "he treated the question as an irrelevant distraction from the real business of receiving God's Kingdom. If Caesar put his head upon the coin, then presumably it is his: let him have what is his, if he asks for it (for such transactions are not the stuff of which true government consists), but give your whole allegiance to God's rule!" according to O'Donovan.

God's laws vs. man's legislation

Two types of law exist – God's laws and manmade legislation. God's laws cannot be repealed no matter how much a legislature might try. For example, the U.S. Supreme Court has made abortion legal. Does that mean U.S. law trumps God's prohibition of murder? Of course not! Murder is still murder with God regardless of what a human law says.

Do human laws have the same character of inviolability? For example, if an immigrant has not followed procedure for entering the U.S. he is considered an illegal alien. But the same group of people who made the laws can give the immigrant amnesty, as President Ronald Reagan did, and declare him legal. Is the immigrant still illegal in the sense that a murderer is always a murderer regardless of the legislation? Of course not! Human legislation is arbitrary and fickle. The U.S. experience with prohibition in the 1930's offers a good example. For more than a decade legislation made everyone who drank alcohol a criminal until the legislation was repealed and the criminals became law abiding citizens overnight without ever changing their behavior. Manmade legislation has none of the authority of God's law. Often, man's legislation violates God's laws.

We have established that God created authorities but did not give them a blank check to do anything they want to do. They have the authority to enforce God's laws but God has not given any ruler the authority to violate his laws and commit crimes against people with impunity.

Why did Paul write this?

An important hermeneutics principle is to look not only at the context in the Bible but the historical and cultural context of the times. Before Paul wrote the passage in Romans 13, he met a Jewish Christian couple named Aquila and Priscilla who had recently fled Rome because Emperor Claudius had expelled all of the Jews from the city (Acts 18). We have to go to secular history to find out the background. The Jews had a habit of rioting and a reputation as trouble makers. In 38 A.D. a riot erupted in Alexandria, Egypt between the Jews and gentiles. After the city sent delegations to Claudius about the riot, Claudius wrote back to the city leaders. F.F. Bruce quoted Claudius in his article "Christianity Under Claudius," which appeared in the *Bulletin of the John Rylands Library 44*:

> The Jews, on the other hand, I bid for their part not to agitate for more than they have previously enjoyed, and never again to send two embassies, as though they lived in two separate cities—the like of which has never happened before. Moreover, they must not engage in contests for such posts as gymnasiarch or games director, but should rest content with what belongs to them by right and enjoy an abundance of all good things in a city which is not theirs. They must not bring in or invite Jews who sail in from Syria or Egypt; this is the sort of thing which will compel me to have my suspicions redoubled. Otherwise I will proceed against them with the

utmost severity for fomenting a general plague which infests the whole world.

Tiberius had expelled Jews from Rome twenty-two years before Claudius became emperor. Claudius had wanted to expel the Jews when he first took power, but the Jewish population had grown too large for him to do so without causing a riot, so he outlawed public assemblies by Jews. A few years later, constant rioting by the Jews of Rome forced Claudius to expel them, two of whom were the followers of Christ, Aquila and Priscilla. Paul would have known this history of the Jews in Alexandria and Rome and he had personally experienced rioting by Jews in Thessalonica. In Paul's day, Christians had not suffered much at the hands of the Romans. In fact, Roman authorities had helped restrain the Jewish and pagan forces that tried to prevent him from preaching. F. F. Bruce wrote,

> Paul was thinking much more of his own experience of Roman justice, which encouraged him to think of the empire as being—temporarily, at any rate—a safeguard against the unruly forces which endeavoured to frustrate the progress of the gospel. On the strength of this experience he could write of the imperial authorities several years later—when Nero had already been emperor two years and more—as "ministers of God"; on the strength of this experience, too, he confidently appealed towards the end of A.D. 59 to have his case transferred from the jurisdiction of the procurator of Judaea to the emperor's court in Rome.

Paul wanted to protect the young church from unnecessary persecution by the Roman state. He may have had in mind Jesus' warning in Matthew 7:6, "Do not give what is holy to dogs, and do not throw your pearls before swine, lest they trample them under their feet, and turn and tear you to pieces." In other words, do not attract the wrath of the opposition when they show violent tendencies; as much as possible, live in peace.

Finally, Paul had already witnessed the threat Christianity posed to the ancient social order. Romans believed that worshipping their gods caused the gods to protect their cities against invaders so not worshipping them would be treasonous, as was refusal to worship the Caesars. Also, the radical individualism of Christianity threatened the ancient pagan hierarchy of society in which patriarchs ruled as tyrants over women and slaves. Larry Siedentop wrote in *Inventing the Individual*,

> Was it an accident that women and even slaves also played an important part in the growth of Christianity, and that, through them, it spread into the upper classes? The Christian movement gained from being marginal. The offer of dignity through belief in the Christ did not openly challenge patriarchy or servitude. But it offered self-respect. A moral revolution was underway.

The Christian refusal to worship the traditional gods or Caesars and its radical individualism threatened to shred the social fabric. As a result, pagans accused Christians of committing treason, cannibalism and of being atheists. Paul did not want the progress of the gospel to be hindered by unruly behavior on the part of Christians giving credence to those charges. Church fathers for the next two centuries defended Christians against the charge of being unpatriotic or treasonous.

Further evidence comes from I Timothy chapter 2 that Paul's and Peter's motives for admonishing Christians to submit to rulers had to do with keeping the peace. Paul encouraged the church to pray for kings and those in authority. In other words, the kingdom flourishes in the hot house environment of peace. O'Donovan added,

> How, then, are these supposed to serve the ultimate horizon? By facilitating a 'quiet and peaceful life' – for their subjects, that is – 'in all religion and sobriety'. 'This', the apostle goes on, 'is good and acceptable to God our Savior, whose will is for everyone to be saved and to come to recognise the truth.'...the goals and conduct of secular government are to be reconceived to serve the needs of international mobility and contact which the advancement of the Gospel requires.

The difference between government and the state

Paul wrote that all authority has been established by God. However, God did not create the state. Theologians often claim that God established human government after the flood when he instructed Noah in Genesis 9:6, "Whoever sheds man blood, by man his blood shall be shed, for in the image of God he made man." The term "image of God" indicated that God had delegated to every human the authority to enforce his laws. However, most of what we know about God's political theory comes from the Torah. That government consisted exclusively of a court system to apply God's laws to adjudicate disputes between free citizens. God provided Israel with no human executive other than a supreme court justice. There was no king or pharaoh and no legislative branch, police force or standing army. Those were the main features of the pagan nations and what we characterize as the state. Israel embraced the state when it rejected God in favor of a king like the nations around them.

So while it is clear that God created government, it consisted only of a few laws and courts. God never created the state with kings or pharaohs who oppress the people. States have always been the invention of men who used force to impose their will on others and rob them of their wealth and enslave or kill them. We need to keep this distinction between government and the state in mind when interpreting Romans 13 and the authority that the state has.

On the other hand, God used mankind's invention of the state for his own purposes. As he warned the Israelis through Samuel in response to their demand for a king in I Samuel 8, kings would oppress them in awful ways. They would take the people's property and their daughters while killing their sons in continual war. By allowing the state, God was doing what Paul told the Romans he has often done to mankind – let them have what they demanded. Paul wrote in Romans 1:18-19, "For the wrath of God is revealed from heaven against all ungodliness and unrighteousness of men who suppress the truth in unrighteousness, because that which is known about God is evident within them; for God made it evident to them." Mankind had rebelled against God and God's punishment was to leave them alone: "Therefore God gave them over in the lusts of their hearts to impurity, so that their bodies would be dishonored among them." (Romans 1:24)

Christians need to keep in mind that God's perfect will for mankind is a libertarian government, as he designed in the Torah, not a state, not even a democratic state. An oppressive state is part of God's permissive will as punishment for rebellion. Individual Christians can refuse to submit to states when states try to exercise authority beyond that which God has given them, but the state will likely crush those who try. God has not promised to miraculously rescue Christians who insist on their God-given rights. Submission to God's laws is a matter of conscience; submission to unjust rulers is a practical affair. Christians are left primarily with the option of fleeing to a less oppressive state as the early Christians did when persecuted.

God will allow the blessings of freedom only to those who embrace him and his designs for government, as he did with the Israelis in the book of Judges. Not everyone has to be Christian and endorse Torah economics, but a critical mass must exist within a nation and when that mass is reached God will allow the people to throw off tyrannical rulers. That happened with the Dutch in the late sixteenth century, England in the seventeenth and the U.S. in the late eighteenth century. However, as each nation has abandoned Christianity it has become increasingly socialist and tyrannical.

With regard to economic tyranny, there is an option between fleeing and civil war, and that is a "black" market. I prefer to call it the free market when it exists in a state with oppressive taxation and regulation. Christians can take part in a free market that follows God's laws of abstaining from theft, fraud and coercion while exercising their God-given rights to free exchange with others. History has shown that as states become more oppressive in economic matters, more people choose to ignore manmade laws and engage in free trade though it may violate tyrannical laws. The numbers may not be great enough to allow them to set up a separate state, but at some point enough people will become engaged in the free market to make it relatively safe to take part in. Such free markets abounded in the old Soviet Union, Communist China and other socialist tyrannies.

Free markets within tyrannical states provide vital services, mostly to the poor and powerless. The wealthy have all of the power within the state they need to make tyrannical systems work in their favor. The poor are the ones who always need relief from oppression. Often, smuggling provided food and medicine that would have been scarce without the "illegal" activity. The most common method of saving by poor people outside of the U.S. is to buy dollars on the "black" market and stash them under a mattress. They cannot buy them legally because the rich and powerful have crafted legislation to give themselves monopolies on foreign exchange. Free markets in U.S. dollars help poor people around the world escape the ravages of inflation inflicted on them by states who insist on "printing" money to pay their bills.

Theologians disagree about who has the authority to rein in tyrannical rulers. Some insist that only God can do it. But then God works through his people most of the time. Godly theologians in The Netherlands during the Inquisition could not decide who had the authority to rebel against tyranny and finally left the decision to the nobility. In the multiple liberations of Israel from tyrannical rulers in the book of Judges, God used humans each time, sometimes with miracles and sometimes without. The difference is that the judges and kings in the Old Testament had the advantage of direct revelation from God concerning when to rebel. We do not have that advantage today. On the other hand, God has given us the gifts of his word and the ability to reason from its principles. We can know what God considered immoral and unjust behavior on the part of ruling authorities by applying reason to God's word.

Consequently, if the majority of a nation is Christian and decides to rebel against the tyranny of the state, as the Dutch Republic and the United States did, God has given them that authority and will bless such rebellion. Until such time, Christians should pay taxes to tyrannical governments, obey the laws as much as possible, and work toward peace and the prosperity of the nation, as God instructed the Jews in Babylon to do.

Christians must keep in mind the principles of interpretation, or hermeneutics, when confronting Romans 13. The Bible is mostly history and to paraphrase Mises, history is so vast and contradictory that people can find support in it for any kind of nonsense. The only way we can have any degree of certainty that our interpretation of scripture comes close to what God intended is by following those principles, which are just common sense. One of those principles is to consider the context, not just the immediate context of the passage, but the historical and cultural context and all of the passages in the Bible that touch on that topic. Most of the scripture that deals with government are in the Old Testament, or the Hebrew Bible. When we include those in the discussion of this chapter we get a different perspective than if it is yanked from its context and used to defend tyranny.

Bibliography

Acemoglu, Daron and Johnson, Simon "Institutions as a Fundamental Cause of Long-Run Growth," *Handbook of Economic Growth*, Volume IA. Edited by Philippe Aghion and Steven N. Durlauf, Elsevier B.V 2005.

Aikman, David. *Jesus in Beijing: How Christianity is Transforming China and Changing the Global Balance of Power.* Washington: Regnery Publishing. 2006.

Anderson, John E. "Economics and the Evangelical Mind." *ACE Bulletin.* Fall 1996.

Arthur, W. Brian. *Complexity and the Economy.* Oxford University Press. 2014.

Arthur, W. Brian. "Complexity Economics: A Different Framework for Economic Thought," SFI Working Paper: 2013-04-012, Santa Fe Institute, 2013, www.santafe.edu.

Alexander, Denis. "Made in the Image of God: Human Value and Genomics," Huffington Post, http://www.huffingtonpost.com/dr-denis-alexander/made-in-the-image-of-god-human-value-and-human-genomics_b_2401494.html.

Alvarado, Ruben C. "Redeemer Nation," *Common Law Review*, 2002. http://www.commonlawreview.com

Bastiat, Frederic. "Academic Degrees and Socialism" in *Selected Essays on Political Economy.* Atlanta: Foundation for Economic Education. 2017. Kindle edition.

Bauer, P.T. *From Subsistence to Exchange and other Essays.* New Jersey: Princeton University Press. 2000.

Baumol, William J. *The Free Market Innovation Machine.* Princeton: Princeton University Press. 2002.

Bleiberg, Edward. "Understanding the Ancient Egyptian Economy," Commerce and Economy in Ancient Egypt, The Third International Congress for Young Egyptologists. 2009. http://www.byblos.org.hu/documents/Bleiberg_Understanding_the_Ancient_Egyptian_Economy.pdf.

Blum, Jerome. *The End of the Old Order in Rural Europe.* Princeton, NJ: Princeton University Press. 1978.

Brooks, Arthur C. and Wehner, Peter. "Human Nature and Capitalism," *The American*, December 11, 2010. http://american.com/archive/2010/december/human-nature-and-capitalism/.

Brown, Peter. *Through the Eye of a Needle: Wealth, the Fall of Rome, and the Making of Christianity in the West, 350-550 AD*. Princeton: Princeton University Press. 2012.

Bruce, F.F. "Christianity Under Claudius," *Bulletin of the John Rylands Library 44*. March 1962.

Cameron, Rondo. *A Concise Economic History of the World*. New York: Oxford University Press. 1997.

Chafuen, Alejandro A. *Faith and Liberty: The Economic Thought of the Late Scholastics*. New York: Lexington Books. 2003.

"Conversations: Vishal Mangalwadi," Christianity Today, January 12, 1998, http://www.christianitytoday.com/ct/1998/january12/8t1042.html.

Constant, Benjamin. "The Liberty of the Ancients Compared with that of the Moderns." A lecture to the Athénée Royal of Paris in 1819. http://oll.libertyfund.org/titles/constant-the-liberty-of-ancients-compared-with-that-of-moderns-1819.

Credit Suisse Research Institute, *Global Wealth Report 2014*, https://www.credit-suisse.com/us/en/news-and-expertise/research/credit-suisse-research-institute/publications.html.

Decock, Wim. "On Buying and Selling," *Journal of Markets & Morality*, Volume 10, Number 2. Fall 2007.

De la Court, Pieter. *The True Interest and Political Maxims, of the Republic of Holland* [1662]. Indianapolis: The Liberty Fund. 2011. http://oll.libertyfund.org/title/85.

De Mar, Gary. *God and Government*. Atlanta: American Vision Press. 1982.

De Soto, Jesus Huerta. *Money, Bank Credit and Economic Cycles*. Auburn: Ludwig von Mises Institute. 2009.

De Soto, Jesus Huerta. "New Light on the Prehistory of the Theory of Banking and the School of Salamanca," *The Review of Austrian Economics*, Vol. 9, No. 2. 1996.

De Vries, Jan. *The First Modern Economy, Success, failure, and perseverance of the Dutch economy, 1500-1815*. Cambridge: Cambridge University Press. 1997.

Devine, Rebekah. "YHWH's Cult Statues: 'Image of God' in an Ancient Near Eastern Context," http://rebekahmgiffone.wordpress.com/2010/08/03/yhwhs-cult-statues-further-study-of-the-image-of-god-in-an-ane-context/, 2010.

DiLorenzo, Thomas. *How Capitalism Saved America: The Untold History of Our Country, from the Pilgrims to the Present*. New York: Crown Forum. 2005.

Dollinger, André. "The social classes in ancient Egypt," "An introduction to the history and culture of Pharaonic Egypt," http://www.reshafim.org.il/ad/egypt/people/social_classes.htm.

Easterly, William. "Does Respecting the Individual Promote Prosperity?" Aid Watch, March 4, 2009, http://aidwatchers.com/2009/03/does-respecting-the-individual-promote-prosperity/.

Easterly, William. "Stories our data tells us: 3 Ways of Looking at a Dictator." Aid Watch, April 5, 2011, http://aidwatchers.com/2011/04/stories-our-data-tells-us-3-ways-of-looking-at-a-dictator/.

Ebeling, Richard M. "Marching to Bismarck's Drummer: The Origins of the Modern Welfare State," The Foundation for Economic Education, December 01, 2007, http://www.fee.org/the_freeman/detail/marching-to-bismarcks-drummer-the-origins-of-the-modern-welfare-state#ixzz2sXzazLRb.

Ebeling, Richard M. "Anti-Commerce and Quietism in Ancient Rome," The Foundation for Economic Education, October 04, 2016, https://fee.org/articles/anti-commerce-and-quietism-in-ancient-rome/.

Edersheim, Alfred. *Life and Times of Jesus the Messiah*. Grand Rapids, MI: Eerdmans Publishing Co. 1980.

Elbadawi, Ibrahim A. "Reviving Growth in the Arab World," World Bank, July 2004. http://siteresources.worldbank.org/DEC/Resources/Arab_growth_revised_July_22_2004.pdf.

"Erasmus," The Internet Encyclopedia of Philosophy, 2001, www.utm.edu/research/IEP/e/ erasmus.htm.

Field, D. H. "Envy," *The New International Dictionary of New Testament Theology*. Grand Rapids: Zondervan. 1975.

Finley, M.I. *The Ancient Economy*. Berkeley: University of California Press. 1985.

Fogel, Robert. *The Escape from Hunger and Premature Death, 1700-2100: Europe, America, and the Third World*. Cambridge: Cambridge University Press. 2001.

Gaidar, Yegor. *Collapse of an Empire: Lessons for Modern Russia*. New York: Brookings Institution Press. 2010.

Gorski, Philip S. *The Disciplinary Revolution: Calvinism and the Rise of the State in Early Modern Europe*. Chicago: The University of Chicago Press. 2003.

"Government and Economy," The Ancient World, Ancient Egypt, http://www.egyptan.sk/en/articles/ancient-egypt/government-and-economy.html.

Graham, Fred. *The Constructive Revolutionary: John Calvin and His Socio-Economic Impact*. Michigan: Michigan University Press. 1987.

Harbison, E. H. *The Christian Scholar and His Calling in the Age of the Reformation*. New York: Charles Scribner's Sons. 1956.

Harrison, Lawrence E. and Huntington. Samuel P., eds. *Culture Matters: How Values Shape Human Progress*. New York: Basic Books. 2000.

Hauerwas, Stanley. *A Better Hope: Resources for a Church Confronting Capitalism, Democracy, and Postmodernity*. Michigan: Brazos Press. 2000.

Hause, Stephen and Maltby, William. *Western Civilization: A History of European Society*. California: Wadsworth. 2004.

Hayek, F.A. "Economics and Knowledge." *Economica*, IV (new ser., 1937).

Hayek, F.A. ed. *Capitalism and the Historians*. Chicago: University of Chicago Press. 1954.

Hayek, F.A. *The Fatal Conceit: the Errors of Socialism*. London: Routledge. 1988.

Hayek, F.A. *Individualism and Economic Order*. Chicago: The University of Chicago Press. 1948.

Hayek, F. A. *The Constitution of Liberty*. Chicago: The University of Chicago Press. 1960.

Hayek, F.A. *The Counter-Revolution of Science: Studies on the Abuse of Reason*. London: The Free Press of Glencoe Collier-Macmillan. 1964.

Hayek, F.A. "The Theory of Complex Phenomena: A Precocious Play on the Epistemology of Complexity," *Studies in Philosophy, Politics and Economics*. London: Routledge & Kegan Paul. 1967.

Hecksher, Eli F. *Mercantilism*. New York: Garland Publishing. 1983.

Hofstede, Geert. *Culture's Consequences*. London: Sage Publications. 2001.

Hollyday, Frederic B. M. *Bismarck* (1970) p. 65, in "Otto von Bismarck," Wikipedia, the free encyclopedia, http://en.wikipedia.org/wiki/Otto_von_Bismarck.

Inalcik, Halil. *An Economic and Social History of the Ottoman Empire*. Cambridge: Cambridge University Press. 1994.

Israel, Jonathan I. *The Dutch Republic, Its Rise, Greatness, and Fall 1477-1806*. Oxford: Oxford University Press. 1998.

Kiersh, Aaron. "Lobbying is a Lucrative Investment, Researchers Find Using CRP Data," Open Secrets, http://www.opensecrets.org/news/2009/06/lobbying-is-a-lucrative-invest/, June 25, 2009

Kirshner, Julius ed. *Business, Banking, and Economic Thought in Late Medieval and Early Modern Europe, Selected Studies of Raymond de Roover*, Chicago: University of Chicago Press. 1974.

Kirzner, Israel. *The Economic Point of View: An Essay in the History of Economic Thought*. Kansas City: Sheed and Ward. 1976.

Kondonassis, A.J. "Economic Development: Issues and Problems." Notes for the class Third World Economic Development. University of Oklahoma. 1990.

Kuran, Timur. "The Scale of Entrepreneurship in Middle Eastern History: Inhibitive Roles of Islamic Institutions," *Economic Research Initiatives* at Duke, March 2008.

Leijonhufvud, Axel. "Life Among the Econ," *Western Economic Journal*, 11:3 (1973:Sept.) http://www.econ.ucla.edu/alleras/teaching/life_among_the_econs_leijonhufvud_1973.pdf

Lewis, Bernard. *Istanbul and the Civilization of the Ottoman Empire*. Norman: University of Oklahoma Press. 1963.

Lewis, Bernard. "Islam and Liberal Democracy." *The Atlantic Online*, February, 1993. www.theatlantic.com.

Lewis, Bernard. *What Went Wrong*. New York: Oxford University Press. 2000.

Lewis, Bernard. *Islam in History*. Chicago: Open Court Publishing. 1973.

Lifshitz, Joseph Isaac. *Judaism, Law and the Free Market: an Analysis*. Acton Institute. 2012. Kindle edition.

Maddison, Angus. *The World Economy: A Millenial Perspective*. New York: Development Centre of the Organization for Economic Co-operation and Development. 2000.

Maddison, Angus. *Dynamic Forces in Capitalist Development*. Oxford, 1991.

Maybury, Richard ."The Great Thanksgiving Hoax," *Mises Daily*, November 27, 2014, http://mises.org/library/great-thanksgiving-hoax-1.

McCloskey, Deirdre N. *Bourgeois Dignity: Why Economics Can't Explain the Modern World*. Chicago: The University of Chicago Press. 2010. Kindle edition.

McCloskey, Deirdre N. *The Bourgeois Virtues: Ethics for an Age of Commerce*. Chicago: The University of Chicago Press. 2006. Kindle edition.

McGrath, Alister. *The Twilight of Atheism: The Rise and Fall of Disbelief in the Modern World*. New York: Doubleday. 2006.

McKay, John P., Hill, Bennett D., and Buckler, John. A *History of Western Society Since 1300*. New York: Houghton Mifflin Company. 1999.

Menu, Bernadette M. "Economy," *The Oxford Encyclopedia of Ancient Egypt*. USA: Oxford University Press. 2000.

Miller, Gregory. "From Crusades to Homeland Defense." *Christian History Magazine*, Spring, 2002. ChristianityToday.com. http://christianitytoday.com/ch/2002/ 002/9.31.html.

Mises, Ludwig von. *Human Action: A Treatise on Economics*. Auburn: The Ludwig von Mises Institute. 1998.

Mises, Ludwig von. *Money, Method, and the Market Process: Essays by Ludwig von Mises*. Mass.: Kluwer Academic Publishers. 1990.

Mises, Ludwig von. *Omnipotent Government: The Rise of the Total State and Total War*. Alabama: The Ludwig von Mises Institute. 2010.

Mises, Ludwig von. *Socialism: An Economic and Sociological Analysis*. Indianapolis: Liberty Fund. 1981, [1922].

Mises, Ludwig, von. *The Ultimate Foundation of Economic Science: An Essay on Method*. New York: D. Van Nostrand Co. 1962.

Nelson, Eric. *The Hebrew Republic: Jewish Sources and the Transformation of European Political Thought*, New York: Harvard University Press. 2011.

North, Douglass C. *Institutions, Institutional Change and Economic Performance*. New York: Cambridge University Press. 1991.

North, Douglass and Thomas, Robert Paul. *The Rise of the Western World*. New York: Cambridge University Pres. 1973.

North, Douglass C., Wallis, John J., and Weingast, Barry R. "A Conceptual Framework for Interpreting Recorded Human History," Mercatus Center, George Mason University, Working Paper 75.

Novak, Michael. *The Spirit of Democratic Capitalism*. New York: Madison Books. 1991.

O'Donovan, Oliver. *The Desire of the Nations: Rediscovering the roots of political theology*. Cambridge: Cambridge University Press. 1999.

Perry, Luc. *A Brief History of Thought: A Philosophical Guide to Living*. New York: HarperCollins. 2011.

Piketty, Thomas. *Capital in the Twenty-First Century*. Cambridge: Belknap Press. 2014.

Prak, Maarten, ed. *Early Modern Capitalism: Economic and Social Change in Europe. 1400-1800*. New York: Routledge. 2001.

Pipes, Richard. *Property and Freedom*. New York: Alfred A. Knopf. 1999.

Quataert, Donald. *Manufacturing in the Ottoman Empire and Turkey. 1500-1950*. New York: State University of New York. 1994.

Reinhert, Erik S. "Benchmarking Success: The Dutch Republic (1500-1750) as seen by Contemporary European Economists" in SUM (University of Oslo) Working paper No. 1, 2004. http://www.othercanon.org/board/about-Reinert.html.

Reisman, George. *Capitalism: A Treatise on Economics*. Illinois: Jameson Books. 1998.

Roepke, Wilhelm. *The Social Crisis of Our Time.* Chicago: The University of Chicago Press. 1950

Rothbard, Murray N. *Economic Thought Before Adam Smith: An Austrian Perspective on the History of Economic Thought*, Vo. I. Auburn: Ludwig von Mises Institute. 2006.

Schoeck, Helmut. *Envy: A Theory of Social Behavior.* Indianapolis: Liberty Fund. 1987.

Schoeck, Helmut and Wiggins, James W. eds. *The New Argument in Economics, The Public versus the Private Sector.* Princeton: D. Van Nostrand Co. 1963.

Siedentop, Larry. *Inventing the Individual: The Origins of Western Liberalism.* Cambridge: The Belknap Press. 2014.

Stark, Rodney. *How the West Won: The Neglected Story of the Triumph of Modernity.* Wilmington, DE: ISI Books. 2014. Kindle Edition.

Stark, Rodney. *The Victory of Reason: How Christianity Led to Freedom, Capitalism, and Western Success.* New York: Random House. 2005.

Schumpeter, Joseph A. *History of Economic Analysis.* New York: Oxford University Press. 1968.

Schwartz, Shalom H. "A Theory of Cultural Values and Some Implications for Work," *Applied Psychology: An International Review*, 1999.

Smith, Adam. *An Inquiry into the Nature and Causes of the Wealth of Nations* [1776]. Ed. Edwin Cannan. London: Methuen and Co. 1904. Library of Economics and Liberty. 8 June 2004. http://www.econlib.org/library/Smith/smwn1.htm.

Tawney, R. H. *Religion and the Rise of Capitalism.* Mass.: Peter Smith. 1962.

Thompson, Derek. "The Economic History of the Last 2000 Years: Part II." *The Atlantic.* June 20, 2012. http://www.theatlantic.com/business/archive/2012/06/the-economic-history-of-the-last-2000-years-part-ii/258762.

Valeri, Mark. *Heavenly Merchandize: How Religion Shaped Commerce in Puritan America.* Princeton: Princeton University Press. 2010.

Ye'or, Bat. *The Decline of Eastern Christianity under Islam: From Jihad to Dhimmitude.* London: Associated University Presses. 1996.

Ye'or, Bat. "The Myth of a Tolerant Pluralistic Islamic Society." The International Strategic Studies Association. Symposium on the Balkan War. Dinner address delivered on August 31, 1995. http://www.srpska-mreza.com/History/pre-wwOne/Ye_Or.html.

Young, Brad H. *Meet the Rabbis: Rabbinic Thought and the Teachings of* Jesus. Grand Rapids: Baker Academic. 2007.

Wallis, Jim. "Seattle: Changing the Rules," *Sojourners*, March-April 2000, http://sojo.net/magazine/2000/03/seattle-changing-rules.

Walton, John H. *Ancient Near Eastern Thought and the Old Testament*. Grand Rapid: Baker Academic. 2006.

Wayland, Francis, D.D. *Elements of Political Economy*. New York: Sheldon and Company. 1873, Kindle Edition, 2017.

Wilkinson, Toby. *The Rise and Fall of Ancient Egypt*. New York: Random House. 2010.

Wilson, Charles. *The Dutch Republic and the Civilization of the Seventeenth Century*. New York: McGraw-Hill Book Company. 1968.

Winkler, Dietmar W. and Baum, Wilhelm. *The Church of the East: A concise history*. London: RoutledgeCurzon. 2003.

Wood, Ellen. *The Origin of Capitalism*. New York: Verso. 1999.

Woodberry, Robert D. "The Missionary Roots of Liberal Democracy," *American Political Science Review*, Vol. 105, No. 2, May 2012.

World Bank. "Poverty Overview." Apr 06, 2015, http://www.worldbank.org/en/topic/poverty/overview.

Index

Made in the USA
Middletown, DE
12 January 2020